Mr. Copacabana

An American History by Night

By
Jim Proser

Copyright © 2014 Jim Proser
All rights reserved.

ISBN: 147526948X
ISBN-13: 9781475269482

Library of Congress Control Number: 2014901309
CreateSpace Independent Publishing Platform,
North Charleston, South Carolina

Praise for Mr. Copacabana

"The book recounts a single place in American entertainment and as The Palace was the premium variety house, the Copacabana was the premium variety and comedy house. It was the best. If you played there, you were the best."

—*Bernie Brillstein, Brillstein-Grey Entertainment*

"Monte Proser was a quiet and dynamic man whose life story will no doubt inspire your readers. Who else could have brought together celebrities, gangsters and the rich and famous in an atmosphere to create the greatest American nightclub?

The Copa is a legacy unmatched by any other nightclub before or since – this book has artfully brought to life the essence of Monte's character and the world in which he dared to live the American dream."

—*Harriet Wright, ex-Copa girl, secretary of Copa Girls Association.*

"I knew Monte and spent a lot of time at the Copa. They were both one of a kind. To my mind, Mr. Copacabana has got all the elements – romance, glamour, gangsters and the best entertainers in the world . . . I was fascinated to read the details."

—*Danny Welkes, personal manager of Milton Berle.*

Author's Note

In 1998, in a book about the singer Dean Martin, my father was described with one sentence saying that he was a "front man" for the mafia. In a dozen other books I'd read that mentioned my father, this description had never been used and it hurt to see it then in print. I knew it was at least partly true, that he was in business with certain gangsters, but I also knew it wasn't the whole truth. What I didn't know for sure was what he actually did and with whom.

What I've found out in the years since then was that my father had been tarred with that brush of the mafia since 1939. That was the year he created and opened the Copacabana nightclub in New York City. That was also the year the FBI opened a file on him. I found out that he had a partner named Frank Costello, the "Prime Minister" of the mafia.

I wrote this book to set the record straight about everything my father was and was not, because a lot has been said. I always hoped that my father was not just a front man but I needed to know for sure. Now I know.

Jim Proser
Nokomis, Florida
2013

For Carrie Dawson, our heart and soul…

Chapter 1

Cocktail Hour

Around Broadway they were starting to say Frank Sinatra was finished, cooked, "…couldn't get arrested." His records weren't selling, his Lucky Strike Radio show was faltering, his flamboyant affair with Ava Gardner was losing him fans and draining his strength. One night, as he hung around the circular bar in the *Hotel 14* above the Copa, not wanting to show his face downstairs in the main room, Toni Williams, a Copa girl, arrived and sat a few stools away. Sinatra sidled over, struck up a conversation. More than anything, he hated to be alone, especially now, when it looked like he might be returning to Hoboken a 25 year-old has-been. He made a play for Toni just as her date for the evening, handsome, young Tom Corbally, showed up. As the couple was leaving, Corbally turned to Sinatra and kidded him, "Next time I see you I'm gonna change the channel." Sinatra was so low he couldn't even rise to the joke. "Don't do that," the demoralized young singer said, "Everybody else is doing it."

This was one of the lowest points in the singer's career and life. Within a few days he would turn to powerful friends for help. The friends made a few calls. One of the first calls went out to the Copacabana.

Monte Proser usually sat at table 4G, just off the dance floor a little to the right of center when he auditioned acts for the Copa. It was the family table, which made him feel a little better. On this typical day at work, which usually started at about 4:30 in the afternoon, Monte wasn't very upbeat. Last night's three shows and five or six Dewar's and soda had left him with a squinting hangover. He turned his attention to the stage where the final bars of "Poor Butterfly" wavered from a young hopeful. A pretty young girl from… somewhere, he forgot exactly where. Monte was starting to enjoy the song as Jack Entratter, the towering Copa manager, placed a heavy black telephone on the table with **Plaza 8-1060** printed in bold black letters on a white paper medallion in the center of the metal dial.

"It's him." Entratter handed his boss the receiver. Monte noted the seriousness on his manager's face. He cleared his head and brought all his concentration to this conversation. He held the receiver slightly away from his tender head, softening the sound, "Yeah."

The caller was Frank Costello, the cordial "Prime Minister" of the *Syndicate*, the united mafia families of New York, New Jersey and Chicago. He was concerned about Sinatra, a trivial issue for one of the most powerful men in the world, but Costello was often like that, very protective of people he liked. Costello just wanted to tell Monte of his concern for the singer. Monte listened closely for other concerns but only heard an older, powerful man trying to give a young friend a boost. After a few exchanges, the conversation ended up about where it started.

"Frank's a good kid, good singer." Monte offered.

"Woman trouble. He's all mixed up," Costello summarized.

Monte agreed. "Yeah, he's a good kid."

"He was upstairs in the 14 the other night. Didn't want to show his face," Frank said.

Monte was relieved there wasn't more on Frank's mind. Even though the two men had become friendly in the 8 years since Frank bought into the club, the power of life and death that Frank held in his hands meant no conversation was truly casual. Monte held his complaint against Frank's man in the club, Jules Podell, for another time.

2

"Maybe you could talk to Cohn and your Hollywood people?"
"Eh..." Monte sighed.
"What?"
"I threw him out last week."
Costello was concerned, "You threw Harry Cohn out?"
"Yeah. He's a bum," Monte said, leaving the details of Cohn's lechery toward his Copa chorus girls drop. "Let me see what I can do here," he added to soften his refusal. In the club, Monte called the shots and Frank C never interfered in his partner's end of a partnership. Harry Cohn was the powerful and much-feared chief of *Columbia Pictures* who had been partnered with Al Capone's Chicago *Outfit* for many years. Even Costello respected Cohn's power enough to be troubled by Monte's action, but Monte was "one-of-a-kind" and Costello let it go.

"Okay," Frank said and hung up.

That was it. Frank never liked to spend too much time on the phone, always assuming that the city, state, FBI or an enemy was listening. Eventually Costello found others to help secure the part of *Maggio* for his young friend in the film *From Here to Eternity* – an event later dramatized in *The Godfather* using a severed horse's head. For Costello, the call was a small favor he felt he owed to a few friends who had an interest in the singer's career. For Monte, it was confirmation that a fly like himself had taken another turn in the spider's web spun by Frank Costello, Lucky Luciano and Meyer Lansky.

The talented young singer was now, somehow, more indebted to the *Syndicate*. Not unusual. Everybody who worked in nightclubs was, but it was never pleasant to be reminded. Particularly since Monte liked Sinatra. The kid was a little hot-headed but he was a stand-up guy, loyal to his friends and had great style.

Two seasons back, in 1946, Phil Silvers was set to perform at the club with comedian Rags Ragland. Two weeks before opening night, Ragland died leaving Silvers emotionally wobbly and stranded as a single. Monte couldn't replace the act, the show had to go on. Silvers begged Sinatra to stand in for Rags but the singer was booked on a movie *It Happened In Brooklyn* that was shooting in Hollywood.

Silvers carried the act himself through opening night but knew he couldn't maintain it. After the first show of the following night, Silvers sat in his dressing room depressed about the other 20 or so shows ahead, when Sinatra knocked and came in. He'd flown from California to help out his pal. Silvers started the next show still as a single and, as if by accident, found a famous face in the audience. He introduced Sinatra who came on stage and did a bit with Silvers and singer Julie Wilson. At the end, Sinatra sat down. When the roaring crowd called him back to take a bow, Silvers suggested they take an extra bow for Ragland. That night made Sinatra into a hero in Monte's eyes and among show folk in general. Everybody knew the kid had heart.

But a lot can happen in two years. Now Sinatra was on the skids. Monte decided he could help the big-hearted singer from Hoboken. He'd move a few things in the schedule and squeeze him in. The kid deserved it and it would make Frank Costello happy - two good ideas.

As far as publicity, Monte knew the big guns, Walter Winchell and Ed Sullivan, were good for a little ink, a mention of the singer in their newspaper columns. The others, Earl Wilson, Mark Hellinger and Jack O'Brian would probably follow. Dorothy Kilgallen you couldn't count on. Sinatra was on his own with her.

The manager of the young hopeful on stage munched *Sen-Sen* like a menthol locomotive and breathed into Monte's face making his headache worse.

"Whaddya think? Isn't she great!" the manager asked with everything he had on the line. Monte looked at the young girl on the dance floor in front of him, who would make a great singing waitress somewhere, smiling wide enough to dislocate her jaw.

"She's really something." Monte said as he shielded his eyes for a moment from the glaring white tablecloth. The manager thought he was contemplating an offer and jumped in.

"She's a humdinger! What dates were you thinking of?"

Monte was thinking maybe the day after he died, which might be tomorrow if his hangover got worse, but he didn't want to be nasty. They looked like nice people.

"I'll call you."

He couldn't manage more with his head screaming for aspirin, Bromo and maybe a little hair of the dog that bit him. The manager's smile started to wobble.

"I'll call you." Monte nailed home as he noticed Irving Lazar, the young music agent, striding across the room toward him. He knew he was in for an earful. Irving was relentless.

The manager knew he was sunk, "Sure, sure. Okay. I'll be hearing from you, yeah."

"She's a terrific singer, really," Monte said. He was thinking of the girl and wanted to salve the rejection he had to inflict on her.

"A humdinger. That's for sure." The manager motioned angrily to the girl, faked a final smile and left with his talented burden without looking back.

Monte nursed his tomato juice, which was supposed to help but wasn't, as Irving sat down, uninvited, and started chewing his ear about Johnny Pineapple. Monte loosened his tie while Irving promoted his "discovery". The truth was that he'd been trying to sell this same band yesterday when it was called the Billy Chesterfield something or other. Now it was Johnny Pineapple, renamed to fit with the Copa's tropical theme. You had to hand it to Irving, he was fast and had more chutzpah than Eskimos got snow.

"Look, Swifty. I'll take the band, Johnny Pineapple, for a week. Three fifty."

"Swifty?" The little agent wasn't sure if he liked having a nickname, but the calculating was over before the thought was even complete. If Monte Proser wants to call me Swifty, and book my guys into the Copa, okay by me. "And there's expenses…"

Monte rubbed his forehead and sighed. Last night's Dewar's was pushing against the walls of his skull. Survival instinct quickly lifted Irving "Swifty" Lazar out of his seat.

"Three fifty's fine, great. They'll be here." The young music agent was out the door before Monte looked up.

"Expenses." Monte said to himself. He was amused by Swifty. He reminded him of himself.

Monte rested his head in his hands. He just hoped the phone wouldn't ring again as he plotted his way around the lineup. Sinatra, for two weeks, I gotta bump somebody, and they'll scream. He needed to lie down. He got up, dodged the young Filipino man vacuuming the carpet and padded delicately toward the bar. He passed by massive support columns that had been made over into stout white palm trees. On the walls, large draped plaster swags were painted in wide stripes of rust red and white echoing the seaside cabanas of the real Copacabana beach in Rio de Janiero. Clusters of tropical fruits hung from the swags and art deco blue lights created the moonlit aura over rust red banquets that lined the walls. Every detail of the Copa décor was pure showmanship and escapism.

Monte climbed from floor level up the two elevated tiers that surrounded the 24 by 40 foot stage floor. The stage was narrow to begin with, but on busy nights, as more tables were placed up front for important customers, it got even smaller. Customers and performers were often so close that Copa girls knocked over drinks with the hems of their dresses when they twirled. Beads of sweat from featured performers, particularly dance teams, often sprayed the front row landing in customers' drinks.

Monte made it to the bar, leaned on it, "Joey," he murmured and nodded ever so slightly to the bartender who slapped down a shot glass and poured a Dewar's. "Tickety boo." Monte saluted and downed the shot. He exhaled the fiery fumes and placed the glass back on the gleaming wood. Everything was quiet in the club except for the reassuring vacuuming of the carpet and the dull clinking in the kitchen as the Filipino chef Pedro Pujal and the kitchen crew started their preparations. Monte looked back over his creation as the liquor started to ease the pain. Above the stage was a bold relief mural of Copacabana beach under moonlight. It was framed by the massive white palms creating the theatrical illusion of an exotically romantic place a thousand miles away from New York City. Monte tried to lose himself in the scene for a moment, to rest and relieve his aggravation.

Except for his hangover, it might seem like Monte Proser should be grinning from ear to ear. He was 44, rich, famous and married to Jane Ball, one of the most beautiful of his Copa

Girls. He and Jane had a healthy one-year old son, Charles, named after Monte's father, and another one on the way. His name had been on the front of the world's hottest nightclub for the past eight years and the mention of it would open any door. He had more fun in a week than most people had in a year and had already lost more money at Aqueduct racetrack than most people would make in their lifetimes. His taste, talent and power as a producer were unassailable, yet he could not control his own creation, the Copa. The first class nightclub that he had created, that bore his name, was being turned into a mobster clip joint and it was making him sick with fury.

At the end of the bar, Jack Entratter was finishing his second coffee and smoke of the day - his eye-opener. It was close to five in the afternoon, which was mid-morning for nightclub guys like Jack who never woke up before noon.

He knew a call from Costello didn't usually help his boss' state of mind. He saw Monte throw back the shot of booze and could see the storm clouds descending. Monte would be turning the problem over in his mind again, for the ten millionth time. The booze was getting to him. For every moment of relief it gave him, it was putting him deeper in the hole. His afternoon naps were starting to be a regular thing. He was drinking earlier and more. By nine or ten, after the first show, he'd be loaded and his conversations were losing their sparkle, taking on a nasty, cutting humor. Entratter mentioned it and got waved off for his effort. He didn't want to see Monte drown in a bottle of Scotch, but if he did, well, it wouldn't be too bad for his own career. Someone would have to fill the gap.

"I gotta lie down for a minute. You uh..." Monte motioned up toward the front door.

"Sure, Boss. I'll open up." Entratter said.

Monte moved off toward the manager's office. He climbed the main stairs toward the lounge and street level, his mind fully clouded with the problem. The Copa was slipping from his control and he was powerless to stop it. The face of the problem, the only part he could get his hands on, was Frank Costello's watchdog manager, Jules Podell. The bigger problem was the quicksand of corruption that had spread to City

Hall, had swallowed entire countries like Cuba and was now engulfing the state of Nevada.

Jules Podell was plundering the Copa like a rum-soaked pirate – padding customer's checks, shaking down concessionaires and grifting vendors with nickel and dime schemes. His last job had been managing the Kit Kat Club, a late night, hand-job under the table, strip joint on Broadway and 50th. Before that he was a leg breaker for Meyer Lansky. He had several convictions for assault and battery and dodged a murder rap due to jury amnesia. In the first years of the Copa, Podell had been confined to the kitchen, technically "off the premises" due to his felony convictions and clear ties with Costello. He had been kept in check by the watchful eye of Mayor LaGuardia's City Hall. Now that the *Syndicate*'s man, Bill O'Dwyer, was in the Mayor's chair at City Hall, Podell was out of his pen and gorging on the Copa like a pig in a flower garden. This was the unsolvable problem that drove Monte to the bottle and then to bed each day. You can't fight City Hall.

To Monte the Copa was more than just a hot nightclub. He already had a string of successful clubs from Miami to Providence, Rhode Island. It was more than the money, even though he had taken the longest long shot of his career and turned a jinxed white elephant into a $25,000 dollar per night Niagara of cash. The Copa was simply everything Monte had learned in twenty years of hanging around the gin joints and backstages of Broadway. It was his mark, his signature, his unique vision.

He had built his creation into the Mecca of the entertainment industry. It was the well from which Broadway and Hollywood drew their talent. Dozens of performers like Frank Sinatra, Nat King Cole, Dean Martin and Jerry Lewis got the boost that made their careers at the Copa. A shot at the Copa for any performer meant they had made it. Monte didn't book headliners, he created them. He revived careers of older vaudevillians like Jimmy Durante and gave new performers like Nat King Cole a place in the Copa's spotlight. This was the special excitement of the Copa – riveting performances by new and rediscovered entertainers. A show at the Copa promised the thrill of discovery.

In the manager's office, Monte sat down on the brown leather couch and untied his gleaming English broughams – the finest shoes money could buy. Across the room, his desk was covered with newspapers. The floor around the desk was piled with press books filled with newspaper clippings dating back eight years to opening night in 1940. This was how he gauged the Copa's success, not in money or attendance, but in ink. What were his friends saying in their columns and more importantly, how often were they saying it?

He aligned his splendid shoes neatly, a personal ritual that signaled a time to rest and contemplate. He slumped into the couch and closed his eyes. In a moment, his mind was calm, the annoyances were put aside and he contemplated the sheer granite wall of the problem.

Simply, he was as powerless as a small boy in short pants before his overlord Frank Costello, the ultimate authority. The sting of recognition opened his eyes. The relationship to Costello was similar to the relationship Monte had had with his imperious father. Both men had the power of life and death over Monte. Neither man was someone he had chosen. Both freely imposed their will on him. Neither could be overruled. Both were civilized and discreet. Neither could be hated. Monte faced essentially the same dilemma that tore him from his family over thirty years earlier. He closed his eyes again, falling asleep to let his mind work on the problem.

He was suddenly 12 years old again, wearing the elegant, black velvet suit with short pants his father bought him in England, as he scooted down the steep gangplank of the massive steel ocean liner, Aquitania for his first deep breath and close look at America. He raced ahead of his father, Charles and his two younger sisters, Isabel and Annette. The young family was dressed as if they were meeting royalty. Charles, the patriarch, wore a monocle dangling from the silk waistcoat of his dark suit, the girls wore matching sailor suits. Meyer Marcus Prosser raced to the end of the gangplank ignoring his father's shouts, pushing past disembarking passengers and luggage, heedless of tearing his expensive clothes. He had to be the first to set foot in America. At the end of the gangplank he stopped. He surveyed the jumble of activity on the dock. Suddenly, he leaped as far as his legs could propel him and landed in America like a swashbuckling musketeer, ready for adventure. He scouted his new home from the fetid docks of Baltimore as he waited for the girls and the old man to catch up. It was the 4th of July, 1916.

That evening, the wild, little Jewish boy saw fireworks for the first time. The terror and beauty of the exploding art tattooed a sense of spectacle and enchantment onto his mind that he would never forget. Charles told him it was created just for them. Monte believed his father just enough to accept this as his personal booming welcome to his new home. The boy leaped with joy at each new explosion as his sisters cowered under their father's arms. The wonder and enthusiasm that would transform Meyer Marcus Prosser into Monte Proser, was ignited that evening.

CHAPTER 2

Makin' Whoopee

The summer of 1919 arrived on a skillet. Daytime temperature reached 108 degrees in the farming village of Flemington, New Jersey about 40 miles south of the Prosser family apartment in Brooklyn Heights, New York. During the day almost nothing moved except the mercury. At twilight, as the black asphalt streets and granite curbstones released the heat of the day into the cooling air, Monte's secret life began.

The family had moved to Brooklyn from Baltimore that spring. Father Charles was desperate to escape the decadence of ragtime music that was pouring out of the bawdy houses of Baltimore and tainting his impressionable eldest son. He heard the American slang and smelled the stink of cigarette smoke that Monte was dragging in from the streets. The enraged father soon ran out of out of ideas to curb his son's waywardness. He couldn't make the boy study or even take his schoolwork seriously. He couldn't honestly use religion since he himself wasn't religious. He could only make rules and enforce them with the tone of his voice which still was commanding and held some waning power over the boy. The breaking point came one afternoon in early spring as school was about to end for the summer, leaving Charles helpless to protect his son against the seductions of a Southern ragtime city. The top-floor apartment was beginning to swelter in the lengthening afternoons. Monte was anxious to get out to the streets after hours of enforced study at school.

"Stop," Charles commanded and Monte suddenly noticed his father as if it was a true surprise, as if this monumental presence could really have been overlooked. In an instant Monte sized up his father and found him unprepared for battle. The old man was exhausted after a day of translating and sorting endless mind-numbing manifests of merchandise. Monte had the advantage of a pressing appointment. He seized it immediately, "Hello, Papa. I was just going."

"Come." The old man commanded and Monte approached. The steel rimmed bifocals were adjusted for punctuation. "I want you to remember your mother when you're out and running wild. She would not have you associating with some of the lower type of characters in these places you go to. Do you understand?"

"Yes, papa."

"Do you really? I want you to think. Stand here and think."

Monte was deeply affected by the memory of his mother, Lena. He clung to it with religious devotion and resented his father for using it this way. It was private, and sacred, and not to be trotted out for lessons in obedience. He stiffened as heat poured through him while he fought against seeing her face, but it was hopeless, as Charles knew it would be. Monte saw his mother's chestnut brown eyes dancing with diamond reflections from the coal fire as she leaned in to kiss him goodnight. He stroked the fine down on her cheeks. Then, just as suddenly, he saw her face as grey and lifeless as the ash in a cold, iron stove.

Lena had died in childbirth delivering her fourth child, a boy, Leo. Monte was 10 years old. The family was living in a drafty tenement house on Swan Street, under the gloom and coal smoke of northern England. The birth had nearly killed little Leo as well. His spine was badly damaged and he was frail, weighing less than five pounds. He was given over to the special care of Lena's relatives since Charles was unequipped to care for Leo and his three other children now that Lena was gone. For months, Leo lingered between life and death.

Lena's death had snuffed out the one, tender hope Charles held for the world. All was now lamp-black and the price of coal, ranks of soulless numbers and stacks of grubby 5-pound notes in the landlord's hand. Life was work and war and what to buy for dinner. How would these children ever grow up and would the Jewish people even survive? His thoughts slowly turned into paving stones, impervious and indestructible. He laid them down methodically, end to end, making a solid, unremarkable road through a filthy world. They were chinked tight permitting no bloom or sprout between them. This is the road his children would follow. To wander from it, even a foot, would bring them only death and horror. Eventually, Charles let the possible funeral arrangements for baby Leo drift from his daily thoughts and turned toward the future. He had three other children to care for and war was about to engulf Europe.

Monte had loved his mother like the sun and she had doted on him, her handsome first-born and prince of her modest kingdom. They had a special language that pretended to treat him as a prince and she as his dutiful Queen. He was born to strike out on adventures and quests of bravery from which she, as a Victorian, a Jew and a woman, had been expressly forbidden. This life chafed like her whalebone corset, yet it seemed these restrictions were the price of love, the one thing above all else that she must have. And so she hid her adventurer's heart like her corset under layers of womanly frill, burying her dreams to fulfill her family's expectations. She was a kind, obedient daughter and became a faithful Jewish wife and mother.

Then Monte was born and she saw her horizons expand. She would live through him. Into his quick and receptive mind she poured all her dreams. Monte was her knight errant, a bright and energetic soul who would stand large in the world. Monte was her Lancelot, and she was his wise Queen.

From the moment Monte looked on his mother's bloodless face and saw the blackened sheets that had soaked up her life, he did not speak for several weeks. The first few days after she was shrouded and carried from the house, he sat silently watching the coal fire in the parlor stove. He didn't look away from the yellow flames, didn't speak. He was sent outside but sat on the front steps silent, inert. The world had shifted on its axis and the familiar was foreign to him. People he didn't recognize said hello and unfamiliar streets drew him in. He avoided the well-known streets to the market and tram stop. On the unknown streets he could walk without seeing her walking beside him. They sheltered him in their shadows. The Queen was dead and the kingdom vanished. The brave knight was a heartbroken little boy wandering mindlessly through a gray world.

Now, the boy and his father stood before each other, captives to the memory of Lena. Without his mother's protection, Monte was subjected to his father's strict and autocratic rule. Without Lena's gentle persuasion, Charles could only bluster with threats of dire discipline. Charles saw the heartbreak and anger crossing Monte's face and knew he'd stumbled. It was hopeless. The boy could not be reached, at least not right now.

"Dissipation," was the word Charles used to distract them as he peered over his pince-nez eyeglasses. He had reduced his lectures to one word so Monte could focus on the meaning. The boy was commanded to look up the word and present its dictionary definition to his father the following day. This was followed by a brief discussion and forced time of reflection. It was an unpleasant and usually unprofitable exercise since the focus of Monte's life was set. His son's true talent was simply unrecognizable to Charles. Monte was really only interested in having fun with people. It had already become his life's work. Charles wanted to grab his son and shake him but the time had passed for that type of discipline. Monte was taut and ready.

"Go," he said. Monte turned away sharply. He grabbed his roller skates by the door.

"Bring me tobacco please." Monte was obliged to turn back. He took the quarter from his father, glanced quickly at his implacable face and was out the door and into his real life. It was the start of a 30 year struggle between two iron wills.

To escape Baltimore's corruption, Charles found work at an import company based in the Red Hook terminals on New York harbor. Although he was an exceptional linguist, and had once translated vital documents in five languages for Czar Nicholas of Russia, the lowly clerk position offered the change of location he needed to save his son's character. Unfortunately for Charles, it was too late. The boy had been seduced by the ragtime anarchy of back alley crap shoots, gin mills and nightlife. The battle for the Prosser family's future would only intensify.

For two years Charles walked home after work, one mile uphill, from the piers of Red Hook to Brooklyn Heights. He arrived home exhausted, ate a quick dinner and then eased into his easy chair, reading about the progress of the labor movement in *The Worker*. By seven, his chin drifted down and eventually came to rest on his chest. Deep, sonorous snores trembled the window glass. As if waiting in the wings of a vaudeville house for his cue, 15 year-old Monte stepped from the children's bedroom in his immaculate evening outfit – his shirt was snow white with subtle vertical striping and expertly pressed. The trousers and jacket were dark, his shoes reflected the soft, gas light.

"I'm off," he whispered. Isabel had her instructions if the Old Man woke up. Monte was just out to Greunwald's Apothecary for some headache medicine. She was then to turn slowly, as if her head was actually throbbing, go into their bedroom and gently close the door. That was it. No more, no less. They'd rehearsed it to Monte's satisfaction and she knew it by heart. Monte always kept a tin of headache powder in his pocket on his evenings out in case he was inspected when he returned. Usually the Old Man would sleep in the chair until Annette nudged him awake. It was generally the younger Annette's job while the ranking senior Isabel finished securing the house and washing up. The youngest child, a little boy, Leo, was too young for a part in the nightly charade. Leo had just joined the family from England. Little Leo always went to bed early. After his difficult birth, Leo spent the first 4 years of his life in an iron machine that attempted to straighten his spine. It was unsuccessful and his small stature was further reduced by several inches by a sharp outward curve of his spine just below the neck.

Many nights Monte had finished his evening business by the time Charles was roused. It was only when business kept him late that the deception might be needed. About 9:30, Annette, in her nightcap and gown, would push the sleeping giant's shoulder sharply, "Poppa, go to bed," she'd repeat until he roused. He grunted and eventually rose with a great yawn, trundling off with a sleepy "Good night". If he did wake on his own he'd usually wobble with his eyes half-mast to his own room without ever coming fully awake. Occasionally he'd glance in the children's darkened room before retiring. He never noticed that Monte wasn't in the room. Annette was unwittingly in on the dodge as well. If asked her brother's whereabouts, she was instructed to say, "Isabel knows, Papa."

Monte timed the closing of the front door to the crescendo of a snore. He stepped gingerly down the first flight of squeaky stairs. Safely out of the Old Man's earshot, his pace would pick up to a fast walk. Usually he'd be at the counter of *Greunwald's Apothecary* just before 8. Gruenwald's did a brisk liquor business along with patent medicines since the two were often used interchangeably or combined for various effects. Old Lady Gruenwald would have Monte's orders of two or three pint bottles ready when he arrived. She always cautioned him not to run or he might spill "the medicine" the boys needed for their headaches. Monte couldn't tell whether she thought he was stupid or she just needed to pretend she was doing something truly beneficial.

He'd arrive at the stage door of *Hanratty's Dance Parlor* at 8:15. The band would be taking their first break. Musicians and a few local boys from the audience would be taking in the night air, smoking cigarettes, reefer and saying very little. Monte would hand them the slim bottles in their paper bags. Before they paid or spoke, the local boys would bite through the wax, pull the corks with their teeth, and take a long swig like they were dying of thirst. It was nauseating. Monte had sipped the stuff and knew it tasted like kerosene. They seemed like very old men to him but they were just a few years older, in their early twenties. Many of them didn't seem to care how they looked. Their clothes were generally cheap and carelessly fitted like the old duffers in the park. After the vile liquid was down, they'd blow hard like they were blowing out a lamp with a high wick and shake all over. The musicians would usually laugh and pass the bottle but the local boys who had returned from Ypres, Belleau Wood and Flanders Field, would take on a sickly look like their minds had suddenly become unhinged.

Monte looked in their eyes, as black and watery as lagoons, their hair dank from dancing, their mouths slack and breath caustic with liquor fumes. Suddenly they'd flip a raw hand into the shadowy lamplight showing flaps of pink scar where fingers had been, or tap their walking stick against a wooden calf or just stare at him favoring a milky, dead eye that had been touched by the gas. Sometimes they marveled at their mangled limb for a moment, but always they'd turn back to him for his reaction. Was he frightened of them? Were they too horrible?

As a favor, Monte gave them no reaction, which was the hope they were looking for. He showed up with their booze, didn't say much and didn't flinch at the sight of their hideous wounds. They were the boys who crowded in front of the bandstand at *Hanratty's* and stared dumbly at the musicians, sometimes exploding into an afflicted sort of dancing. Then they went out back and drank until they fell to the paving stones senseless, in a dreamless sleep. Alone or in pairs they began to wander the streets of Brooklyn Heights, eyes flaming red from liquor, skin crusty with black city filth like the trench mud and gunpowder they wore in the Great War. They were America's new world travelers. They brought home the real news that wasn't in the newspapers - of a changed world that was unimaginable in its brutality and horror.

The scenes came to Monte in his dreams and he began to fear sleep. He didn't speak to Isabel about it, protecting her from it. He could only talk to other night walkers like him on the street corners. He stayed with them, out on the streets, running his business while the daylight world slept.

The first mechanized World War, the war to end all wars, had just sputtered to its shameful end. Through the early fall and Indian Summer the boys came home to families in Brooklyn, Chicago and California in pieces and in pine boxes, with shattered minds and empty souls. 10,000,000 young men of all nations had been slaughtered in four years. The number was mind-numbing. The innovative ways they devised to kill each other caused public revulsion and nausea – poison gas, incendiary bombs, germ warfare. The war had shattered more than individual soldiers, society itself was largely destroyed. European royalty were clearly buffoons, national leaders were cowards and God was a useless myth. What was important now was to forget, to drink and grieve and somehow get on with life. America trudged on, forgetting Europe and all that had ever happened there, looking for a new way, its own way. The Old World was dead.

Summer fled south down the Hudson and East Rivers leaving behind a tapestry of red and yellow. It blew across the harbor and through the Verrazano Narrows sucking the chill down from Canada behind it. The kitchen windows came down and the "season" in the city began. The pace on the street quickened as people ready to do business, ready to make their mark, returned from their summer idles rested and bored.

The collapse of the Old World blew through the streets. Anarchy, a world without governments and the corporate bosses that supported them, was the only way humans could hope to live together in peace. This wind of defiance blew into Monte's sails and set him straining at his moorings. Anarchists stood on the pedestals of war heroes in the park and cursed the tyranny of the states that had led them all into hell. Leaflets declaring freedom for all working people were slapped insolently on private property and public lamp posts. A new society of disrespect and cynicism was being born screaming and bloody. Riots swept up to City Hall and bombs were hurled into the federal building on Adams Street.

Winter fell heavily. The East River froze over and the deep snow of 1919 was dotted with blood. Anarchists and socialists cloistered in coal cellars to plot vengeance on the capitalists who built the war machine and enslaved the workers. On the street corners, the ranks of truants swelled, scouring the gentry in their beaver hats and fox coats with hard eyes while quietly the second rider of the Apocalypse, following on the heels of War, had already arrived from Europe.

A strain of influenza swept out of Spain and hitched a ride on the American boys returning home from battle. Within 7 days of arriving in America, it had spread to all 50 states. It would kill another 20 million Americans who had survived the war. Before it lodged in the lungs, the disease infected susceptible minds. This was surely God's judgment on all mankind for the wickedness of waging this new kind of war, for promiscuity, for the usury of the Jews, for poor farm practices, for all the real and imagined evils of the human race.

In Brooklyn Heights, the wide-eyed, foam mouthed evangelists vied with the anarchists for street corners to shout from. Hysteria electrified the winter winds. Polite society retreated to their parlors for a sherry in front of the fire, but the talk soon turned dour and strident. They had endured war and now suffered with disease, which rider would appear next, pestilence or famine? The fun had gone out of life and the fearful stayed home. Parties broke up early or were cancelled without excuse. Only the young, the desperate and the fearless refused to stay in. They spit in the devil's eye and went to *Hanratty's* to dance the tango. They went over Niagara Falls in barrels and walked on the wings of barnstorming airplanes. They began a bacchanalia of the doomed and swept into Brooklyn's dimly lit carpet joints for a couple rolls of the dice, a few shots of untaxed booze and a little whoopee with an enterprising good time girl.

Monte, who was still using his Jewish name Meyer, watched the traffic and followed its flow. There were jobs around for errand boys who kept their mouths shut and their eyes open. You took your chances or you stayed home and waited for the next horseman.

Business was bad through the holidays. The streets were empty, lamp wicks were turned down low to conserve kerosene and coal stoves were banked up early for people who just wanted to get under the covers and forget. A freezing rain had covered the streets in a filthy slush so that simply being on the street became a test of willpower and footwear. Yet Monte endured and continued his clandestine errands to dancehalls and pool rooms where the atmosphere hung in low clouds of tobacco, wet wool and rose water. It seemed people had been stampeded into these overheated rooms. They thrashed about with the same white-eyed fear Monte had seen in the holding pens of the kosher butcher.

These places now shuddered with frantic foxtrots and tangos. The solemn waltz, the stately quadrille and the light-hearted polka were as dead as everything else in Europe. When the band struck up the new ragtime tunes it brought on the energetic one-step and the *Maxixe* pronounced *ma sheesh* – a wild, unhinged sort of Brazilian waltz that caused frequent collisions. The young crowds were seething, barely controllable. The few older people who had ventured out stayed pushed up against the walls as if by the centrifugal force of the gyrating youngsters who danced to defy the death and madness they had inherited. Monte soon found himself in the middle of the dance floor sweating like a stevedore, bouncing girls with painted faces around the room, spinning on the balls of his feet, all restraint vanished.

Then the State of New York clamped a lid on this roiling stewpot and screwed it down tight. In January, they finally bowed to religious zealots and joined the other states to ratify the 18th Amendment, the *Volstead Act*, outlawing the manufacture, storage and consumption of alcoholic beverages. To the young and disaffected of Brooklyn Heights, this was the intolerable act of a discredited, tyrannical government. A wholesale revolt erupted overnight. Respect for the law was thrown onto the bonfire along with the bobble-headed royalty of Europe, the greasy politicians and God himself. The 1920's began to roar.

At the street corner parties near *Hanratty's*, teenage Monte nurtured his reputation as someone who knew where the action was. He made it a point to find out names before he met other young people and a bit about their business. He also learned that being polite and well-mannered got you nowhere.

"Hey Gent!" the kids called him Gent for his English manners and natty clothes, "Hey Gent! Where's the party?"

"Far away from you, my friend," he'd shoot back. "Far away from you."

Nothing was more important to Monte than making new friends, lots of them, all kinds. While the dance halls were sweating through a lot of wholesome activity, a small group of boys would trade a nod and split off from the general crowd. They would gather quietly near a new type of clandestine club that was springing up like mushrooms on every block - speakeasies. These clubs had no bright, inviting windows or festive striped awnings. There was nothing on the outside that announced they were a nightclub. You couldn't just walk in and get a table. You needed a secret knock, a password or a special business card. If you didn't look like a government dick, the double-locked door would open.

Inside, it was said, you could get anything you wanted. The back storeroom of *Gruenwald's* had become a "speak". The loading door to the alley behind the store now had a slot at eye level where identity was checked. Their liquor business doubled then tripled in the weeks after the new law was decreed. They just moved it from the store shelves to the back room. Monte was no longer allowed to walk out carrying bottles in paper bags, he had to tuck them under his belt and cover them with his coat. He was told which cops were customers and which would be trouble if they caught him.

Monte joined the other boys who waited across the street or down the block from a place where nothing seemed to be happening. They lied and gossiped, chewed tobacco, waiting for patrons to stumble out and walk past them. They got precious shreds of information in exchange for their offer of a cigarette. The ladies would give one of the boys the eye while she leaned on her equally unstable date. The patrons reeked of booze and smoke and sweated perfume. They carried guns and knives and would make a subtle display of them in case the boys were thinking of something other than offering free cigarettes. A tip could be earned for hailing a cab while the clubbers sat on a stoop with the other boys. Pitching pennies gave way to a pair of dice and they soon learned the intricacies of the game and the impulse that named it crap. It was all illegal, it was all fun and it went on all night.

Monte watched and learned. He was an observant private eye in one of his pulp novels. The clue to scram was when the cheap suits showed up. You could always tell a government dick, a fed, by his shoes – down at the heel, no shine. And they always came in pairs because they didn't even trust each other. If one arrived alone, he always left with booze on his breath and a roll of the club's cash in his pocket. The local cops sometimes got dragged along on a raid but somehow when they were involved, the place would either be empty or serving root beer when they arrived. After a while the Feds didn't tell the local cops what they were up to. This was how the game was played. They called it Prohibition.

Just across the East River from Monte's operation, his future partner, Frank Costello, was making new friends and growing an operation of his own. The fortunes of Frank and Monte rose together on a sea of illegal booze. Frank was ten years older than Monte and had been making money helping friends like Louis Rao in his Upper East Side Manhattan neighborhood manage their gambling operations. Prohibition suddenly made Frank Costello and all of his friends incredibly rich, in cash. The volume of cash soon became a problem and one of Frank's first business investments was for dozens of waterproof, zinc trunks to hold his money. Soon the money needed trucks and eventually boats to move it. The illegal liquor business started strong and got stronger every month for the next 13 years. It was a spigot of cash that quickly grew to a river. Business was so good that Frank built an ocean-going navy to ship his product from the distilleries of Ireland across the Atlantic to New Brunswick, Canada. One of the first moves that indicated his emergence as an unparalleled black market leader was to secure a distribution terminal on the tiny, rocky island of St. Pierre off of Canada's east coast. St. Pierre was the sole remaining French outpost in North America and thus immune to the Prohibition treaties Canada enforced for the US. He negotiated to pay the Mayor of St. Pierre two dollars per case of liquor transshipped through the little island. Soon fleets of European ships of all kinds, rusting scows and ancient schooners, arrived at St. Pierre with their intoxicating cargo. From St. Pierre, a sleeker, faster supply fleet sailed south into international waters off of Montauk Point on Long Island and down to the mouth of the Chesapeake Bay.

In another demonstration of Costello's bold innovation as a criminal mastermind, his ships were provided with security from armed seaplane escorts. At this time, airplanes were an expensive novelty with almost no commercial uses. Rumrunners like Frank were among the pioneers of commercial aviation. Frank ran a tight operation and as people who knew Frank would later say of him, nobody got killed who wasn't supposed to. Other gangsters, of course, got killed quickly if they tried to rob him. But after a few tries, nobody ever tried to rob Frank again, and business grew smoothly.

Costello restricted his activities to "legitimate" businesses meaning liquor and gambling - things that later became legal. He never involved himself in drugs, prostitution or loan sharking. But, as he often said of himself, he was no Bible salesman.

He'd grown up desperately poor in New York's East Harlem where the newer Italian immigrants were preyed upon by the established Irish clans which included the New York police. When Costello arrived from Naples with his mother, father and brother, the Irish already controlled city politics, the labor unions, the police force and large swaths of real estate – all the social institutions with direct influence on new immigrants. By the age of 15, Costello had served 10 months of a one-year sentence for being caught with a gun and for having the reputation of being a gunman for the emerging Italian gangs. He realized that he'd been convicted only because the gun reinforced the suspicions about him. He vowed never again to carry a gun and in the 40 years of his rise and dominance of the highest echelons of organized crime, he never did.

Miss Creel of Flatbush Avenue, tutor to the Prosser children, smelled faintly of cabbage and camphor and suffered frequent headaches. This gave the children plenty of free study time while Miss Creel lay on the floor in the study with a damp cloth over her eyes.

Two blocks from the apartment on Green Street, a glimpse of Manhattan and New York harbor could be had from the vantage point of a cigar store where Monte established his headquarters free of Miss Creel and her lessons. Travel to the city was forbidden by Charles and was reinforced by a nightly recounting of child kidnappings and murders that were apparently epidemic and printed in the newspaper every day.

At the corner cigar store, Monte read the same newspapers and didn't find the dire situation that his father described. Charles was lying to maintain his control by fear, and as Monte came to realize this, the crack in the relationship between them widened.

Monte's nemesis became the truant officer who prowled the pool halls and cigar stores looking to catch children out of school like Monte. After Monte's first snaring and return by the truant officer, Charles put Miss Creel on notice to better supervise Monte's education or find other employment. Monte came to an understanding with Miss Creel that absences would need to have legitimate errands associated with them. The strain of deception was too much for Miss Creel and her headaches worsened. She couldn't protect Monte and backed out of their deal. Monte was now in a dilemma that had no easy solution. He was stuck again in the endless lesson plans his father prepared for the children, trapped in the sweltering room with Miss Creel who was still terrified to open the windows to the fresh spring breezes. The sun beat in all day, overheating the room to a swelter. The children droned on through endless pages of useless information as the minutes tumbled away.

It soon became clear that Monte had no intention of studying hard to get into college for what he foresaw as just another stretch of dusty classics and classrooms. This was mortifying to Charles. He could not conceive that his eldest son, the heir apparent, protector and vanguard of the new generation was not committed to getting a formal higher education. It was simply unthinkable and an explosive topic.

But it could not be helped, the shimmering world outside the two kitchen windows entranced Monte like twin exotic dancers. The sheer abundance of America drew him into daydreams of powerful rivers and vast forests. He saw cities of soaring buildings with thousands of smiling, jazz-crazed friends all waiting to welcome him to parties on the great rolling lawns of their family estates. America was the freedom to just jump on a train and cross the country, the exuberance of flappers, the open expanses of the West and the hilarity of Charlie Chaplin. It captured his imagination completely. America itself would be his classroom and he abandoned any thought of a profession, trade or job that would support him. He would simply do whatever came along and he knew he couldn't fail. There was just too much opportunity for someone with their eyes open and a willingness to work.

He read the popular rags-to-riches life story of Horatio Alger and the dispatches of Horace Greeley on the abundance of the West that waited for any man with enough energy and courage. The model for his life was set. He would become rich and powerful; he just had no clear idea of how. He literally could not sit still – too much was happening in the world and he wanted to be a part of it desperately. Old European society was dead, new American society was bubbling over like a shaken magnum of champagne.

A young Westinghouse engineer had started broadcasting a regular schedule of records from his garage in Pittsburgh on a new invention called the radio. In Hollywood, Charlie Chaplin had just turned 30. He and movie icon Mary Pickford, just 27, were millionaires and had formed their own independent movie company. Just across the river in Manhattan, 33 year-old Al Jolson was electrifying audiences with his high energy, soul-wrenching performances. Everywhere one turned, the Old

World had been swept away and replaced by a new eccentric society.

Charles' lectures on caution and prudence were part of the Old World and Monte would have none of it. It was nonsense. Terms like propriety, restraint and forbearance held no more force than the cooing of pigeons in the eaves. He let the lectures fall on him like a chilling rain but kept his mind constant on the words of his fallen Queen that glowed inside him like a low, coal fire, glowing red and yellow. He was born to stand tall in the world. He couldn't fail. It simply wasn't possible.

On the streets, Monte was slowed to a walk as he held Leo's hand. The little boy still had a strong British accent and Monte tutored him continuously on proper American pronunciation so they wouldn't get singled out as foreigners. One day as Monte jumped into a neighborhood game of stickball, Leo was nearly crushed under the wheels of a butcher's wagon. A quick thinking neighbor snatched him out of the way at the last second.

When Charles heard of this he exploded, "You nearly killed the boy!" In a blind rage, he swung and slapped Monte hard across the face. Monte was confined to the apartment and Isabel was assigned the duty of tending to Leo. Unknown to Charles, Monte had been saving money for months that he had earned from his secret life after dark.

He had almost twenty dollars saved and it would have to be enough. The following day, after Charles had left for work, Monte packed his best clothes into a bundle and tied them with string. He called Isabel aside as Miss Creel was settling for the day's lessons in the front room. He told Isabel that he was leaving and he would write soon and not to worry.

He shook her hand goodbye. She asked him where he was going and he replied, "As far as twenty dollars will take me." With that, he turned and walked out of the apartment. He would never return to the family. It was late in the summer of 1920 and Monte had just turned 16.

Chapter 3

Freeport

Monte walked into Manhattan across the Brooklyn Bridge carrying his bundle containing one white shirt wrapped inside his dark suit, two pairs of white cotton underwear, a cloth napkin containing a few matzo crackers and a movie magazine. He wore a tweed motorman's cap, a white cotton shirt and a Buster Brown suit with knee pants. He walked quickly with his face down to avoid detection by the truant officers until he got halfway across the bridge at which point, according to the crime novels he'd been reading, he was out of the truant officer's jurisdiction. He felt he was a free citizen of the United States now and it would only be a short while before he was rich and could return to Brooklyn in a gigantic black car with pockets full of money.

As he reveled in his glorious future and the slightly superior talk he'd have with his father upon his return, he walked off the bridge onto Canal Street and turned up the Bowery. In his first 5 blocks of Manhattan he'd already seen more different kinds of people than he had living for a year in Brooklyn.

The gentility of Brooklyn Heights seemed part of another country. This was where the poor from a few dozen countries lived literally on top of one another. It was loud, it was fast and it was dangerous. It was the Bowery. A drunk sprawled across the sidewalk, his crotch soaked and buzzing with flies. Filthy children held their noses while they rifled his pockets for coins. Huge trucks loaded with furniture ran up on to the curb to avoid gaping, axle-busting potholes in the street. Crap games were out in the open. Three-card monte hustlers held suckers spellbound while the shill picked their pockets.

When he first saw the late morning sun splashing off the five story glass windows and crowning Beaux Arts stonework, he felt butterflies in his stomach. He almost walked into oncoming traffic as he crossed 33rd Street. Grand Central Station was as magnificent as they said in the papers. From here you could take a train to anywhere in the country. It was the towering golden gateway to his life of adventure and fortune.

He picked the destination Freeport, Long Island because the name fit his new status. On the train ride out of the city he passed through neighborhoods of factories and out into vast tracts of farmland. He saw the Atlantic Ocean swing into sight on his right and seemingly endless forests of hardwood stretch out inland to his left and suddenly there it was, he let himself imagine, the vast forest of the frontier. Somewhere beyond these trees were the great cities of St. Louis and Chicago, the vast prairies, towering mountains and a desert where it never rained.

Freeport was a movie-perfect American small town with a white church steeple in the center of town standing guard against all forms of corruption. The sea breezes cooled the shady town square and children played on the streets free of the fear of kidnappings and evildoers. Monte looked around for about an hour walking down the wide, shady streets past the barbershop, the library, to a pier. It was small and clean, intended for pleasure boats only. It was nothing like the massive structures he'd been around most of his life. There was no stink of fish or diesel. Just the clean salt sea. He decided he liked the place. Freeport was where he would start, he decided. Now all he had to do was see the top man and let him know he was in town.

Monte waited for about an hour until Mayor Howard Disetel could see him. In that time he rehearsed his presentation to the mayor. He decided he was ready to make the change he had been thinking of for some time. This was a fresh start and required a fresh approach. He would change his name from Meyer Prosser.

The church steeple, like a giant exclamation point, clearly punctuated the territory as non-Jewish. He needed something that sounded solidly American. Meyer Marcus Prosser became Monte Proser. He chose Monte from the square-jawed movie actor Monte Blue who stared out at him from the movie magazine he had packed in his bundle. The sound was right – Monte. It was masculine, impressive. The last name was more difficult. Prosser was too harsh sounding, too foreign. A name had to sound right. It had to have music and Prosser had the staccato rhythm of a Prussian marching band. Foreign names were always too long, American names were short –Smith, Jones, Brown. He took the hard "s" out, slipped in a more musical, jazzy "z" sound - Proser, like prose and poetry. Monte Proser, better.

The newly named Monte Proser was shown into the Mayor's office. He shook the Mayor of Freeport's hand with a firm grip and steady eye. He took the chair offered and sat very straight. He explained to Mayor Disetel that he was available for work and hoped the Mayor might suggest something suitable. Monte was certain local business people would be eager to hire someone so obviously enterprising, well-dressed and well-spoken as himself. All the Mayor had to do was introduce him. Mayor Disetel considered the proposal. He stared with some disbelief at the incredibly confident and admittedly well-spoken young gent facing him, then suddenly the corners of his mouth turned up and he burst out laughing. This confused Monte terribly. Had he said something wrong? When the Mayor had calmed down and dried his eyes from laughing, it was clear that Monte had rolled a seven, as he never doubted that he would, but not exactly as he had imagined. Disetel had a son Gregory, the same age as Monte. Perhaps Monte would like to come to the house and meet him? "Yes, that would be fine." Monte said, somewhat upset that a job had not been offered.

Within hours Monte had charmed his way into the Disetel family. It was an effortless conquest, as natural as sunrise. It probably never occurred to him that this might be an unusual situation – that a stranger would open his home to him after a brief chat and that the stranger's family would welcome him almost like a returning son. Monte was completely unaware of his talent, which at this point was brand new and dazzling. It was still unstained by the betrayals and heartbreak that would come. It was not clouded by liquor or the compulsion to gamble that would eventually encroach. It was simply the talent to draw people to him, to instantly become a friend, someone you invited home. It was a talent that built an empire without a formal education, family connections or money. Eventually he developed an educated wit and an ability to spin entertaining stories but his essential quality was optimism - an intoxicating sense that anything was possible.

Monte was invited to stay with the family and share Greg's room. Greg was also an avid fan of detective and popular adventure books, so the two spun out their versions of stories they'd read on the Freeport beaches at night, performing all the parts.

The job Monte expected arrived just as he expected it would. He and Greg were introduced to the manager of the swanky new restaurant and summer theatre, *The Lights Club*. The two boys were assigned as general help and were started off in the kitchen washing dishes for the lunch business. The boundless energy that had made Monte a valuable messenger in Baltimore made him a valuable dishwasher and busboy - one who managed to charm customers while clearing dishes. He could put on a proper English accent and play at being an English butler. Americans loved the act and a shower of nickels, dimes and quarters fell into his outstretched hand like spring rain. Monte was certain now that his fortune would soon be made.

After busing tables, he haunted the backstage area of the club, poking his nose into everything that happened and offering to help in every task he saw. Eventually he maneuvered himself into the position of assistant stage manager. His limited wardrobe gave him a choice of his brown tweed, which was too hot for the summer evenings, or his fine black dress suit. In his black English tailored suit he was the best dressed assistant stage manager in the history of *The Lights Club* and possibly all of Long Island. When the time came to move scenery or clean out the paint shop, Monte noticed the stage manager diverted this heavy and dirty work to stagehands. He assigned Monte to help organize costume storage and run errands for the band. Monte realized his clothes were elevating the type of jobs he received. He remembered his father's insistence on using the finest cloth and meticulous tailoring on the suit. He appreciated this fact about his father and for the first time in the few weeks since he'd left home, was beginning to think of him without bitterness. He wrote his father a brief postcard and let him know how he was getting along. He thanked him for the fine suit that was part of his success.

"Come in!" the command boomed from inside the dressing room. Monte stood looking at the gold star on the door and took a moment to shine his shoes on the back of his pant legs. Inside the room was the biggest star of vaudeville. Her gowns cost hundreds of dollars – nearly a year's wages for many of the fans who poured in to see her. She stood as tall as most men and ran her business with as much authority as any Rockefeller – hiring and firing men in her band like a field general.

Monte entered the jumbled up room. It was crowded floor to ceiling with sprung open traveling trunks, drawers pulled out spilling lingerie, fur and jewelry from one side of the room to the other. Sophie Tucker squatted on her divan, cigarette dangling from her lips, huge white legs like tree limbs descending into an enamel basin. Daisy, her Negro assistant poured hot water into the basin. Monte judged her to weigh at least twice as much as he did. She closed her eyes and drew in a breath of painful relief.

"I'll kill that Goddamn shoe-maker." she exhaled at the ceiling. Monte looked at the snow white, rhinestone encrusted high heels on the floor next to the basin. She lowered her head that was piled high with light blonde hair, took the cigarette out of her mouth and motioned to Monte to approach. He did and felt something was required by way of introduction, "Good evening Miss Tucker. My name is Monte Proser."

"Well, well. Is that so?"

Monte wasn't sure whether to offer his hand, so he made a slight bow. He looked into her face and she started to smile.

"Hello totteleh." She had chosen the Jewish familiar address of mothers to children and youngsters, a term of matronly kindness.

"Hello," he responded impulsively. He hadn't heard the phrase since his own mother had held him in her arms and hummed a tune into his freshly bathed hair. It was all he needed to hear. He was her devoted champion from that moment.

"You know where to get cold cream in this town?"

"Yes, M'am"

"You call me Sophie. This is Daisy."

In Sophie's three weeks of sold out performances at *The Lights Club*, Monte became her shadow and Daisy's right hand helper. He was there as she arrived every afternoon at the theatre and escorted her to each entrance on stage. He watched every moment of every performance as she finessed song after song, infusing each one with an emotionalism that was genuine and unaffected. She was so completely herself and in her element that nothing could shake her. If a light fell backstage or she missed her lighting mark, it became part of the act. She cursed her luck or apologized as naturally as if she was in her own kitchen and people loved her for it. She was their own good-old Sophie – a regular gal. Between songs, she would seem to rest as she chatted with audience through practiced patter and jokes but Monte realized she was listening with an intensity that made her pause from time to time. Sophie was certainly not the most attractive woman to look at or even nearly the best singer. She was simply Sophie; unadorned, emotional, honest. She captured the heart and fired the emotional memory of everyone within the sound of her voice.

Monte let it all pour into him. He had found the echo of his own heart – as true as a harbor beacon. He had had no stomach for the rough work of bootlegging or running a gambling operation. Through Sophie, he witnessed the true measure of talent and it would guide him perfectly.

Charles and the family ventured for a weekend to Freeport late in the summer season. They were greeted by the Mayor at the train station and invited to his house to relax after dropping their bags at their rooms in a summer hotel. Monte arrived in between his job at the restaurant and before going to the theater. The Mayor gave a glowing account of Monte's visit and Charles was stoically impressed. Charles asked his son, without using the new name of Monte, what he had been reading. Monte told him he'd been re-reading Aristotle. He knew that was what Charles wanted to hear. In fact, he'd only glanced through "Poetics" since he left home. Mostly he'd been reading movie magazines and pulp novels that Greg had in his room. Shockingly, Charles asked if Monte was seeing any of the local girls. This was as close to a fatherly chat about sex as the two would ever get. It was informal and highly personal and Monte recalled that it seemed almost to question the supervision of Mayor Disetel. Monte responded that he'd seen a few he had wanted to talk to, but was usually too busy working. The issue dropped. Charles seemed satisfied that his son's moral slide hadn't progressed too far.

That evening Charles sat out in the cool ocean breezes with Mayor and Mrs. Disetel in a box seat of *The Lights Club* listening to the lively saxophones of a big band and eating freshly made vanilla ice cream. Life in that moment was everything America had promised to Charles. His British formality softened under the melodic waves rolling from the bandstand. The oppressive heat and ever-present dangers of Brooklyn were far away. His small children were safe to wander outdoors at night and chase fireflies. In his few weeks on his own, Monte had lost the agitation Charles remembered and seemed light-hearted. He was applying himself to his work with an energy Charles wished he had shown for his studies. His young face had the healthy rose and tan cheeks of an outdoorsman and most startling of all, he had impressed this small community as an extraordinarily capable and charming young man, an example to be emulated. It was clear that his son, once called Meyer, had passed forever out of his control and beyond his influence. The boy was now

Monte Proser, an independent young man making his own way in the world.

In the early part of the train ride back to Brooklyn, Charles crowed to the girls and little Leo about their older brother. He was to be admired. Monte was undisciplined, headstrong to be sure, but nonetheless he was to be admired. Charles left his three remaining children with that lesson. He pulled his pince-nez glasses from his vest pocket, placed them gingerly on his nose, turned to his newspaper. Leo asked him if Monte was coming home and he said no. He read his newspaper and was quiet the rest of the trip.

The productive days of summer had lined Monte's pockets with easy money. He had invested much of his summer earnings in a three-piece Brooks Brothers blue, pinstriped suit and fine brown brougham shoes, a shocking extravagance to some, but to Monte it was both confirmation of his ability and preparation for the destiny he felt sure he was soon to fulfill. As summer faded, he was faced for the first time in his brief successful career, with a narrowing of his options. Greg was due to go off to college and he suddenly had to make the choice to stay on in Freeport, go back to Brooklyn or think of something else. His ambition pushed him into the unknown.

Transportation was an unnecessary expense when the spaciousness and romance of open boxcars were available to anyone with a fast pair of legs. Monte thanked the Disetels for their hospitality and informed them that he was off to seek his fortune. The send off was as warm and gracious as their welcome. A very special closeness had developed between them but their lives couldn't have diverged more completely. Greg followed a well-worn path to adulthood, Monte wandered where his whims took him. That first summer in Freeport was a cherished memory for Monte as long as he lived. In later years it was often recounted to remind him or instruct his children on the basic goodness of people, and also on how far you can get with a good suit.

CHAPTER 4

THE 500 MILE DEATH RACE

The crucial difference between a bum and a hobo is that a bum is just a bum, but a hobo is a noble and free-spirited itinerant worker. A bum lies around and bums things; a hobo lives the promise of free enterprise with the fearlessness of a pioneer. They are not to be confused lest a grave insult be laid on a class of men who built much of America in the 1920's. Monte was always insistent on that point. A bum could be known by his tattered clothes, a hobo carried his meager belongings in a neat bundle often depicted in paintings as wrapped in a red patterned handkerchief, and dangling on the end of a long thin pole resting on the shoulder. The vaudeville clown, Emmett Kelly used the pole and bundle as his comic prop and it is seen in most depictions of him. In Monte's later homes a picture of the clownish Kelly in the kerosene footlights with his blackened face, white lips and bundle pole was always in a prominent place. The pole was a universal tool used by the hobo as a fishing pole, tent pole, weapon, and in the case of a bundle, as luggage handle.

The bundle, because hobos are relentless innovators, became commonly known as a bindle, and the hobo, because hobos were relentless physical laborers, became known as a working stiff. Thus, among themselves, the elite and cognoscenti of hobos soon referred to themselves as bindlestiffs. This separated the seasoned bindlestiff who was totally self-sufficient, from the novice, common hobo who may occasionally swipe a pie cooling in a kitchen window or chicken from an unwatched barnyard.

Among bindlestiffs, Monte developed the unique style of mailing his fine Brooks Brothers suit and brougham shoes to a hotel at an intended destination. He would then 'ride the rails' to his destination, check into the hotel as a bindlestiff and emerge later in the lobby as a dapper young man of promise. This curious partnership, the carefree bindlestiff and the dashing man of fortune, were the two essential elements of Monte's developing character. His simultaneous disregard for money and yearning for acceptance into stylish society would make him into the perfect high stakes gambler – a nightclub impresario. As with all partnerships, one of the partners began carrying most of the weight. He had been misled and somewhat spoiled by his early success in Freeport. He came to rely on his clothing to open the arms of influential strangers and secure him the key to any city.

He leapt from his rolling boxcar outside the Keokuk municipal rail yard and beyond the reach of the railroad bulls. The bulls were the lowly salaried detectives of the railroad companies. They were universally disdained by bums, hobos and bindlestiffs as being lifeless wage slaves. Bulls were the hobos' principal enemy often inflicting crippling beatings on the unfortunate late-sleeping or slow-running hobo and robbing them for the trouble. The best way to avoid them was make the running leap from the train well outside the depot as it slowed when approaching a destination. For the same reason, boxcars toward the back of the train were prime hobo real estate.

Monte made his way to the hotel for a rendezvous with the Brooks Brothers that had arrived by US mail, and an afternoon of social prospecting. After washing the road dust off, shaving, powdering and pomading he brushed out the midnight blue wool of his fine suit, polished his broughams and dressed for the afternoon. Then fully inflated with naiveté, he promenaded through town displaying his invisible but, to him, obvious ability to the citizens of Keokuk. He'd have a light meal, buy the local newspapers and retreat to his hotel lobby. There he waited in anticipation of his discovery by a prominent citizen who would certainly recognize him as his heir apparent, offer him the keys to the office and his daughter's hand in marriage. Of course, the day would pass with Monte having read the paper, eaten a light meal and having met only other retired or indolent lobby rats like himself. The next day he would be pressed to find any type of work to pay for the next night's hotel and meal.

He tried his audition with the Mayor routine. That served as a quick lesson on how rare people like Mayor Howard Disetel are in the world. Clearly more was being asked of him than his ability to wear a good suit and he rose to the challenge gradually.

The adventure of new towns, new people, new jobs and the traveling brotherhood of bindlestiffs was more than enough to keep Monte entertained and believing that he was just around the corner from stumbling into some great opportunity. In the cold months he washed dishes, waited on tables or any other indoor work he could find. He picked up occasional stints as a general stagehand in the vaudeville houses around the country. In the warm months he picked fruit, dug ditches and cleared brush. The infectiousness of his love of for the cult of the open boxcar and his unshakeable faith in his ultimate good fortune continued to draw people to him and protect him. As long as the towns, the jobs and the people were new, he continued to happily roll the dice. In the next town or the next boxcar could be the guy that would make his fortune. Slowly, with the grudging acceptance of a gambler walking away from a cold deck of cards, Monte accepted that hard work and diligence were the only ways he was going to find his fortune.

Chicago in the winter of 1923 rattled with the sound of sheet metal being shaped, stockyards groaning, hot jazz and Thompson sub machine guns. The Taxi Wars were leaving scores of perforated gangsters leaking all over city streets. Monte arrived with enough money for a few weeks and a Brooks Brothers suit that was beginning to fray at the cuffs. For nearly two years he'd been "riding the rails" as a hobo, working as a circus roustabout and picking up odd jobs, along with thousands of other fortune-seekers. It was time to begin directing his career instead of being blown by the winds of chance, and Chicago seemed as good a place as any to start.

Monte found a small room above a hardware store in a region of the city called Near West Side, north of the Chicago River. It was a spider web of streets ten minutes by trolley from the Loop downtown and populated with a riot of what-not markets, pool halls, saloons and dance joints. It was the territory of George "Bugs" Moran, the affable, singing, folk hero and gangster whose North Side Irish Gang fought it out with Al Capone for control of the bootlegging business and was soon to be the guest of honor at Capone's Valentine's Day Massacre. Soon after Monte moved into the neighborhood, Dion O'Banion, Moran's business partner, was assassinated by Capone and an advertisement appeared in the local newspapers sponsored by Moran and two other North Siders announcing that in respect to the assassination of their leader they, the survivors, would share the running of the organization as equals. They signed the ad, "Board of Governors". The city was half shocked but amused by the gumption of the gangsters posing so brazenly as a group of legal businessmen. Prohibition had so corrupted respect for the law that criminals felt free to advertise and corrupt politicians were unafraid to operate in the open. Bootleggers became respected men of The Cause. The Cause was to repeal the 18th Amendment. The North Siders now headed up by Moran and company and the South Side run by Italian Johnny Torrio, whose confrere or chief lieutenant was Al Capone, both paid tribute to the country's most corrupt Mayor William Hale "Big Bill" Thompson. Chicago Daily News columnist Howard Vincent O'Brien called Thompson "…a prince of demagogues" and his political machine one "…that made the efforts of such men as Tweed (a convicted corrupt politician) seem bungling and inexperienced."

This corruption in the highest and lowest strata of society was accompanied by outlandish public fads such as flagpole sitting and dance marathons. Flappers bobbed their hair in defiance of the long tresses revered in popular culture, smoked cigarettes, had multiple lovers and talked back to men whenever they felt like it. In nearby Dearborn, Michigan Henry Ford was rolling a Model T off his assembly line every 10 seconds which were reviled by many of the upright citizens who supported Prohibition as "…brothels on wheels." But overall, Prohibition was good for legitimate business and great for illegal business.

People who had never touched alcohol before Prohibition, began to drink to be part of the fun and danger of it. Cocaine was used freely and often combined with alcohol, notably in a popular wine called *Vin Mariani*. Likewise, marijuana was legal, inexpensive and a favorite of musicians at the time. Many of the speakeasies that offered these legal intoxicating treats also provided illegal diversions such as gambling, loan sharking and prostitution on the premises. The line between legal and illegal activity was sufficiently blurred so that average citizens felt comfortable breaking the law, and it was certainly more fun than the hell-fire preaching of Temperance meetings.

In order to operate efficiently, the speakeasies shoveled cash into local political coffers and into patrolmen's pockets. A river of bribes, kickbacks and payoffs washed through American society from top to bottom. In Chicago, virtually all local, regional and federal officials were supplementing their government income directly or indirectly from the profits of bootleg liquor and associated activities. Because of their access to the whiskey mills of Canada and the grain fields of the Midwest, independent minded Chicagoans brewed the headiest mix of lawlessness and the wildest nightlife in the country. Into this cacophony of corruption and public misbehavior strode the adventuresome young Monte. He found work soon after his arrival with the jeweler Sam Klein.

Klein was a moderately successful neighborhood merchant who fancied himself a car racing sportsman and purveyor of quality goods. Monte was put behind the counter as a salesman. This soon proved to be much too boring a position for the energetic former barker and roustabout. He spent his afternoons spinning notions of how to promote Klein's business. He soon impressed the enterprising Klein with a series of remarkable promotional notions. Calling on his experience as a circus barker, Monte first engineered a simple handbill campaign to bring the jeweler's name out into the neighborhood. Monte stalked the street in front of Klein's shop proclaiming his slogan, "Meet Klein and wear diamonds!" as he handed out the handbills with the name and address of the shop. On the handbill was the offer to own a diamond for a dollar a month, a sum most could afford. Klein's business began to grow steadily as a result.

Monte spent his off hours haunting the speakeasies especially the dimly lit, smoky *McGovern's* cabaret on North Clark Street where gangster Dion "Deany" O'Banion part-timed as a singing waiter. While he held forth with lilting ditties in his fine Irish tenor, his mates Moran and others, picked the pockets of drunk customers or rolled them for their billfolds in the men's room.

In 1923, Moran had just been released from a 5-year prison stint after staying quiet on a robbery charge and taking a dive for everybody in his gang. He had been given a hero's welcome on his return to *McGovern's*. The cabaret was the hottest of the North side hangouts.

In spite of its seedy side, McGovern's was the favorite hangout of politicos and union bosses who showed up for a song and a drink after work. In neighborhood pubs like *McGovern's*, neighborhood gangs were increasingly looked upon as Robin Hoods and popular pirates who lived a life of excitement outside the boring 9-to-5 of most working people.

Deany grinned to his political friends for whom he would find much work intimidating voters and stuffing ballot boxes, "We're a diverse lot. And we wear our brass knuckles with style, sir!"

Monte spent most of his free time at *McGovern's* and places like it, meeting people, listening to the music and developing his taste for hard liquor. It was hard not to admire these rough and colorful characters – characters like Sammy Morton who called himself "Nails" and fenced stolen cars on the West Side, Louie Alterie, a union breaker with a fascination for the Old West and "Dapper Dan" McCarthy, an army deserter and plumber who strode *McGovern's* like a peacock in the finest, most expensive suits. Beyond the free spirit of these characters who stayed up singing all night, woke up late and did exactly as they pleased, Monte was attracted to the fact that they were all fantastically rich. Prohibition had made them all more money than they had ever dreamed of and Monte was ready for his share.

Sam Klein adopted Monte like his long lost son, who also happened to be turning his pokey jewelry store into a bonanza. Advertisements with Monte's dollar a month scheme and "Meet Klein and Wear Diamonds" slogan appeared in newspapers, billboards and on "sandwich boards" portable signboards worn over the shoulders of hawkers who shouted Monte's slogan down the city streets as they passed out handbills. Klein's success left Monte with free time to dream up ideas. He soon came up with his first publicity stunt. Inspired by the newsreel films of Barney Oldfield racing a locomotive in an open top roadster, Monte created *"The World's First 500 Mile Death Race"*. The title was both outrageous and misleading since there was no "death" intentionally involved, but was nonetheless sadly prophetic. Klein leaped at Monte's idea to race his new Packard V12 Phaeton roadster against the Santa Fe's *Super Chief*.

Monte devised a city-wide publicity campaign using all the newspapers, handbills and sandwich board barkers he could muster. The stunt was promoted with the grandiosity of an arriving World's Fair. With characteristic flair, Monte persuaded Mayor "Big Bill" Thompson to fire the starting pistol. A gigantic local turnout was now assured. Monte had the "starting gate" constructed on either side of the Union Pacific railroad tracks just beyond Union Station in downtown Chicago. The gate was a circus-gaudy affair with banners and huge letters proclaiming "Meet Klein and Wear Diamonds". Klein was coached by Monte before his newspaper interviews to portray himself as a brave, selfless local hero who risked his life to prove that one man with determination could defeat the powerful forces of wealthy railroad barons. This was such an important part of his personal creed that he had dedicated his life to making sure any working person could own a diamond, just like Mr. Rockefeller – or something like that. Klein got the drift and didn't need much coaching after the first few interviews.

The newspaper exposure generated letters from all over the region wishing Klein well and included a few marriage proposals from impressionable young women. For a moment, Sam Klein, neighborhood jewelry merchant, was a local Lindbergh. He even began to believe some of what he was saying and took to wearing his white silk racing scarf full time around the shop. Monte was astounded at the reaction and unprepared. He raced to have extra handbills printed and sandwich-board hawkers hired to take advantage of the large crowd expected at the starting gate.

The fateful day arrived and the *Super Chief* approached right on time. Of course, the Union Pacific company and the engineer of the train had no idea they were involved in a race with Mr. Sam Klein. The 12:05 *Super Chief* bound for points West roared out of Union Station and was a mile down the track, nearly at full speed when the engineer noticed a crowd of hundreds of people massed around the tracks and some type of construction on either side. He blew the whistle as a warning.

This was the signal Monte had been waiting for. He announced through a megaphone from a raised platform near the starting gate, "The Great Race is on! Mr. Klein start your engine!" Monte improvised the last part, which confused Klein. He looked at Monte through his partitioned driving goggles and threw up his hands in futility; his engine had been running for several minutes. Monte stumbled on in his best circus barker inflection," Mr. Mayor, ready your pistol!" Thompson struck a pose worthy of marble and Monte counted down with the crowd as the *Super Chief* approached at 60 miles an hour blowing its mighty air horn continuously. "On your mark, get set, go!" The *Super Chief* roared through the starting gate, the Mayor fired his pistol and Sam Klein stomped his accelerator to the floor. He sped away alongside the massive train. Photographers snapped photos and the crowd cheered the intrepid local hero. The two racing machines disappeared toward the horizon and the crowd thinned out through the gauntlet of sandwich-board hawkers who stuffed their hands with handbills. Mayor Big Bill Thompson shook Monte's hand and handed him the starter's pistol. The Mayor naturally assumed the race was fixed and asked Monte, "Whose gonna win?" Of course, he was right.

"The car." Monte answered. Big Bill smiled and invited Monte to visit him at City Hall anytime.

Light-headed and jubilant, Monte retired to *McGovern's* to celebrate and pass the time until the photo finish the following day in Omaha, Nebraska. Certain members of the North Side Irish Gang who had been at the start of the race congratulated the young promoter. Monte had his first taste of celebrity. They wanted to know the odds on the race since gambling was a necessary part of any public event. Monte assured them that Klein was going to roar ahead to win by a nose in a beautiful photo finish. He had it all calculated, Klein would be reported to be losing by scouts set up along the route. They would telegraph progress of the race to Chicago. The ace in the hole was that the train had to slow down as it approached the finish line outside the Omaha station. All Klein had to do was stay even with the train, or a little behind, which he thought should be easy to do, and roar ahead at the last moment. Heavy odds were touted throughout the North Side and Monte got stinking drunk for the first time in his life as the honored guest of Deany O'Brien and his North Side gang.

When Monte awoke in his hotel room sometime in the afternoon of the following day, the race had already been over for hours. He threw on his clothes and staggered with a crushing hangover to the hotel lobby telephone. He rang up his contact at the Omaha newspaper for the news of the finish. The news was not good. In fact, it was very bad. Sam Klein had been killed outside of Des Moines when his car overturned on an unmarked culvert. The train had won.

Monte had become very fond of Klein, who was in his way an adventurer like Monte. Crowds of mourners gathered at Klein's Jewelry Store to stare at the last place their local hero had been before his fateful race. Word soon arrived to Monte that several members of the North Side gang were paying off through the nose on a bad tout from some wiseacre kid, and they were not pleased. The romance of the open road suddenly bloomed again for Monte and he skipped town in a yellow Nash roadster that he bought in a hurry with no questions asked.

CHAPTER 5

Hollywood Dreams

In 1924, Hollywood had many more orange trees than people. Miles of rutted dirt roads connected dusty farms that had been converted into outdoor movie mills. Silent movies were ground out under sun-diffusing muslin canopies. Directors shouted instructions over whirring camera noise and the shouting of other directors working next to them in the open air. When the cameras stopped, the crickets took over and the city quickly reverted to a pleasant farming community with a dim and nearly lifeless downtown. Monte quickly discovered that the glamour of Hollywood was mainly on the screen and the day to day life in the movie business reminded him more of the rhythm of mill and factory work of northern England than anything else. It was the common reaction of many Easterners who found the utter lack of nightlife unnerving and the rarity of social interaction depressing. It was a very long way from the noise and tumult of the big cities of the East.

More than anything, Monte craved the crush of other people, the excited interplay of conversation and music. Where was the music in Hollywood? While flappers and jazz were tearing up gin joints in Chicago, nightspots in Los Angeles were likely to be full of ranch hands, oil workers and citrus farmers quietly munching peanuts to the strumming of a homemade guitar. The entertainment in Los Angeles was generally packed up in steel film cans and shipped to Pathe' distributors in New York for delivery to the gilded movie palaces around the country.

Yet, millions were being made in movies. The only problem was most of the movies at this time were still being made in the East. Paramount Studios wouldn't move to the West Coast for another seven years. Monte was stuck at the dusty end of the continent having done a "Horace Greeley" and gone west as a young man.

His fate, common to new arrivals in Hollywood then and now, was to work as an extra. Young men of Monte's Semitic features of dark hair and rounded noses frequently found themselves in buckskin loincloths with turkey feathers in their hair. They would stand arms crossed defiantly in the distant background as Two Gun Bill Hart or Monte's namesake Monte Blue, swapped blankets for bullets with the big Chief by an Indian campfire. As the cameras ground through yards of celluloid, they stood and nodded with bare shoulders under the blazing sun. Heatstroke and sunburn felled many Jewish braves early in their careers and Monte was another faceless casualty in the white man's incessant drive for entertainment.

Perhaps because of his disappointment in Hollywood or his realization that he had reached the end of his carefree, vagabond youth, his sterling enthusiasm and self-confidence seemed to leave him. He no longer put on his Brooks Brothers suit and read the local paper in his hotel lobby waiting to be discovered by powerful benefactors. He didn't cajole a studio or shop owner into letting him promote their wares. Instead he fell back on his first and most basic gift, his raw energy. He went to work as a physical laborer doing anything he could find. He soon found steady work on a road crew as Los Angeles desperately tried to come up to the standards of a modern city with paved streets.

It was miserable work – slathering hot, stinking tar in the merciless Los Angeles heat. Yet he applied himself with a focus and energy that soon brought him to the attention of the road boss. What luck and the Brooks Brothers could not provide, he would carve for himself from dirt and rock. He simply would not allow himself to be a failure. It wasn't remotely possible.

He would retreat to his hotel at night exhausted and reeking of tar. At least it satisfied his basic needs for money and he didn't have to stand in line at the "shape up" with other movie extras hoping to break into the movies – and maybe not work at all. After months of mean labor without even hope of relief, he began to lose heart that he would ever recover his enthusiasm for life. His salvation arrived by mail.

Carl Erbe, his ever-faithful, fellow hobo, had tracked him down and sent a letter to Monte's sweat-stained Los Angeles hotel. Carl and Monte had met years earlier, late one freezing cold night, in a boxcar rolling across the Great Plains toward their unformed futures. Carl had devised a portable cooking stove out of an oil can and generously, in proper hobo etiquette, offered half a heated can of beans to Monte. Monte immediately recognized Carl as a true, noble hobo – not a lowly tramp or even worse a bum – and obviously with his oil can stove, a man of science. The two fell in together immediately and partnered over the years in adventures including entertaining campers at *Yellowstone Park*, promoting a young fighter around the Milwaukee area named *Kid Jabs* and working as roustabouts and side-show barkers for the *Snapp Brother's Circus*, a one-ring mudshow out of Long Island, New York.

Now, instead of riding the rails, Carl was in the movie business in New Jersey. The details were sketchy but they were more than enough to put Monte in the next boxcar leaving Union Station. In his farewell boxcar tour of America, Monte made no appearances along the way as a working bindlestiff. He was a young man who had graduated the School of Hard Knocks and had been selected to join in the great enterprise of entertaining America. Or so he imagined.

The great enterprise of entertaining America had been put through the keen business mind of Carl Erbe and had come out as smooth and featureless as milled lumber. Carl seized on the principles of mass production, so profitably demonstrated by Henry Ford, and applied them to movies. Although this has been attempted by nearly every movie producer in history, Carl hit upon the misinterpreted element – interchangeable parts. Every producer soon finds out that the stories can't really be duplicated but the basic elements or formulas can be. A formula that emerged in Carl's mind and had already become a staple of Hollywood by then, was the old chestnut; boy meets girl, boy loses girl, boy gets girl. The problem Hollywood could never solve was how to repeat the winning formula but make it different enough so the audience thinks they are seeing something new. Carl didn't try. Carl discovered he could make exactly the same movie indefinitely. The interchangeable part that Hollywood could not grasp was the audience.

The set up was simple. In an increasingly movie-mad public, all that was required was the application of Monte's charm, a movie crew and a small town with a local theatre. Sometime mid-week, when advertising rates were low, a 2-inch ad would appear in the local newspaper of a small town somewhere in New York, New Jersey, Pennsylvania or Connecticut. The ad announced that the small town had been selected as the location for a major motion picture by *New Era Motion Pictures. New Era* was looking for new faces to screen test and would be holding auditions in one week. The lucky winners of the audition would be screen tested the following week.

Suddenly drama clubs at the local high school were jammed with a rash of new actors brimming with emotion, singing instructors around town enjoyed a rush of new clients bursting with song. Elocution, fencing and dance schools filled with intensely animated teenagers, housewives and tradesmen. The Mayor ordered long overdue repairs to town facilities – particularly the ones that showed. Police were instructed to remove vagrants to the city limits and issue them a stern warning not to return. Barbershops and beauty parlors snipped, pomaded, curled and waxed a phalanx of native Valentinos, Pickfords and Fairbanks'. As the week matured, a coolness settled over the small town and sauntering was widely practiced. Cigarettes were smoked with rakish attitude, shots of liquor were knocked back with dramatic flair and small disagreements flared into soul wrenching soliloquies.

The day finally arrived. A gleaming roadster, waxed to the luster of a dressing room mirror rolled into town. It slowly circled the entire downtown area, its driver calmly inspecting the inhabitants and their facilities behind his arc-light proof sunglasses. The car stopped first at the newspaper office. Out stepped Monte, once again immaculate in his tailored pin-stripes and broughams. By now the word had gone out from the donut shop, the filling station and the Lady's Emporium – the movie people were here. Monte strode into the offices of the *Altoona Daily Bugle*, the *Paterson News*, the *Poughkeepsie Crier* and asked to see the editor in chief. The Chief received the news with forced calm while the secretary/receptionist smiled significantly at Monte and angled the framed photograph of her daughter on her desk in his direction. The local reporter tipped back his fedora with the press card in the hatband and peered over the smoke from his dangling *Lucky Strike* like Bogart sizing up a mark.

These performances and many like them continued throughout Monte's two-day stay in the town. After granting the Chief newshound an exclusive interview that would generally run on the front page the following day, Monte made his way to the Mayor's office. As with his first meeting with Mayor Disetel of Freeport, Monte impressed the town leader with his infectious enthusiasm. He painted a picture of *New Era*'s hopes to make quality, family pictures. The details were filled in by the galloping imaginations of the Mayor and anyone else who had waited all week to meet the man from Hollywood, although *New Era* never got further West than Altoona, Pennsylvania. Monte always inquired as to whether the Mayor had any teenage or young adult children, if so, they should audition for his picture – you could never tell, a Hollywood contract and a fortune could be in the stars for them.

As luck would have it, the Mayor's son and the Police Chief's daughter almost always got the starring roles in *New Era* productions. The two fated hopefuls reenacted a classic tale of romance, danger and redemption; boy meets girl, boy loses girl, boy gets girl. An opening sequence established all the major businesses in town and their happy staff. This was the setting for the adventure. At the fateful moment, when all the local businesses who could be potential advertisers in this *New Era* production had been photographed, the boy and the girl met. It was always love at first sight, since the cameraman/ director was under strict orders from Carl that the lovers had to meet before 150 feet of film was shot. The courtship was brief and included major landmarks of the town - but danger lurked. Without warning, the doe-eyed maiden was suddenly a damsel in distress. A speeding car, an approaching train or a prominent town burgher who had always wanted to play a bad guy suddenly threatened the tender lovers. The dashing young man would spring into action. A chase of some type would ensue past the most prominent faces and businesses in town. With a stroke of selfless heroism the boy vaulted his love out of danger's icy grip. Once again, all was well as they held each other tightly, gazing into each other's eyes. For all eternity, and perhaps the third time that week, the boy got the girl. The End.

Monte had made sure that all the prominent people in town had been greeted and knew that their businesses would be featured in the movie. He usually dined that evening with a town dignitary. The following day he would hold auditions at the firehouse, high school or town hall. These were usually limited to asking the name, particular talent and performing experience of the person. There were always dozens and often hundreds of people eager to be seen, heard and discovered – yodeling plumbers, tap dancing mechanics and warbling wait-resses. He made his selections and sent them to Carl in New York who directed the schedule of the production crew. Monte moved on to the next town.

It was a lonely existence, worse in some ways than working on the roads in Los Angeles. At least he had his friends on the road crew to socialize with. Now he was isolated by design, a permanent stranger trading on the dreams of everyday people he knew would be disappointed. He knew it was far more likely they would get hit by lightning than be discovered as a movie star. He also knew that nothing in the world would stop them from trying and hoping. The stock market crash and Great Depression that would crush the life out of many of these small towns were still years away. It was a time of peace, prosperity and innocent optimism. As far as anyone knew, anyone could become a movie star. Anything was possible.

It certainly seemed that way to Monte, who finally had all the freedom the world could possibly provide; money, his own car, absolutely no obligations except to promote *New Era* in every little town within 100 miles of New York City. Carl had found him and led him to the pot of gold at the end a small rainbow but for Monte, it only created his next and much larger problem. In every town, Monte's final stop was the speakeasy, roadhouse, carpet joint or blind pig. These were the names for the havens that provided the three distractions he craved; socializing, liquor and gambling. The more isolated he became in his travels, the more he needed to connect with people who were having fun, swapping stories and commiserating at "the great equalizer" as he called it, a bar. Monte believed that bars were one of the best social structures ever invented to address several common human needs. Bars were America's adult playground, confessional, safe haven and town hall. Bars were a place where people spoke their minds freely and social stature didn't matter. He and millions of his future customers found the human connection they needed only in bars. Since bars were illegal, they also brought people together against a common enemy – the government. The lessons in humanity Monte learned at the bars were an invaluable but lonely education.

A few days after Monte moved on to his next town, a front-page story appeared in the local paper announcing the selection of the cast for *New Era*'s upcoming production. In the text of the story was a quote from *New Era*'s executive producer, Carl Erbe, inviting local businesses, which he mentioned by name, to support their local stars by advertising in the printed program notes that would be circulated at the premier in three weeks. It was gangbusters. The souvenir program featuring the names of the local stars and supporting cast looked like a real Hollywood playbill, except that the last three or four pages bulged with advertising.

The movie crew of 4 arrived in an enclosed truck with a hand-cranked camera, tripod, shiny board reflectors, canvas director chairs and a small make-up kit. They had breakfast with the stars and cast of the day and explained how the filming would proceed. For that day, the town effectively became the property of *New Era*. The police were *New Era's* security force and the town's inhabitants became enthusiastic, unpaid volunteers. Without fail, after a full day of chasing and melodramatic overacting throughout the town, at sunset the boy got the girl. They gazed longingly into each other's eyes, but did not kiss, as the sun set over the most picturesque part of town. The crew then packed up, waved goodbye to the exhausted and exhilarated cast, and drove off into the night.

The following week the newspaper announced completion of the film and its date of premier at the local theatre. After the announcement, Carl called the local theatre owner and discussed ways to boost the ballyhoo for the picture. A favorite suggestion was to organize a "Parade of Stars" featuring the local leading man and lady. Once again a committed core of citizens found a reason to celebrate their brush with Hollywood. For a few hours they commandeered Main Street and paraded in support of "their" film. Theatre owners soon discovered local interest was so intense it often overshadowed the scheduled Hollywood features.

On the appointed day, the dapper representative of *New Era* reappeared in his polished sedan. He carried with him 1000 feet of film packed with familiar faces and places dear to a small audience. Often premier celebrations were already underway when Monte arrived. Many had distinctly local features like livestock judgings and traditional ethnic dances. Monte stepped into the hoopla like Jason returning with the Golden Fleece, which wasn't far from the truth. Carl Erbe's 12 minute assembly-line movies played for weeks. Every relative of every bit player, which meant everyone in the surrounding area, came at least once. Many came dozens of times to marvel at themselves and their neighbors who loomed in front of them twenty feet tall on the screen. The little movies broke house records for the longest runs. They ran until the film literally fell apart and couldn't be run anymore.

Monte had learned his lessons from the heartland. He understood people's passion for drama. He understood their need to escape routine. He understood their childlike thrill at emotion. He understood that he wasn't really delivering what they wanted, not really. The passion they needed, that he needed, wasn't in the film cans of machine stamped stories. It was in his bones. It rang in his ears. It was ragtime piano, hobos belting bawdy songs and murderous gangsters weeping as they sang of their dear, sweet mothers. It was a feast of passion and he was only delivering an appetizer. The feast was somewhere near the loud music and glare. It was near the danger, the games of chance, the stench of excess. It was in the smoke and the crush and the millions of eyes desperate for love. It was in New York City. It was time for Monte to come home. He would return triumphant, in the big shiny car he had envisioned years ago as a young runaway to Freeport.

CHAPTER 6

THE STAR OF TEXAS

Monte returned home with pockets full of cash in a big shiny car just as he had predicted. At 21, his transformation from naïve youth, to hobo, to sophisticated man of the world was nearly complete. Under the sharp business eye of his boxcar mentor Carl Erbe, he was beginning to hone his natural abilities with language into a marketable skill - publicity.

He was becoming a press agent. The months he'd spent promoting Hollywood dreams to the small towns around New York City opened his eyes to what people wanted. They wanted to be known. They wanted to be recognized. The public hunger for fame, even to be remotely associated with it, was etched in his mind by the hundreds of expectant faces he had seen.

They wanted to be famous, wealthy and just like the stars in the newspapers and movies. They believed that they could leave their aprons and druggist smocks behind and live a life of privilege, attended by adoring fans. All they had to do was let someone know how special they were, how talented. Someone with connections like Monte could introduce them or their precocious daughter or their handsome nephew. He could make their daydreams into real life.

Monte's first uncertain steps into the emerging field of publicity were plagued by problems of inexperience. Before he found his niche as a promoter of speakeasies, Monte took on clients that, with a little more savvy, he might have avoided. Carl Erbe knew there was trouble when his young partner, fresh from his advance work for *New Era Pictures* in the wilds of New Jersey, arrived for lunch at *Delmonico's* with a beaming smile and announced his terrific news.

"My first client." Monte said proudly.

"Yeah?"

Monte pushed a tattered handbill toward his mentor. On it was emblazoned in large type, "*Dean, Doctor and Professor Kaufman. Astrologer, phrenologist and handwriting expert.*"

"What the hell is this?" Carl growled quietly. He was anxious about the new business and 3 cups of black coffee weren't helping his patience.

"He's got people standing in line. On the East Side."

"He's a carnival act."

"He's paying 25 a week."

"He is?"

"That's right."

"Watch he doesn't skip on you. No "*Pay you Tuesday…*" strictly cash on the barrel-head." Carl was uneasy about Monte's easy success. He had been disappointed over Monte's abandonment of their successful movie business and wondered if his young partner had the gumption to stick it out, to make a business work. Even though Carl had grown bored with the movie business himself, the prospect of steady money wasn't surrendered without a fight and it had strained their friendship. He also worried that Monte's taste for the most expensive clothes was a sign of general extravagance that would sink him before he had a chance to get going. It was the same generalized fear that had worried Monte's father. Almost as aggravating to Carl as his partner's willfulness, was the fact that no matter what, Carl just couldn't stay mad at the young wisecracker. Monte would always be the whimsical little hobo full of big dreams and good-natured wit. He was a free spirit, a dreamy-headed optimist and in regard to business, not completely logical or reliable. Just as the business-minded Carl would get up the steam to vent his frustration, Monte would crack his crooked smile, apologize and disarm him with a comment off the subject like, "How's your girl?" or "You sleepin' okay?" It was an amusing, frustrating sort of hell.

The profitable development with Professor Kaufman lightened the mood somewhat. The younger man sat in front of Carl happily reviewing Delmonico's menu for his hero's lunch, completely unfazed by Carl's testy remarks and at peace with the world. In spite of himself, Carl smiled. The kid had done it again. Monte's blind optimism won him over, just like it did to everyone else. He raised his water glass over his businessman's lunch, "Congratulations. You can pay."

Monte went on reading and humming to himself. Then he said, "You're a rat. Which is actually a very clean animal, I'm told," as he raised his glass with a short pause on the way to his lips.

"Honored, I'm sure. What's phrenology?" Carl asked.

"Bumps on the head. He reads them." Monte worked his fingers over an imaginary skull like a blind man reading Braille. This set Carl back in his seat. "What if you get knocked on the head in a fight?"

"I guess he would read that you were in a fight."

Carl spent a full second hashing out the philosophy behind it. "Here's what you do with this guy..." and Carl got busy mapping out a strategy to bring Professor Kaufman to the attention of the phrenology-starved citizens of New York City. Since nobody knew what phrenology was and even fewer believed it was on the level, Carl reasoned that they'd need bona fides to vouch for it. He saw phrenology readings of science students, or better, science teachers. No, even better, science professors. They'd get a couple of eggheads from City College and give them a hot lunch in return for their expressions of amazement at the accuracy of Kaufman's insight from their noggins. Monte felt the first twinge of headache – the signal that someone was crowding him, making plans for him – as his father had once tried to do.

The late editions of the *Mirror*, *Times* and *Herald* hit the newsstands as the working world was heading home for dinner.

Monte grabbed his copies of all three and searched them for mentions of the celebration party for Mayor Jimmy Walker at gangster Larry Fay's speakeasy, the *El Fay Club* featuring headliner Texas Guinan. The party was a publicity stunt Monte had invented to land the job as the mouthpiece for the notorious Guinan. It would be a score that would put him prominently up the list in the social register of Broadway hustle merchants. People would talk. There was only one, small hitch in the plan. The Mayor didn't know anything about the party. Monte figured he would show up if he saw it in the papers – a calculated gamble.

Fay opened the *El Fay Club* at 105 West 45th Street in 1924 and started selling outrageously overpriced Canadian whiskey as fast as it could be poured. The sound of raining money soon attracted Texas Guinan, a fading movie star. She had discovered late in her career that she could hold the attention of a roomful of boozers with a few songs, a wooden ball and stick clapper and a lot of wisecracks. Texas was soon presiding at the *El Fay* with a sexy chorus line and free rein to say and do anything she wanted. She didn't worry much about where Fay got his money or that a large part of her audience were his friends making the circuit from Sing-Sing. All she knew was that the rapid downward slide of her modest career had been reversed. As she entered her 43rd year, she suddenly became a star pulling in a top salary. No qualms about the legal status of her associates bothered her or any of her hundreds of guests she greeted with "Hello, sucker!"

No one before, or since, could hold sway over a rowdy barroom like Texas. She drew suckers from all walks, crooked and straight, into Fay's overheated, overpriced, overcrowded cellar where she insulted them, took their money and sang to them as best she could. And they couldn't get enough.

Texas soon became the incandescent, reigning queen of illegal nightlife. In her clubs, you did anything but speak easy. The places were loud, more like alcoholic glee clubs than clandestine nightspots. They were raided so often and she was arrested so often, that it became routine. To celebrate her notoriety, she had a necklace of padlocks made for herself. She always made sure the club's band was arrested with her so she could entertain the other prisoners in the City Hall jail. All the way downtown in the paddy wagon they sang choruses of "*The Prisoners' Song*". Texas knew how to make whoopee and the newspapers couldn't get enough of it.

Monte had come up with the plan to snag the Mayor a week earlier, just moments before he'd walked into the *El Fay*. He'd spent the previous weeks plotting his pitch to win Texas Guinan and the *El Fay* account, but had come up empty handed. His meeting had already been set and he wasn't going to cancel it. He had no idea what he was going to tell her until his brainstorm about Mayor Jimmy Walker arrived just in time as he entered the front door of the *El Fay*.

Texas was rehearsing. He moved to the bar, where he waited quietly until she finished. He'd come to her rehearsal the day before when the place was dotted by people who wanted her time. When she finished she made the rounds greeting friends and doing business. Monte waited patiently for two hours. Texas finally left the club to rest and prepare for the evening. He couldn't shove his card into her hand and start talking as he'd been encouraged to do by a half dozen small time agents. His ambition was constrained by the fact that first and always, he was a proper English-style gentleman, especially toward women. The hard sell American style was impossible for him. That day he left his card with the bartender and offered him a free steak dinner for two at one of the unlucky steak houses he represented at the time. In return, the bartender promised to get his card into Texas' hands and told Monte she would be rehearsing the next day too but at a different time.

Monte returned at the scheduled time and again sat with the bartender waiting for Texas to finish. The place was nearly empty this time. He'd get his chance to make his pitch. Texas had learned her limited moves that allowed the chorus girls to form a tableau around her and so concentrated on her singing. She was extremely mediocre as a singer, even on her best day. She finished the rehearsal at close to performance level singing nearly full out. Her last notes died off. Polite applause sprinkled out from the few people in the audience and faded, except for Monte. He continued to clap politely after the others had stopped. This drew her attention. He continued until she acknowledged him.

"Why thanks partner." Texas said. She preserved her West Texas twang, never wanting to blend in and become a New Yorker. If there was one thing Texas never wanted, it was to blend in. She made her rounds again, ending up at the bar where Monte introduced himself as one of her supporting cast in Hollywood, years earlier. She'd made over 300 two-reel Westerns, according to her, although the actual number was only 35, and couldn't exactly place him. That didn't slow him down. He'd only been a background extra anyway and had never spoken a word to her. He played an Indian brave, one of the Ashkenazi Hollywood tribe who looked Indian-enough from a distance.

Monte went right into his pitch for a tryout. He'd place articles announcing a party to celebrate the Mayor's recent election victory. Mayor Jimmy Walker wouldn't miss a chance to blow his own horn. Texas heard Monte out as she sipped from a mug of beer checking the bartender for his reaction. The bartender gave Monte the nod of endorsement and pushed his card toward her over the bar. Monte said he'd place the party item in every major column. She had to admit, she liked the young fella's style. He was calm and polite and listened thoughtfully when she interrupted. He wasn't much like the hard-edged Broadway characters she dealt with who pushed hard and never listened to anybody. For a Southern lady, it was nice to meet someone with refined manners. He had all the confidence of a young man but also the sense of someone who'd been around a bit and taken a few hard knocks. And he dressed like a real gent. When he finished, Texas looked him over top to bottom for any obvious signs of mental defect and then hitched her wagon to his vision.

"How much?" she asked.

"It's a tryout. If you like what I what I do..."

"I like _you_. And I figure you can do what you say you can do. You gonna make me ask you again?"

"50 a week," Monte said.

Texas didn't like the sound of that at all. "50? Horseshit. You can't be any too good if all you get is 50."

Monte looked at the bartender for a clue, he shrugged his shoulders. "100?" Monte guessed.

"150, and that's final." She pretended to spit on her palm and stuck her hand out to him. He took it and was in business with the top cabaret act in New York. Now all he had to do was pull off the stunt he dreamed up.

Monte, an itinerant hobo and freelance promoter, and Walter Winchell, an itinerant hoofer and gag man on the vaudeville circuit, both left the dusty back roads of America and entered the "suffused glow of a thousand lights" of Broadway in 1925. They made a pact over Lindy's cheesecake late one night to lure Mayor Jimmy Walker to a party at the *El Fay*. From modest schemes like this, Walter went on to re-define polite social reporting as bruising entertainment and pointed political commentary.

Monte and early press agents like him were the primary sources of the shocking human stories that Winchell would report unashamedly to the public. The voice that emerged from Winchell's daily column in the Hearst organization's *Daily Mirror* turned movies into "moom pictures", divorces were irreverently referred to as couples being "Reno-vated" and births became "blessed events". At the time, many newspaper editors were squeamish about even mentioning a private event like the birth of a baby. It was thought by many readers to be immodest. Winchell smashed this taboo and tore up the social contracts on privacy, discretion and modesty on his way to becoming one of the most powerful voices in America. Eventually even Presidents Franklin Roosevelt and Harry Truman sought Winchell's advice and assistance in swaying public opinion at difficult moments.

Winchell and the columnists that came to prominence with him like Mark Hellinger and Damon Runyon, were the primary outlets for the publicity Monte generated for his clients and later for himself at his own nightclubs. It was a natural relationship that put them both squarely at the center of the action. Together, with the lesser nightclub operators and columnists, they built the reality and perception of a new society, Café Society, on the ashes of the old world.

The day of the Mayor's party, Monte walked up Fifth Avenue toward the newly constructed *Ritz Hotel*. In the barbershop of the hotel, he'd have his second shave of the day and a shoeshine. It was the make-or-break night with Texas and he wanted to rest under a steam towel to think for a minute. If the Mayor didn't show up for his own party, and the evening flopped, he'd need something else planned, a make-good.

He turned a corner and saw him before he was seen. His first instinct was to turn away, hide his face, but he kept walking. He felt embarrassed and didn't know why. The presence of the man created an uncomfortable, weakening effect on him and he resisted it, raising himself to his full height and power. His father recognized him when they were a few feet apart. They slowed and stood silently assessing each other for a moment.

"How are you, son?"

"I'm well, Papa."

Charles offered his hand stiffly, not sure if it was the proper form of greeting for a son who had abandoned his home. Monte shook his father's hand.

"How are the girls?" Monte asked.

"Jim-dandy. Is that the word they use now? Just jim-dandy I think it is. Quite American. I was glad for your letters. We all were."

All the threat and accusation were gone from his tone. Monte had continued to write home every few weeks when he was on the road. In the past few months, since he had moved into Manhattan, the letters had stopped. He visited Brooklyn once in a shiny, new sedan he'd bought a few months after he'd come off the road. He gave everyone a ride out to Coney Island for ice cream. That was almost a year ago. Since then it had been silence. Charles seemed eager to tell him about the progress of Leo. He was healthy as a horse, a little wastrel he called him. It was clear that he had found a tenderness toward Leo that he had never shown toward Monte. It was clear as well that

Charles had lost a step. His punishing schedule of work and the responsibilities of the children had chastened him, dissolving the haughtiness Monte remembered.

Charles was mired hopelessly in the struggle of the middle class. There was no way out and no moment of complete rest. He wouldn't permit discussion of re-marriage or even becoming involved again with a woman. This avenue of relief and solace was closed to him for his own private reasons. Monte saw the grinding routine of his father's life in stark relief against the complete randomness of his own. His own life was rising with the force of a full moon tide while his father, whom he realized had devoted every moment of his life and invested every dream of his heart into him, was being slowly worn away by the same tide.

The shock of seeing this former colossus as a frail and trapped man, stopped the glib and reassuring words in Monte's throat. He comforted his father, telling him what a good job he was doing and how much he was admired by his children. It was the settling of a lifetime of accounts, pouring out suddenly, in the middle of a busy Manhattan sidewalk. It wasn't effusive or emotional. It was a gentle acknowledgment of debts. It was the first sketch of an adult relationship between them. Monte spoke his mind and Charles listened as he would to a young colleague. Darkness deepened around them. The gas street lamps began to glow a dull orange. Life was pushing Monte on. Their time was up. He offered his hand to Charles who took it and held onto it. The old man wasn't going to let it end as it would with a colleague. The gaslight revealed a tuft of whiskers on the old man's chin that had been missed by his morning razor. Decay was beginning to settle on this once impeccable monument. His top shirt button was loose, hanging on its threads, showing clearly that fastidious daughter Isabel was no longer focused on her father. Monte pictured the old man alone, silently reading his newspaper in his easy chair, falling asleep with no one left in the house to wake him and show him to bed.

Dead leaves scuttled like brown crabs around their feet in the rising evening breeze. The scent of mold and dry paper filled the space between them.

"You write well," the old man said. "Colorful. Look to it."

"I will." Monte assured him.

"We're off then. Warmest regards, dear boy." It was one of the few tender phrases Monte had ever heard from his father and emotion suddenly flooded into his chest and face. He could only motion, a hesitant wave goodbye, as the old man finally let go of his son's hand. The old man nodded and walked on.

In the *Ritz* barbershop, Monte laid back in the barber chair and let the fragrant steamed towel cover his face. Finally in solitude, his thoughts surfaced. He realized he loved his father and that his childhood family was scattering. He felt he'd been given his father's blessing and was finally free of the stinging judgment that had pushed them apart. All was forgiven. In the solitude of the steam towel he was finally free to feel what had happened on the street. Tears of relief and love were soaked up into the hot towel.

One of the first and most important lessons Monte learned about being a press agent was that when a customer in a joint you represent invites you to have a drink, you have a drink. The joint he now represented, providing the Mayor actually showed up, the *El Fay Club*, was heaving with waves of conversation, people talking over one another. A heavy hand fell on his pinstripes and he was told to pull up a chair so he could toss one back with owner Larry Fay's gun-packing gangster pals. Texas was late getting the first show started and the crowd was turning toward its own forms of entertainment, like finding sober looking people and getting them drunk. Monte was an obvious target as he walked among the tables greeting individuals he'd invited.

When Fay's tough guys collared him they had a different diversion in mind, a more practical one. They wanted to see him risk his own internal organs on the house hooch. That way they knew the stuff was okay and he was okay too. Monte polished off a straight *Dewar's* scotch that he'd come to rely on as one of the least damaging selections. He hobnobbed with the boys until Texas made her appearance and started to take control of the room. No sooner had he gotten out of the hoodlums' headlock than he was lassoed by rubber-faced Broadway funny man and *El Fay* regular Francis X. Mahoney and his stable of gay chorus boys who, unlike the strapped gunsels, packed only powder puffs. They savored thin cigarettes of marijuana and provided Monte with some relief since they didn't care if he drank whiskey or water or nothing at all. They were more interested in Texas' gown and enjoyed singing along with her opening number and vamping for each other. Francis poured Monte a welcome shot from his own bottle of *Cutty Sark*, another reliable brand efficiently smuggled by Frank Costello's navy directly from Ireland to Frank's colleague Joe Kennedy, future patriarch of the political clan.

Monte caught the hand signal from the side of beef who worked the front door indicating that a line was forming on the sidewalk. The night was shaping up to be the home run he'd been counting on when he first proposed the scheme. He and Francis saluted, glasses in hand, and downed "...milk from the tit of Mother Ireland".

He toddled off from the gay boys and made it a few feet before he was pulled over to a table of Long Island socialites by the son of someone who owned large parts of the state. This was an unhappy group ruled by dark gods. They joined the party by throwing a raccoon coat over one shoulder to hide the fact they were injecting heroin into their jeweled arms. This habit dulled the conversation considerably and propelled Monte on his way.

Not far from the socialites, he got snagged into a private session with an impatient young patron known as Legs Diamond. Legs wanted information about joints upstate along the old speakeasy trail up the Hudson, but Monte was having none of that conversation. Nonetheless, he was obliged to stay and drink with Mr. Diamond - at least one. Monte rested at the table and endured the forced hospitality.

The ambitious Legs was at the time employed as an enforcer for gangster Arnold Rothstein. Rothstein owned a small part of the *El Fay* in a cooperative deal with George "Big Frenchy" DeMange and Owney Madden who participated in Rothstein's gambling operations on the West side. Legs was in the club spotting marks and recruiting them for Rothstein's nightly game that was a short cab ride away near the docks on 28th street. Legs sometimes escorted the marks to the festivities making sure they arrived safely. Later on, he often escorted the big winners from the place for the same reason. The place was a furniture storage warehouse full of dusty packing crates. Down a narrow canyon of crates, behind a steel door it opened up into a huge, carpeted and chandeliered casino reminiscent of European salons except for the preeminence of crap tables instead of baccarat or chemin de fer. It was a place with friendly women, soft music and free liquor – a place where you and your money were safe. Once you were done for the evening, especially if you were a big winner, the neighborhood around the casino was particularly unsafe for someone with pockets full of cash. That's where Legs earned his keep and his nickname.

Legs was a high-energy type who paced nervously when kept inside to watch over the action. It made people nervous. Eventually he spent more time outside "stretching his legs" than inside where he belonged. Legs took over outside security for the organization, walking people to their destinations. Unfortunately for the very big winners, with Leg's protection their destination was frequently beneath a Westside pier, while the destination of Mr. Rothstein's money was safely back home to the casino. It was extremely unsafe to walk around with pockets full of Arnold Rothstein's cash in the company of Legs Diamond.

Legs was making a move to open his own territory up the Hudson toward Poughkeepsie and Kingston and he insisted on knowing Monte's ideas about places that might need a supply of his beer. Monte avoided the issue claiming alcoholic amnesia until Legs started to bear down. The enforcer knew Monte had been all over the area with a one-reel movie production racket cooked up with Monte's pal Carl Erbe.

Legs also knew that Monte had a habit of visiting roadhouses while fronting Erbe's operation. Legs wanted names and addresses so he could visit these joints and suggest they buy their liquor from him. The last thing Monte wanted was for Legs to muscle in on the little Mom and Pop hideaways he'd become so fond of in his travels. He finally delivered a totally useless load of misinformation while seeming to be absorbed in Texas' belting the drinking song *Show Me the Way to Go Home.*

"Show me the way to go home." Texas sang and the crowd joined in, *"I'm tired and I want to go bed. I had a little drink about an hour ago and it went right to my head…"* Monte joined in the singing too, hoping to end Legs' interrogation.

The next valuable lessons Monte learned about surviving in speakeasies were liquor selection and pacing. In this era of unregulated distilling, he learned the best way to avoid blindness and organ failure was to stick to scotch whisky with the white paper government seal still on the cap and avoid bourbon or rye which might come from a backyard "still" patched with lead soldering or gin which was likely to come out of someone's bathtub with a tincture of drain cleaner. He gravitated to *Dewar's*, the lightest of the scotches which, for the purpose of pacing, he diluted with soda water. Drinking with the customers was part of the job in representing nightclubs. It reassured them, built a bond that was vital and, equally as important, helped move the merchandise. There were many reasons customers invited Monte to have a drink and none were because he looked thirsty. Once ensnared this way, it was expected that hard liquor would be shared. Ladies could be excused from the social tyranny of drinking straight, hard liquor but men were not. To be able to "hold your liquor" and to "drink like a man" was the standard of behavior. He couldn't very well accept a guest's invitation and nurse a soda water or a glass of milk. It would have made him and the club's liquor suspect.

After a few bouts of socializing with clients, he'd pick his way to the bar at the back of the room using the shoulders of seated patrons for balance as needed. At the bar he'd drink seltzer water hoping to dilute the liquor further and that's where Winchell and other colleagues of the press would regroup from their own table-hopping and pump him for items. From this dizzy dance sprung many of Winchell's early career-making and startling columns about who was on the skids professionally or financially, who was cozy with the underworld, which famous face was having a secret affair. All the naughty, unspoken secrets that humanized the stars and suddenly made their private lives part of the public record were Winchell's stock in trade. This pirate's bazaar of personal information was navigated on a sea of liquor. Young pilots like Monte steered clear of heavy seas and delivered their cargo of gossip or shipwrecked on the shoals of stupor.

Monte was finally rescued from Legs by the arrival of a nearly topless chorus girl who was working the crowd, filling glasses and providing the best view of two natural promontories since Lewis and Clark.

"They wanna see you," she indicated the bar, Monte took the cue. He slipped away with her, giving a nod to Dutch, toward his seltzer and safety. He thanked her, eye to eye, with a smile and a nod. The tough cocktail waitress and sometime dancer, stuck her chin out at him – still posing like a tough girl. But he knew Helen Pinoyer better than that. She put on her scrappy, no-nonsense show, learned some from Texas and some from her head-knocking, metalworker father. But away from *El Fay*, Helen purred under Monte's arm sometimes, soft as a kitten. Something about dancers in joints like this tugged open his hidden heart. How did they shine so beautifully through the smoke and vulgarity all around them? She smelled of sweat and faint lavender. He grabbed her hand as she moved back into the crowd. She squeezed and nodded "You're welcome" back at him.

Monte rested at the bar for a moment like a fighter in his corner, watching her wade back into the melee of fanny pinches, wolves' eyes and sex banter that was her workplace. Bruised knucklebones were in his near future as he watched her dodge the male hands directed at her thighs. A knight will defend the honor of his lady, as he'd learned at his mother's knee. It was his most deeply held law. That's when Winchell corralled him.

Monte was feeling his power drain slowly away as the evening got later and Mayor Jimmy Walker stayed away. Winchell was there to collect on their setup, to catch Mayor Jimmy at an illegal speakeasy and report on it first. If the Mayor didn't show, the celebration of his election victory at the *El Fay* might end Monte's brief career as mouthpiece for the loudest speakeasy in New York. Either way, Winchell was there, salivating to capitalize on this bubbling cauldron of gossip he had helped create. Like Monte, he was new in his field and still needed to prove himself.

"Hey Monte, whaddya know?"

"I wish I remembered." It was a wisecrack Monte had been delivering to some effect recently but Winchell was all business.

"Whadda we know about…? Winchell indicated with a tip of his head the heated discussion at the table of a minor film star.

That's when two of the most delicious ladies to ever wear high heels walked through the front door and posed for the hungry crowd. The chatter fell off a notch as the ladies scanned the room while the feathers settled on their thick boas. Almost everybody took a drink to cover their silence as they watched the two take in the room. They were waiting for someone. A rowdy greeting sounded for someone just beyond the door and grew louder and closer. Monte felt him before he saw him – someone big coming in the door. A gust of wind ruffled the glossy black neck feathers of the two imposing beauties as Mayor Jimmy Walker himself stepped in between his two appetizing escorts. Winchell only had to glance at Monte once – a tip of the hat. Monte was made.

The two ladies led a winding arc to a table at the far side of the room, giving everyone plenty of play. A line of backslappers rose before the Mayor and nearly pummeled him across the room. Everybody loved Jimmy. The chatter roared up to full blast and Texas struck up the band with Mayor Jimmy's hit song *"Will You Love Me in December, Like You Do in May?"* Mayor Walker wrote the hit song 8 months before winning the Mayor's seat in a landslide. It was a good year to be Jimmy Walker.

Winchell went back to work, "Mayor Jimmy looks like he's having a good time."

"Yes he does."

"Is that his wife?"

"No question, definitely. Both of them." Winchell didn't even nod to acknowledge the attempt at fun. It just annoyed him. He prodded into a dangerous area to dampen Monte's wisecracking and get some items he could use. He didn't have time for cute jokes, he had ten inches of column to fill.

"What's with Legs?"

Monte diverted that line of inquiry instantly in a reflex of self-preservation. When one gangster is making a move, any move, the healthiest option is to know nothing about it. Unfortunately Monte knew plenty and Winchell knew that he knew. Monte clammed up, "He's thinking of becoming a chicken farmer."

Now Winchell was really annoyed. "C'mon with that crap."

"The man loves chickens."

"What the hell am I gonna do with that?"

"Walter, I'm surprised at you. We're talking about a young man's career."

"Yeah, yeah. What else?" It was a truce. Monte threw him a bone.

"Texas is gonna open a place for Mr. Fay in Florida."

Walter got out a pad and started to make a note. Monte put his hand down firmly on top of Winchell's, stopping him and hiding the paper. He wasn't taking any chances that Legs might mistake the type of information he was giving out.

"Just remember it." Monte checked to see if Legs was watching them. He wasn't. "Young Mr. Diamond gets embarrassed if he thinks other people can read and write."   S u d d e n l y , Walter got slammed into Monte. They were both knocked back several feet as a whirlwind of fists and feet crashed into the bar. Glasses were swept off the bar onto the floor and crushed under the dancing feet of two drunks bent on killing each other. Walter had bruised his forehead on Monte's chin. They both moved to seats at a small table as the fight raged up and down the bar. Other participants joined in.

Walter rubbed the spot over his eye while Monte checked his teeth for attendance.

"I'll get you some ice." Monte offered. He walked to the bar, dodged a flying champagne bottle, reached over and grabbed an ice bucket, brought it back to the table.

On stage, Texas didn't miss a note in her number. The doorman trotted over toward the melee from his post at the viewing slot in the front door.

Winchell filled a napkin with ice and put it on his forehead. Monte did the same for his chin. They turned and watched the progression of the fight. The injury had knocked Winchell off track and he was content to sit for a while.

"Brown suit by a decision." Monte said as he pulled out a roll of bills from his pocket. Winchell watched for a moment as the combatant in the brown suit got his head smashed against the bar. "You givin' odds?"

Monte saw his champion's head hit the bar. "Ow", he sympathized. "Looks like even money." Winchell slapped five bucks on the table. "Even money." He said. "I think Checks has the reach", referring to the fighter with a checkered coat who now clearly had the advantage. The doorman grabbed one of the men and took a hard shot in the face intended for the opponent.

"Lost a point there." Monte said.

They continued to chat about Helen, whom Monte was seeing socially as the fight spun towards them. Monte swung the ice bucket at the fighters, a defensive move that narrowly missed Winchell's head. The doorman recovered from his punch in the face and pulled the clinched fighters back toward the bar. Walter started to dig for details on America's Sweetheart, movie star Mary Pickford who was just too clean to be believed. Her rival, silent film star Mabel Normand had just referred to her as a "prissy bitch" in an interview and Winchell smelled a story. Monte didn't know anything about Pickford who never came in to joints like the *El Fay Club*. He continued to steer Winchell toward the adventures of his benefactor, Texas Guinan - her gowns, her music selection, who she had dined with about a possible return to her movie career. He tried to make it as entertaining as possible and some of it was even true, but Winchell was a bulldog on a beef truck - divorces, affairs and run-ins with the law were his interest.

The bartender finally got a good hold on the checkered coat of Winchell's man and came across the bar with a horse cock - a stout wooden billy club that cracked against the man's head and opened a gash that spurted blood across the bar. Monte and Walter hopped up from the table to avoid the spray, "Ah Christ," Monte was upset.

Simultaneously on the other side of the room, a flapper who'd had too much to drink pulled a small silver pistol from under her table and waved it in the face of her companion who apparently thought he would find something else under the table. Pandemonium. Tables turned over as people dove for cover. Texas tried to take control from the stage,

"God damn it, everybody just hold your water a damn minute."

The flapper's amorous companion blanched white as he stared at the gun. He vomited across the table forcing the pistolera to stand and scream her insults at him.

"Ah Christ" Monte said again.

"Let's get some air" Winchell suggested. The two men walked to the door leaving Texas to command the room of terrified, cowering guests except for the dozen or so young men like Legs who had calmly drawn their guns and held them down at their sides, out of sight. Monte and Winchell reached the unattended door, unlocked it and went out.

"Hungry?" Winchell asked. Monte thought that was an odd question after what they'd just witnessed. Winchell was in the street waving for a cab when Monte realized that Winchell hadn't really paid much attention to what had just happened. He was too focused on getting leads for his column.

They rode across town to *Lindy's* and checked in with the other roving night owls. From nearly every table it was, "Hey Walter, whaddya know?" or "Monte, where ya been?" Monte had a light dinner mostly by himself since Winchell was busy working the room for leads. It was exhausting being with Winchell but nobody knew the ins and outs of Broadway better and nobody worked harder. You had to admire the guy.

Monte returned to the *El Fay* after a decent interval to gin up the party. Things had been sorted out and the music and booze were flowing again in a tide of whoopee. The rest of the evening was taken up with congratulating the new Mayor Jimmy Walker on his win. It had been a dirty campaign against the incumbent Mayor but it confirmed that the Celtic gang of Tammany Hall was now firmly in control of the city with their boy Jimmy at the head. Now the rackets could run freely and the Irish were sure to get their cut. Best of all, Monte's gambit to attract Mayor Jimmy to the *El Fay* had worked. He was now Texas Guinan's press agent, her new golden boy.

CHAPTER 7

THE MAIN STEM

It was the *Glittering Canyon, The Great White Way, The Main Stem.* The mythical district of Broadway represented freedom, just as Hollywood represented glamour. It was around the clock whoopee, the hotcha haven for wild flappers and their raccoon-coated Gatsby's who were dedicated to excess and determined to die young. The stock market posted explosive record highs, flooding the city with easy money. Darkness never settled on the sidewalks of Broadway. When the sun quit, the street lit up like a midway with electricity doing the barking from every direction. Pomaded swells in two tone broughams and snappy suits swaggered down the avenue past stumblebums who had snagged a lamppost for a date. Jalopies honked for headroom as they flew down the *Street of Broken Dreams* like fillies in the last furlong. Monte had found his place and it was squarely at the center of the nightly party of New York City. It was a love affair for a young man who learned the slang of Broadway like a sonnet.

The phone rang at the bar of *Leon and Eddie's*, Monte's new field office. The bartender handed it over, Monte answered, "You got me."

"Monte, Joe Russell." Russell was a new bird dog for Winchell and a loyal colleague, very discreet. Bird dogs like Joe were poorly paid, widely disrespected and were among the most precarious of the uncertain professionals in the twilight world of illegal nightclubs. They lived item to item and could be cut off either from the suppliers like Monte or the buyers like Winchell for a single unchecked fact or ill-considered comment. They sniffed out the stories Winchell had overlooked or was too busy to follow up. Monte liked Joe and always made time for him.

"Hey whatta ya know, kid?"

"I gotta line on the actor who shall remain nameless, who did the thing we're not talking about."

"No go, Joe. I got nothing for ya there."

"That's what I figured. Whatta ya know?"

"I'll have an item for you later. We're gonna beef about the latest roust. They're treatin' her like she's a common criminal, Joe." Monte referred to Texas, his flamboyant chanteuse and speakeasy operator.

"Well, strictly speakin'...." Joe implied the obvious fact that she <u>was</u> a common criminal along with just about everybody else in the country as far as Prohibition laws.

"3 grand a week ain't common," Monte zinged him.

Joe snickered as he wrote that down. The quip was a sure sale to Winchell. Monte spent his morning, which was most people's afternoon, feeding the newshounds like Joe scraps from last night's meal. Then it was over to the office of *Erbe and Proser – Press Agents* to clip the afternoon columns that mentioned his clients and paste them in his press book. Carl had followed Monte into press agentry in the wake of *New Era's* untimely demise. Carl put up the rent for the office and so got first billing on the company stationery. The hobo pals were partners again and the world was their oyster.

Frank Costello, Monte's next partner, moved a step closer to Monte's orbit. Frank was at that moment in Atlantic City with his own senior partner at the time, Lucky Luciano. Frank and Lucky had organized a three-day sit-down with counterparts from Chicago, Detroit, Miami and Cleveland including Al Capone and other significant players, at the first national gangster consolidation. That year, 1927, a convulsive wave of killings, started by small-time operators were upsetting the public and bringing the heat. At the meeting, Costello used his considerable talents as a businessman on the assembled Jewish and Italian mobsters to deal with the problem by forging the *Syndicate*. By uniting, they could command that any killing must be ordered from the top, and they were the top. Frank was smooth and soft-spoken as always. Within minutes, his unification plan was adopted and the constitution of the *Syndicate* was written in oaths and signed by handshakes. Jewish and Catholic criminals embraced each other for the common good, bringing organized crime into the modern era. They forged a business partnership that within 30 years controlled a larger part of the US economy than the Department of Defense and that continues to endure at all levels in the world economy today.

Further, Frank proposed a division of the *Syndicate* that would operate under a very strict chain of command and was responsible for only such assassinations as were absolutely necessary to keep order. With modern business efficiency, the division came to be known as Murder Inc. and was headed up by Frank's loyal ally, Albert Anastasia.

The columns from Winchell, Hellinger, Runyon and Ed Sullivan rolled off the presses every morning. Among the spicy tidbits in each column were the mundane items that Monte relied on – who was appearing at his client's club and which famous faces were seen at the bar. He gathered these gray strips from the *Post*, the *Daily Mirror*, the *Herald Tribune* like falling fruit and pasted them into press books, then took them to Texas' apartment in Greenwich Village.

Over an afternoon coffee, he'd watch her pour over the week's notices, commenting with her West Texas twang on "… that sum a bitch!" or "… now that boy can write!" if she liked what she was reading. Mostly it was about the clothes, he realized. She made the *El Fay* sexy and herself distinct by dressing herself to the teeth and undressing her chorus girls to the skin.

Texas was 44 and had an unerring instinct for what attracted the big spenders, the "big butter and egg men" she was so fond of referring to and insulting in the crowd. These same garrulous, red-faced moneybags were the marks that received invitations from Legs Diamond or other recruiters to Rothstein's crap casino. But while they were in the *El Fay*, Texas kept their attention fixed on her with oversized floppy hats, gigantic fabric begonias on her hip and the wand-like clapper she rapped on table tops or distracted skulls as a noisemaker, like an indoor bullwhip and gavel. She didn't use the sophisticated approach of speak operators like Belle Livingstone or the tender-hearted charm of chanteuse Helen Morgan. Texas was big and raw. She was outrageous and loud and knew what men wanted. As wild as the *El Fay* got on most evenings, she knew it was genteel compared to what was going on with the flapper girls at "petting parties" and in the backseats of cars all over the country. She knew polite society was rapidly going to hell and she was having a "…shitload of fun." helping it along. It was also making her very rich.

Monte learned everything about nightclubs from Texas. She was more than twenty years his senior, the most recent in a line of maternal substitutes who had taken him into their hearts and confidences. Monte and Texas spent Monday afternoons lounging on Texas' overstuffed, frilly divans sipping coffee, smoking Chesterfields and plotting stories that they knew would start the ink flowing like the Pecos in spring.

Texas wanted to stage a shoot-out in the club like she had done in almost every one of her western two-reel movies. Monte vetoed the idea and kept the focus on bringing in the leading lights of the city who would shy away from places known for gunplay. They came up with the idea to crown her "Queen of the Nightclubs". It was an angle Monte knew would play for Winchell and Ed Sullivan since they liked to back sure things and no one could dispute the title. It also played to Texas' personality as bigger than life, bigger than her competitors and bigger than anyone else would even dare to be. Because of all the social fervor for the common man, Monte knew instinctively that people would respond to the idea of a tongue-in-cheek royal title. It was his second experience, after changing his own name from Meyer Prosser to Monte Proser, of engineering a public persona.

It worked. Texas Guinan "Queen of the Nightclubs" became a featured character in columns and magazines. She was discussed across dinner tables, pool tables and poker tables. She rose to become a local legend, a national icon and eventually entered the language with the fictional characters of F. Scott Fitzgerald and Hemingway as a representative of the gin-soaked excesses of the Roaring Twenties.

Quietly among the legend-makers of Broadway, the reputation of the ex-hobo press agent rose along with his client and co-creation. The buzz around the name Monte Proser was starting in press rooms, producers' offices and backstage dressing rooms.

By afternoon, the morning news columns of Winchell, Sullivan and Hellinger were wrapping fish. By nightfall, the boys on the Broadway beat were out and ravenous again for fleshy morsels of gossip. There was no telling them no or fobbing off some pleasant anecdote. They needed news; facts, names and places. They could not afford to come back empty handed and face a scowling editor with some fluff about a minor escapade. It was a daily grind that demanded shocking news of blood and heartbreak. If they didn't get something, they'd make it up which might ruffle some very important feathers. Monte was in the middle. He needed them as his mouthpiece but if he let slip the wrong detail about the wrong person, or if they got something he said wrong, he could wind up explaining his mistake to catfish in the East River.

Over time, the pace of the nightly feeding frenzy began to coalesce into a political minuet of alliances and small favors where insiders like Monte who operated in the top tier spots were at the center. The reputations of Monte and Walter Winchell grew at a similar pace. Because of their nostalgia for their early careers around vaudeville and circuses, the two men maintained a particularly close association. If they weren't stooled up at the bar of the *El Fay* watching Texas cut her herd of "suckers" from their money, they might catch the late show at *Dave's Blue Room* or skip out to *Lindy's* to meet up with a fluid group of bookies, ball players and newspapermen.

In this new type of drinking room comedy, promoters like Monte were typically behind the scenes pulling the ropes and mouthpieces like Walter were out in front of the footlights hoofing the old buck and wing with a line of snappy patter. Soon it was the coin of the realm in show business and politics to be mentioned in Winchell's column. It was called "getting ink" and few had the access to Winchell that Monte had. He was there at the creation.

With the success of Broadway and with Texas Guinan as his fairy godmother, Monte achieved the rank of "up and comer". He and Texas spent so much time together that rumors began to float from hushed lips to cocked ears about their relationship being more than professional. It wasn't, but neither made any effort to deny it. A rumor, after all, was still publicity and often the most effective kind. The only one who began to have a problem with the possible arrangement was Larry Fay, proprietor and namesake of the *El Fay*. Monte was filling Texas' head with dreams of a bigger career, drawing her attention away. Texas was Fay's meal ticket. Without her, the club would fold in a week.

By 1927, with Texas, Monte and Fay working the levers, the *El Fay* netted $700,000 in one ten-month period, all of it illegal and therefore tax-free. Texas' many clashes with the federal "dry agents" of Prohibition were publicity gifts for Monte that no amount of money could have bought. She was front-page news from the stately *New York Times* to the skeevy tabloid *Evening Graphic*. "*Two Senators See Guinan Club Raided*"; "*Texas Guinan Jailed in Dry Raid on Club*"; "*Freed on $1,000 Bail with Nine Employees After Nine Hours of Mirth in Cell,*" screamed the headlines that Monte cut and pasted in his press book like badges of honor. Texas played into all the hoopla like the cool professional actor she was. "I like your cute little jail," she tossed to the cops, who were all her customers, after a night in the West 30th Street slammer, "...and I don't know when my jewels have seemed so safe." Texas' jewels were very safe. So was delivery of the bottled gold that paid for them.

Owney Madden, in an historic negotiation equivalent to the straight world's Magna Carta, had cut a deal with the United States Coast Guard to escort his shipments of illegal booze to a convenient West Side dock where Fay's swastika-clad cabs could shuttle them to the clubs. Fay chose the swastika to decorate his cabs long before the Nazis adopted and tarnished that good luck symbol. He also had swastikas embroidered on his shirts and engraved on his cigarette lighter because it was the symbol on the warm-up blanket of a long shot horse named *Scotch Verdict* he picked out one day at Aqueduct Race Track. Anything with scotch in the name had always made him money, so Fay took the long shot at 18 to 1 odds. The horse placed and Larry Fay took home enough money to end his cab driving days and open the *El Fay*.

The story circulated around Broadway for months after that and eventually came out of the pen of a young newspaperman Damon Runyon, a regular at the *El Fay*. Runyon used Larry Fay and his horse story to model his character Harry the Horse in his classic fable of Broadway, *Guys and Dolls*.

Every time Texas was arrested she was released from jail the next day. With all her attendant publicity the police began to look ridiculous. They were finally forced to raid the *El Fay* like they truly meant it and with only minimal advance notice to the owners. To their shock they found booze on the premises and padlocked the club for the cameras. Later that week, Texas and Fay launched the *Texas Guinan Club* at 117 West 48th Street. The cycle progressed for almost a year until once again the authorities were forced to stage a public padlocking ceremony. Again within days, the *Del Fay* opened its doors back at the old *El Fay* address. If anyone was paying attention to this poorly directed farce, they weren't doing much about it because the *Del Fay* raked in more money than first two places. Texas continued to apply her trademark greeting "Hello, sucker!" to all new arrivals in the clubs and added her standard segue for female performers, "Let's give the little lady a great big hand."

Monte's star was also rising due to the wild success of Texas and the *Del Fay*. He took on Billingsley's *Stork Club* that was also supplied by Big Frenchy and Owney Madden. He handled Belle Livingstone's place on the East side, as a personal favor since he knew she didn't have the toughness or tough partners that made Texas a success. He was proved right. Belle was soon hounded out of the business by the Feds.

1928 roared in and Texas and Fay pressed their luck by opening another *Del Fay* club in Miami. Although the place fizzled, by this time, with Monte's creative scheming and Fay's unlimited bankroll, Texas had become an odd national hero. She was a sort of Robin Hood who cleverly robbed from the rich, or at least those who acted like it, and then pretty much kept it all for herself.

It was very clear that the people were coming to see her, not the various clubs that employed her and she began to see Larry Fay as just a landlord with a large piece of her action. She decided to make a break. Just as Fay feared when he saw Texas and Monte getting chummy, he was being cut out. Fay agreed that cutting was a good idea but felt that Texas' body parts would be a better target than his income. This was seen as a poor business decision by big boss Owney Madden since Texas pushed more of Madden's booze than one of his hired Coast Guard cutters could carry. Madden offered Texas his protection. She opened the *300 Club* with her own money and continued her raucous act with the insurance of additional hired muscle and a heavily armored car. Monte could not afford either and had to make-do with a cautious attitude.

Monte made himself scarce at the *300 Club* for a while. He started to spend more time down the street at the *Stork Club* working a new angle for owner Sherman Billingsley. Billingsley was convinced that he had to seed his place with beautiful young girls, not a new idea, except that he wanted debutantes, sorority girls and daughters of the upper class. Again Monte was thrown in with the society columnists and social register types. These were people who always had two or three last names, each indicating an ancestral revenue stream. They were the Walter Lippmann readers representing the views of the first families of New York with an icy zeal that gave Monte the familiar sinking feeling of being a Jewish outsider. Also, compared to Texas and her crowd, they generated about as much fun as an iron lung.

Monte's fees were ratcheting up dramatically leaving partner Carl Erbe behind. The teacher became the student as Carl began to drop doctors' accounts in favor of following Monte's lead into publicizing entertainers and nightclubs. Monte began to look toward Broadway theatres and movies as the next targets for his ambition.

CHAPTER 8

HOLLYWOOD ON THE HUDSON

By late 1928, Monte's most loyal client after Texas' was movie producer Walter Wanger – pronounced like "ranger". Wanger called Monte one day as Monte was packing his suitcase for a trip to Hollywood for private meetings with Joe Schenk, United Artists' head of production. Monte's boss was in trouble again.

Wanger had insisted on hiring Viennese actress Elizabeth Bergner for his latest UA extravaganza, *Catherine the Great*. It was a huge, expensive production and although his instincts about Bergner were exactly right, she was perfect in the part, no one had heard of her. Opposite Bergner was Douglas Fairbanks Jr. who didn't pull in ticket sales like his old man. Test audiences in California had been luke-warm about the picture and Wanger was panicked. He had to have a big opening in New York or he was finished. This time it would be permanent. The picture would open at the *Astor Theatre* and it had to open big.

Monte turned the title over and over in his head. *Catherine the Great*, Russian royalty, the Romanoffs, imperious, incestuous and paranoid. Were they all murdered or did some escape? An angle formed. He sketched it out on a cocktail napkin. He saw it unfold in his mind's eye unlike anything ever done before, almost. It was huge, great like Catherine herself. It would have to be.

It was a complete story, a life, not just an aspect of a star's life or a soft angle on history. He would recreate history and bring it roaring back to life. By the time the train pulled into Grand Central station he was so excited he couldn't sit down. He would reach back into history, his history, to one of his earliest lessons. He would reincarnate a member of one of the most influential royal families ever to grace the city of New York.

Unemployed actor Harry Gerguson did a little bird-dogging around town sniffing for stories like Joe Russell and Eddie Jaffe, and a little whatever else paid a week's rent at his hotel. He was hungry and not a terrible actor but most importantly he had a set of brass balls that made statues of stallions in Central Park jealous. Monte invited Harry to dinner at *Dinty Moore's*, a surefire tactic that guaranteed Harry would show up early and sober. After the scale of Monte's plan was revealed to him, the light went on and Harry negotiated his terms like a team of Philadelphia lawyers, shrewdly settling on a bowl of beef stew, $50 dollars walking around money and an unspecified amount of cash when the job was over, depending on his performance.

The first stop was the *Hollywood Barbershop*, next door to the *Palace Theater* in the subway arcade at Broadway and 47th Street. Harry had a decent head start on a beard having recently reallocated his grooming expenses toward food. Monte directed John the barber to clean him up except for the moustache and goatee. That was enough excitement for one night. Monte had concerns that Harry might abscond with the fifty and fresh goatee to racetracks unknown, so he set a schedule to test him.

The next day they were set for an early Broadway start. At noon they were to meet at *Sulka*, the top drawer men's haberdashery. Precisely at the stroke of 12, Harry strolled through *Sulka's* front door in his best blue suit with a remarkably un-Harry-like demeanor. Naturally Monte assumed he'd been drinking. But it was an entirely different Harry who then surveyed *Sulka's* merch. He was sober as the Pope and living his role, years before the Method was invented. He began to swagger with the haughty air of one accustomed to greatness. Monte was more than relieved; he was giddy, but kept his amusement hidden from Harry. Harry was fitted for a white tie and tails, dinner coats with striped pants and a top hat. They visited a theatrical wardrobe and prop facility where a shoebox full of royal insignias, emblems and pins was secured. A chauffeured Rolls Royce was rented for a week and finally, since Monte represented the swanky *Ritz-Carlton Hotel* as their publicist at the time, the former Harry Gerguson was delivered to the hotel where they had prepared a reception normally reserved for royals and major movie stars. Monte, of course, had called the hotel earlier and using his best London accent, informed them that the Russian Prince would be arriving. As Harry strode into the lobby, calmly reviewing his new regiment of servants, Monte had to admit to himself that Harry really wasn't a bad actor, so far. Or maybe he'd finally found the part he was born to play.

Harry, in his elegant suit, approached the front desk with a wan smile on his lips indicating royal forbearance. He lifted the silver Tiffany pen from the inkwell and signed the register in large, florid script - *Michael Romanoff*. He finished his new signature with a royal flourish and put the silver pen in his pocket. Monte saw Harry nick the pen and his heart dropped. He realized Harry would still need some direction in his performance.

The next day several papers ran unobtrusive items about the prince staying at the *Ritz* after a season of grouse shooting in Europe. That night Monte directed Harry in the chauffeured Rolls on the way to the *Stork Club*. He knew Billingsley would wet himself to have royalty in his saloon and he didn't want to miss an opportunity to expose him as a sycophantic horse's ass while he could.

Years earlier, Billingsley had employed Monte briefly to weave stories of the *Stork* for the columns. When it became apparent that Billingsley was an anti-Semite, Monte reared back and took a swing at his boss, missing his nose by less than an inch. Now, as he rolled up to the *Stork* with the Prince becoming more princely by the moment and Walter Winchell inside the club primed to unleash a river of royal ink, he was sure

Billingsley would never see this roundhouse coming right at his head.

Winchell was in on the joke of Monte's fictional Prince Romanoff but would later claim he was fooled as well so he could maintain a good relationship with Billingsley. Winchell wrote a glowing account of the Prince that opened the kingdom of Broadway to the Prince like a pearl-laden oyster. As expected, with Monte's advance notice, the *Stork* welcomed the bogus prince with every courtesy and privilege. There wasn't much chance that Harry's previous circle of friends would be dining at the Stork so he was free to put on princely airs without fear, and he did.

His $100 allowance for the evening was barely touched as drinks kept arriving from admirers. Billingsley picked up the Prince's dinner tab and by night's end several starlets, business magnates and hopeful society widows were crowded around the Prince's table. Harry was brilliant, exactingly vague and completely convincing. The next day the columns were abuzz with the worldly, witty Prince Romanoff whose American friends called "Mike". Monte laughed so hard, John the barber had to stop shaving him. John finished reading the columns to him while Monte lay back in the chair, his face half-shaved and roared.

Unfortunately Walter Wanger was not as happy. It was just two days before the opening of the picture that might end his career and so far the picture's name had not even been mentioned anywhere. He was more than nervous. He felt slightly worse after Monte told him the payoff to all the royal buildup. Monte could hear the producer grinding his teeth on his pipe stem all the way from California when he told him to go prepare the front office for the bomb he was about to drop. It was going to be big and it was going to be loud. Poor Walter Wanger mumbled anxiously, "Jesus Christ..." and missed the cradle with the phone receiver several times. The next part of the plan required Monte to step back further into the shadows while he directed the coup d'etat through a front. There was only one man for this job - Eddie Jaffe.

Eddie and his sometime partner Joe Russell had been bird-dogging around Broadway since the early days with Texas and

Larry Fay. Eddie had the theatricality and nerve required to see the attack through and he still had a low enough profile so nobody would recognize his voice and be tipped off that there was funny business afoot.

Eddie sat in Monte's apartment and called every newspaper contact in Monte's little black book. Eddie introduced himself as Prince Michael Romanoff's secretary. He informed the media that the Prince was suing United Artists for $5,000,000 for degrading his great, great Aunt Catherine in a movie of the same name. The following day, one day before the premiere, the story broke like thunder across page one of every New York newspaper. Later that day the *Associated Press* and *United Press* news wires picked up the story and blasted it across the country where it landed in twelve point type on the front page of the *Los Angeles Times* and Walter Wanger's breakfast table on the opening day of the picture. Wanger's career was a series of nail-biting, cliffhanger events like this. Eventually, they wore out the poor man's nerve.

In New York, Eddie administered the coup d'grace. The Prince would attend the premiere in person so that he'd have specific evidence of slander when he hauled the disrespectful money-grubbers into court. Monte went to work getting the Russian eagle emblem of the Romanoff family stenciled onto a long red carpet that he had laid to the curb in front of the *Astor Theatre* to cushion the arrival of the royal feet. That night, over 50 photographers including several newsreel cameramen, lined the walkway to record the historic scene as the Prince stepped from his Rolls Royce into the adoration of hundreds of new fans and strode purposefully into the theatre. The stars of the picture had arrived moments earlier and were barely noticed. When the movie was over, the Prince returned to the blazing lights and grinding cameras on his royal carpet, he exploded in a screaming fit of accusation. Somehow during the nearly 90 minutes of the movie he had acquired a clipped British accent. He howled at the cameras in a most un-British fashion that, "My family of 800 years of royal lineage has been slandered I say! And the transgressors will pay the price! It is an outrage, I say, an outrage!" He improvised on the theme for a few moments doing what he felt was a credible impression of Lloyd George and his best work in years. He then stalked back to his limo escorted by two glamorous Hollywood starlets and decamped to an evening of nightclubbing where Monte kept him fed with plenty of cash to spread around. At eight the next morning, the party broke up. The Prince gave his two lovely escorts sixty bucks each and kissed them farewell. Monte and Harry shook hands.

"Dinty's, six o'clock?" Monte asked.

"Okay," Harry confirmed. The two conspirators had a last laugh and split up.

The next afternoon Monte and Harry met at *Dinty Moore's* for an early dinner. Monte handed Harry an envelope with $500 cash in it.

"Keep the clothes," Monte offered. Harry accepted. They passed a pleasant evening as Harry laid out his plan to go to Hollywood. Monte gave him a few names to look up in the studios. Harry made it an early night, excusing himself once Monte paid the check. He returned to his apartment but was locked out. He hadn't paid the rent. The Prince spent the night at the YMCA.

The next day, Harry Gerguson left New York on a train headed west and never returned. Four days later, Prince Mike Romanoff arrived in Hollywood. The Prince began a charmed 40-year career as a some-time actor and eventually famed restaurateur of Romanoff's, well known for its Russian savories, favorites of the royal family. The Prince became an icon of Hollywood nightlife and an indispensable confidant of the movie elite.

CHAPTER 9

THE PARTY'S OVER

In the early 1930's as the Depression deepened, Costello's main rival, Dutch Schultz, was the indispensable business partner of many nightclub operators in Manhattan. Arthur Flegenheimer adopted the name of Dutch Schultz at the age of 16 in an attempt to transfer some of the fear and respect associated with that name to himself. The original Dutch Schultz was a gangster who terrorized New Yorkers at the turn of the century with unusual cruelty. When the teenage Flegenheimer made his first bones by killing a rival policy runner, he invoked the name and reputation of his hero in crime with a bravado that marked him as the natural successor.

He continued his rise in bookmaking in the semi-rural Bronx of the 1920's, eventually heading an executive council of Jewish experts in the business. Morris "Abbadabba" Berman was Schultz' chief financial officer. Berman was nicknamed with the shortened version of the magic command "abra cadabra" for his ability to work magic with numbers. He was known to keep the tallies of dozens of bookies in his head going back months. This was an invaluable talent to Schultz' criminal enterprise since Abbadabba's method of accounting was a code known only to himself, so the only evidence of illegal payments were inside his head. Lulu Rosenkrantz was head of security for the operation and commanded platoons of gunmen and fleets of vehicles. Dutch became known as the Beer Baron of the Bronx after taking over the breweries north of Manhattan shortly after Prohibition arrived. His interest in nightclubs grew along with his power base as Prohibition continued to pour millions into his operations. He edged out the less capable but incredibly lucky Legs Diamond who survived even after being shot four separate times by Dutch and others. Legs took twenty slugs in all from the four incidents. Legs finally got the message and moved operations to the Catskills area north of New York City to supply those villagers with his own line of distilled products. Dutch took over Manhattan, Legs' inheritance from Owney Madden, who was then appearing at Sing-Sing for an extended engagement.

Texas knew Schultz' reputation and didn't welcome his takeover. She realized her armored car might discourage a small time operator like former partner, Larry Fay, but it wouldn't do much against a warlord like Dutch especially since she didn't have Owney Madden to back her up anymore. Instead, Monte became her first line of defense. The first time Dutch and Texas met at her new *Club Intime*, he introduced himself,

"Hi, I 'm Dutch. I'm your new partner."

To Texas, this was a familiar tune. She took the measure of Dutch the way she'd looked over Monte. She knew the score, but also knew a top predator when she saw one. His teeth were yellow and long. She immediately sang along.

As with Legs, Monte was assigned to sit with the new partner, so the gangster wouldn't have to drink alone. The movie business was looking better every day. Monte had had about enough of gangsters and was having a harder time holding his tongue in their presence. His pal of years, singer Joe E. Lewis, had just had his throat cut by Chicago mobster, Jack "Two Gun" ("...and one ain't metal", as they said) McGurn.

Joe had returned to his hotel room a few weeks earlier after work at the *Green Mill*, a rival club McGurn had warned Joe not to play. McGurn and Sam Giancana, one of Capone's men, an enthusiastic young murderer who would graduate to prime suspect in the murders of JFK, Robert Kennedy and Marilyn Monroe, were waiting for him. They cracked Joe's skull open with an iron pipe as promised. McGurn then took out his hunting knife and cut Joe's throat from ear to ear. This was a signal to all performers who thought they might want to speak up and direct their own careers. They left Joe for dead.

In New York, Monte took the news badly. He was sickened by the brutality of the attack. As he sat at the bar of Leon and Eddie's with the newspaper open to the article about Joe's attack, the heat came up into his arms and face. In a vision he saw McGurn on the floor with his own throat cut and himself standing over the body with a knife and he felt good about it. The news of Joe's survival arrived a few days later. Joe survived, but as a comic, not a singer. His scarred vocal cords could never again carry a complete tune.

Joe Lewis wasn't just another acquaintance to Monte, he was special. He was more than a fellow nightlife gypsy. He lived the same life and spoke the same language like a lot of friends, but he was someone Monte instantly trusted. He was a guy you could relax with, who was just so essentially good-natured that there didn't seem to be a problem in the world. That world was gone now for Joe and for Monte. The power and cruelty of their masters was unmasked.

A creeping fatalism chilled the atmosphere in clubs as the excesses of the 20's were beginning to extract their full compensation. Flask wielding frat boys became unemployable drunks, wild flappers became young mothers and pressed their good time Johnnies into dutiful matrimony. The Victorian Era finally ended with sexuality being freely discussed, often while dancing cheek to cheek. Even homosexuality crept cautiously out of medieval superstition into more public display and dared whisper its name.

The rambunctious, glittering nightclub floorshows that Texas specialized in turned more thoughtful and ironic with popular songs of social strife like *Brother, can You Spare a Dime?*, *In a Shanty in Old Shanty Town*, *River Stay Away from My Door* and old fashioned romantic ballads like *Night and Day* and *Someday I'll Find You*. Crooners like Rudy Vallee and Bing Crosby found large audiences and the clubs spawned their own versions of the romantic nightclub singer to carry the popular sentiment. The floorshows thinned to a comic, a singer and maybe a few girls. The girls, who had been bouncy, sexy playthings, were now tough, tight-corseted survivors in heavy makeup. The lights were dimmer, the brass horns were muted and nightclubs were transforming into smoky, little cabarets. Many began to cater to distinct specialty clientele such as white men looking for black women, openly gay, deeply closeted gay, white only and black only.

After the attempted murder of Joe, Monte couldn't stand the sight of tough-guy gangsters like Dutch, a pale, muscular brute with a sour milk expression whose hospitality was only slightly above his hostility. Dutch tended to drink alone because he was a caustic, moody companion with a sociopathic sense of humor. Keeping the Dutchman placated and entertained took all of Monte's social skill. The *Beer Baron of the Bronx* drank only wine preferring *Vin Mariani*, the unremarkable red wine fortified with cocaine. Dutch liked being alert. Unfortunately the cocaine only further de-stabilized the Dutchman's volatile temperament making Monte's job even more difficult. Monte winced inside every time his companion sucked the cocaine-laced wine through his canine teeth. It was an annoying, nervous habit that qualified social time with the Dutchman as the first level of hell. He had to baby-sit this Bronx thug to protect Texas and to discourage Dutch from shooting holes in the customers. Monte had to accomplish this while somehow keeping himself from getting killed for his trouble. Privately, the young press agent complained to Texas, describing Dutch as having the personality and sense of humor of a cod, maybe a little worse. Texas was unmoved. She had a show to run and if the Dutchman felt he was being ignored, things might get ugly.

Sitting at a back table "on the cuff" of the main room where special guests were treated to the hospitality of the house, Monte passed the hours in halting conversation, sticking to pleasantries and generalities without somehow becoming boring and obvious. Long lapses in the conversation with Dutch were oases of rest. Monte took full advantage of them to pull passing colleagues into a dialogue hoping they would find a subject that needed hours of discussion. When a suitable dupe was roped into joining them, the drinks kept coming, no charge. This went a long way toward making Dutch feel like he had a social life of his own. Conversation would bounce along with Monte making sure that his unwitting guest was well aware that the Dutch they were chatting to was Dutch Schultz, *the* Dutch Schultz. Frequently, the conversation dried up or suddenly became very sketchy as to names and details. Memories suddenly failed and bladders quickly filled making an abrupt exit necessary. Dutch's affection for Monte grew as he began to feel he'd finally found someone he could spend time with who wasn't being paid. Monte, of course, was being paid, just not by Dutch.

In the gloom of one particularly off night, conversation became difficult. Receipts were down, distracting conversational partners were rare and the restful silences in Monte and Dutch's conversations stretched into awkward chasms. Dutch was annoyed by business concerns and was drinking more than usual. It was shaping up to be a very unpleasant evening.

"Dis place is getting on my noivs," the Dutchman grumbled. This was a line Monte later recalled to hundreds of people and eventually turned up in dozens of plays and movies.

"Yeah, slow nights are tough. Maybe I'll turn in early," Monte faked a yawn hoping to induce one from his companion.

"You're going nowhere." The old Schultz charm was warm as ever. On stage, a lanky chanteuse slithered her boa suggestively between her breasts and cooed a love song to the thin crowd. Dutch watched her seduce the suckers in the first row and felt the first stirrings of tender romance, "Maybe I'll throw a fuck inna that one."

"Nah, she's not your type, Dutch."

"Fuck d'you know about it, heh?"

"Take it from me."

"Yeah, sure. You got your hooks in her already, I bet." He smiled broadly at the singer and gave her the nod. The performer sensed a fish on the line and slunk toward the back riveting the gangster with her eyes. Dutch flicked imaginary dust off his powder blue homburg hat, flashing his diamond pinky ring like a deep-sea lure. She was hooked and reeling in fast. She finished the blowoff to her number on Dutch's table, her boa lashed around his neck and her stocky calves close to Monte's worried face.

"Like the show?" she said. Her deep voice struck Dutch's ear like a tin can. He sat back slowly taking more of her into view. She sensed the act had gone too far and slid off the table taking her boa with her. Dutch grabbed the end of it and pulled. She was pulled off balance, stopping herself from toppling back onto the table with her hand. Dutch saw her small adam's apple bob and fear flick into her eyes.

"Hey, hey come on…" Monte tried to move her out of the way but Dutch had already zeroed in on the shaved stubble on her chest that had been powdered over and was now riven with beads of sweat. Up front, Texas saw the commotion and was on her way toward the back under full steam. Dutch stood up from his chair to his full height like someone was threatening him with a baseball bat. The singer made an inoffensive gesture of apology by flicking his/her boa toward Dutch and was about say something when Dutch's fist slammed into her ruby kisser and launched her across the next table. In mid-flight, she was revealed to be a "he" as her wig spun off in a separate orbit from her head. Dutch stood at the table surprised and proud of his accuracy as she swept across the table and crashed in a clump to the floor.

"Eh, look at that!" he crowed. "How ya like that, eh!" He hopped over to the far side of the table to take another shot at the wounded entertainer. Monte got in his way.

"Lay off!"

Dutch turned on him, lowering his eyes. "Whadda you talking?"'

"I told you she wasn't your type."

By this time Texas was protecting the singer. Blood was pouring onto the floor from her busted nose and jaw.

"It ain't even a girl and what kind of creep joint are you runnin' here?"

Monte forgot himself. He'd had enough of this clod and it just jumped out of his mouth, "Who the hell cares what you think?"

Dutch was rocked back. Nobody talked like that to him, "Izzat right?"

Monte wasn't quite ready to die but he wasn't ready to back down either, "Yeah."

Dutch stepped up close, put his finger on Monte's chest and pushed hard, pushing Monte back a step. "Meshugeneh." He grabbed his homburg and fine silk scarf from the back of his chair. He gave Monte a hard look, like he was sizing him up for a casket. Adrenaline dumped into Monte's blood suddenly weakening his legs. Dutch walked out. Monte went to the bar, grabbed the phone. Behind the bar, Gus packed ice into a clean bar towel and brought it out to the stricken singer. Monte dialed up the operator to get a doctor as a bird dog for one of the columnists landed at the bar to get the details.

"What happened?" the leg-man asked.

"Son of bitch should be put away." Monte was boiling. He wanted to get back at the low-lifes like McGurn and Dutch, make them pay for what they'd done.

"Dutch?" asked the newsman.

"He's a goddamn menace. They oughta lock the bastard up!" Monte was shouting. He shook the phone receiver in his hand. The man knew he had an item but it was tricky. People like Dutch didn't like being in the papers.

"Who are you calling?" he asked.

"Who the hell do ya think?" Monte turned away, end of interview. The young man slipped out, leaving Monte to his phone call. The band struck up and things returned to normal except for Texas and Monte hovering over the downed singer. A young doctor arrived who had opened a practice on the West side specializing in late night calls involving gunshot and barroom injuries. He had a mild southern accent, maybe Maryland or Virginia and drank rye, but otherwise seemed to know what he was doing. He bound up the singer's head like a Christmas package, immobilizing the jaw and trundled her off to a cab for the short ride to *Roosevelt Hospital* uptown.

Monte was sickened by the incident. Texas took him in hand again, giving him a Texas-sized earful but Monte was in no mood for it. The old friendship was unraveling by the second and neither one seemed to be able to back away from the fight. Around and around they went like an old, unhappily married couple until Monte walked out for what might be the last time. He steamed north on Broadway blind to everything but the war in his head with just about everyone and everything he knew. At 48th he stopped by the newsstand.

"I'm looking for Gregory's game," he said cautiously to the newsie.

"Warehouse. West 40th corner of 9th."

Monte put his hand in his pocket, folded the first bill he found into the palm of his hand and shook the man's hand, covertly transferring the money. The newsie handed Monte a paper and Monte walked on.

That night Monte fell in with Mayor Jimmy Walker's special brand of pizzazz at his honor's floating crap game. The finest names in New York; congressman, social register regulars and even some clergy, spent the night dotted with the special sweat reserved for addicts. If Texas could get away with gambling in her place, she'd take the business away from them all, but as things stood, the Mayor's game was the place to be. Since Arnold Rothstein's assassination, the Mayor had a lock on this easy money. The Chief of Police was a regular player and owed the house several thousand, so the likelihood of a raid was minimal. Things were so good for the Mayor that he sometimes worked at City Hall only two or three days a week. He revealed in an interview that he owned 150 pairs of silk pajamas. It was obvious that he couldn't afford that kind of extravagance on his city pay of $25,000 a year, so he gave himself a raise to $40,000. When a political writer expressed his outrage given the nation's economic situation, Jimmy shot back, "That's cheap! Imagine what it would cost if I worked full time!" Jimmy was always good for a laugh.

Monte spent the night as the Mayor's guest, shooting dice, concentrating on the small problem of making his point rather than his larger problems. In the morning, his larger problems of the night before seemed small by comparison.

The *Daily Mirror* carried a small item on page 4 without a byline that drew Monte's eye like a magnet. "Schultz wanted in Westside Brawl". The short article went on to say how the well-known gangster had attacked and hospitalized a performer at Texas Guinan's *Club Intime* and was wanted for questioning by the police. Adrenaline shot through Monte like electricity and he grabbed the phone. He needed a retraction and an apology printed or he foresaw a long, furtive exile in his immediate future. His contacts at the *Mirror* said the article was legitimate news and they couldn't print a retraction of something that was hard news and true. He called Winchell but his old friend couldn't see any way to undo what was done. That was it, he decided. He'd take it on the lam, disappear. He knew he was going to disappear one way or the other, better he did it his way than let Dutch handle it.

That same morning, in the second story office over a garage in the Bronx, Dutch read the same article. He dropped it in Lulu Rosenkrantz' lap and jabbed at it with his thumb, "Get that paperboy," he said. Dutch always called reporters or press agents paperboys. Lulu made a mental note to kill the Jew who worked for Texas Guinan and then turned back to the sports section. Lulu loved the Yanks. Lou Gehrig was on fire but the Babe was in a terrible slump.

Monte couldn't afford to take it on the lam. He'd been off Texas' payroll while he was settling his personal business and now looked like he wouldn't be collecting this week's check. The Mayor's game had pretty well cleaned him out of any ready cash and his reserves in the bank were minimal. He had to keep working which meant he had to be in New York among his clients. Belle Livingstone had recovered from her humiliating arrest but had moved on to Reno, Nevada where gambling and boozing were openly smiled upon by the local authorities. Carl Erbe, his old hobo buddy, had begun to work for large corporations as a publicist, so wasn't much help with leads in the nightlife world. Monte did what he had to do.

He moved from the Knickerbocker to a cheaper hotel that he picked at random where nobody knew him and he knew no one. He checked in under an alias, Halston Thurgood, and paid cash for two months' rent. He never wore hats but that day he ventured out and bought a new hat, a drab, brown, wide-brim fedora, exactly like a hundred thousand others worn on the streets every day. He wore it low on his forehead, shading his eyes. He changed his regular eating spots to unknown and unpopular cafes among the Broadway crowd where he ordered meals to take with him to his room. During the day he stayed in his room reading and occasionally venturing to the end of the hall to a payphone.

After sundown, he ventured into the streets to keep his appointments. Winchell and Runyon knew where he was and what was happening. He didn't trust anyone else with the information. Even Texas thought he'd skipped town. Word came back through Winchell that the Dutchman had, as expected, reacted badly to the publicity and had fingered Monte for a long dirt nap. Lulu and a few friends were looking for him. Dutch apparently wasn't angry enough to put on outside contractors, so it was on the regular job list for Lulu and the boys along with collecting policy money and shaking down restaurant owners to hire union waiters from Dutch's Local 16.

By night, Monte ventured out to the *Heigh-Ho* where Toots Shor was on the door. The *Heigh-Ho* was discreet - lights were low, walls between private booths were high. It was a place for people who had business or pleasure they didn't want conducted over an open café table. It had one piano player for entertainment and Tiffany lamps for decoration and navigation. Other than the lamps, everything was in shadow. Monte took up rotating residence between the *Heigh-Ho* and two other clubs. He picked the other clubs based primarily on their doormen. These were men, like Toots, he now entrusted with his life and who knew what Lulu and Dutch's boys looked like. He colonized tables in the clubs that were nearest the staff escape routes used during police raids. From these tables, with his back to the escape route and his eyes on the doorman, he conducted his business.

Newspapermen came and went, news was exchanged and items were suggested. People had to come to him in his fortified locations. He frequently changed his mind on the way to his regular places, and changed the location of meetings at the last minute. It was just a gambler's hunch, but he never ignored it. The truth was he was getting jumpy as a cat. Sleep was difficult and car backfires took years off his life. During the six months of this routine, he rubbed the fur off of his lucky rabbit's foot.

Luckily for Monte, Dutch had bigger problems than knocking off press agents. Twenty-eight year old Thomas Dewey was the youngest chief assistant U.S. attorney in New York State history. He may also have been the most effective. Within weeks of taking office, a torrent of indictments overtook con artists, crooked contractors and lower echelon hoods who were caught completely off-guard. Legs Diamond, who by that time had survived a fourth assassination attempt and was awarded the title "Clay Pigeon of the Underworld", was first to go. Dewey put him away for 4 years for operating a still. Next was Jimmy Hines, the Tammany district leader who controlled much of Harlem and was Dutch's partner in the Hotel and Restaurant Employees International Alliance and Bartenders Union, Local 16, commonly known as the Waiter's Union.

Local 16 was actually a multi-million dollar shakedown racket that extorted restaurant and café owners in all five boroughs. If Dutch's threat of violence didn't make restaurateurs loyal union supporters, Jimmy's withholding of their city operating license would. Dewey had successfully turned Jimmy against Dutch and Dutch then took a powder to parts unknown. Lulu, Abbadabba and the boys all followed the boss into thin air, otherwise they expected to be the state's guests at Sing-Sing until they sang. Then suddenly, the heat was off. The Dutchman was out of the picture at least as long as Dewey was in office. Monte crawled out of his low-rent hole like Puxatawney Phil on Groundhog's Day and saw no shadow following him.

He held a small coming-out party that was well attended at the *Club Intime*. Texas opened champagne and proposed a toast to the fact that she'd lost her banker but had gained a pain in the ass. All in all a real bad deal. They all drank champagne until the house was dry. Customers were let in on the fun. Texas incited an elderly banker, one of her oldest and most faithful patrons, to play leapfrog in his top hat and tails with a chorus girl all around the club. She bought a round of drinks for everyone, something she never did. Her generosity was matched by the leapfrogging banker in mid-leap.

"And another round on me!" he'd bleat.

Others joined in this spontaneous generosity. The band broke into the old Charleston and the place erupted into a frenzy of flailing limbs. For a moment, it was like the old days. The fear was gone, people were giddy, the booze was flowing. In the middle of it all, Texas turned to Monte. She hadn't caught the giddiness of her guests, some of whom had been coming to her for over ten years. They were playing like children at recess. She'd done it again. She'd brought back the magic, but it was a sand castle against the tide and she knew it.

"We ain't gonna make it, kid," she told Monte. The club was doomed. With no one to provide protection, the Feds and the small sharks would be moving in fast. She started giving away Dutch's liquor because she didn't want to move it all to the next place, if there was a next place. By daybreak even the waiters were drunk, the bar shelves were empty and the place had become one large sleepover and drunk tank. It was the party to end all parties. People were helping each other into cabs late into the next afternoon.

As the sun was peeking in to break up the party, Texas and Monte and a few of the chorus girls loaded into Texas' armored car and were driven out to a deserted Long Island beach. It was a quiet, reflective time. Discussions about business dwindled as they drove into the rising sun.

At the beach all shoes came off. Jewelry and jackets were left in the car. Texas kept her huge floppy hat on and they wandered onto the cool sand in a loose pack. They stood ankle deep in the cold water quietly mesmerized by the spangles of sunlight on the surface. The night was over, the jokes were played out and the gulls took over the conversation.

The odd little troupe ended up nestled together for warmth and comfort on the sand like a feral wolf pack. The others often fell fast asleep but Texas usually only rested, half-asleep, never completely surrendering to fatigue. She would sometimes stroke the hair of one of the girls allowing herself this maternal gesture perhaps missing the children she never had with either of her two husbands or dozens of lovers.

Monte lay as close as possible to his Helen, the jet haired, green-eyed beauty from somewhere in Connecticut. Helen had first gotten his attention with her deep, explosive laugh, almost like a man. It seemed to signal her distinctive, fearless nature. At least Monte was convinced that it did. She was also by far the best dancer in the line. She performed the dance routines like the other girls but between shows would ask Monte about notables who came and went during the evening. The other girls were mostly oblivious to the audience, needing all their concentration just to get through the routine. Not Helen, she saw everything that went on.

He watched her sleeping on the sand on her cloche hat with the side of her face pushed up toward her nose. He was falling in love with her. He'd felt it coming on but pushed it aside as one of the endless chorus girl infatuations he'd learned to ignore. He couldn't very well make a play for every chorus girl who lit his lamp, it was bad for business. He learned to let his infatuations cool for days or weeks. With Helen, his initial reaction had grown stronger over several weeks of watching her. Now here he was, his tired eyes wide open hoping she would feel the same rushing emotions. She slept on, lifeless and trusting as a child. He inched closer on the sand to feel her warmth. He drifted toward sleep hoping for a natural disaster or marauder to appear so he could defend Helen and win her love forever.

Texas was correct, the end was near for speakeasies. The novelty of arresting her was wearing off. *Club Intime* was raided and closed, prompting the opening of *Club 300*, down the street. Texas was running out of names for places and just took the number address of the location where she landed next.

The sixth raid of the *300 Club* began one evening, less than a year later, with a phalanx of officers smashing in the front door. Perhaps to make up for the lack of subtlety, the arresting officer had prepared for his supporting role in that evening's show by delivering his parody to Texas' trademark introduction for performers, "Let's give the little lady a great big hand." The clever cop stood in the middle of the club and did his duty by informing the guests they were under arrest. After the pandemonium and cursing had died down he turned to Texas and said, "Now let's give the little lady a great big handcuff." The line got a decent laugh for which the officer offered a small bow of appreciation. The band, which had suddenly shrunk to the solitary trumpet player, took his cue from the officer's line and struck up *The Prisoner's Song* as contracted. The mournful tune continued to play from the back of the police wagon as it sped down Broadway toward justice.

At the 47th Street police station, Texas entertained nearly 200 former guests, now her cellmates, and her hosts including apologetic beat cops and federal agents with several renditions of the song. The station house rocked as the party continued, off and on, for the next nine hours until just after noon that day when lawyers for the *300 Club* managed to post bail for everybody. Again, patrons went home exhausted but thoroughly entertained.

Within days the *300* was padlocked again for the last time. Texas was handed a summons and escorted to the sidewalk to witness the dispersal of her guests into the night. There was no rousing procession to the jailhouse for another festival at the city's expense. The trumpet player couldn't summon up *The Prisoner's Song* because they weren't prisoners. Texas sensed the sea change that had occurred immediately. She was uncharacteristically quiet as the last of her guests finally gave up waiting for something else to happen - something wicked and liberating, the capper to the evening. Texas quietly wished the remaining revelers goodnight. They wandered off bewildered and unsatisfied.

The *Queen of the Nightclubs* summoned her car once again and her private group of beach friends. They took the long drive together. On the ride, Monte realized there wasn't going to be a publicity hook in what had just happened. There was no ending, the evening simply stopped. It was a bad show, a stinker that everyone wanted to forget. Texas didn't seem much interested anyway. Her thoughts were turning to the future.

She sensed the way that things ended more keenly than the young people who rode with her, she'd had more experience with it. She had plenty of money so her normal terror of the future was calmed. For now, all she wanted to think about was the endless ocean.

Helen clung to Monte as they walked the beach. It was a restless evening. Everyone had caught the sense of sober contemplation from Texas and was unnerved by it. Conversations started with humor then sputtered without finding a response and ended. No one knew what the matter was except perhaps the trumpet player, an older gent, who lay out on the car's hood to absorb the remaining engine heat and rested. He had his trumpet, his ticket to the future, wrapped in his arms. For him, things ended, shows closed every day. He packed light.

Monte and Helen found themselves far down the beach, out of sight of the group. She wanted a fire so they gathered driftwood. Monte instructed her with great care on the proper construction of a campfire so that it would only take one match to light. A true hobo only ever needed one match. A bum would need more. She sat close to the fire, he wrapped himself around her. They watched the flames, silently letting their minds go blank. She kissed his encircling arms.

His face rested on her back as he inhaled her warm scent. She turned around inside his arms and planted a leg on either side of his waist. Her skirt fell back to her navel. The tide of an ancient, warm sea filled him. The eyes that had tormented him now waited for him. The lips he couldn't look at were swollen full and touched red from the fire. He devoured her.

He descended on her like a season of tidal waves. Rushing under the pull of the full moon toward the black beach, waves formed into ranks; endless ranks stretching endlessly out to sea. They flew toward the beach, thrust up, crested and pounded down - wave after wave after wave until the beach shook under the assault. The lovers threw themselves at each other in a sexual frenzy, unleashing months of frustration. They were dissolved in the ancient, milk-warm sea.

Moments stretched into hours. The blood-red sun rose out of Long Island sound, splashing them with color as the hobo's campfire died of neglect. Gulls sailing on the morning wind wheeled overhead, screaming their approval as the tidal waves receded. Then they started again.

When they awoke they were under Texas' Arctic fox coat. The sun was high and white. The car was gone. Their friends were gone. The gulls stood off at a distance eyeing them, hoping they had died of exertion and might be an easy breakfast. Sand was in every crease. They were dehydrated. They were mostly naked. They were in love. Suddenly, Helen found her deep, easy laughter again. Monte just lay there on his back, listening to the laughter of his woman, grinning at the sun, not caring if the gulls ate him or the sea rose up and swept him away.

The *300 Club* stayed padlocked, missing the start of the new season in New York. The cooling north winds blew into town once again like an honest Canadian cousin reminding sluggards dozing in the summer hammock that time was short and life was fleeting. Heat and summer lethargy were swept into New York Harbor and New Yorkers picked up the pace. The decade was slipping away.

CHAPTER 10

I OWN THE JOINT

Monte looked around the 800 or so square feet that up to a few weeks ago had been a shoe repair shop. The Italian shoemaker, a fine craftsman, had drowned in shoes. Everywhere rows of unclaimed shoes were stacked in neat rows with paper tags on them. Some had been repaired four and five times and were a skillful patchwork of old and new leather but they were all unpaid for. The Depression had slowly ground the shoemaker's business down to nothing. People couldn't even afford to repair a second or third pair of shoes anymore. He walked out one afternoon to join the long, gray line and never came back. The shoes were now the landlord's problem.

Monte sat among the shoes wondering what his own place should be. Speakeasies were dying but they weren't dead yet. As precarious as the clubs were, the truth was they were his most reliable source of money. Wanger was being eaten alive by the movie business and was going to be bounced out of *United Artists* at any moment. Monte needed a saloon, a home base. He was ready for a joint of his own.

He thought of using the shoes somehow. He could do a Cinderella theme. He'd take the nicest pair of ladies' dress shoes and promote a contest that matched a lady's foot to the shoes. She'd get to keep the shoes and get a free round of drinks for her party. It was crap. He loaded up several burlap sacks, dragged all the shoes to the corner of Broadway and gave them to the first panhandler he met. For several weeks the man had a thriving second hand shoe business at that corner.

He had limited money to create a place where his friends would be comfortable. A fresh oyster and clam bar eliminated the need for a kitchen and cook, so he put a single gas ring in a storeroom to make chowder, displayed the clams and oysters at the bar on a bed of ice, buried the illegal beer under the ice and called the place *Monte's Clam House*. It was a simple saloon with burnished dark wood walls and furnishings supplied from the defunct *Club 300*. He booked a piano player who played at an after-hours place in Harlem and could play any tune especially the new jazz by Louis Armstrong. As long as he kept the prices low and the patrons high, he figured he'd turn a decent profit. Like people said, all you needed to open a speakeasy was one room, one bottle of booze and one customer.

Monte's Clam House opened in the spring of 1931. He greeted friends and the curious at the door in his sleek blue suit and his lucky gold and blue patterned bowtie. Veterans of *Club 300* had gotten the word and made the pilgrimage. They needed another place to go since Texas had packed her bags, and were visibly relieved that the prices were in line with the new realities. They carried on the Texas tradition of raucous fun by belting out songs along with the piano player who had his coffee cup constantly refreshed by their hip flasks.

For the first few days, Monte bought more drinks than he sold. The shock of the empty register turned him against his bartender, Boaty McGinn, an ex-fighter with a nose like a turnip and lips segmented by scar tissue. Boaty knew absolutely nothing about bartending except how to pour beer and fight, but he knew Monte and had the foresight to work out a simple accounting system. Monte thought Boaty was stealing until the man showed him a tally sheet of Monte's own generosity. Monte had gotten used to giving away other people's liquor and now faced the sobering shock of ownership.

Business was good in the first weeks as the weather heated up, but outside clients continued to slip away as his time was taken up by the new place, increasing the pressure for profits. After the first month, traffic settled down to a fairly steady pace. Winchell put *Monte's Clam House* on his regular beat as did Ed Sullivan and a few others. This put pressure on Monte to keep notable people coming through the brass door of the place. He added the expensive door partly because he thought it added to the nautical theme of the place but mainly because he had learned the value of strong metal doors against the forces of the Federal government.

In one of the downtown fight clubs, his protector Toots Shor, introduced Monte to a promising young fighter named Jack Entratter. Entratter was a gentle giant with a shuffling kind of footwork caused by a childhood bout with polio that left one leg shorter than the other. Entratter could swat but he was probably never going to get up into the big prize money because of his limited mobility. It wasn't thought to be that important in the heavier weight classes but it still made Entratter an easier target. His strategy was to be able to take punches and counterpunch. Any way you looked at it, it wasn't going to be an easy road.

Entratter was a humble and gentle guy out of the ring. He made you feel you were important because he listened closely to whatever you had to say. He even had a sense of humor. Toots and Monte adopted the big galoot and set him up at the front door where he towered over patrons like Gulliver. He was a hit with the young ladies and added an element of Broadway style and authenticity to the place that Toots and Monte appreciated.

Toots and Monte were two like minds. They fell into a natural friendship that was instant and heartfelt. Toots had a mind open to the world and all the people in it. He was big, unafraid and felt a responsibility that everything in his city of New York should operate so that a regular fellow and his lady could have a good time. He didn't like foul language, cheapskates, clip joints, wise guys or smart aleck dames and never had any hesitation letting each of them know his feelings. There weren't too many layers to Toots. He was a gentleman of the old school. He stood between all good people and trouble like a knight of the Round Table, exactly as Monte had been instructed to do as a young boy at his own mother's knee. A real, stand-up guy.

As his first business rolled on toward its first successful quarter, Monte immersed himself in a self-taught course of restaurant management. He was awful with numbers and record-keeping but managed to apply the basics needed to survive. The place was given a boost by U.S. Attorney Thomas Dewey's prosecution juggernaut that was sweeping mobsters from the city and creating a brief holiday for small club owners from pay-offs and shakedowns. The supply of booze, as always, continued uninterrupted as Frank Costello, Meyer Lansky and Lucky Luciano efficiently went about the importing business out of the public view.

Monte had his feet up on a table and was enjoying a seltzer and the write up Winchell gave him as the newest "hush house", Winchellese for speakeasy. A late spring breeze was blowing off the Hudson bringing the smell of warm mud all the way through the *Clam House's* open door. Winchell was now getting his own publicity. That same day in the *Herald Tribune,* Percy Hammond, the portly drama critic had apparently caught the Winchell bug and wrote glowingly, "He is young, fearless, sophisticated, and he combines a common sense with good Broadway taste, endurance and a forthrightness of prose expression." It was the validation from the old guard that Monte knew would send Winchell through the roof. He would be even more insufferable especially now that he was indispensable. But Winchell was a loyal pal in true show business tradition and gave Monte the benefit of his readers for free while the *Clam House* was getting on its feet. He turned back to the front page that carried a picture of the Empire State Building. It had just been completed and was drawing crowds that overflowed the sidewalks on all four sides.

The chill came over Monte when two husky men blocked out the soft yellow sunlight in the doorway with a peanut vending machine.

"Where ya want it?"

"I didn't order it." He knew it was useless to protest and the men ignored him in agreement. They moved the machine in the door on a hand truck wheeling it toward a spot near the piano.

"Over there!" Monte re-directed them to a place around the back of the rectangular, four-sided bar instead where the lonely boozers bounced their nickels on the bar punctuating conversations with themselves. Maybe now they'd at least put the nickel in the peanut machine, not that he'd see any of it. That nickel and all the others would be going straight back to Dutch Schulz. Dutch was making over ten million a year with all his rackets, why he bothered with peanut vending machines was just one of the many mysteries about Dutch. But one mystery was now cleared up – when he would return from exile.

Dutch found a lawyer who delayed Dewey's attack, giving Dutch time to resume his business and plan his counterattack. The machine might as well have been an engraved announcement notifying the recipient that they were now a part of the greater Dutch Schultz empire and that the Dutchman had returned. Monte was frozen at the table. It could as easily have been Lulu or Dutch's giant leg breaker, Bo Weinberg, who walked in with a Tommy gun instead of a peanut machine.

"To whom do I owe the honor?" Monte razzed the delivery men.

"Dutch."

He knew that but hoped Dutch had been iced and a rival had taken over the peanut business.

"Tell him thanks a lot."

"Tell him yourself. He's on his way over."

The words ran down Monte's spine like ice water. He leapt up from the table and sprinted into the tiny back kitchen. The boys shucking oysters near the kitchen sink were knocked out of the way as Monte climbed on the sink to get to the window that could drop him into the alley.

Out front, Abe Landau, Dutch's main bodyguard, took up the whole doorway himself as he cased the joint before allowing Dutch to enter. Dutch came in and looked the place over, then crossed to the bar.

"Where is he?"

Boaty slowly pointed with his thumb toward the storeroom/kitchen. Dutch reached into his coat pocket and Boaty started jabbering, "Ah Jesus, Mary, Dutch I got kids, please. I got kids..." Dutch didn't even acknowledge the man's terror as he pulled out a roll of bills as big as his fist. He peeled off five 100's and slapped them on the bar.

"Go get him."

The bartender moved faster than he had since high school. In the kitchen, Monte was stuck in the window. His legs kicked at the air trying to force his hips through the impossibly small space. He was panting hard with the effort.

"Dutch wants ya!" Boaty yelled. The legs stopped kicking for a moment, then started kicking again, harder. Dutch and Landau were suddenly in the kitchen.

"Get him out." Dutch said. Landau stepped up on the sink and grabbed Monte by the belt and pulled him back inside. Monte was too humiliated and exhausted to do anything but stand at the sink panting in his shredded, dirty shirt.

Dutch looked Monte over and asked, "How about a drink?"

At the bar, Dutch shoved the 500 in cash at Monte. "Put it in the till. For good luck." the gangster instructed. Monte pushed the bills across the bar to Boaty who put them behind the bar into the metal strongbox, then moved as far away as possible, to the other side of the bar where there was nothing for him to do but loudly stack, wipe and re-stack clean plates.

Dutch sat there straight-faced while Monte tried to figure out why he wasn't dead on the floor of the kitchen. He never did figure it out completely. Another mystery of the Dutchman.

Soon, it was just like they were back at their old table in the *Club Intime*. Dutch wanted a complete update on everything since he'd been away. Monte filled him in on the late night characters and recent action. Dutch never mentioned the article that almost got Monte killed. The spring sunlight in the doorway turned deep honey color, then steel blue and finally black. The brass door was closed and locked. Customers drifted in after tapping the code of two short knocks, then two more, since it was well known that Federal dry agents always knocked three times.

Mugs of beer dripping with moisture skidded over the bar to Monte and his guest until Dutch had finally heard enough of the news. He got up, twisted his sapphire pinky ring around and back. Monte thought, "Here it comes. Here comes the gun. He just wanted to know who I've been talking too…"

Instead, Dutch leaned in close and said, "Don't never do that again. Put me in the papers like that." He turned and took Landau with him into the river-scented night air. Monte turned to his bartender who was already pouring himself a shot of brandy. The poor man's hands were shaking so badly he spilled most of the stuff on the bar. The knot in Monte's chest slowly unwound.

The first thing he noticed was the sweetness of the music that calmed and quieted his small group of friends in the club. He marveled at the scent of perfume and hair oil that blended with the pale blue clouds of tobacco and floated up to the ceiling. He knew now for sure that his life was charmed and that he was protected. He thought about all the times he might have been killed - from dodging streetcars on his roller skates in Baltimore, to dodging knives and pistols in Brooklyn and Chicago, to his near murder at the hands of Dutch. He calmly watched his mind's movie screen as he absent-mindedly lit a match and dropped it onto the spilled liquor on the bar. It ignited with a cold blue flame. He folded his arms on the bar and rested his cheek on his forearm as he watched the flames dance harmlessly on the surface of the booze.

CHAPTER 11

ANARCHY IN ASTORIA

In the odd calculus of Hollywood, Walter Wanger's multiple disasters at *UA* added up to his next job as head of production for Paramount. By 1931, under his direction, *Astoria Studios* developed into a hotbed of anarchy in an industry that prided itself on the efficient production techniques developed in Detroit by Henry Ford.

But in Astoria, movies weren't made like cars. Wanger imported unwashed avant-gardists of Europe, mixed them with the independent minded powerhouse actors and writers of Broadway and sat back to watch the fireworks. All he asked Monte to do was make sure everybody knew about it. The place was a press agent's dream. Every star was competing with every other star for attention and would dish dirt on each other that made teamsters blush. Of course, the real stories never got out because the bosses could still control the press department. They made sure that the wholesale debauchery, scandal and wild-eyed mayhem of their employees penned up in the asylum across the river was presented as a wholesome day's work suitable for discussion at church socials.

But actually, the Marx Brothers were running amok during the shooting of their film *Animal Crackers*, giving stars like Clara

Bow a hotfoot while Jack Barrymore roamed the halls, eyes inflamed with liquor, looking for any chorus girl who wanted private acting lessons in his dressing room. The costume shop was frequently infested with rutting couples and triples. Certifiably insane directors screamed curses in five languages and shot pistols into the fly loft to get the reaction they wanted on film, ignoring the men overhead setting lights. Monte never felt so at home, in the working studio, among his friends.

The front office across the river in Manhattan, with his bosses, was a different feeling completely. The newspaper fiction he created about movie production in Astoria was like sworn testimony compared to the lies Jesse Lasky, a pioneering Hollywood producer, was telling in the sales meetings. Film distributors from all over the country would convene in Paramount's impressive boardroom overlooking Broadway. Monte and Wanger would smile and nod in agreement as Lasky hailed the next Paramount release as the grandest, most expensive production in the studio's history. Project after project would roll out of Lasky's mouth, each one grander than the last, as if Paramount controlled every literary work in the English language. Often Wanger hadn't even secured the rights to produce the projects yet. Some he hadn't even heard of. Lasky wrapped up his whole package of lies and tied it with a big bow proclaiming that stars like Gloria Swanson and Wallace Reid, whom no one had even spoken to, would be starring in the pictures. He once became so enraptured by his own nonsense that he spouted, "Gloria Swanson and Wallace Reid! I can hardly believe it myself!" This drew an excited round of applause and allowed Lasky to momentarily regain his common sense.

This was Monte's introduction to the prevailing ethics of corporate boardrooms. It was a world of puffery, innuendo and bluff, quite a contrast to the small saloon operations he was used to, where not lying well could get you killed. He sensed the pervasive treachery and felt off-balance. In a few late night discussions, he found that Wanger had made his peace with the situation. It was how this game was played. As Wanger said, Lasky's word wasn't worth the paper it was written on.

Lasky closed the fun house in Astoria and sent everyone packing for Siberia in the sun, Hollywood. "Where," as comedian Fred Allen commented, "no matter how hot it got during the day, there was still nothing to do at night." In Hollywood the streets were empty at 10 PM, the gin mills were quiet and the worst trouble set-bound swordsmen like Barrymore could get into was a dose of the clap. Or so the bosses hoped. The real reason was because Paramount was in dire financial trouble. If they didn't step up the box office receipts and quick, they weren't going to make it another year. That meant increased production and that meant they were heading for the 350 days a year of sunny shooting weather in Hollywood.

Monte was invited to join the company since Wanger had grown very used to having the street smart and energetic young man as his sounding board. Monte would split his time between New York and Hollywood, sometimes acting as associate producer for Wanger. Often on his return trips to New York, the Paramount bosses would sit him down in the boardroom and grill him for the inside dope on who was drinking, showing up late on the set and who was screwing whom. Monte played the part of the dutiful errand boy, all the while promoting the remarkable job Wanger was doing. But Monte couldn't disguise the continued overages and delays and the persistently mediocre returns on Wanger's pictures. Wanger was increasingly and typically on thin ice.

Monte arrived in Hollywood for the second time in his life but this time instead of a sunburned background extra or road worker, he was a fully-fledged member of the movie community, an insider. Hollywood had come a long way in the six years he'd been away. Instead of a pokey factory town, he found a widely dispersed but active enclave of moral refugees. Maybe it was because he was in a different crowd now but in saloons and nightclubs around town, what young men were strumming between their legs weren't the guitars he remembered.

A year before, in 1930, a very popular place called *Jimmy's Backyard* had opened and was followed in rapid succession by a series of "pansy clubs" which were all the rage. In these places, men and women dressed like men and women but not strictly in that order. There was a sense that Hollywood was a remote desert outpost where the morals of the old East Coast establishment took a holiday. There were entertainments of every sort that spoofed sex roles and couplings using everything from kitchen utensils to farm animals. Some of this raciness began to spill over into the explicitly sexual story lines of films. The first lady's dress was unzipped that year in *Just a Gigolo*. The Hays Office, created specifically to protect the public from the obvious moral decline in movies, mobilized all their forces when they saw that scene. Once again, Hollywood's producers were forced to proclaim their collective outrage while stalling any action against the film until the first few weeks' box office receipts were safely deposited in the bank.

Hollywood, like every region and industry in the country, was under enormous stress. As the Depression deepened, it looked like the movie business might be engulfed as well. Even though its millionaire stars were gorging on caviar in publicity stories, its customers were starving. It seemed as though this tension was being relieved out of the public's view in a nightlife steeped in sexual decadence. This wasn't entirely comfortable for the young press agent who maintained a deeply British reserve in sexual matters but it was at least an improvement over the cowboy yodelers he recalled from his last visit.

The Marx brothers were shooting *Monkey Business* their second picture for Wanger in a dusty barn converted to a movie studio and rumors were flying that they weren't getting along. Chico was chafing in the role of second banana to Groucho's manic lead. Suddenly, there was plenty of work diverting the press' attention from the friction on set by providing endless puff pieces on Paramount's historic decision to move from New York to Hollywood. There were also individual interviews with stars of the production to arrange. This took up most of Monte's time and satisfied snooping gossip writers like Louella Parsons. The first wave of disaster passed without incident and work settled into a routine of sniping, backstabbing and threats; veiled and unveiled between Wanger and the bosses.

Monkey Business was Wanger's best and possibly last hope to produce the box office smash the home office was looking for. Monte was sent on a barnstorming mission with Groucho to promote the picture in New York, Chicago and Philadelphia while Chico was left in Hollywood to stew, hopefully quietly. Monte pulled in every favor and contact he had ever known to promote Groucho Marx as the greatest comic genius that ever lived and his new picture *Monkey Business* as the funniest thing ever filmed.

In Philadelphia, Groucho had had enough of the publicity routine that included answering the same inane questions that other reporters had asked in Chicago and New York. He complained to Monte who informed reporters assembled in the sitting room of Groucho's suite that they would have to ask more intelligent questions than their colleagues in Chicago or Mr. Marx would not answer. Some reporters who objected to this treatment left without interviewing Groucho. Those who remained were subjected to Groucho's nonsense answers and being pelted with olives if their questions displeased the Grouch. The publicity tour was clearly over.

Monte returned to New York under instructions to see every show in town and report back on anything that might add another strand to Wanger's rapidly unraveling rope at Paramount. Although he had pockets full of money and a job, Monte couldn't celebrate his luck with the same freedom he once enjoyed. Walking the streets he met too many friends who had been out of work so long that they were literally starving. He ended up giving away almost all of his expense money. The weeks on the road with Groucho had been fun and the two men had developed a friendly working relationship.

But the trip accented Monte's growing sense of isolation. The move to California and heavy workload as a small cog in the very big publicity machine of Paramount, often left him with hundreds of new acquaintances and no old friends. Now back in New York, it seemed his old friends were either gone or were suffering beyond his ability to help them.

One night at the Paramount Grill on Broadway, while swapping stories of the pansy craze and sexual Olympics of Hollywood, he was introduced to 16-year old first time chorus girl, Julie Jenner. Echoes of Helen shuddered through his chest – beautiful, fearless Helen, who laughed like a man. Helen had disappeared with the speakeasies.

But Monte had tracked her down, at her parent's home in Naugatuck, Connecticut, a few years later. She had grown fearful in the years since they last saw each other and became uncomfortable as they continued to talk at her parent's kitchen table. Something was not right, something was not being said as he felt the cold eyes of her parents bear down on him. He left her there without demanding an answer, returning on the train to New York City, fully absorbed in the mysterious problem. Weeks later, a letter from Helen found him at the bar in *Monte's Clam House*. There had been a baby. The Catholic Fathers of Naugatuck parish had found a good home for the little boy far away, out west somewhere, but it had broken Helen's heart and erased her confidence in life, seemingly forever. Monte felt the pin-prick in his heart as he crushed the letter into his jacket pocket. His picture of innocent, dream-like first love with his beautiful, fearless Helen on the beaches of Long Island, was now stained with heartbreak. He ordered a shot for himself and threw it back quickly. It did nothing for the pain.

He was once again captivated by a bold, dark-haired beauty. Julie Jenner was fresh and feisty as any teenager who knew she could command the rapt attentions of a table of older men. She was clearly comfortable in the spotlight and clever enough to stay there without being a bore. It was quickly apparent that she had reviewed and sorted the men by order of power and suitability. That night Monte was clearly the frontrunner. He was a young man with plenty of cash and a firm foothold in café society and Hollywood. His manners and his clothes were impeccable. He spoke the lingo of a crapshooter but had the refinement of an English Duke. Monte couldn't help staring into her huge, flashing eyes but held himself back. Starlets on the make were a hazard he had long since developed a healthy immunity against. And there was the shadow of Helen that still chilled him whenever he thought of falling in love with another chorus girl. Julie's boldness dispelled Elaine's shadow. He would never have to wonder what Julie was thinking, or so it seemed.

Soon private comments were being shared between the two and the fellas at the table were feeling the ebb of the tide in their direction. Mayor Jimmy's crap game was happening somewhere close by and Monte felt he had a hot hand. Julie wanted to come but the guys including Monte weren't too keen on having a nice girl tag along with them.

Other kinds of girls were more welcome, but innocent looking kids from somewhere in the sticks didn't belong at an illegal crap game. They might sap vital concentration away from rolling sevens. Julie took it for a minute and then flashed her money, "I can shoot the eyes outta any man here." She got her way. Joe Frisco, the jazz dancer, was always in awe or maybe just wary of beautiful, young women. He preferred large, mature, less attractive ladies who could give a skinny guy like him a more comfortable position in the world. He pulled Monte aside and whispered in his usual stutter, "Sh-sh-she's a bell ringer. B-but I'd hold on t-t-to your clapper."

Julie seemed to hold her own at the game and made a few respectable passes before crapping out and losing her small wad. Monte let her drift away so he could focus on the task at hand. A few hundred dollars later he finally came up for air. She was in a circle of new friends near the piano leading them by the nose as she had done with his group earlier. He let it go and figured she was making the play he expected, but suddenly she looked up from her entourage and caught his eye. Of all the powerful, rich and well-connected men in the room, she was staring at Monte. How did she know, how could she tell he was looking at her at just that moment? A powerful shock went through him. The invisible lines of communication had been laid between them when he wasn't even looking. How could he miss those eyes of hers? They were huge. He fell into them head first. Julie Jenner was going to be his new girl.

Life galloped along with Monte traveling between New York and Hollywood on promotional tours and scouting missions for Wanger. Julie continued her senior year of high school by day and filled out chorus lines on Broadway by night. It was a chaste relationship filled with romantic farewells and exuberant returns. Letters between them became increasingly intimate. She had her dashing young man, he had his virginal young woman. It was a relationship built almost completely on fantasy. The fact was that Julie was too young and too ambitious to do much more than play at romance. There was always a new stage door Johnny or a new talent manager who needed her attention and she couldn't very well ignore them. Her family depended on her steady income. Her mother, in typical Depression-era style, was vocal about her expectations for a "comfortable" marriage. It was a handy Victorian sentiment readopted to address the financial realities of 1932. Save yourself for marriage – to someone well off.

Maybe his innocent lover gave Monte an emotional refuge from the sexual cauldron of the Hollywood movie colony. The hijinks that flourished in Astoria, if anything, got worse in California. Contrary to Fred Allen's complaint about Hollywood, now there was something to do at night. Even as the Hays Office was beginning to crack down in response to public pressure caused by increasingly risqué newspaper stories about movie people, parties of excitable young starlets swarmed in gardens and living rooms every night. In spite of his reserved and gentlemanly approach to sex, Monte was never one to spoil a party. Sometimes after a few drinks and few laughs, a pair of friendly eyes would rock him to sleep. He would awake disoriented and in a strange bed with a brand new friend. Those mornings were a shock but his training saved him. He never neglected to offer a proper introduction, leave his business card with his home phone number and seek a gracious exit. Sometimes he felt bad and sometimes the feeling lasted all the way to lunch. He would write a love letter to Julie in New York and chalk up the previous night to research. It may have been that Monte wasn't really recovered from Helen. It certainly seemed so looking at his hollow pursuit of

Julie, but the pursuit continued. He was playing the game and Julie was a well-matched partner.

Wanger's discovery, Clara Bow, the *IT* girl, was getting quite a bit of *IT* of another type at a few of the parties Monte attended. Bow's life-long, devoted assistant, Daisy DeVoe attempted to blackmail the star and the floodgates of scandal opened wide. Bow made the mistake of taking her confidante to court. This backfired into a detailed public expose of the star's personal habits. DeVoe was only too happy to lay out the lurid details of her employer's sex life in open court. The newly established tabloid *Coast Reporter* saw the opportunity to give readers the juiciest scandal in years. In the past, Monte and his publicity colleagues at the studios could often divert friends like Billy Wilkerson of the *Hollywood Reporter* and other industry insiders from printing hard facts that could destroy a career. They often resorted instead to innuendo and code words that winked at the true sex preferences and practices of stars. But *Coast Reporter's* publisher Frederic Girnau, was a different sort of reporter. He wanted dirt; the dirtier the better and he paid well for it. Girnau took DeVoe's testimony added liberal embellishments of his own which included claims that Bow was simultaneously mistress to a number of married men and lesbian lover to an equal number of starlets. He even reported that Bow's overall favorite partner was her Great Dane and tabloid journalism was re-born.

The *IT* girl became the first *"gotcha"* girl. In May, 1931 Bow was shown the gate of Paramount Studios. Not long after, perhaps because his spunky star was the last straw, Wanger was also bounced from Paramount with all the warmth and ceremony of kitchen scraps being tossed out an alley window.

Monte went with Wanger to Columbia where Wanger's next picture *Washington Merry Go Round* pointed a finger directly at the past Coolidge administration's Attorney General, Harry Daugherty, his involvement in the Teapot Dome Scandal and his financial interests in bootlegging. It was a shocking and nearly unprecedented thrust into political muckraking by popular entertainment. It exposed the general public to what Monte and his Prohibition peers had known for years – that large portions of the United States government had the integrity of a wrestling referee. As the nation slipped into the deepest trough of the Depression in 1932, the notion was gaining acceptance that lawmakers were the ultimate gang of carpetbaggers and swindlers, who had robbed the country of its vitality and sunk it. The new socialist experiment in Russia looked like the new land of the people, by the people and for the people. In Russia, everybody had a job.

CHAPTER 12

FAMILY ENTERTAINMENT

Sex scandals were breaking wide open and the Hollywood studios were running for cover. The gentlemen's agreement with papers like the *Hollywood Reporter* that had always protected stars with divergent sex lives was breaking down. Any remnant of the freewheeling 20's was being publicly dragged out and stoned in a new, moral witch-hunt. Revealing stories began to appear on Jean Harlow, Tallulah Bankhead, Howard Hughes, Cary Grant and Randolph Scott. Some of them were tagged as "confirmed bachelors" and "temperamentals" – code phrases for homosexual. The *Hollywood Reporter* was now in competition with the vicious new tabloid *Coast Reporter* to catch stars at the newly popular "pansy clubs" like *B.B.B's Cellar*, a notorious and very dimly lit meeting place that featured a chorus line of 10 female impersonators.

As if the sex scandals weren't enough bad news, box office receipts were off by nearly 20 percent. It was the first decline in the history of the movie business. Rumors circulated that it was the beginning of the end, the jig was up and no one would survive the Depression. It was a difficult time to be a studio publicity man. Every week brought another publicity disaster and many former allies in the press were expanding their readership by trumpeting the disasters instead of helping to cover them up.

William Haines, the top box office leading man in recent years for Louis B. Mayer and MGM, was apparently caught in the act with a young sailor in Pershing Square. The studio, through its close working relationship with Los Angeles District Attorney Buron Fitts, managed to have all arrest records disappear but not soon enough to prevent unsubstantiated stories from appearing in the papers. Jean Harlow's camouflage marriage to producer Paul Bern ended in Bern's suicide. A note was found hinting at the "comedy" of their union. Now the hounds smelled blood and were at full cry. News reports were coming back from Europe about Garbo dressing in pants, boots, a black wig and cruising the clientele in a lesbian nightclub in the Montmarte.

It was distant but threatening thunder to Monte as he sat at the bar of *Dave's Blue Room* on Broadway nursing his Dewar's and soda. A cold spring drizzle slid down Dave's front window and made him glad for the steamy animal warmth crowded around him. He was relieved to be away from the hornet's nest of bad news on the West coast but he still felt the sting reading about Garbo cruising in a Paris lesbian bar. It wasn't helping him pump *QUEEN CHRISTINA,* Garbo's new picture and Wanger's last lifeboat. Nobody wanted to talk about the film - all they wanted to talk about was Garbo's women.

Dave's was packed with the usual crowd of athletes, actors, sports writers and agents. The place was like a thousand other New York saloons, short on decorations and long on the pour from the bartender, except that it was located at 49th and Broadway, a convenient spot for the night people. Because it was on such pricey real estate, the sawdust was swept up and the dark wood floor was polished until it shined like the customers' shoes. There was nothing in *Dave's* but decent food, good hooch and people, generally men, occasionally a girl dancer or two. It was a transit spot. Nobody spent the evening in *Dave's* unless their string had run out and they were there to commiserate. Broadway guys on their way to swank joints would hoist a quick one, check the score and sniff the wind – which there was plenty of – for action. The story on *Dave's* was that more money changed hands there than in *Chase Manhattan* bank. It was mostly in well-worn ten's and twenty's and mostly between men who wore their hats indoors, low over their eyes. Some had stubby pencils behind their ears. Some chewed gum while they smoked cigarettes, a few smoked cigars. The place was always clouded up with smoke exhaled from a hundred flapping mouths. When you walked into *Dave's*, you walked out smelling like a brush fire.

The whiskey took the chill off the evening. Monte felt it loosen his tongue and lighten his heart. Dewar's was still making the same, reliable straw colored juice. With all the up and down he had in his life, he was beginning to look for things he could rely on and Dewar's seemed as constant as things got. For ten years it had been his constant companion and was as pure as chamomile tea, he thought. It was his familiar habit now, his harmless entertainment. It sparkled gold in the glass, winking at him like a friend recently out of jail and up for some mischief. On cold nights he'd start off with a shot, neat, soda and ice back. The first shot of the night slid down easy with just little nip at the back of the throat – a friendly kick in the pants. Suck a little ice and it was all over.

The heat from his shot of Dewar's sank into his belly and the giddy feeling came up slow and warm, pouring over his brain like a mineral bath, relaxing all his joints. He opened his eyes and there he was, a little unsteady, but happy and in *Dave's*. He looked down at his shot glass and it was full again, like magic. His man Boaty, transferred directly from *Monte's Clam House*, poured openly, figuring nobody was going to pinch them now. Roosevelt was in and the whole Prohibition shebang was about to get tossed.

Carl Erbe was holding court that night and hailed his old hobo buddy and partner. Monte plunked down at the table surrounded by familiar pals who were likewise handicapped. Carl and Monte were referred to frequently as "these two bums". Monte got tired of correcting his disrespectful cronies that he and Carl were hobos, bindlestiffs to be exact. The comfort of barroom hospitality closed in around them. Joey Fay, the young comic, had ordered *Dave's* special lamb chops. They slid by on a blue plate, sizzling and fragrant, tipped with white paper cuffs. Joey must've hit the numbers, those chops could feed a family. Nobody said a thing. The constant news chatter continued – a tip on the Jack Sharkey fight at the *Garden*, the new 3.2 beer (Roosevelt's campaign promise) and everybody agreed that it was what got him elected. Waxey Gordon already had the deal sewed up on the stuff with his *Red Monogram* brand. You'd get dizzier from all the pissing you had to do than from the alcohol in it, but it was a step in the right direction.

"Roosevelt's alright, for a soft-head." the commentary at the table continued from radio producer Walter Batchelor. Batch rarely said anything really bad about anybody but the soft-head dig was sure to get a rise. He shifted his thick body and knocked wood on the table for good luck. Batch was like Puck, Monte thought, like Shakespeare's little mischievous sprite, but in the body of a professional wrestler. He was self-conscious about his size because it made him a natural target when fights broke out, which was several times a night, so Batch got used to ducking and heading for the door at the first hint of violence. He didn't mind a little poking to rile up his pals though. His comment sparked the instant reaction that he expected.

Carl was celebrating some new account or something and was already pretty loaded. He growled, "He'll knock sense in these sons of bitches, get things going again." Nobody dared disagree with this. Among working age men at the time, pessimism was dangerous. It could push someone who couldn't pay his rent, or feed his family, over the edge.

"He's a New Yorker, right?" the boosterism went. "He knows the score." Everyone agreed and then they all felt better. There was hope.

Other young men of Monte's age were home, exhausted after a grueling day or tending babies while their wives, if they were lucky, were out doing shift work in a garment factory. Monte was as free as a young man could be. He had no responsibilities and pockets full of money. On the outside, it looked like the world was his oyster. But inside, it was a different story.

His confidence in women was badly broken by his first love affair with his dark-haired dancer, Helen, and in subtle ways he had retreated from them. His pain had sunk far below the surface, like an old splinter. He was most comfortable now in the company of other men in a bachelor's den like *Dave's*. He even kept his distance from his new flame, Julie. When Carl mentioned Monte wasn't bringing Julie around much and asked about her, he got the brush, so he dropped it. Monte was quiet on the subject, except that it was all over his face. When the piano player struck up a tune from Julie's show or a girl who looked something like her walked through the place, his eyes would light up then slowly go to the floor. To the few like Carl who knew him well, it didn't seem normal. It seemed like this new girl was more of a protégé or a casual date than the girlfriend Monte claimed her to be. She was too loud for Monte, too flirtatious. Even so, Carl knew that Monte would defend her like she was the Queen of England. They called it "carrying the torch". They said Monte carried the torch for Julie and he let the half-truth stand. The truth was that he carried the torch for his dead and buried dream of Helen.

Dave, the boss, didn't help Monte's state of mind when he leaned in and gave him the news along with a few of the postcards that had been waiting for him behind the bar. Monte heard the news and but instantly rejected it. It was too much and too hard. He stared at the postcards in his hands. Dave patted Monte on the shoulder, then his words came back to Monte. Suddenly it seemed like the world had gotten old.

Dave had told him that Texas Guinan had died in a hospital on the other side of the continent in Vancouver – just about as far from New York as you can get. The saloonkeeper gave the sketchy details about some kind of infection but it was like a radio signal that wouldn't tune in. Monte only heard snatches of what Dave had to say.

Texas was his youth, and now suddenly, she was gone. She was his mentor, his confessor and surrogate mother. She helped nurture his first love, she stood up to Dutch Schultz and saved his life. She held him when his heart was breaking from Helen. He hadn't seen her since the big scram from Dutch and always felt sorry that shooting his mouth off had brought Dutch down on them both and finished her in New York. She had forgiven him years ago but he never got around to forgiving himself. He knew that Dutch himself had come into the *Club 300* and threatened to put her in a hole somewhere unless she coughed up the paperboy, but she never breathed a word. That was Texas. And it was the end of Texas and speakeasies.

Her first move was to leave the country. She grabbed most of her chorus line and headed to Europe to open a "sucker joint" in Paris. She was apprehended in Cherbourg and placed under house arrest in a local hotel pending her summary deportation. The Minister of Labor denounced Madame Guinan to the papers as an unsavory character. Her long association with Dutch and his predecessors had tarnished her beyond redemption, even in France. Monte read of her humiliation as he lay in his hotel room hiding from Dutch and his men. He felt responsible for her problem with Dutch but was powerless to help.

On her return voyage, she once again typically turned the tide of bad publicity into a flood of cash. She cooked up a show that she called *Too Hot for Paris*. The entire week of the voyage she worked the communications officer of the ship like a stevedore, cabling every contact she and Monte had ever discussed. The idea was a hit and by the time the ship docked she had a tour for the show booked around the states. She toured *Too Hot* for two years, playing everywhere except, of course, New York.

The occasional cards he got from all over the map were always short, no more than two sentences usually about the weather and the "kids" who were sticking with her through all the small town theaters that had been converted to movie houses. They often played a double bill, Texas was the warm up act for the movie. She never complained or seemed depressed in her notes, and they were always signed, "So long sucker, T." There would be nobody like Texas ever again. She had been the lighthouse of his career and to a large extent his life. The party of his early life had finally died. It was him, not the world that had suddenly gotten old. His lighthouse had gone out.

The sleety March rain drizzled down Dave Kleckner's front window as Monte bought another round for his pals. He stood and proposed a toast to Texas, almost everybody stood up except the low hustlers in the back booths. He caught sight of one and yelled at the man, "Get up!" The man looked around at the shaming eyes on him. He slowly got to his feet.

"To Texas Guinan, my pal, and a hell of a dame," he said. He downed what he had as the next round arrived. He was going after that one too hoping it would sting bad enough to distract him from crying, when in walked a woman in her forties who definitely did not belong.

She had naturally blushed cheeks and clear blue eyes like mountain lakes. She was dressed for a blizzard. She stopped short in the smoky haze, clearly hesitant about stepping further into the rough saloon. She was definitely a spark, a light and something for Monte to focus on. Her gentlemanly young escort, Milton Blackstone, followed her in and took her by the arm urging her forward. Milton was one of the strangest birds on Broadway. Not only did Milton Blackstone not drink, gamble or swear, he did not know how to work an angle. He couldn't connive, finagle, cajole or schmooze. In short, Milton was not Broadway material. He didn't hustle in the sense of bouncing from client to client. He had only one account, the lady on his arm. But for that one account he pioneered a new branch of press agentry. He did this because his account, Jenny Grossinger, couldn't afford to buy newspaper or radio advertising for her Catskill hotel. What Milton developed would eventually be called public relations.

Milton wrote letters, personal letters, hundreds of them. As a young desk clerk at the hotel, he started writing letters by hand in the evening after he finished his regular work. He wrote a letter to every customer that ever visited Jenny Grossinger's country hotel thanking them for visiting and asking them for their ideas on how to improve the place. He wrote an individual letter to every Jewish workingman and woman he could find in the five boroughs of New York inviting them to *Grossinger's* for a very modestly priced vacation in the clean air of the Catskill Mountains. When the budget allowed, he followed up the letters with a personal phone call. He wrote to single girls, *"Even if you are coming by yourself we know you'll have a wonderful time. You will meet a lot of fine, friendly people, and you can be sure that you will get our personal attention."*

Milton was a straight-arrow and a mensch and Jenny Grossinger treated him like her own son. More than that, she entrusted him, at the age of 26, with the uncertain future of her family's hotel. The Depression was threatening to shutter the place for good. Only Milton's letter writing campaign was keeping the doors open. Now he needed ideas and he needed his friend's help.

Milton had been picking Monte's brain for months about affordable entertainers who would make the trip to the mountains, and Monte had always been glad to help, no charge. Doing favors had become a completely automatic response and the natural currency of Monte's life. Once again almost everyone he knew was only a few bucks away from an empty belly – like hobos, his first social group.

Milton pulled a chair out for Jenny that was still warm from the guy who surrendered it to her. All the men stood and shook hands until Jenny was seated. Monte could tell she was uncomfortable. He sized her up immediately as the kind and hardworking lady Milton told him about. He put aside his whiskey and ordered tea for the table. Everything stopped for a second at the table. One by one the men took their hands off their liquor and contented themselves with the chasers of water and soda.

Jenny spoke to Monte for a few moments about their situation and Milton's faith in him. She was so obviously an uncomplicated, country lady that Monte instantly relaxed. As she spoke further he saw that she was simply a warm-hearted Jewish mother whose first thoughts were for her family. She included in her family the people who worked for her. Without expecting to and without hesitation she had just, in effect, invited Monte into her family. The invitation sank all the way in and touched him deeply. All he needed was for Al Jolson to walk in and sing a few bars of "My Yiddishe Mama" and he would have started crying. Instead he looked at Milton and knew he had found a safe harbor. It made perfect sense that someone like Milton would work so hard, for so little, for someone like Jenny. He felt these were people he could trust with his life.

Monte leaned in to Jenny, "There's a nice guy," he indicated a slim, dark complexioned man slouching among a group of celebrities. "His name is Sol Gold and he trains fighters. If things are going well with him, the big cigar he smokes is always straight out. If things are bad, it droops down to his chest. Sol must be in trouble."

The cigar drooped from the man's glum lips. Monte hied Sol over and he seemed happy to get away from his boisterous and successful companions. Sol was introduced to Jennie and Milton and sat with them. He knew the others at the table, Carl, Joey Fay and Batch. The reason for the Sol's long face unspooled before them.

He handled Barney Ross, the champ from Chicago, who was slated for a title bout in New York. The problem was Sol couldn't find a decent training camp. Jennie had almost no idea what fighters did or why. She was upset by the idea of two young men beating each other for money and lost the thread of the conversation a few seconds into it. Monte reeled her back in.

"Milton's always talking about getting something different for the hotel. You know, some gimmick. Well the gimmick is sitting right here at this table."

Jennie listened carefully, looking deep into Monte's eyes for the meaning of what he was saying. She nodded, indicating that she understood what she just heard, but turned to Milton and asked, "Gimmick? What is it?" Milton did his best to unravel the new slang. He picked up Monte's thought and instantly saw the possibility.

He explained to Jennie, "Remember a few years ago, a fighter named Sid Terris from the East Side came to the hotel for a weekend? Everyone made a big fuss over him?" The light was going on for Jenny. Monte took over, "This kid of Sol's is named Barney Ross. He's a two-time world champ and he's going to fight Jimmy McLarnin, another champ in six weeks. Any place where either of them trains will get national press."

Monte launched into a flight of promotional imagination that had the whole table leaning in and grabbing their drinks again for support. Milton translated for Jenny and interjected elements into Monte's vision of a national promotion blitz that the hotel could provide. An unprecedented media extravaganza was woven before their eyes. Carl and Batch got into the act, suggesting corporate sponsors and radio features that could be broadcast live from the camp. This was Monte's long suit. His vision exploded in a burst of enthusiasm that swept all doubts aside. The scale of what Monte saw had never been done before. The thrill of his innovation impressed even the hardened Broadwayites in the group and elevated his reputation from one of the better press agents to a visionary. When Monte finally wound down and sealed the deal with a toast, even Jennie was enthralled with the grand scale that Monte envisioned, and Sol's cigar had levitated to the tip of his nose.

Within weeks, *Grossinger's* built a regulation size boxing ring and a separate cottage for the champ. Barney Ross arrived with an entourage of several dozen sportswriters just as Monte said would happen. Suddenly every room in *Grossinger's* was booked. Every afternoon as part of his regular training, Barney Ross climbed into the new ring and proceeded to whack the hell out of various sparring partners under shade of the tall pine trees. Every guest in the hotel crowded around to see the champ. Milton trucked in dozens of folding chairs and started charging 50 cents admission. Within a week the cost of the ring and the cottage was paid off. Jenny had been worried that the wrong elements would be attracted to the fight spectacle and she was right. The top sports writers from New York, Chicago, Philadelphia and the wire services infested the place from the first day. They drank everything remotely alcoholic in the hotel and then trucked in their own. Cigar butts on the ground multiplied like roaches and their language made the blue mountain sky pale by comparison. However, they kept it generally to themselves. Regular guests seeking the healthy, restful respite of the Catskills were only as disturbed as they might have been by renegade flock of noisy, messy crows.

Under Monte's tutelage, Milton worked his first angles. He got the writers to dateline their dispatches, "Grossinger, N.Y." instead of "Liberty, N.Y." which was the closest Western Union office. When the sparring match was cancelled because of rain, he worked the "human element" by feeding the press corps feature stories about the hotel and Jennie's family going back to 1914 when they decided to move to the mountains from New York City. As Monte predicted, the hotel gained national exposure worth millions. The *New York Daily News* dubbed the place *The Big G* and from that point on, no resort in the Catskills could come close to the star power of *Grossinger's*.

Ross went on to win an unprecedented third world title. His victory breakfast was celebrated at *The Big G* with gigantic portions of herring, kreplach, kugel and strudel. It was a very big day for Americanized Jews like Monte, Milton Blackstone nee Schwartzstein and Barney Ross, who was born Bernard Rasofsky. Barney was feted like a king but at heart he was just a nice Jewish boy. Throughout his career he swore to his mother that it didn't hurt when he got hit. Ross' third title was a boost even Monte hadn't anticipated but he was prepared.

No Jewish man, which included the biggest stars of Broadway, radio and movies, could resist Monte's invitation to have victory breakfast with the champ. Al Jolson, Eddie Cantor, young Milton Berle, the Ritz Brothers, composer Abe Lyman and another dozen leading lights all made the trip to nosh kippers and kibbitz with the new Jewish King of the Ring. This was the final gusher in a virtual Niagara of ink that had flowed from *The Big G* since the day Barney Ross arrived. Where the stars went, the press followed and when Damon Runyon knighted the place "*Lindy's* with trees," the word was out and *Grossinger's* was in like Flynn. In a little less than 3 months, Monte and Milton had transformed *Grossinger's* from a sleepy mountain hotel for asthmatics into "big time" show business.

Although Jenny and Milton said they could never adequately pay Monte for what he had done, they nevertheless insisted that he share in their bounty. Monte always put them off with, "I'll bill you later." He eventually submitted a bill for his services for 1 million dollars marked in bold letters "No

Charge". What he gained in reputation was worth more than anything the hotel could offer and more importantly, he had tacitly accepted Jenny's invitation to become part of the family.

He was given carte blanche at the hotel for as long as he lived. He was free to come and go as he chose, no charge. It was as if he had inherited a huge country estate. He could retreat from the pressures of the city to his mountain getaway and stroll the landscaped grounds. He had time to think now. Offers were pouring in to handle nightclubs and Broadway shows. His name had magic attached to it. He and Milton took long strolls around the property just after breakfast. They discussed their futures and the future of the hotel. It was springtime in the Catskills, the air was rich with stirring life. On July 14 Monte would be 30 years old. It was time to look for a place to have a family.

In the little general store in the village of Liberty, he found a plain, handcrafted walking stick made of ash wood. He adopted the habit of using the walking stick on his jaunts about the hotel and kept it with him when he returned to Manhattan. He liked the heft of it in his hand. It helped him focus on his vision of the future. He saw himself as a sort of English gentlemen, a man of property, a country squire.

CHAPTER 13

MR. CAPONE SAYS HELLO

Returning to Hollywood for a new assignment after the successful run of QUEEN CHRISTINA, Monte found a place transformed from just a few months before. The wild, all-night "anything goes" style of partying was suppressed to whisper-quiet private dinner parties under the heavy hand of the embattled studios. Studio press agents or "flaks" as Monte and his colleagues were called suddenly were pressed into service as enforcers of studio policies dictated by the newly invigorated Production Code.

Not only were the studios suffering through sex scandals and their second year of falling revenue, 1933, they were also being squeezed from the inside by a branch of Al Capone's Chicago mob. That year, studio workers struck for higher wages under the direction of Capone protégé Johnny Rosselli and Rosselli's front man at the *International Alliance of Stage and Theatrical Employees* union, Willie Bioff. The studios responded by immediately slashing their costs. Louis B. Mayer of *MGM* cut salaries of actors, directors and producers by 50 percent across the board. Only Columbia Studios was spared by the IA strike. Apparently, Harry Cohn, head of the Columbia, was in on it with Rosselli. Cohn had helped Rosselli cut all his competitor's throats. Cohn used this advantage, including muscle supplied by Rosselli, to extort his competitors. He bought contracts of popular stars and promising properties from the other studios at discount prices. He controlled the movement of equipment trucks into and out of every competing studio in town through the IA office and was merciless toward his colleagues, driving a few to bankruptcy and suicide.

In celebration of their great partnership conquering Hollywood, Rosselli gave Cohn a ruby pinky ring. The studio executive slipped the ring on eagerly and wore it proudly. He and his new pal, Johnny Rosselli, now called the shots. When Columbia called Monte for an interview he declined, saying he was booked. He and everyone else in Hollywood hated Harry Cohn's guts and would never forgive him.

Publicity staffs at studios throughout Hollywood were cut, creating an anxious pool of unemployed press agents who subsisted on per picture assignments. Fortunately Monte had his recent notoriety from *Grossinger's* and a healthy roster of top New York clubs including *Chateau Madrid* and his alma mater *Leon and Eddie's* that continued to seek his services. Freelance assignments suited him fine and allowed him to continue to expand his career options on both coasts.

Almost everyone in the world seemed to be foundering in the undertow of the Depression while Monte's star continued to rise. Luck clung to him and increasingly people wanted to be close to him hoping some would rub off. Paramount, his old shop under Walter Wanger, hoped they could somehow attract a little of his luck too. They contacted him for an important and delicate assignment.

Paramount's publicity chief knew Monte was friendly with many vaudeville performers including W.C. Fields. The studio wanted him to use his relationship with Fields to keep the comedian in line during the filming of *The Man on the Flying Trapeze*. Fields had begun to worry the studio with his increased boozing on the set and off. He had begun keeping liquor in his ever-present coffee cup which prompted the noted outburst, "Who put grapefruit juice in my grapefruit juice!" when some novice actually put fruit juice in the cup. The studio wrote into

Field's contract that he was not to drink on or off the set for the duration of production. It was Monte's task to make sure Fields lived up to his end of the bargain – no boozing until the picture wrapped. It was a somewhat depressing assignment and one that perfectly reflected the new restricted atmosphere of Hollywood, but Monte thought he might actually have a few laughs with his old drinking buddy who used to juggle live clams at the bar of *Monte's Clam House* for their amusement.

Billy Wilkerson, publisher of the *Hollywood Reporter*, had just opened his second club, the *Trocadero*, on Sunset Strip. Monte was among the first week's guests anointing the place with industry approval. He and Wilkerson had a friendly "nodding relationship" at that point since they frequently traded studio related stories for Wilkerson's paper. On the night Monte was there, Chicago's man Johnny Rosselli was entertaining a table of mutual acquaintances. At some point in the evening, Monte swung by the table to say hello and was introduced to Rosselli. Rosselli looked like a movie star and hinted broadly at the idea he was ready to step in front of the cameras just in case there were any bona fide producers in the group. He was serious about wanting to be a star but didn't want to appear as actually striving for it. He simply thought he was a natural and eventually someone would wise up to the fact. From his point of view it had to be easier than shaking down the studios. As far as most people at the table knew, Johnny was just one of many wealthy playboy businessmen who hung around the studio crowd looking for a lucky break.

It was impolite to delve too deeply into anyone's livelihood since many in Hollywood had embarrassing second jobs that actually paid the bills. Those who had been in the higher circles of the movie business for a few years knew Johnny started with Longy Zwillman, the labor rackets king of northern New Jersey, then graduated to Al Capone in Chicago. Zwillman and Capone were both movie fans and were as impressed with movie people as movie people were with them. Several of the starlets Johnny escorted regularly were actually babysitting assignments from Longy.

For most of the group at the table, Johnny was just Johnny and nobody asked or cared what he really did. He was charming without being particularly witty and loaded with cash. He gave the impression of a regular Joe, a guy who could be counted on to stand up with his friends in any kind of fight and who treated ladies with deference and respect but was definitely not the marrying kind. He was reserved in his personal habits, drinking very little, smoking occasionally and avoiding the bravado and exaggeration common to wealthy playboys. He would quietly pick up the check for an entire table of guests and refused to acknowledge any expression of gratitude except a simple thank you. Johnny was just a great guy and everybody liked hanging around with him.

The conversation turned to certain friends of Johnny's in Chicago, important friends of comedian Joe E. Lewis. Monte caught on that Rosselli's line of work didn't involve honest labor in any traditional sense. He had to be working for Joe E's guardian, Al Capone. Rosselli even told a story about his boss coming to Hollywood a few years back and wearing a banana yellow suit with pink silk shoes. The boss thought it was a style coup that the movie people would appreciate. Johnny called it a "pimp outfit". Capone's garish outfits were noted in many of the local papers and Monte recalled reading them. He always made a mental note on anything about Capone in the papers because he knew that as long as Capone was alive and well, his friend Joe E. was safe.

Monte, who was happy to be free of Dutch Schulz and Legs Diamond in recent years, recognized the familiar signs of mob encroachment. Where there was a smiling showboat like Johnny, there were dozens more unseen men working in the shadows. He didn't know Rosselli's angle yet and didn't much care, he figured Johnny was in with Wilkerson on the club. Nobody would know Johnny's real angle on the movie business for some time yet.

Monte excused himself from the table to make a call. He was going to check in on Bill Fields one last time for the evening, even though he dreaded making the call. It was a nightly ritual that both men had to endure for the next few weeks and things had so far been pleasant. On his way to the phones, Monte spotted Fields at the bar. He considered ignoring the unlucky accident but decided he might as well get it over with. If Fields was going to blow the picture and everybody's job on it, at least Monte was going to try to do his. He walked over and leaned in next to Fields just as the comedian was taking a sip from a cocktail glass.

"Bill, what're you doing? You know you're not supposed to be drinking."

Fields finished calmly and appraised the dainty drink in his hand, "Kid," he said, "I'm not drinking. This is sherry." He turned to Monte to make his point, "Sherry's for faggots."

Monte had to admit, there was a certain Fieldsian logic to the statement. It was funny of course, that was the easy part for Bill Fields, but it was also heartbreaking because obviously he couldn't stay away from the booze. Whatever demons had kept him hidden away in *Monte's Clam House* to avoid seeing destitute panhandlers were now keeping him hidden behind a fog of alcohol. In spite of his gut-wrenching first experiments in film at the old Astoria studios, W.C. Fields was now a major star and very rich, but that didn't seem to help. He was killing himself.

Fields was at work the next day on time and Monte didn't say a word to anyone hoping his old friend would straighten up, but within days it was clear, at least to Monte, that Fields was back on the sauce. If anyone else knew about it, they weren't saying. By the time the picture wrapped Fields had completely "fallen off the wagon" and was back to his coffee cup routine.

The end of the picture was a sad occasion. The old Bill Fields was gone, replaced by an irritable drunk. There would be no more light banter and clam juggling to pass the time. He didn't show up for the small cast party on the set before it was torn down. Fields went on to make more pictures but his circle of friends, including Monte, dwindled as the bottle pushed them out of his life. Finally, he retreated to his mansion and self-imposed exile. Monte would never see him again.

The long distance connection to Brooklyn was barely audible but Monte could tell Julie was hysterical. He had been drinking at the *Clover Club* on Sunset Strip where he ran into pal jazz pianist Henry Nemo, a veteran of the speaks around Greenwich Village, and a few of his sidemen who were playing around town. Nemo was an anarchist, free-love bohemian, who believed music would soon destroy all nations and unite mankind in its natural, uncivilized state. Nonsense was the highest expression of art to Nemo, or so he said, and so he spoke in poetic, disjointed sentences, "Let the pipes play," was a favorite catch-all phrase and "Euphonious" was a common Nemo compliment. Nemo had black girlfriends in the European jazz tradition who were the sisters, cousins and aunts of the cats he shared the bandstand with.

Monte and Nemo's merry band had nipped into the private back room of the *Clover Club* where an elegant and illegal crap table exerted its overwhelming gravitational force over them. Only Monte and Nemo were real shooters, the others just kept them company. Soon the sidemen needed more stimulation and started passing hand-rolled Mexican marijuana to each other. They treated the herb smoking like a sacred ritual, making the sign of the cross several times and studying the plumes intently like written scripture. They started snickering among themselves, then chuckling and soon were laughing like hyenas. Nemo got drawn into their separate reality. As much as Monte loved Nemo and the boys, there's nothing more annoying to a man under the gravitational influence of a crap game than to be surrounded by people who aren't concentrating. It got so bad that they blew the heat right off Monte's dice and the box man was going to 86 the whole crew. Monte retreated to a neutral corner with the new *Red Eye Quartet* and attempted to talk sense into them. Strictly in the interest of social harmony, he sampled their coveted vapors of Montezuma. Soon he too was laughing at hats, convulsed by neckties and rendered completely unsuitable for gambling.

They retired back to the bar where the party continued until Monte realized he couldn't remember where he lived. For a moment it was raw panic. The weed had dislodged a fundamental hinge of consciousness and it scared the hell out him. Normally he had a sense of direction like a homing pigeon, but now he was without a compass in a crew of hophead jazz crazies. Nemo had chug-a-lugged an entire tumbler of maraschino cherries and taunted the crew with his crimson clown lips and scarlet dragon's tongue.

The only antidote for the mind-bending smoke seemed to be Scotch whiskey that Monte downed like a man dying of thirst. The *Clover Club* management was beginning to form up into a frontal attack. It was time to go, but where to? Monte had to get some sleep for an early appointment the next day but as much as he wracked his brain, couldn't remember where he lived. He'd only been back a few weeks from New York and was staying in a new place. He started asking people in the club if they knew where he lived. He figured he might have forgotten people as well as his address, maybe someone knew him and could tell him in what direction to start looking for his place. The club management moved in and suggested it was time to find another club to host the party.

Nemo and the guys had to drive Monte home. It took a large part of the evening with a stop at *Schwab's* drug store for coffee, but they eventually found his place near Formosa Avenue by trial and error.

Now, in the early hours before sunrise, with Julie hysterical on the phone he couldn't tell if the static was on the phone line or a side effect of his Mexican vacation. She had heard all about the sexual shenanigans of Hollywood press agents. It was all over the papers. Hollywood was a sex free-for-all with directors doing starlets, agents doing writers, producers doing pretty much anybody and the press agents were apparently the worst of all. Because they traveled from city to city promoting the movies, press agents, it was said, had girls in every town and were consummate liars. She was sure she had been played for a fool and had embarrassed herself in front of her family and friends.

Monte was helpless, caught completely unprepared. He agreed to things and said things that were not what he felt but only what she needed to hear. She had convinced him that he had treated her badly and that she deserved better, he agreed.

By the time the call ended, he had confessed his undying love and fidelity. He promised he would be back soon and they would go away together, if her parents approved. As he hung up, he felt like a hooked fish gasping its last breath of life on a dock. He had promised things he could never deliver and said things he didn't mean but was now bound by his word. He blamed it on the marijuana and trundled off to bed cursing Nemo bitterly.

One of the disgusting developments in Hollywood during the moral inquisition of the mid-1930's was the new practice of character assassination by publicity. Perversely, it frequently rewarded press agents who failed to protect the reputation of a certain star with more work than ever. Monte's fiasco with Bill Fields was followed up by another doomed mission; make the recent divorce of Mary Pickford and Douglas Fairbanks look good for Mary. She was one of the owners and biggest earners of United Artists. The studio couldn't afford to let her fans think that she was just another godless Hollywood floozy. She was the public's "Little Mary", pure as the driven snow, plucky heroine of a dozen tearjerkers. She'd made the transition from silent films to sound with a voice that stirred their heartstrings and a moppet head of curls that made you want to just hug her and take her home. Doug Fairbanks, on the other hand, could be made out to drink blood and rape nuns for all UA cared. Even Fairbanks understood that he would have to pay some price for his abandonment of their storybook Hollywood estate and Little Mary. Exactly why Monte got this dirty plum he never figured out entirely, but he was enjoying his time in Hollywood less and less.

After a brief meeting with Pickford at the magnificent *Pickfair* estate, Monte arranged for a publicity photo shoot in Griffith Park. It was immediately clear that this would be no ordinary studio "smile and snap" job. He was instantly buried in memos from the executive offices with notes on hair, makeup, the "feel" of the shots and lighting. A production manager was assigned to him to secure the transportation and care of Miss Pickford's special trailer and support vehicles. He was in effect directing the production of Pickford's newest starring role in what might have been titled *Our Mary: A Little Lamb Lost.*

It was a production on the scale of any major film of the time. On the scheduled morning, Griffith Park was invaded by an army of technicians and vehicles. Pickford arrived exactly on time in her chauffeured town car. She went into make-up an enormously powerful and wealthy corporate executive and came out a heartbroken, curly haired waif – a good wife, naïve in the ways of the world, abandoned by a Hollywood cad. She wore a drab, lace collar dress - something that women all over America were making for themselves from the cheaper cotton fabrics available. Her face was a studiously crafted version of a no makeup look with the exception of modestly rouged "bee stung" lips. Her trademark hanging curls looked homemade, even a bit distressed suggesting her emotional turmoil. Everything was a complete fake to match her onscreen persona, except for the pain that drained her face of expression. She was in fact, deeply hurt by the erratic and cruel abandonment by Fairbanks who was having his own emotional crisis.

She moved through Monte's suggestions for poses without a word of comment. She was in no hurry to leave or interested in the work being done at all. She simply moved herself like a manikin from position to position with always the same dour expression on her face. Very quickly Monte ran out of ideas and turned to the photographer for his input. The photographer suggested a few things that were concerned primarily with his technical interests in lighting. Pickford waited patiently in the heat from the large silver reflectors as the man fooled around with lens diffusion and lighting adjustments.

"May I get you something? A drink?" Monte asked the star.

"No, thank you." She answered quietly, barely managing a smile. He felt sorry for her but didn't dare let her know it. He knew the photographer was just experimenting, probably for extra shots that he'd swipe from the studio darkroom and sell later to magazines.

"We're done." He told her. She seemed surprised. He assured her. "That's it. Thank you." She shook his hand and walked to her dressing trailer looking very much like a poor, abandoned wife even though she could have easily bought Griffith Park if she wanted to.

The photographer was beginning to discuss bringing the big arc lights off the equipment truck when Monte told him it was over. He was shocked and sputtered about the great idea he had worked out but Monte ignored it and offered his hand, "Nice job." The man was too angry to even accept the handshake. As Monte walked away, the man mumbled something about "Jews" which turned Monte on his heel. He came up closer to the man than he normally might have and asked to repeat what he just said. The man just turned away and started packing his gear. This wasn't the first time Monte had heard the resentment of Jews from some of the local crews and studio support people. They worked for the Jews, but it didn't mean they liked them. Monte plopped into a canvas camp chair under a eucalyptus tree and wished he were back in *Dave's Blue Room.*

The assignment with Pickford was his last. Monte didn't see himself scrambling to stay in the good graces of a two-faced cut-throat like L.B. Mayer of *MGM* or a snipe like Harry Cohn of *Columbia.* He'd already seen enough of the corporate movie culture watching Jesse Lasky lie and cheat his board of directors and then lay the blame for the lies on his friend Walter Wanger. Wanger, who could think them all under the table, was treated like a dog by these pishers and Monte was tired of them.

He returned to New York and the problem of Julie. Was he going to continue to bet on her? He didn't seem to be able to make up his mind. He chewed Carl Erbe's ear trying to figure the angles. Around town, showgirls who were working their own angles towards personal retirement via matrimony were thick as fleas on a dog, so it took some thinking.

"So y'love her?" Carl asked.

"Sure." Monte answered.

"You don't sound sure."

"I'm sure."

"I don't know." Carl said. "What about her?"

"Yeah." Monte still didn't sound convincing. He was a terrible actor, Carl realized.

"Yeah? She said she loves you?" Carl asked for what seemed like the tenth time.

"Yes, she did. Whatta you think? I'd do this if…"

"I'm saying she's maybe too young. Give it another year."

"Nah, this is the one." Monte was firm.

Carl took a drink to keep from saying "shit" because that is what he was thinking. Monte wanted someone to find something wrong with the idea but nobody could point to any one thing and Monte was stubborn when it came to women. He treated them all like fine China. It didn't matter what kind of woman they were. He treated them all like that. There was something strange about it as far as Carl was concerned. It was one of Monte's many stubborn quirks and it was frustrating.

The conversation was going nowhere so Carl said, "So good luck and mazel tov. Marry her."

"Yeah, I'm gonna marry her," which came out with the enthusiasm of, "I'm going to the store."

"Well that's good 'cause now my mother is safe."

"Why do you say filthy things like that?" Monte wasn't much fun to be around. Carl laughed because he was annoying Monte almost as much as Monte annoyed him.

"You can give her a pearl necklace on your wedding night." Carl continued to dig at Monte by alluding to the common practice of birth control by pulling out and ejaculating on a girl's neck and chest. Monte went silent, a prelude to what would have been with anyone else, a haymaker aimed his chin. But Carl was too close a friend for that. He was family. So Monte sat and stewed.

Carl was sorry and tired and a little jealous. His old hobo partner and protégé had left him in the dust of his zooming success and it still nettled him. Carl's old boxcar buddy didn't seem to have much time for him anymore except then he needed something, like now. So Carl got annoyed and took a shot sometimes. It just came out before he even knew it. Now they both went quiet, finished one and ordered another drink, neither one offering to buy. That's how they were sometimes, kind of prickly and uneven.

Monte and Julie got married on March 5, 1935 in Julie's mother's apartment under a Jewish canopy where Monte smashed the glass to shouts of "Mazel Tov!" The bride and groom fed each other cake and Monte danced with several of Julie's lavender and rose-scented aunts.

Leo Proser, now 20, and the sisters, Isabel and Annette, had arrived with father Charles who spent the afternoon assuring Julie's melancholic mother that Monte had always been a hard worker and would take good care of the girl. The dour woman tried to smile but could not be satisfied. Her little girl was still only 18. She sighed, resigned that her only daughter had married a man who worked for gangsters.

After the ceremony, dancing in Monte's arms, Julie took up her mother's overriding concern and asked for a teeny, tiny favor.

"Sure, kid, anything." Monte felt he could give her whatever she wanted. He had people lined up waiting to work with him in New York and Hollywood. If he couldn't afford it now, he soon would be able to.

"It worries me, the gambling and hanging around with these tough guys. I want you to bring the money home." She made it about the money but the truth was she knew that sooner or later Monte would say the wrong thing, like he did with the Dutchman, and they'd find his hat in a fisherman's net. She'd seen him, after a few drinks, go over a table at a fellow who made the mistake of saying something that sounded like "dirty Jew". It could have been "dirty shoe", "thirsty too" or just about anything. It didn't matter. Monte launched himself like an Olympic high jumper over a perfectly good steak and fried potatoes dinner to attack a mumbler and potential anti-Semite. She was terrified when he went out nights to his games in the dirty warehouses, garages, even somewhere in the sewer system. Sometimes, when things were on his mind, booze made him crazy, like he wanted to fight the whole world.

Monte was dumbfounded. It was like she was asking him to row a boat to the moon. He ignored the attempted clamp on his money. "They're in the places I go."

"So don't go, is what I'm asking." She continued to smile sweetly.

And Monte thought, "So it's like that. The cuffs aren't on two minutes and she's starting." A cold panic gripped him causing him to miss a step in the dance, followed by a hot flush of anger. It all suddenly felt like a terrible mistake but what could he do? After a few quiet turns on the parlor floor the sacrifice required for marriage was sinking in. He bowed his head and accepted the yoke of married life.

"Okay," he said and he meant it. He would change. He'd lay off the dice for a while.

As America emerged with agonizing slowness from the Great Depression, FDR's government, arguably, further retarded recovery by launching the most expensive publicity stunt in history. They invented thousands of often ridiculous federal make-work jobs, like digging holes by the roadways and then filling them in, to convince citizens that America was getting back to work.

One of the few sectors where the American economy was truly growing was organized crime. The maturation of the *Syndicate* into a modern, diverse corporation and the recent repeal of Prohibition gave Frank Costello his first taste of legitimacy. He and his *Syndicate* partners bought distilleries, breweries, trucking companies and liquor distributors. They diversified into real estate, banking, hotels, publishing, shipping, food service as well as expanding their holdings in the traditional revenue streams of labor unions, gambling, prostitution, illegal drugs and entertainment at all levels.

Frank recruited Moses Annenberg, a heavy set, very tall and distinguished-looking man who had been circulation director for the *Hearst Organization* in Chicago. Costello had been introduced to Annenberg by Al Capone at the Atlantic City confab in 1927 where the *Syndicate* was created.

As circulation director for *Hearst*, Annenberg's job description included discouraging anyone from selling a rival newspaper. His staff included Monte's old mentors, financiers and nearly his murderers, the gangsters Deany O'Banion and partner Bugs Moran who received salary bonuses for killing a few reluctant news distributors during the bloody circulation wars of 1910-1911.

Annenberg had outgrown *Hearst* and now owned the *Daily Racing Form*, the *Philadelphia Inquirer* and his real moneymaker, the *Nationwide News Service* that provided results of racetracks across the country. Costello saw the profit margins on liquor falling with legalization and realized a partnership with Annenberg would lock in the high margins still available in gambling by controlling the results of every racetrack in America. It was a heady time, maybe even better than Prohibition. Meyer had sewn up a partnership with Fulgencio Batista, the corrupted president of Cuba, and was building casinos as fast as they could pour concrete. Miami Beach was being readied as a beachhead for legalized casinos in the US with opulent hotels and resorts going up just as quickly as Havana. Luciano, against Meyer's advice, took on the dirty parts of the business like prostitution and heroin retailing that Frank and Meyer wouldn't touch.

Technically Lucky was Meyer's boss, so he went ahead and developed the drug trafficking routes through Marseilles and Mexico City, the prostitution, loan sharking and union corruption schemes with his crew of Joe Adonis, Longy Zwillman and Waxey Gordon. Everybody was busy, times were good.

With Meyer and his childhood pal Bugsy Siegel developing casinos and taking over numbers operations on the west coast, Frank concentrated on racetracks. He was particularly fond of the summer playground of the genteel leisure class north of New York City across the Hudson from the Jewish Catskills in the more Christian area of Saratoga. For a moment it seemed like Frank Costello could quietly go about his business of providing the federally taxable sins of liquor and gambling to America.

Walter Winchell's *Stutz-Bearcat*, a present from Dutch Schultz for a flattering comment in Winchell's column, hummed along the winding mountain roads leading to Monte's Catskill retreat. Winchell lent Monte the car as a wedding present.

Monte drove as Julie extended her arm from the passenger window letting the rushing spring air buoy it weightlessly off the sill. Everything was going to work out fine, Monte thought. All the dark misgivings of the wedding reception were fading like the empty fears of a sleepless night. The commitment was made, the course was set. Julie was a good kid, she'd settle down to being a wife and mother soon enough. Once Jenny Grossinger took her under her wing, Julie would be truly part of the family and everything would be peaches and cream. Pop! Monte looked over and saw Julie working an explosion of gum off her lips with her tongue. She was like a little kid. A messy little kid. She worked the gum as her arm rode in the air. All the glamour and womanly pretense stripped away, she was a child amusing herself with simple distraction.

A terrible thought exploded in front of Monte's mind. He drew a sharp breath, as adrenaline reached his heart and lungs. What had he done? The minute he'd finished his bit as an older brother to his family, he had signed on to shepherd another child, a child bride, to adulthood. He felt the wedding cake churn in his stomach like it might come up. He rolled down his window blasting cool air into his face. He focused all his energy on the road ahead leaving no more room for reflection. He stepped on the gas.

CHAPTER 14

THE HONEYMOON

Monte flew up the gravel roads toward *Grossinger's* like the Devil was chasing him. Julie was exhilarated, squealing with fright at every turn. The powerful *Stutz* drifted laterally through the turns like a speedboat sweeping in an arc through water. He was dying for a drink and could taste the Dewar's on his tongue from memory. The faster he went, the louder Julie squealed until they were both screaming with laughter. It looked like the wind had brought tears to Monte's eyes as he pushed the overheated machine up the mountains through the top ranges of its gears, but it was Monte's overheated mind bouncing between hope and dread that pushed the tears out.

He worked over the angles of the emerging story of his new marriage. They were young, just married and it would be like this forever. Or, their perfect future was dashed by a tragic turn in the road and a thirst for speed. What was happening to him? He was thinking in headlines, bad ones, like a hack churning ink for *TRUE ADVENTURE* magazine. But he didn't seem to be able to help himself. His life was unfolding like a tragic pulp novel. They roared into *Grossinger's* driveway in a cloud of road dust almost an hour ahead of schedule. Monte may have set the world speed record from Manhattan to the resort.

He sat in the car motionless as Julie checked her face in the mirror, flicked away the last crumbs of chewing gum and got out. The sudden quiet was startling. Monte let the calmness soak in. He didn't move a muscle. He saw nothing.

Slowly, the world re-assembled in front of him. He was safe at his mountain fortress in Walter's car. He had a new bride. He was a man of ability and success. He was on his honeymoon. Julie's voice came through to him, insistent that he get out and help with the bags.

He obeyed. A primary and second bellhop recognized him, "Hello, Mr. Proser." He was home. He opened the trunk and that was his last act of responsibility.

"Hi ya, fellas," he said distantly. He still wasn't completely back in his body but he knew he was safely in the loving hands of Jenny Grossinger's extended family. He let it wash over him. Finally, he was the one being taken care of.

The word had gone out, Milton was already on his way out the front door to greet them. Milton kissed Julie on the cheek, reassuring her about the prince of a husband she had. Jenny was next out the door. They couldn't wait to see Julie and lay hands on Monte.

In the lobby, Malke, Jenny's mother, waited for them with other members of Jenny's immediate family. They were smothered in welcome and congratulations. Jenny was so excited that she didn't want to go to the honeymoon suite. She wanted to see hotel before the sun set completely. Jenny took her personally and Monte was grateful to be left with Milton. They went on a separate walk.

Like dutiful princes of the realm, they walked the perimeter as they customarily did. Monte wanted to know about the flow of reservations, the schedule of talent, all the vital business aspects. Milton laid out the facts; reservations were months in advance, the top names of Broadway and radio were fighting each other to get a shot at *Grossinger's*. Monte had put them on the map and there was no end of success in sight. Monte was talking to comfort himself and Milton sensed it.

"And how are you?" Milton asked.

"On top of the world, old pal," Monte lied. "She's a wonderful girl, just wonderful."

The sun slipped behind the pine green mountains as they returned. Julie was in the dining room with Jenny, still excited and recounting her dazzling Broadway courtship with Monte. Jenny was serene. She seemed interested but not engaged, like an ancient oracle calmly auditing the feverish charade of human life.

Anyone who knew Jenny, as Monte had come to know her, knew she had at least a dozen urgent details of the hotel racing through her mind. A perceptive conversationalist would have noticed Jenny's lack of involvement and inquired, but Julie barreled on. Monte saw what was happening and stepped in to relieve Jenny. He escorted his young wife toward the Bridal Suite. Jenny, without the slightest hint that she had been inconvenienced, slipped behind the front desk with a parting kiss for them both.

Night crept across the mountains. The hotel filled slowly with the rich smell of roasting meat. Monte escorted his child bride toward the huge, rustically ornate Bridal Suite. The carpeted hallway soaked up even the sound of their footsteps giving a hint of the rest and solitude to come. They glided along silently, the anticipation of their first full night alone, looming larger with every step. The thirst came back. Scotch whiskey was as smooth and comforting as mother's milk. They passed a junction of hallways where direction signs for the pool, the card room and the front desk showed guests the way.

They stopped before the heavy double doors. Monte unlocked the doors, turned to Julie, lifted her into his arms. She was small and strong, heavier than he anticipated. He kissed her with authority. Whatever she was, whatever she had, belonged to him now. He turned the knob and shoved the doors open with his shoulder.

They stepped into a fairy tale – fieldstone walls surrounded picture windows overlooking the twilighted Catskills. A canopied, four-poster bed overflowed with floral printed bolsters and pillows. On a central table, wedding presents were stacked in a small, irregular pyramid. Huge vases of forest and field flowers were in every direction. Monte carried Julie to the bed and laid her down gently. She was speechless with awe and joy. She grabbed him and kissed him roughly.

He laughed, pulling away from her. At that moment he fell in love with her all over again. Her eyes were blazing. She was a free woman, not a child. His dark, punishing thoughts retreated.

"Isn't it just completely perfect?" she asked.

"Yes," he said. "Why don't you rest, take a nap before dinner." A dinner table was set for two next to the picture window. They would be dining privately, all they had to do was pick up the phone.

"I'm going to play a hand of cards, unwind," Monte tossed off quickly. She barely heard him, fascinated by the feel of the rich fabric and thick goose down comforter. "You are?"

"Just a hand. It helps me relax. You just take it easy for a while. Unpack if you want."

"Oh, fine." She said, turning back to look at him. "Whatever you want, darling." She didn't often call him darling. It was a mature word that she was still fitting into.

The card room was nearly empty. A few grandfathers were there, happy to have peace and quiet away from the in-laws and grandchildren. The lighting was low, the octagonal poker tables with green felt centers looked like small life rafts in a calm sea. He took a seat.

"I need a drink," he said. Three of the four grandfathers produced flasks.

"Don't drink that shit," said the flaskless one. "Use the phone." He indicated a house phone on the wall. Monte calculated room service would take under ten minutes. Life was slowly getting back to normal.

Julie woke up suddenly. It was after 10. She had slept through dinner. For a moment she didn't remember where she was, the altitude and mountain air had conspired for the famous restful atmosphere. Had Monte come and gone? Had he left her to sleep and gone to dinner? She called the dining room, no one remembered seeing him. She ordered dinner for herself and waited. She unpacked until the food arrived. He was probably with friends. The hotel was full. Runyon was right, it was like Lindy's with trees. It seemed like every Broadway character, good and bad, was in the hotel tonight.

Eddie Cantor was playing the main room. That must be where Monte was. He should have called or left a note. She called the front desk, no note.

Dinner arrived. She ate slowly, hoping he would come in and join her. It was their first night together, they should at least eat together. What had he said on the way up to the mountains? Something about getting away? What was he getting away from? He certainly seemed to be in a hurry to get away from something. He'd be back any minute now, the show would be letting out, maybe he'd stop for a nightcap with his friends. She'd take a bath and put on her silk robe. Just wait until he got in the room.

She'd lock the door and show him she wasn't as young as he thought. The hot water didn't relax her. Her mind was flitting from one snatch of conversation to another trying to fit together some idea of where her new husband might be. It was after 11. Enough. She pushed out of the tub, splashing water over the floor.

On the phone, she grilled the front desk for her husband's whereabouts. They assured her they would look for him. Now she was pacing. What the hell had he said about getting away? Maybe they had followed him, whomever it was he was getting way from.

Anyone of the leg-breakers he crossed paths with might have a score to settle. What better place to do it? Nobody would ever find him up here. She was panicked now. She got dressed and went out.

First, she stopped at the card room. An attendant was cleaning up. He told her Mr. Proser had been playing but left hours ago. She ran to the front desk. It was after midnight and no one had heard a word from Monte. Julie was convinced that something had happened to him. Milton was awakened. Security was called. They pressed a few late busboys into service searching the hotel. Milton arrived in his shirtsleeves. He comforted

Julie, assuring her that Monte would turn up. Milton reminded her that Monte liked to take walks around the property.

He was probably out taking a walk. Julie imagined him being escorted by gun-wielding brutes down a dark path through the woods. A thorough search of the hotel turned up nothing. He was not in the hotel. All eyes turned to Milton for the next step. He ordered the grounds searched. Waiters, cooks and fitness instructors who stayed for the entire season in bungalows around the property were summoned from their beds. Search parties were organized and dispatched to the furthest points of the property using all available vehicles. Julie stayed in the manager's office with Milton monitoring reports as they came in. No Monte. Finally, the last patrol came back from the farthest end of the property and beyond. Nothing, no trace of him. Milton called the police.

The town of Liberty had one sleepy patrolman snoring in town hall. The phone rang for the first time in years and the startled patrolman picked it up, annoyed that he might be asked to do something. He reluctantly agreed to take the cruiser out for a circuit of the local roads and roadhouses looking for a five foot eight, 145 pound, 30 year old Jewish man, possibly intoxicated.

A re-examination of the card room attendant's account of the night included Monte having had quite a few Dewar's and soda. The attendant couldn't remember exactly how many. Julie was convinced her husband's vices had caught up with him. Sinister types must have been waiting for him in the hotel. Milton tried to calm her. He ordered seltzer reflexively. Jenny Grossinger showed up in a housedress and farm boots, ready to do whatever was required. She took command. She ordered the hotel to be searched again. He may have fallen asleep somewhere or, though she wouldn't say it, he might be involved in a crap game in a storeroom. The minutes passed slowly. The policeman reported in. No sign so far. Jenny ordered the front desk register checked for unsavory characters or obvious aliases. Her husband, Max, made quiet arrangements for his shotgun to be loaded and brought to the back of the hotel, out of sight. The night clerk checked each entry in the front desk register for that day and made a shocking discovery.

The door to room 1401 was opened with a passkey. There in bed, fully clothed and unconscious from whiskey, was Monte. He had gotten drunk at the card game and in a telling lapse of memory, forgotten that he was married. He had checked into the room and then fallen asleep. Julie threw herself on the bed crying with relief. Monte barely roused. Jenny and Milton wearily closed the door on the newlyweds.

CHAPTER 15

THAT OLD FEELING

In Hollywood, everyone, and especially Monte's client Walter Wanger, was under constant pressure to top his or her last, best effort. Wanger and the other movie people tended to band together to stave off the effects of the endless demands of their careers. As stable family ties collapsed under the strain and long-time friends fell away, only movie workers who suffered together under the same constant threat of professional annihilation stayed close. Particularly actors and actresses found it almost impossible to maintain relationships outside the movie business. It was required that even a minor star's free time be offered in sacrifice to a ravenous public, a public who couldn't care less about them personally and would tear the clothes off their backs if they could. A public that fed on the strange debilitating syndrome which successful actors acquired called celebrity.

Monte was now part of this lonely club as his deteriorating relationship to Julie went from bad honeymoon to worse marriage. It became clear that Julie expected a career boost from chorus girl to actress and Monte could not or would not deliver it. It was then also clear that he had married a client, and a bitterly disappointed one at that. His dream of a creating a family, a refuge from the pressures of show business, was a mirage. Suddenly he found a pressing need to be in Hollywood, away from the accusing eyes and sharp tongue of his new wife.

Now Monte and his movie friends were all stranded on the island of Hollywood together. They all needed a private, secluded place where they could share their grief and triumph, where they could unwind and unleash the pent up rage against their patchwork lives. This could not be done in the mainstream nightclubs like *Ciro's*, the *Trocadero*, the *Clover Club* or the famous restaurants. These places were also open to the public, so famous faces had to be on guard and could only attend with studio approved companions. There was a need for something more private. Monte opened a little club on Fairfax Avenue to fill that need and called it *La Conga*.

It was the sixth nightclub that Monte was operating simultaneously at the time, all of them financed by the publicity assignments from Wanger. So far, he'd owned or worked in over 50 clubs and was well aware that each one had an unpredictable life cycle. Some were stillborn and some never made it to adolescence. Some were gifts of wealthy men to new girlfriends, some were investment schemes of athletes who had had a few good years, some opened on Friday night and were in flames by Saturday afternoon for the insurance money. But they were, to the exclusion of his grander dreams and more bankable talents like publicity, where Monte truly excelled. His clubs succeeded because he needed to be in a nightclub, especially now, to be close to people. Nightclubs were his refuge, his tonic and soothed him with a sense of control over his own life. His clubs succeeded because he loved the people who, like him, needed company at night. *La Conga* was created primarily to keep the people he loved and admired close to him.

La Conga's trademark was "Peanut Night", a particularly unglamorous evening that featured peanut vendors dispensing free hot roasted peanuts from carts brought from the streets of New York. Customers were expected to throw the shells on the floor. Peanut fights were frequent and tolerated. Peanut Night was always Tuesday, when civilians – people not in the movie business – would be least likely to show up. It was a night when the movie colony entertained themselves with inside jokes and vicious send-ups of well-known movie executives. No one dressed up. Stars came in gardening pants, riding attire or bathrobes as they saw fit. They came with whomever they liked and no one paid a bit of attention to them.

They bought their own drinks and made their own introductions if they wanted to meet somebody. It was the only night that a greeter was placed at *La Conga's* door whose assignment was to only admit people who could verify that they were working for a movie company. If not, they were told it was a private party and invited to come back another night. For publicity people, who frequently free-lanced under pen names for tabloids, a strict code of silence was observed. Any news about anyone on Peanut Night was off-limits. Any infraction was enforced with more than ostracism from *La Conga*. An offending writer could find himself outside the studio gates with his Underwood in his arms. Stars were not without power. Peanut Night was the needed escape valve for the Hollywood pressure cooker and was guarded jealously by its patrons.

But even *La Conga* and "Peanut Night" couldn't completely blot out the heartbreak of his ill-considered and failing marriage to Julie. He looked back at his naïve assumption that Julie would forget show business and turn over a new leaf once she realized that she wasn't a very talented actress. He had imagined she would get over her disappointment eventually and become his contented helpmate and housewife. He blamed himself and pined for the vivacious young girl he had married, who had turned bitter, he thought, by his neglectful and haphazard life. She had called from New York to say that she had scrounged up a bit part in a play without his help. Her tone and the implication were clear, this was the excuse she needed to end it. He was on a plane that evening.

A salt breeze blew all the way up to mid-town lifting a few freewheeling gulls up from the harbor and sailing them over the stone spires of Manhattan. The ocean tide rolled up the Hudson, pushing against the tarred posts of the West side piers and churning the salt marshes across the river in New

Jersey. The tide breeze cut through the exhaust of Times Square subtly confirming the start of a new season. The season this year, 1935, was going to be a real season. People had a little money in their pockets. The apple-sellers had mostly disappeared from the street corners. The popular and venerable evangelist Billy Sunday, now 72, was everywhere on the radio assuring people that the years the locusts had eaten would be given back to them, and the redemption was just beginning. He still condemned the drinking of alcohol and the repeal of Prohibition but he was now a lonely voice in the wilderness. Prohibition, like the Depression, was rapidly moving into history. The Depression had scarred the minds of millions around the world, leaving fearful, miserly people who would forever save bits of string and scraps of food. Those who survived intact were driven to get back in the chips – to find the new, the fresh and the profitable. It seemed like everybody was working an angle and on the make. The farms of the Midwest and the South were emptying of young people, white and black. Everybody was headed for either Chicago or New York. That's where the money was.

Monte headed up 7th Avenue taking in the sea-scent. His two-tone wing tip shoes, chalk white arches in rich calfskin brown, made a stylish accent under his mahogany mohair overcoat. He was headed home which was now a two-bedroom penthouse apartment on 54th street and 7th.

He stopped in at *Izzy's Cigar Store* on the corner of 48th for a pack of Chesterfield's. Izzy's wife, Mabel, made hand rolled cigars in the back and Monte always bought one or two just to have a chance to chat with the old man, an immigrant Russian Jew like himself and Monte's touchstone to the vanishing Old World. Izzy was the male counterpart of Jenny Grossinger and his cigar store was the sidewalk equivalent of her resort. He was everybody's favorite uncle and had a drawer full of nearly $10,000 worth of bad checks to prove it. Izzy never refused to cash a check for anyone who came to him with a good reference. Somehow he felt it all balanced out in the end. Mabel, on the other hand, would let fly a shock wave of cursing in Yiddish and English that cleared out the little cigar store from embarrassment if she caught him accepting checks. Everybody knew to wait until she was in the back.

"Mr. Proser, so how are you?" Izzy greeted in his lilting Yiddish. He sat, arms folded like the prophet of 7th avenue behind his glass counter. A few pairs of eyes looked up from the employment section of newspapers. The old wooden chairs creaked as the eyes dipped back to their reading.

"Izzy, whatta ya know?" Monte replied.

"My Mabel says, not enough." Izzy couldn't understand why Monte picked Harry Gerguson instead of him to be the Russian prince Romanoff. Izzy was actually Russian. Since the stunt, practically everywhere Monte went he was set upon by actors, comics, singers and now Izzy, the cigar store owner, who were all convinced they would have been a better Romanoff than Harry Gerguson. "I am Russian." Izzy pointed out once again, preceded by nothing. That started a conversation that went on for some time. Monte explained his decision until Izzy eventually shrugged it off as Monte's poor judgment.

Izzy's was where the bust-out, down-at-the-heel Harry Gerguson types were found, or could be located for a price. It was where news of a certain sort was traded; news of a day job or a 50-cent lunch special, merchandise that fell off a truck or the funeral of a friend whose lifetime achievements didn't rate a write-up in the papers. It took Monte over an hour to buy his pack of Chesterfields and two cigars. He started out again up 7th and bought a handful of carnations from a boy on the street.

By the time he got home, Julie was gone. A note on the little kitchen table said, "Gone out." She'd taken all her belongings with her and at that moment was putting them into dresser drawers at her parent's apartment in Brooklyn.

A few days later, Monte ran into Lew Brown at *Dave's Blue Room.* Lew was the composer of the title song *Strike Me Pink* for the failed musical where Monte had given the then actor/singer Joe Lewis the nickname that distinguished him from the world champion prizefighter of the time, Joe Louis. When Monte suggested the name Joe E. Lewis, or simply Joe E. - after the common name in England for a clown – a Joey, the name stuck and Joe E., like Lew, remained Monte's oldest and closest friends in the nightclub business.

Lew Brown and Monte went back even further to Texas Guinan's early places where Lew played piano while he dodged shot glasses that were thrown at him. Lew and Monte were on Texas' beach trips to Long Island together, so Lew remembered how hard Monte had fallen for Helen and how he suffered when they broke up. Now Lew saw Monte nursing his marital heartbreak from Julie at the bar.

Lew sidled up and saw the look on his friend's face, "Monte, what's wrong?" Lew asked. There were tears in his old friend's eyes. He needed a drink first before he said anything. The drink came, Monte started to pick it up but lost interest in it.

"Ah Lew", he said finally, "I saw her last night and got that old feeling." It was the simple, unadorned admission of a broken heart. Monte drank his drink while Lew began to hear music. The two veteran saloon rats sat together silently while Lew poured out a tune of heartbreak onto a bar napkin. Lew knew, in his gut, that the song was a hit. After a few drinks he played it for Monte on the club's piano. He didn't have all the words yet but the melody floated across *Dave's* – soft and low, minor chords. *Dave's Blue Room* was never bluer than it was that night. It made Monte cry into his handkerchief.

The next day Monte got Wanger on the phone and Lew played *That Old Feeling* for him. Wanger bought the tune there and then as the signature song in his dreadful flop-in-progress *Vogues of 1938*. In spite of the picture, it was the only song that ever got Lew nominated for an Academy Award. For the rest of his life, Monte could never hear the song without feeling the tears come.

CHAPTER 16

KILL THE DUTCHMAN

Frank Costello was also ending a close relationship. A few days earlier, Meyer and Charlie Lucky had called with an alarming story about a meeting they'd just had with Dutch Schultz. Dutch was panicked. Dewey was on the warpath. The unapproachable young prosecutor was empowered by a new grand jury investigation into the rackets. His confidence in nabbing gangsters was at an all-time high. A few years earlier he successfully hobbled Legs Diamond for a four-year prison stint and recently waxed Waxey Gordon for ten years with the new secret weapon of law enforcement - income tax evasion.

Now he was after Dutch. Dewey had turned Dutch's chief counsel for his lucrative bookmaking operation, Dixie "Kid Mouthpiece" Davis, into a stool pigeon. Davis laid out the details of the Schultz operation – times, places and people. Although Dutch had successfully avoided the lawman for five years, it was now just a matter of time before he was caught. And if that happened, Dutch was on Dewey's dance card for a 30-year stretch. One of them had to go. It was simple arithmetic to Dutch - Dewey was the one to be subtracted.

Dewey kept a regular morning routine. In the company of two bodyguards he walked from his Westside apartment every morning at 7:30 AM to a corner diner for breakfast. The report back to the Dutchman from his eyes on the street was that Dewey could be taken.

Meyer and Charlie did their best to talk Dutch out of it. The heat that would come down on all of them would cost millions and high ranking men would have to be given up. But Dutch wouldn't listen. It was him or Dewey. He'd do it without their approval and made the fatal mistake of saying so to their faces. Soon after Dutch stormed from the meeting, Frank got the call. In keeping with Costello's Atlantic City protocol, the bosses decided collectively that it was Dutch, not Dewey, who would have to go. Frank agreed.

Charlie would handle the details. He soon realized that this was more than a simple assassination, it was a coup. When Dutch was iced, one or more of his top enforcers Lulu Rosenkrantz, Abe Landau or Marty Krompier would instinctively move into Dutch's position and probably retaliate to protect themselves. Lulu, Abe and Marty would have to go too.

It was now the appointed day for Dutch's exit and Frank Costello carefully made his arrangements for the evening. He made sure that he would be seen in public places in the company of reliable eyewitnesses. He'd have dinner at his regular haunt, the *Waldorf Astoria*, with his lawyer, George Wolf, and then take in the show at the *El Morocco* at a prominent table where he was sure to be noticed. By the time the headline act was finished, it would all be over.

The *Hollywood Barber Shop*, like *Izzy's Cigar Store*, was one of the quiet eddies along the fast flowing stream of Broadway. But unlike *Izzy's*, it was a hangout exclusively for men. The presence of the pretty, female manicurist tempered the conversation toward more polite observations and that was the way John preferred it, being a temperate, quiet man. The place wasn't decorated or designed in any way except as a functional barbershop. It wasn't promoted or advertised, and only identified by simple block lettering on the front door. It was the same as a thousand other barbershops except that it was conveniently open until midnight and its proprietor, John Sideri, whom everyone knew as John the Barber, was a talented listener. John didn't care if you spent money there or not. The *Hollywood* was just a hangout, a quiet place with no ambitions beyond providing men's grooming for a reasonable price. It was a place to get out of the action for a while and relax.

Winchell was in the chair. John the Barber was just finishing up a late shave on the now famous wordsmith while the very nice looking manicurist buffed his nails.

Monte assaulted his old pal Winchell, "Get up, you bum!" He whacked him on the soles of his shoes with a rolled up *Racing Form* like a cop rousting a bum on a park bench. Monte had taken to reading the *Racing Form* as Joe E. had encouraged him to do. Since he was losing so much money on horses, he felt he should at least get to know them a little better.

"Hey, pal," Winchell murmured, half conked, in deep relaxation. Monte went to the pinball machine in the corner to distract himself.

"Whaddya say, John?"

"Hey, don't bother my customers. Especially the ones with money." John the Barber joked. John was like that. He'd joke around if you felt like it. If you were blue, he was quiet. Monte passed by Abe Bronson, manager of vaudevillian Willie Howard, and Harold Scadron, proprietor of light heavyweight champion Bob Olin who were smoking and swapping news at a small table stacked with magazines and sections of newspapers.

"Boys," Monte offered. They each returned a greeting.

The manicure girl finished rubbing lanolin into Winchell's cuticles and patted his hand gently. It was his signal to wake up. His eyes opened and John let him lay there for a few seconds until he was fully awake. John pulled the big white enamel lever on the side of the chair and gently hoisted it upright, spinning it at the same time to face the mirror wall. Winchell checked both sides of his shining face while John splashed *Lilac Vegetal* from its pale green bottle into his hands, rubbing briskly, then turned back to his famous customer to finish him off with a light touch of the floral scented alcohol over his face and gleaming hair that brought him fully awake. John unbuttoned the white drape and pulled it free with the paper neck cuff like he was unveiling a new statue by Michaelangelo. He snapped the drape smartly which signaled Barnes, the coat and shoe man, to fetch Winchell's coat. Winchell stood up as John whisked away any errant snippets of hair from his neck with a soft, talcum-powdered brush. Monte turned to watch the unveiling, appreciating John's mastery, the precision of the familiar ritual. Winchell spoke into the mirror as he checked the details of his suit and tie. He was right back on duty, not a moment wasted. "Whattya got for me?"

"I gave it to ya," Monte answered.

"Still on the wagon?" Winchell jabbed.

"Who the hell told you that?"

"A little bird."

"Runyon's a liar." Monte jabbed back. "But a pretty good one. I was taking a night off."

Barnes, a tall, thin black man, approached with Winchell's overcoat. He brushed Winchell's shoulders and lapels with a little straw hand-whisk and held the coat open. Winchell slid in. He duked Barnes with a buck and likewise the manicure girl.

"Y'wanna come along, the count of something or other's in town. Real royalty." Winchell smiled. Everybody was still giggling at Monte's Prince Romanoff stunt.

"Nah, I'm okay. Can't stand that place." Monte meant the *Stork Club* but actually meant Sherman Billingsley, whom he still detested as a bigot and snob. The fact that Billingsley had captured the social register's limelight with his ploy of handing out expensive gifts to well-connected society ladies meant that Winchell had to be there. Winchell knew the rap on Billingsley but that meant nothing compared to the *Stork's* position as the irreplaceable listening post for news on the better elements of society and the hoi-polloi who strove to be near them. Without Winchell, it was doubtful Monte would even be allowed in now. Word was out that Billingsley didn't appreciate the fake Prince Romanoff using his place to grab headlines.

"I'll give the boss your love." Winchell teased.

"Yeah, you do that."

"We'll be around Lindy's later. Take a drive." Winchell invited. He palmed a five to John the Barber and headed out the door and up the arcade steps to 47th Street. Before the door closed behind him, a short, wide-shouldered character in a black fedora and dark coat stepped through followed by two others. It was Marty Krompier along with his brother Jules and Sammy Gold, a bookmaker in Marty's employ. Marty was the chief policy enforcer for Dutch Schulz. He kept the money flowing from the sometimes reluctant Negro, Puerto Rican and Cuban bookmakers who occasionally made the mistake of demanding a larger cut of Dutch's public gambling operation. Marty convinced them otherwise. For this important work and his other duties which included keeping the bite on over 240 restaurants and bars that were paying protection money, Marty was paid $1,500 a week all through the Depression and up to the present. He was also the man Lulu Rosenkrantz had handed over the responsibility of killing Texas Guinan's Jewish press agent - the same one who was currently nodding in acknowledgement from the pinball machine.

"Monte, whatta ya say?" Marty greeted him.

"Okay, Marty" Monte answered.

Marty took the empty chair, throwing his coat to Barnes. The old business of trying to kill Monte was forgotten, no hard feelings. Marty had even apologized to Monte in his own way, later after it was over, joking about it. He really wanted to be liked, especially it seemed, by Monte. Everybody liked Monte and Marty wanted that too.

A few years after the contract on Monte was lifted, Marty confided that if he could ever find a fighter without a glass chin, he might quit strong-arming for Dutch and go into the fight business. Monte recounted his own brief experience in his scuffling days managing a young fighter named *Kid Jabs* in Milwaukee. After that, Marty was convinced he had found a friend. It was a one-sided relationship as apparently were most of Marty's relationships.

Monte, the eternal soft touch, even though he wanted no part of a friendship with Marty, saw how trapped Dutch's enforcer was. Marty and Monte were like a thousand other young Jewish guys caught up in the Broadway life. They were the same age with the same overwhelming drive to do things differently, to be somebody special. Marty was considerably brighter than the average hood. He was a product of the same Jewish tradition that revered education, but unfortunately he had no particular talent. He found his niche, like their contemporary Meyer Lansky, as a *schtarker* – muscle for hire. He was 31 and old enough to begin to regret his choice, but now he knew too much about Dutch's operation to just walk away. He knew that his daydream of managing fighters was just that, a daydream. He belonged to Dutch now, for life. Monte felt a little bit of sympathy for him, not much, but enough to say hello. Barnes asked Marty as he was being lowered in the chair for his late shave,

"Shine 'em?"

"Nah." Marty said. Barnes retreated to his pinochle game at the coat rack with the manicurist. She didn't approach Marty. She didn't like to work on men who might have blood under their fingernails. Sammy Gold, the younger brother of Sol who managed the new world champ and graduate of *Grossinger's* fight training camp, Barney Ross, joined Monte at the pinball machine, standing off to the right. Monte turned to the machine and put in his nickel so he wouldn't have to talk to Marty. Sammy took bets for Dutch's operation and also moonlighted making odds and taking bets on Marty's fighters – a skill he'd learned from older brother Sol. He let Monte in on the action for the evening. They were going uptown to take in a few rounds of boxing at the *New Park Casino*, a hole-in-the-wall club where some fighters from Marty's own *Lenox Athletic Club* were going to try their skill.

Skill was in short supply with Marty's fighters. This was a constant disappointment to Abbadabba Berman in Dutch's front office. It was the one division of the operation that never produced much revenue. Lulu and Abe Landau, the personal bodyguards to the Dutchman, teased Marty continuously that whatever he knew about fighters, he should forget. Lulu was a prick as far as Marty was concerned. Marty considered himself a good judge of talent but a victim of bad luck. The way he saw it, Lulu and Abe sat in the office kissing the boss's ass while he was out cracking heads and bringing home the bacon. Pricks, the pair of them. He'd settle up one day for all the wisecracks made at his expense.

Marty started in on John about how he'd double his money on a new kid he'd brought in from Cleveland or someplace but John was real quiet. John didn't like Marty either but Marty never noticed things like that. He just kept jabbering on while John laid on the hot lather and then stropped his straight razor. Marty just liked to talk and since no one ever answered, he figured they were listening to his every word. He offered the bet to Monte. He went on and on, a cloud of words, half thoughts, jokes to himself as John struggled to shave without cutting him. John the Barber had a trick of accidentally smearing a little lather across the corner of a customer's lip which tended to cut out the chatter. Marty just reached up, wiped it off and kept right on talking.

Monte only paid half-attention. He caught Sammy Gold's expression out of the corner of his eye which was "Whattya gonna do?" Sammy went back to following the silver ball shooting around in the pinball machine trying, like Monte, to distract himself from the unpleasantness in his life. The chatter stopped suddenly when John pushed Marty's chin up with a finger to shave his neck. This was a maneuver that never failed to quiet the place. Depending on the customer, John might keep his finger there through the entire shave. He wouldn't risk that with Marty. The razor scraped lightly, slowly over the gangster's throat, returning the peaceful atmosphere to the *Hollywood.*

Across the river in Newark, Dutch got up to take a piss. Lulu Rosenkrantz and Abe Landau stayed at the table. This was the temporary command post of Dutch's $20 million-a-year operation - the corner table at the back of the narrow, 60 foot long *Palace Chop House* on East Park Street. Dutch's chair was strategically placed giving him an unobstructed view of the distant front door. He had good intelligence inside the Newark police that would tip him off to any attempt of Dewey's New York cops to cross jurisdictions and nab him. It would give him enough time to disappear. Until he resolved the problem with Dewey, he wouldn't even venture into New York. He moved his common law wife Frances Flegenheimer, bodyguards and staff across the Hudson River to the classy *Robert Treat Hotel*, just around the corner from the *Palace*. The Newark police were so cooperative in Dutch's relocation that they issued Lulu an Essex County Deputy Sheriff's Badge, number 74. The badge gave Lulu the right to carry his .45 without fear of being molested by lawmen who weren't in on the arrangement.

For the past three weeks, Dutch had been conducting business at the *Palace*. The business agenda included Abbadabba's usual glowing financial reports and increasingly, planning the move against Dewey. This included calculating the possible counter-measures of the *Syndicate* and the government after the shooting was over. All that time, his sources inside the Newark police department were also providing information to other people about other things, including Dutch's movements of the last three weeks.

Abbadabba's meticulous spreadsheets were laid across the table with a craftsmen's pride. The master mathematician earned his $10,000 a week by diluting the odds at select racetracks with instantaneous mental calculations performed over the phone. He placed last-minute bets that guaranteed that Dutch's customers in Harlem wouldn't win quite as much as they deserved. Abbadabba's figures showed that in the last six weeks, with his split-second computations shutting out the most heavily played numbers, the banks – people like Sammy Gold - had taken in bets of $827,253.43 and paid out winnings of only $313, 711.99. Abbadabba, Lulu and Abe were so entranced by the numbers that they didn't notice the two men who strode quickly through the front door. The Palace's piano player continued to hammer away at a lively ragtime tune and bellow it's suggestive lyrics at the top of his voice. Dutch insisted on loud music during his business hours to disrupt any eavesdropping on his discussions.

The executioners hesitated for a moment after they stepped through the ten-foot passageway into the dining room. The Dutchman was supposed to be in a chair facing them, under the orange-tinted light in the far corner - the proverbial sitting duck. But his chair was empty. The front gunman went to work anyway. He unleashed a .38-caliber pistol on the trio in the corner, firing accurately 30 feet across the room while walking toward his targets. His husky partner cut loose with a covering spray of lead from the sawed-off shotgun that rose up from the folds of his overcoat. Seven pellets ripped into Lulu's back, piercing his chest and abdomen, one lodging in his right foot. Even as he was falling, the muscular hood was grabbing for his .45 to return fire. Abbadabba was hit six times in his compact, 220 pound frame, all on the left side. He hit the floor next to Lulu. Three bullets nailed Abe Landau, the most agile and deadly of Dutch's gunmen. One pierced his left shoulder, one went through his upper left arm and one blew a hole in his right wrist while he too was getting his .45 into action.

Within seconds, the first gunman had passed the table and kicked in the men's room door where Dutch was caught turning away from the urinal with something less dangerous than a gun in his hand. Obviously a professional of some experience, the executioner had unholstered his .45 for close-in work. One thick slug tore through the Dutchman's abdominal wall, large intestine, gall bladder and liver, lodging on the floor close to the urinal. The Dutchman fell and though mortally wounded, was still alive. He was saved from a second slug and instant death by the fire directed at his attacker by Lulu and Abe who managed to fire wildly in spite of their wounds. A second shot at Dutch missed entirely as the gunman retreated under the counter-attack. The shotgun operator turned and ran out.

With blood spurting out of a severed artery in his neck and a hole in his shooting arm, Abe staggered after the first assailant firing inaccurately. Backing him up was Lulu who looked like he was drunk and shot like it. Lulu poured blood from his seven piercing wounds, three of them in his shooting arm. Shots flew around the place wiping out rows of display bottles, the front window and a cigarette machine, but never coming close to the escaping shooters.

Abe somehow got all the way to the street, firing all the way, until the hammer clicked on an empty chamber. The executioners escaped in a waiting car, west toward Park Place. Abe reeled toward a garbage can near the *Military Park Diner* a few feet away and sat on it like a drunk taking a breather. His chin came to rest on his chest and the blue steel .45 fell from his hand, clanking onto the sidewalk. Lulu never made it to the door, he collapsed on the tavern floor.

The Dutchman wobbled from the bathroom to the bar, holding his hand over the hole in his side, just as bartender Jack Friedman poked his head up from behind the bar. Dutch didn't say a word. He went over to a table, put his left hand on it to steady himself. Then he plopped into a chair and fell forward. His head bounced on the table. He stayed like that for a few seconds, then he said, "Get a doctor, quick." Just then, like the mummy in a horror movie, Lulu got up again off the floor. Now he was soaked with his own blood. He made it to the bar and to the shocked bartender Friedman, the normally gruff Lulu looked like he was going to cry. He threw a quarter on the bar and said, "Give me change for that," which Friedman did. Lulu was always very thrifty, a habit he and Dutch shared in spite of their millions. Lulu clung to the wooden bar while he waited for his change. The bartender dropped the dimes on the bar, Lulu picked them up, kicked over a spittoon inside the bar rail as he turned unsteadily toward the pay phone near the door. He tottered slowly across the room and sagged against the phone booth. He managed to dial O, waited patiently, then gasped, "I want the police, hurry up." Lulu continued to prop himself up as patrolman Patrick McNamara took the call at Police Headquarters. Patrolman McNamara heard Lulu mutter softly, "Send me an ambulance, I'm dying." Lulu was correct.

Joe the Barber was finishing up Marty Krompier, his last customer of the day, as Barnes pulled down the window shade signaling the end of business. It was 12:01 AM about an hour and a half after the *Palace* shoot up. Upstairs at the newspaper stand, reports in the late late editions had just arrived with sketchy details about the attack. Monte finished his second or third pinball game having successfully avoided further conversation with Marty. It was time to move on.

Monte turned to Sammy Gold, "See ya, Sam," he said. He was eager to get out before Marty put the arm on him for company. Marty stepped out of the chair and had his shoulders and lapels brushed by Barnes. As he slipped into his outstretched coat, the front door banged open and four men stepped through. The noise from a passing BMT Express muffled the first shot from the .38. The first slug went into the ceiling. It was theoretically a warning shot for the benefit of Barnes and John the Barber who instinctively stepped back. The theory is supported by the fact that the next two bullets were accurate shots into Marty's chest and belly. The two that followed blew holes in both of his arms. He was spun around by the force of the slugs and collapsed into Monte's arms. He slid to the floor grabbing at Monte's suspenders, taking Monte's pants down to the floor with him. Bright red blood smeared down the front of Monte's white shirt. The press agent cradled his one-time murderer's head in his hand, keeping it from crashing to the hard tile. He laid him down gently. Marty didn't seem at all surprised or even very upset. He looked up at the man he had so desperately wanted as a friend and said, "They got me."

Two ricochets hit Sammy Gold who had taken Monte's position at the pinball machine. The slugs punctured his left side and left arm, knocking him to the floor. The four marauders left, dropping one of their smoking tools on John's doorstep. It still had two out of six bullets left. The lead gunner had used up all six of his bullets and kept his gun.

When the cops arrived, no one could remember a thing about what the gunman looked like. Monte told them, "I just saw this big gun. I couldn't tell you even if it was a six-foot brunette with a machine gun in one hand and an automatic in the other. My pants were falling down." They let him go. He fastened up his suspenders and threw on his coat, covering his gory clothes. His first stop was the payphone on John's wall. He called Winchell's office, the newsman was still there, "You blew it, pal" he said. "They just shot Krompier in here." Winchell ran the nine blocks from his office at the *New York Mirror* to the *Hollywood* in under 5 minutes.

The cops laid Marty out in John's chair as he begged them, "Do something for me. Do something for me." They tried to stop the bleeding with towels while they waited for the ambulance.

"You know the guy who shot you?" a cop asked.

"If I saw him again, I would," Marty cooperated.

"Okay, you ever seen the man before?"

"No. I don't know him, but I'd know him if I saw him again."

"You hear they shot Dutch over in Newark tonight?"

Marty hesitated. Then he said, "How do I know? It's gotta be one of them coincidences."

The cops turned their attention to Sammy Gold who was leaking blood onto the other chair. They wanted to know who the shooter was. Sammy didn't have to think, "No, I never saw him before."

"Do you know Dutch Schultz?" The cops asked.

"I wouldn't know him if I fell over him." Sammy lied to avoid further questions. The ambulance arrived and they moved Marty and Sammy to *Polyclinic Hospital* four blocks away.

When Monte got home, he went to the bathroom, took off his bloody clothes and wrapped them in newspaper. He showered, taking extra time to lather twice. He changed quickly into fresh clothes, there would be no sleeping that night. He slipped out onto the street again, taking his bundle of newspaper with him. He dumped his bloody clothes in an alley trashcan. The next stop was an all-night newsstand where he got the early version of the story about the move on Dutch Schultz. It was hard to imagine that there was anybody powerful and bold enough to make this kind of a move, but apparently there was and Monte knew, eventually, he would meet him. If anybody knew the score on this new kingpin, they'd be in *Dave's Blue Room* tonight.

Frank Costello left the *El Morocco* just after midnight and went straight home. He had spent the evening in the company of his lawyer and other reputable business associates. He made a point of saying goodnight and spending a moment with Pat Lionel, proprietor of the *El Morocco* before leaving. When he got home, he expected a call from Charlie but the call didn't come. He eventually went to bed but, as usual, couldn't sleep. Something had gone wrong.

A few hours later the sun came up on a sparkling clear autumn day, the kind that brings the red up in children's cheeks. In Newark, Dutch and Lulu lingered at death's door and in Manhattan, Marty Krompier was chatting with policemen from his hospital bed.

Charlie Lucky, as he was sometimes called, decided his reputed luck was not with him at the moment. His coup had left 3 of the 5 targets alive. He decided to take over and personally finish the job. The day nurse at *Polyclinic* remembered a man with scar down his right cheek demanding to see Marty.

"And who are you, please?" the nurse asked.

Charlie pushed his NYPD gold detective shield toward her face, "That's who I am," he informed her. Before the nurse could reply several genuine cops came by to see if they could pry anything more out of Marty. The scar-faced man and his two accomplices shrunk away at the sight of the arriving police. Charlie's luck was still running against him, except in one important aspect. Marty was not talking.

After hours of grilling by police, Marty finally refused to answer any more questions, particularly about who had shot him. "Tell us who shot you, Marty," the cops persisted.

"I can't." Marty said, "The doctor told me not to talk."

The reign of Dutch Schultz ended at 8:14 PM that day. Lulu, as ever, preceded his boss to the next location. Abe Landau and Abbadabba Berman hadn't lasted through the night. Dutch's last words were a disjointed, fevered soliloquy delivered to Newark Police stenographer F.J Lang, who had sat at the bed of the dying gangster through the night, "Look out for Jimmy Valentine for he is an old pal of mine. Come on, come on, Jim. Ok, ok, I am all through. Can't do another thing. Look out mamma, look out for her. You can't beat him. Police, mamma, Helen, mother, please take me out. I will settle the indictment. Come on, open the soap duckets. The chimney sweeps. Talk to the sword. Shut up, you got a big mouth! Please help me up,

Henry. Max, come over here. French-Canadian bean soup. I want to pay. Let them leave me alone."

Of Dutch's top men, Marty Krompier was now the lone survivor. After several weeks in the hospital, he recovered completely. In return for his silence and years of faithful service to a former *Syndicate* chief, Marty was deeded a linen service that supplied tablecloths to *Syndicate* nightclubs. It was a profitable venture that didn't require a great deal of Marty's time once he installed his brother Jules as the manager. It allowed him to continue his search for a fighter who could go the distance.

Frank and Meyer's *Syndicate* took over Dutch's race wire, bookmaking and brewing businesses. They sent Benny Siegel to Hollywood to take over bookmaking and race wire operations there. He continued the *Syndicate's* enlightened Italian/Jewish cooperative structure by enticing West Coast tough guy Mickey Cohen into the fold. They now had a seamless nationwide operation from Miami to New York to Chicago and Hollywood.

They were making legitimate inroads as well. Frank Costello's old bootlegging partner Joe Kennedy had been appointed head of the newly created *Securities and Exchange Commission*. Now instead of selling boatloads of *Cutty Sark*, Kennedy oversaw the selling of corporate stock. Meyer Lansky was buying into the opulent casinos of Havana. Soon he would recruit dozens of major American corporations like *AT&T* to join him and his soon-to-be partner, President Fulgencio Batista, in the economic development of Cuba. It was an exciting time to be a gangster. Like the new Fred Astaire song on the radio said, "… nothing thrills me half as much as dancing cheek to cheek."

CHAPTER 17

Monte Proser's Copacabana

After the messy business with Marty and Dutch, Monte took every opportunity to duck out to the countryside. He wanted to be out of the public eye and away from the questions about Julie that he couldn't answer. Old pal Walter Batchelor's farm outside of New Hope, Pennsylvania gave him solitude and Batch was always more than happy to have Monte for company. The place provided a little too much solitude for Batch's taste even though he had owned it for years.

They drove south from New York in Batch's cream-colored Packard, taking the two hours on main roads through New Jersey, then back roads into farm country and eventually dirt roads as they approached Jericho Mountain. As the roads got worse, the conversation dwindled. Green waves of clover and corn rolled away to the horizon, hypnotizing them into silence.

English names came into view - Bucks County, Makefield Township, Yardley, Solebury. Deeper into the heart of the land, on the forested lanes that ran along sun-dappled creeks, the Lenni-Lenape Indian names echoed from a time before time-keeping - Delaware, Neshaminy, Nockamixon. In this sacred place, no one knew or cared a thing about Broadway. A man could start over.

The first demand of the new environment was sleep. As the Packard crested the peak of the hill called Jericho Mountain and rumbled over the graveled, dusty clay of Eagle Road, Monte's eyes would begin to feel heavy. By the time the huge nose of the car swung into the canopied forest driveway, his mind had cleared of all thoughts except cool linen sheets. As they pulled up to the farmhouse, road dust settling around them, all Batch had to do was point to Monte's room window, which in the spring was directly over the lilac bushes.

Often it was just Monte and Batch for the weekend. Monte would spend lazy days by the huge field stone swimming pool reading new novels like Caldwell's *Tobacco Road* and Mitchell's *Gone with the Wind*. All around him the sheltering woods sang with blue jays, sparrows and warblers. Frogs and toads demanded access to the conveniently located swimming pool and were frequently bathing companions. Occasionally a black, garden or copperhead snake would join them. The air was sweet and heavy with woodland vapor that congealed into a low-lying mist at twilight. When the last glow of the sun drained through the bottom of the sky, fireflies rose through the mist like floating Japanese lanterns. Monte never tired of this particular performance. He was often in a front row seat on the edge of Batch's lawn in front of the house. Instead of popcorn, he ate a perfectly ripe tomato, still warm from a farmer's garden, like a sloppy apple.

The second order of the new environment was food. Country taverns and inns kept the two supplied with simple family-style meals. On the first or second night at the farm, a tavern was selected to provision them with enough fried chicken, roast beef and vegetables for a few days. For Monte, it was a return to the simpler ways of his hobo youth. Holing up at Batch's woodland hideout provided some of the simple joys of living he'd forgotten about.

When he could get away with it, Monte stretched weekends into the week. Batch, since he had the ability to adjust his schedule as an independent radio producer, stayed on as well. The two toyed with the idea of operating from a local town out of a joint office but the realities were that they were bound to the city. Country life was a chimera they indulged in like an opium dream.

The day of reckoning eventually arrived when the two weekend hobos shaved, donned expensive suits and prepared for the trip back to New York City. After a brief, silent ride over country roads, Batch's Packard rolled up to the intersection of Bridge and Main streets in New Hope. Late morning heat brought up the scent of the Delaware River. Their first appointments of the day were cocktails at *Leon and Eddie's* or *Dave's Blue Room*. They looked right over the Delaware toward New York City, they looked left toward the taverns of Bucks County, then looked at each other. Batch hesitated behind the wheel to read Monte's face. The old quote would roll from his smiling lips, "Go west, young man." That was Batch's cue. He swung the great wooden steering wheel to the left, back into Bucks County. It was, after all, near lunchtime and driving all the way to New York on an empty stomach was a terrible idea.

Often, they went west, back to obscurity, away from the lights and the Broadway life. Later, at the bar of a country inn, they resolved to try again tomorrow and often wondered aloud how they maintained any careers at all.

When Monte finally got back to his empty penthouse apartment, there were notes that had been slipped under his door. Some were a few days old. Wanger was looking for him, obviously entangled in another emergency. But how many times can you save the same drowning man? Julie had come in and taken more of her clothes. The place reeked of spoiled food. The telephone stared at him, demanding that he get back to work. He ignored the little beast and made a cup of tea instead. He pulled up a chair to his front window and stared out at the Manhattan skyline. Endless blocks of buildings piled against each other, chock full of people and their struggles. For the first time, he wished he had listened to his father and gone to college.

Herschel Grynspan was outraged. He and his parents had been given 10 minutes to pack. They were then dragged from their beautiful Berlin home and put on a train. They were given a choice of where they wanted to go and then told they were never to come back. It was February, 1939.

Their home now belonged to the Nazi party. They were expelled like gypsies who had been caught stealing. They were then pushed from place to place by the tidal wave of anti-Semitism cresting throughout Europe. Herschel was determined to avenge the humiliation of his family and theft of their property. On November 7, in Paris, he pulled a pistol from his coat and fired three bullets into German diplomat Ernst Von Rath, killing him. Two days later, on November 9, the Nazi SS, SA and coordinated German local police forces attacked Jewish businesses, homes and synagogues in a convulsion of violence known as Kristallnacht – Crystal Night – named for the broken glass that littered the streets of nearly all German cities. 91 Jews were killed and thousands more were rounded up and deported to work camps. It was the beginning of the Holocaust.

In New York, Monte read the news with a sense of dread he thought he'd outgrown. The terrifying stories of murder and mayhem visited on Jews were now front-page news. For the second time in his life, madness was loose in the world. Hitler was a living dybbuk, a devil, who walked the earth ravenous for Jewish blood. Isabel called from Baltimore frantically wanting to know, "What do we do?" Annette was an organizer with radical socialist groups in the East Village. She had taken on the cause of raising money to help Jews immigrate to the US. Monte sent her a thousand dollars.

Jews in America were incensed. They mobilized to help in hundreds of organizations, yet the country as a whole was unmoved by the events. The significance of a new wave of pogroms was lost on most Americans. Most didn't know what the word meant.

The wind buffeted the *Beachcomber's* front window. Monte sat at the bar. The sun blasted into the window from the white drifts of snow outside. Every crumb on the carpet was exposed, every spot on every glass, each wire artfully suspending a palm frond. The fantasy of a South Seas island hideaway evaporated in the glare. There was only the wind clawing at the front door and the news of death in black and white.

Monte was 34 years old and about to be divorced. Julie had finally asked for it and he was through fighting with her. He was a man adrift and without purpose in the world. Success had come too easily. He didn't have hard fought battles of achievement to look back on. His life was just a big, sweet gift that he'd done nothing to deserve. He didn't have a mission that he could remember. After all, he realized, he was just a saloonkeeper. It was nothing to be ashamed of but it was nothing very special either. He wasn't going to save the world from Nazis, gangsters, crooked cops, movie executives or anybody else. For all his high flying, coast to coast, party life – he ran joints and sold booze. If he didn't have a mission, it was okay, he accepted his fate. Saloonkeepers don't need missions.

His close friend and fellow press agent Jack Diamond walked through the front door, shook the snow off his overcoat and saw Monte at the bar staring into the blackness of a mug of coffee. Jack was a long time veteran of the circuit including *Leon and Eddie's*, the *Cafe Madrid* and a half dozen other joints. He distinguished himself around town with his dedication to hard work and lack of guile. You could count on Jack's account of the latest rumor to be closest to the truth. He pulled up a stool and laid out the photos he'd taken on his two-week vacation in sun-soaked Rio de Janiero.

Monte was having a hard time focusing on Jack's vacation. After a moment, Monte started to hear what Jack was saying. Jack knew what was on Monte's mind and the mind of every other Jew in the world. That's why he'd taken a powder to Rio for a few weeks – to get the hell away from it. He knew Monte and knew the man was a sucker for exotic locales where beachcombers, hobos and other vagabonds might be comfortable. He shoved the black and white snapshots in front of his friend and pointed out the local nightclubs and the shacks on Copacabana beach that served tropical drinks. Monte picked up the tiny photos for a better look. Jack saw the wheels start turning, the smile slanted up and Monte's eyes turned to him, then moved off to a vision just over his left shoulder.

"I got it." Monte said, and it was done. The vision of a nightclub with a Brazilian beach theme hung in the space just over Jack Diamond's shoulder. The *Copacabana*, the nightclub that would outshine and outlast every other nightclub ever created, sprang complete and intact from the void. It would be a natural expansion to his tropical themed *Beachcomber* clubs that stretched from Miami to Rhode Island, but this new club would have a hot, Latin beat.

Excitement crept into Monte's voice now that he heard the music that went with the vision, "What's that music called? Calypso?"

"I dunno, I'll find out." Jack said.

The fear, the pain and the disappointment of Monte's life were pushed aside once again by his enthusiasm, this time for the music and culture of Brazil. Brazil was new, it was sexy, the music was hot, they liked to drink and dance. It seemed to provide the antidote to the loveless, aimless life he found himself in.

He threw himself into the creation of this new club and through it, into a new life. It was worth everything - all his money, all his connections and all his time. He laid his whole bundle on the bet and shot the dice for a seven. It was the kind of high stakes, winner-take-all tumble that made his heart pound.

Part of the excitement was the long odds against him. The location, 10 East 60th Street, on the fashionable Upper East Side of Manhattan at the threshold of the most expensive section of Fifth Avenue, was considered worse than a risky area for a nightclub. The place had a history.

Nightclubs and the boisterous crowds they attracted were traditionally located in the rough and tumble West Forties between the garish lights of Broadway and the dark alleys of Hell's Kitchen on Tenth Avenue. 10 East 60th Street was particularly jinxed. Ten years earlier Rudy Vallee, then the biggest movie star in the world, bombed there with his club *Villa Vallee*. Zero business. After that, it sat empty for ten years. No one even tried. The *Hotel 14*, which owned the space, was using it as a storage cellar.

When Monte saw that the cellar had enough room for a small stage, his ambition took over. He had to have the place. It would need everything – plumbing, electrical, a kitchen, a sound system and something would have to be done about the huge support columns that held up the *Hotel 14*. The investment and the overhead would crush him in two months if it didn't hit. He knew the only thing that could fill a place that size and that far uptown was entertainment. To survive, the Copa would need the best in the business of cabaret. It would have to have the best food as well as entertainment, otherwise people would tire of it and not make the trip. If the Copa didn't hit it big, right away, it would bust him and he'd lose more than money. This was a game for high rollers, winner-take-all and he wanted in badly.

The wager on the table was, could he fill the same stage that Rudy Vallee couldn't? Some friends, like Nick Kelly, who worked the door at his *Beachcomber* were privately touting the odds at 3 to 1 against. Nobody could make that place work.

"Why that joint? It's got the jinx." Kelly warned.

"I gotta hunch," was all that Monte would say.

"I gotta hunch." Kelly said to himself over and over. "I gotta hunch."

The question buzzed in Monte's head constantly. It kept him awake at night. Could he fill that stage? He didn't need Kelly to tell him the odds, he knew the place was a white elephant. The question haunted him.

Monte took on the financing of the renovation of the old *Villa Vallee* himself and quickly his enthusiasm outstripped his business sense. He spent lavishly, building an entire Chinese-style kitchen from scratch with custom built-in copper woks and new plumbing for steam cooking. He leased hotel rooms on the floor above the club in the *Hotel 14* and renovated them into dressing rooms. He renovated the elevator, the ventilation, the walls, the ceiling and the floor.

Youngest sister Annette, a budding young Socialist, watched Monte's wildcatter capitalism with growing anxiety.

"Monte, why this one? What's so important?" she asked.

"You'll see. I gotta hunch." He told her. "Start taking Samba lessons," was his advice to her.

Annette started coming uptown to see him since he rarely made the effort anymore to get to her neighborhood. He was becoming too busy. Every night he was going somewhere to meet someone about some deal. Isabel had moved to Baltimore with Ted, the tiresome stockbroker and Leo was busy working as a writer of radio shows. It was up to Annette to keep the communication in the family up. She made it a point to track Monte down when he was in town. She knew his heart had been broken once again and maybe permanently. She was under orders from elder sister Isabel to look in on him. Monte told her he was fine, he knew what he was doing,

"Wait'll you see the place." He told her, happy as a kid with a new bike. "Just wait and see."

There was a touch of madness to his pursuit of the place. He was proving something to himself. Most clubs took a month to six weeks to open. The Copa took almost two years.

He called in Miles White, one of the top production designers on Broadway, to bring his vision to life. The walls of the Copa downstairs were covered with custom-made mirrors that reflected the mural, bandstand and dance floor, creating the illusion of doubling the size of the place. Green palm fronds were painted on the mirrors' surfaces to disguise them and create the effect of lush jungle foliage. The vibrant color palette of bright and dark greens, rust red and white with accents of brightly colored fruit was wildly theatrical. Even the El Morocco with its blue and white zebra striped banquets was pale by comparison. The Copa swayed with color and sparkle. Five hundred settings of glass, silverware and snow white plates on white linen, would light faces from below, sparkling in the eyes, flashing over the surface of the teeth. The lighting overhead from the pink baby spotlights warmed the skin and softened laugh lines.

The support columns, thick as barrels, were covered in plaster and sculpted into white palm trees. Pastel green top fronds rested against the ceiling. The palms glowed under their own special blue baby spotlights when the house lights got low. They dominated the view of the club. White palm trees had become emblematic of Monte's places. They first sprouted at the *Beachcomber* in Miami, popped up again at the *La Conga* in Hollywood and now were the overwhelming icon of the Copa. From back in "Siberia" the most distant table up on the third tier, the palms framed a moonlit painted panorama of Rio's curving Copacabana beach at night that hung over the stage. The illusion, with the moonlit palms in the foreground, was of a balmy tropical night. A full equatorial moon glowed over pale blue sand and shimmered on the surface the sea.

The club was a three-tiered rectangular amphitheater that surrounded a 24 by 40 foot stage floor on three sides. A large center aisle divided the room, ending at the stage. Ranks of men in snappy uniforms would flow up and down the levels from down front, up to the kitchen and service bar on the long north wall.

The service bar ran the length of the wall. It was the business end of the business – a mechanical river of booze. Every drink that Monte had ever encountered in his long stagger along the bars, cabaret tables and betting parlors of Manhattan and Hollywood, was on the menu.

The back page of the Copa menu was devoted to categories of drinks listing 35 whiskeys including several ryes, bourbons and scotches. Then there were the gins, vodkas and liqueurs. Then mixed drinks that took up the entire inside facing page. Name your poison.

The wall headed west along 60th, turned left, ran south for hundreds of feet behind the kitchen. The kitchen was built to feed 2,000 guests a night. A field of custom fitted, stainless steel work surfaces surrounded the steaming copper woks, optimizing every inch of the kitchen space.

The dressing rooms nestled into the far corner of cellar underneath the lobby of the *Hotel Fourteen*. They were the carpeted and mirrored preparation rooms for the chorus girls and supporting guest acts.

When it came to sorting out the Copa's finances, Sol Meadow, a meticulous, business-savvy, young lawyer, walked into Monte's life about six weeks too late. Not yet realizing

Monte's true nature, Sol came in and tried his best to map out the framework of the business with things like projections of cash flow and time to recoup, business concepts distantly familiar to Monte. It quickly became apparent that the damage was done and the situation was critical.

Everything Monte had built up to that point, particularly his credibility as a smart club operator, was now in serious jeopardy. He would need even more cash than all six of his current clubs were producing. Word raced down Broadway like wildfire that Monte was up to something big on the East side and was in trouble.

Frank Costello survived by keeping a low profile. Hotheaded Charlie "Lucky" Luciano was being kept cool at *Dannemora Federal Penitentiary*. They called it Siberia because it sat under the hard snows near the Canadian border four months a year. Lucky's room at the facility was reserved for 30 to 50 years, courtesy of Thomas Dewey, prosecutor.

At nearly the same time, Vito Genovese had been fingered in the killing of small time hood Ferdinand "the Shadow" Boccia. Prosecutor Dewey also hung an indictment on Vito who promptly packed and sailed to a new home in Mussolini's Italy. Vito's millions bought a lot of expensive jack boots for the Dictator.

Frank Costello had quietly been gathering up many of the businesses left behind by the sudden departures of his two colleagues but avoided their largest earners. He didn't pursue Vito's lucrative heroin trade or Lucky's extensive prostitution empire. Instead he consolidated his hold on his traditional "legit" businesses of liquor and gambling. He now sat unopposed as acting Boss of All Bosses. Lucky was locked up, Vito was vacationing and Meyer was busy in Miami. No one was left to vote on it. Except Thomas Dewey.

Dewey turned all his skill against Frank but couldn't manage to get a grip on him. As he perfected during his early bootlegging prosecutions, Frank left no tracks of his illegality. Frank had a different view on Dewey's legal pursuit, "He couldn't touch me 'cause I was legit." meaning he was "legitimate" in mob terms. By rejecting the drug business and prostitution, he felt he was simply providing entertainments that the hypocritical government wanted to regulate for its own profit. He had been proven correct regarding liquor, which was once again legal and taxed, and expected the Feds would take gambling before long. Before his career was over, he would be proven correct once again when state lotteries and Off Track Betting took the bread out his bookie's mouths.

Frank's other business and the future of the *Syndicate*, was real estate. He owned an office building at 79 Wall Street where he kept his own office and operated his legitimate business, the *79 Wall Street Corporation.* He also held a variety of other real estate holdings including hotels. Real estate held no particular attraction for him. It was the brainchild of his lawyer George Wolf to provide legitimate investments. He made a little money as a landlord, but the money was small potatoes compared to his liquor and gambling empire. Profits from rents at the 79 Wall Street office building were donated to charity. Like Meyer, the business Frank preferred was gambling. He was a high stakes crapshooter and horse player himself and most at home in his own stylish casinos and in the nightclubs that catered to night people.

Steadily over months, as the threads of the Copa were being woven together, Monte's finances were unraveling. Monte had bet his entire bankroll on the most ephemeral quality then in vogue, the one that was most pursued but rarely captured, the one that all the hoopla and gimmickry of Broadway missed, the one that made anything it touched transcendent, timeless and unique. He bet on the quality known as class. The Copa would have class.

Other clubs had singers, dancers and comedians but none would have the precision timing and elegant design of a Copa revue. It would be an intimate revision of classic vaudeville extravaganzas, but instead of overpowering audiences with opulence, he would charm them with style. Class.

The dancers for the chorus would be young women selected for their elegance and gentle personality. Copa girls would be small, young, intelligent and expressive, with bodies of normal female proportions. These girls would look like the beautiful sister or cousin everyone had and loved. They would look like the first loves of men and the first true best friends of women. They would each be given dance solos, moments alone in the spotlight, so patrons could savor each one. They would be each season's perfect blossoms, calmly confident and thrilling in their athletic grace. Class.

He would surround his performers with a Broadway-quality production and his audience with an exotic, exciting and carefree world. Every time the Copa girls strode back onto the stage between acts, they would have a new outfit. The mink costumes had to be real mink so that everyone close to the stage would recognize the opulence as authentic. Class.

For Monte, class was inclusive, most people had it. It didn't require wealth but it did require money, a sense that all was well. Like Monte himself, the Copa would welcome anyone. It was going to be a joint, a saloon, and so an equalizer, where any lady or gentleman with a good suit of clothes and proper manners could sit with swells of every stripe. Class.

Timing, the other essential element of entertainment, meant the design of the show had to complement the main business of the saloon – drinking, eating and seduction - so highly emotional singers would be followed by light-hearted comedians. Interspersed dance acts including the Copa girls would allow the emotions to dissipate while the life-blood of the nightclub evening, the intimate conversation, resumed.

Every trick of the trade he had learned in the carnivals, circuses, gin mills and movies would find a spot in the Copa. The design included the intoxication, if not by liquor then by the atmosphere, of his guests. He understood that the early stages of drunkenness made people more sensitive to emotion. His revue would first disarm the audience with humor allowing them to get in their first drink order, then overpower them with an emotional charge, the singer, and then relieve them with comic relief. The pacing anticipated the second or third drink, when people became much less sensitive and had to be shown the door. Polluted patrons had to be replaced with fresh ones three times a night. First, the usually sedate dinner show at 8 PM would be tempered for working people, then the rowdy midnight show at 12 would cater to seasoned club-goers and finally the outrageous 2 AM show would be delivered "no-holds-barred" to fellow showfolk and people of other uncertain professions who were not expected anywhere before noon the next day.

In spite of all that Monte knew, all his talent and all his energy, opening day seemed to be getting further away. Everything was taking longer and costing more. The missing element, he decided, was luck. He tacked a mezuzah and a Christian cross just inside the club's front door, "In case of a tie," he said. Inexplicably, even covering his bets with both religions also failed to turn his luck. Weeks were turning into months as he continued to pour money into the unlucky cellar.

After Charlie Lucky's exile to the frozen north, Joe Adonis, a handsome, quiet gangster who operated from Brooklyn, became Frank Costello's closest business advisor. Adonis took Lucky's place as Meyer Lansky's trusted representative and so became a frequent companion and also advisor to Frank. While Meyer and Joe A. advised him on business, Albert Anastasia, Frank's longtime friend, founder and former top man of *Murder Incorporated*, continued to handle Frank's security. Fortified with the best brains and brawn in the business, Frank continued to say little and rule New York, the traditional capital of organized crime, with a light touch.

It wasn't a strategy, it was Frank. He disliked being in the spotlight. Being the *Syndicate's* top man was dangerous and forced responsibilities on him that he didn't need or want. Frank had always been a friendly co-operator with buddies who operated outside the law but he also had always been independent. Because he was never part of any "family", he was the ideal unifier and mediator. He mediated between the families, then between the families and Jewish mobs and ultimately between the unified *Syndicate* and the "straight" world of politicians and businessmen. Frank bought and sold judges, aldermen and presidents of large companies like used cars. He derived his power both from the enormous money he made and from his skills as a negotiator. Becoming the default leader of the *Syndicate* did nothing but distract him from his core business and make him a target for attacks.

New York Attorney General Thomas Dewey was at least professional in his persecution of Frank, refraining from implicating Frank in public statements. Mayor LaGuardia however, never missed a chance to smear him, calling him a "bum" in print and on the radio and using some of Frank's confiscated slot machines for his famous publicity stunt - smashing them with a sledgehammer on the West side piers for the assembled news cameras.

Frank's opinion of LaGuardia was also clear, "He's a two-bit hustler. Anybody could've looked good coming in after Jimmy Walker."

To Costello, LaGuardia was a blue-nosed bureaucrat and a professional actor who was performing a "get tough" attitude for votes. But LaGuardia wasn't play-acting when it came to nailing Costello. The Mayor used all his considerable power trying to put Costello in prison. If he got him, he might be able to make a run for the White House and even win. The constant pressure was starting to keep Frank awake at night, pushing him to find relief with a few drinks, a few songs and the distracting conversations found in nightclubs.

The *Hotel Fourteen*, host of the developing nightclub in its cellar, also came under the piercing gaze of Mayor LaGuardia. Building code and fire safety infractions were found, delaying construction and opening the hole in Monte's pocket a little wider. He was being bled to death with a thousand small cuts. He now had only a vague idea of how much money he'd spent and no idea how much more he might need. He only knew that he needed Broadway-sized money to keep going.

Coming to Monte's aid once again, as he had with his restorative weekends at his Bucks County farm, Walter Batchelor found a small theatre in Hartford, Connecticut. Early in its long history the place had been a pearl of the vaudeville circuits but now, 30 years later, it was a carbuncle on the behind of Broadway – a low-rent tryout house between New York and Boston, a decrepit relic of a glorious past. The theatre survived even though it wasn't grand enough for the movies. The newer movie theatre, a few blocks away, was a palace that hosted the emperor idols of Hollywood, but Batch's place, the *Elmont Theatre*, got by with the occasional burlesque revival, an itinerant hell-fire preacher or a local civic meeting. It was large enough to support a run if the show hit with the locals but the real purpose was to put up new shows in hopes of finding one that could make it to Broadway. Monte needed one that could move to Broadway and quick. Then a small miracle happened, indicating that the dangerous Miss Luck had arrived.

Batch made a grand gesture. He got a loan against the Farm in Bucks County and laid it all at Monte's feet. This was one of the few times that Monte was confused about Batch's motives. Batch was known to be tight with money, so it was more than shocking that he did this for Monte without being asked. They'd discussed the idea but Batch went ahead on his own and literally bet the Farm on the remote chance that Monte could bring in a hit. Batch's last attempt on his own was a play called *Sentinels* eight years earlier that closed after 11 performances.

Since then he'd been too discouraged to try again. Monte was overwhelmed by his friend's generosity. For one delicious moment, he felt lighter than air, like he might float off. His luck was running so strong that it levitated him. He breathed in deeply, hands rising weightlessly at his sides, and floated effortlessly in the palm of Lady Luck, suddenly understanding why investors like Batch were referred to as *angels*. He'd been saved from certain disaster by a true miracle.

The result of this magnificent gesture of faith and friendship was a string of hopeless failures. Monte was simply stretched too thin. Miss Luck left, again, without a goodbye. The delays and harassment by LaGuardia's legions at City Hall directed at the Copa were drawing all Monte's energy. He couldn't focus on the productions enough to avoid pitfalls that became obvious well after the plays were into rehearsals. By then, it was generally too late. To re-write, re-cast or re-hire a director would be ruinous. So they went on with minor fixes while the two producers prayed for another miracle. After three flops in a row, the last one being an embarrassing disaster named *Daddy's Dandy*, the jig was up. Batch was about to lose the Farm. Monte did what he vowed he would never do, he diverted money from the Copa. He paid $20,000 toward Batch's mortgage at the bank and saved the beloved Farm from foreclosure. It was the second uncharacteristically sentimental gesture in their short producing partnership and it cemented their friendship for life.

It also put Monte in an even more desperate situation regarding his club. He was now actively looking for partners, another situation he vowed never to get into. He knew his temperament was completely wrong for partnership. He could be a hired hand or a boss, but being a partner was an altogether different and much tougher proposition. The partnership with Carl Erbe had soured eventually although they managed to stay close friends after a cooling off period. The recent debacle with Batch left him feeling frustrated. He couldn't separate friendship and work easily. Partnerships always seemed to pull him into uncomfortable compromises of both business and pleasure. It was better to be on your own. Besides, no one, not even Monte himself, could predict the course of his own thinking. If he had had a partner, the Copa would never have been attempted. Any rational person would have walked away and found something else. It was his *Moby Dick*.

Monte and Sol Meadow sat quietly in the sawdust, under the pounding of hammers and rasping of wood saws. The figures Sol had penciled neatly into rows seemed to paralyze Monte. He was looking into the abyss. His string had run out and the numbers confirmed it. Even if he sold all his *Beachcomber* clubs, there wouldn't be enough to finish the Copa and operate it for two months. The bar still hadn't been built, the walls were still unfinished and plaster dust hung in the air. They had spent the last week going over Sol's neat rows of calculations and financing schemes that now lay in front of Monte like a death warrant. It was apparent that he'd wildly overspent. Class was expensive. But Monte's jackpot finally arrived that day in a full-length camel hair coat.

Frank Costello walked down the stairs, dodging plaster-speckled workmen, looking like a tanned and prosperous banker or insurance executive. Sol saw him immediately while Monte was scratching his neatly pomaded head over the grim numbers in front of him. Costello walked over to Monte and offered his hand, "Say hello to your new partner." Monte looked up. A look passed between Monte and Sol. The saws went silent, leaving only a workman's trowel scraping dry plaster. A whiff of sweet cologne floated by as Sol watched Costello's outstretched hand move toward Monte like a dagger. Sol felt the urge to speak up but his tongue failed him, staying motionless and mute in a bath of bitter coffee. Monte's hand met Costello's and took hold, sealing the deal before any discussion happened.

"That was it", Sol recalled, "It was over before anybody could say a word. Not that I would have."

"Hello Frank." Monte said as he stood up. They shook hands. Searching his face, Monte found something so familiar in Costello, then realized they loosely resembled each other. Frank could almost pass for an older brother. He indicated a chair for Frank, introducing Sol. They all sat and said nothing for a moment. Frank took a good, long look around the place then settled on Monte, lingering eye-to-eye a bit longer than was polite. Monte held the stare and gave up nothing. Frank watched and waited calmly. He was looking for a twitch, a tell, any break. Monte watched and waited as well, focusing on the Prime Minister's glossy black eyebrows for a crease or movement. Frank enjoyed the contest and moved on, smiling in appreciation. Monte gave another look to Sol, who got the message, stood up and walked upstairs for some air.

Instantly, Monte's cash problem was solved. He had heard all about the Prime Minister and now felt the compelling charm up close, face to face. He quickly sensed that Frank was quiet and intelligent, may even someone he could trust. The man looked rested and relaxed, with a healthy tint to his Mediterranean skin, his chestnut eyes clear and his nails expertly trimmed and buffed.

It was a brief negotiation. Monte held only one card. He could walk away. He would be finished in New York, he would lose everything and insult a man who, with a slight nod, could turn him into mulch under the Meadowlands. Costello also held only one card. He had a packing crate full of cash from his Saratoga casino that needed a home. Frank scanned the place quickly and came back to smile at Monte, "I hope I'm not too late."

Monte surrendered to the inevitable and accepted the Prime Minister's friendly negotiations. "Your timing couldn't be better." Monte replied.

"Tell me about your place." Frank wanted to know everything.

Monte started to tell the story of Jack Diamond's photo of Copacabana beach. Frank listened as he looked around the four white walls picturing scenes of Rio de Janiero at night. Frank loved what he saw.

About 45 minutes later, Costello got into the back of a cab on 60th Street. Sol saw him, realized he'd had enough fresh air and went back inside. Monte was motionless in the same seat, elbows on the table, face resting on his folded hands. He was staring at what would be the Copa stage. Sol sat down and they both stared at the stage area for a long while. The workmen sawed and hammered. Plaster dust drifted down past bare light bulbs, covering everything in a filthy snow. Speaking over his hands Monte conveyed the deal to Sol, "Fifty fifty."

Sol nodded, "Good," accepting the terms as fair.

Costello's visit wasn't much of a surprise. Monte expected that someone of Frank's circle would eventually stop by with an offer of partnership, but usually it happened a few weeks after opening, after a place proved to be successful. Cash flow attracted gangsters, not investment opportunity and risk. Why shakedown a place that might flop? It was significant that Frank came himself, sat down man to man and negotiated a fair business arrangement like any other investor. Things had changed.

Compared to partners like Dutch Schultz, Frank was a walk in the park. He was the most powerful mobster in the country yet he traveled without bodyguards and never carried a gun. In his own mind he was simply an investor and a gambler who was simply faster to the cash than the government. He and Meyer were in perfect harmony and agreement about how business, modern business, should be done. Monte had to agree with them both.

On the outside, Frank was always calm, unrushed and gentlemanly. He knew that unless Dewey or LaGuardia could catch him with a great deal of untaxed cash, he would remain untouchable. But inwardly, the relentless pressure from LaGuardia, and from business partners, wore on his mind. His trouble sleeping worsened. At first it was part of his business, then it became part of an obsession to stay on guard at all times.

The only things that relaxed him were smooth Scotch, fast horses and swing music. Some form of all three enchantments he soon found with Monte. What made the two men almost family was the fact that Frank trusted Jews, did all his business with them and married one - his cherished Roberta Giegerman, nicknamed Bobbie, a childhood sweetheart from the old neighborhood around 114th Street and Second Avenue. When Frank and Bobbie wed, mixed marriages between Catholics and Jews were seen as a betrayal of culture by many. Frank and Bobbie couldn't have cared less. They were Romeo and Juliet.

Frank spoke lovingly and discreetly about his wife, "When I met Bobbie it was like meeting one of my own people. She didn't talk Italian, but the German dialect of her parents was foreign, like mine. Bobbie and me got along great from the first, although neither of our mothers was too happy. Bobbie's thought her daughter could do better than a poor Italian kid from East Harlem. And my mother naturally was hoping for an Italian girl."

Monte, like everyone else, was charmed by the romance. It was hard to believe that Frank did the things they tried to pin on him. For his part, Frank was almost giddy about having a playground like the one Monte was building. He honestly couldn't wait to be Monte's partner and deferred completely to Monte's talent and experience. The charm Monte first felt about Frank turned to enchantment. He'd met charming killers before like Deany O'Brien in Chicago and Owney Madden in the early days with Texas, even Larry Fay had a style about him. But Frank wasn't like any of them. He was a devoted family man, discreet, tolerant and wise. He also loved to play the ponies. Racetracks were his second home. Maybe things really were different now that Dutch was gone. Maybe Frank Costello was the new generation.

Monte let himself be seduced. He had been staring into the abyss of financial ruin and humiliation when Frank Costello walked into his life. Now he had an endless supply of cash and one of the most powerful and influential partners in the world. He was made. But his new angel was also New York's public enemy #1. The most powerful Mayor in the country working with the most effective prosecutor in New York State history were hunting him and anyone near him, with all their skill and power. From that moment on, Monte Proser was in the files of law enforcement as part of the *Syndicate*. This was the hidden chain attached to his jackpot.

Sherman Billingsley was delighted by the news. Winchell had only to mention the name now involved at the Copa and Billingsley knew instantly that he had his first useful weapon against the man who had misused his *Stork Club* as a staging ground for his humiliating publicity stunts and stolen a valuable employee in Jack Entratter. The promise of vengeance energized his step and he wasted no time in arranging a very private party to announce his finding, or rather, let the information slip.

FBI chief J. Edgar Hoover and his life-partner Clyde Tollsen adored the *Stork*. After all, the voice of New York, Walter Winchell himself had dubbed the place "...the New Yorkiest" of all New York nightlife. Whenever J. Edgar – called by friends Jedgar - could slip away from the pressure cooker of Washington, he and Clyde packed their best evening clothes and hopped the express to Pennsylvania Station. A private car whisked them from the station across town to their favorite suite at the Waldorf Astoria. On the trip across town they began to unwind as they felt welcome anonymity cloaking them and their love that could not speak its name.

For too brief respites, they lived as princes in an enchanted kingdom. Days were spent luxuriating in private baths, at elegant luncheons with discreet and powerful friends and, of course for Clyde, shopping in the best shops in the world. But it was at night, when shadows protected them from snooping reporters and gossips, when they could truly enjoy time together and were accepted just as they were – two princes in love.

Billingsley always came to greet them personally at the door. He showed them to their regular table and on a particular night in 1939, introduced them to his private party attended by only himself and Walter Winchell. Winchell, in spite of his reputation as a purveyor of scandal, impressed Jedgar as a fellow master in the art of collecting personal information. Just as Billingsley planned, the two were soon trading on the most intimate details of citizens from entertainment and politics. They were addicted to other people's secrets and couldn't help themselves. All Billingsley had to do was keep Clyde distracted while the men talked. That was easy. Clyde couldn't resist couture fashion and the women who could afford it. The *Stork* was full of them. Clyde found himself guest of honor among the best people who were dressed in the best that money could buy. It was heaven.

Jedgar and Winchell were also thoroughly entertained. They reveled in each other's treasure trove of naughty tidbits. Just as Winchell, a Jew, was compelled by his lust for power and legitimacy to embrace the openly anti-Semitic Sherman Billingsley, he was likewise compelled to open his vault of secrets to J. Edgar Hoover - even if it meant providing damaging information about his oldest friends. Jedgar knew the enticements of power as well as anyone and played them like a fishing lure.

Eager informants were common but the type and detail of Winchell's information was not. It was a highly profitable partnership for both. Winchell kept his readers well-informed and Jedgar kept his FBI agents well supplied with leads. Pleasantly enough, the business was done largely over cocktails at the *Stork*. Sometimes Billingsley even picked up the tab. As hoped by Billingsley, Monte's new affiliation with Frank Costello generated a new FBI file in 1939 and agents got to work filling it. Monte's business was now a federal matter as well as a city and state concern. Billingsley savored the sweetness of his revenge, served as recommended, cold.

CHAPTER 18

PARTNER TROUBLE

Down in the raw bump and grind of Times Square, the *Kit Kat Club* hosted an all-night revue featuring the hoochy-kooch and tassel-twirl of dancing girls *Misty Morning* and *Taffy Delish*. It was a low ceiling, second floor place, thick with cigar smoke and rank with old beer.

It was a place where sailors who didn't speak English and mechanics who didn't want to, got their rockets polished under the cocktail tables for the price of a watered down whiskey. Complaints about service or the outrageous prices could get a patron thrown head-first down the flight of stairs to street level.

Presiding over this desperate entertainment was Jules Podell, leg breaker turned club manager. Podell grew up in the Brownsville section of Brooklyn around friends of Louis "Lepke" Buchalter, future co-operator of *Murder Incorporated* with Albert Anastasia, another Brownsville native. The Boys of Brownsville were a separate society with a specialized language that depended on inflection, hint and gesture because much of what was said was incriminating. The workhorse of Podell's vocabulary, the expression he used dozens of times a day was "Eh". It meant yes, no, maybe or get the hell away from me, depending on how it was said. A nod, a gesture and an "eh" was most of what Jules and his friends had to say on most subjects.

Podell learned his restaurant management skills operating a hotdog pushcart on Coney Island. Shaking down pushcart operators was the early meat of Lepke. But instead of being intimidated, Podell saw his future as preying on other pushcart competitors as well. He joined Buchalter but quickly became a liability. He had no finesse as an enforcer. A simple rough-up for collection purposes became a near murder. In 1934 he was tried for attempted murder and acquitted due to sudden jury amnesia. From then on, Podell was strictly a manager, a watchdog in mob operations.

When Lepke merged operations during Prohibition with Luciano and the *Syndicate*, Podell moved up from hot dog carts to a series of restaurants, nightclubs and strip joints. Soon after Costello introduced himself to Monte in the Copa, Podell got a new assignment. He was leaving the *Kit Kat* and moving uptown.

Monte quickly filled key positions in the Copa with men loyal to him – press agent Jack Diamond, manager Milton Pickman and three of the biggest, toughest doormen in New York.

The first was Jack Entratter, who had walked away from Billingsley's high-hatters, debutantes and paranoia, with Toots and Monte a few years back. Jack was hired on as inside security. Entratter was an unusually kind man for the rough business he was in - a lovable giant. He was forced to become tough both because of his size and because of his limp. Polio had shortened his left leg. He was a big, lopsided target for certain cruel drunks and had learned to deal with them early in his career.

Next was Toots Shor. Toots had also done a stint with Mr. Billingsley and was currently employed at the *Club Versailles* as the all-around guy, meaning he knew as much about running the club as anyone and was trusted by the owners like family. Toots, like Entratter, was a gentleman of the Old School. If he gave his word of honor, it was a sacred trust. Rude behavior or inappropriate language in his club was out of line and was dealt with severely. He was so trusted that the owners relied him to close up at night, count the night's cash and walk it to the bank's night deposit, alone. If he was skimming, they would never know it. It was unthinkable that Toots would ever steal from anyone.

Toots was ready to open his own place, he just couldn't get his stake up yet. Like Monte, he invested much of his available cash in slow racehorses. He also wouldn't take start-up money from the hoods he worked for. He'd laugh them off, tell them he didn't need partners. He'd use his own money, thanks. People liked Toots, they loved him, so he could tell almost any hood to get lost and they'd laugh. He was a tough guy and didn't need anybody. They liked that. The only problem was he ended up working for everybody else, guys like Monte, who did take the money.

Nick "Kelly the Belly" Kelly was the third of the three stout oaks who made and enforced the law of the Copa. The Belly was outside security. He greeted patrons at curbside and directed them to Toots who opened the club's door where Jack took over. Nick had handled all the security for Monte at the *Beachcomber* but Monte needed him out front at the Copa. Out front was where the work could get very dirty and nobody cleaned it up faster than Kelly the Belly. He was squat and round, which got him his name, but he was a brawler in his prime and nearly impervious to pain. Or that's the legend he promoted. In his career, his fists occasionally went through car windows, doors and plaster walls. He'd never suffered more than bruises or so he said. He carried enough concealed weaponry to accommodate any security situation and always had backups hidden a few steps from his position. Nick had done some amateur boxing, but always made his rent money guarding other people's nightclubs. His dream was to be a singer. He had a soaring Irish tenor that was often called upon at wakes or late at night after the saloons he guarded closed for the night. Monte generally had him in for a nightcap, a filthy limerick or two and an Irish ballad before locking up for the night. Monte spent as much time with Nick as he did with anyone. Nick wasn't as lucky with the ladies as Toots and Entratter. He generally had no place to go after work, no one to see. The loneliness made him want to stay up and sing.

The experienced arms of Jack, Toots, Nick and company could carry a fighting drunk from a front row table seat to the gutter outside the club in seconds with minimum damage. It was called the "bum's rush" and it was a skill long practiced and highly valuable in saloons.

Men of controlled violence who could wear a tuxedo and smile were worth more than a good chef, even more than a bartender who didn't drink, if they had decent social skills. Toots, Jack and Nick were the best in the business.

When they ran a place, vulgarities or rudeness won an offender a tap on the shoulder from the very large finger of Jack Entratter. If immediate and sincere apologies weren't offered, or if the offense was grievous enough that no apology would do, a polite suggestion of, "Let's have a talk." was offered as your dinner table was suddenly whisked away. If you were at the bar, your glass would suddenly be moved out of reach. Sitting exposed and by this time surrounded by "the redcoats" - all the serving captains wore red waistcoats - it was obvious that accepting Entratter's offer to "talk" in a quiet, dignified way was the healthiest option. Once you were up, Entratter's walk-and-talk maneuver propelled you toward his staff and the front door. You were then passed off to the firm embrace of a muscular employee who encouraged you with momentum or conversation as needed. Whether you ended up walking or flying out the front door depended entirely on the nature of your brief chat with Entratter.

One last addition to the main crew was made in the last week before the club opened. Prince Michael Romanoff was visiting from California. It seemed that his movie career was not going as well as he had hoped. Once again, the Prince's timing was extraordinary. Monte put him on the payroll immediately as a greeter, an unofficial position, somewhere between a doorman and maitre d'. The Prince was extremely grateful to have the work. For his first few weeks back in town, he slept in the manager's office and showered upstairs in the star dressing rooms in the *Hotel Fourteen*. During working hours, in his tuxedo and rented military medals, he would lend an air of Old World elegance to the place.

Poland fell to the Master Race of the Third Reich in two weeks. In four weeks, they divided the country and gave half to Joseph Stalin as a reward for signing the "Non-Aggression Pact" that promised Russia would not interfere with German aggression. This gave Adolf Hitler the confidence to send his Nazi mechanized blitzkrieg rolling over Austria, Belgium and soon the Champs-Elysees. His dream of taking all of Europe was suddenly possible.

At the same time, American newspapers reported that 937 European Jewish refugees on board the ocean liner *St. Louis* were refused entry into Cuba, then the United States. The ship was steaming back to Europe. It was the tacit *Non-Aggression Pact* of the rest of the world. 40,000 Cubans in Havana demonstrated against admission of the Jews, while the Americans, particularly President Roosevelt, merely stayed silent and would not relax immigration laws even for humanitarian purposes. No one would interfere with Germany's persecution of its citizens. The Jews sailed back to the emerging holocaust.

In America, all anyone talked about was this new European war with the same, old enemies and if America was going to get into it – again. While the Americans talked, the royal families of Europe began pouring into New York bringing everything they owned. They were soon followed by the wealthy, who were then followed by the middle class, followed then by the lucky and finally the desperate. After FDR finally woke up and spoke against the Germans, New York became a safe haven, even for Jews, who could get there. It represented the heart of the free world. Hollywood had the looks and Washington had the brains but New York was the heart.

The city was becoming flooded with the loot of Europe. Jewels and furs arrived at New York vaults. Fleets of the most expensive cars, entire stables of the finest riding horses, storage barns of wine, mountains of silverware, rare art, books, and furniture – essentially anything portable that had any value came to New York.

The social climate suddenly shifted under the weight of thousands of new, wealthy immigrants who were eager to be accepted. Gruff New Yorkers were overrun with painfully polite

Englishmen who were exceedingly keen on being helpful and desperately in need of good places to put their money. The English came to America like someone needing refuge in his neighbor's house and willing to pay double the value of the house for the privilege. It was good for business. It was the biggest boom since Prohibition. Nightclubs expanded again to accommodate small orchestras and a full line up of stage acts. The number of clubs swelled to over 1,000 in New York alone, entertaining 2.5 million patrons a year. A new vaudeville circuit was formed, but of nightclubs. Nightclub entertainers traveled the deeply worn paths of extinct vaudeville acts. They played New York to Hollywood and everywhere in between. Dance schools sprung up just for tap dancers. Voice lessons were advertised on almost every corner. Entire neighborhoods would host amateur talent contests hoping to attract Broadway's attention. Four major newspapers and dozens of local magazines slugged it out for readership. New York developed a thirst for culture to help all the cash go down more easily. British elocution lessons infected a generation of impressionable Americans with a British tinge to their slang. The result often sounded merely pompous, like a snooty old time New Yorker putting on airs. It was certainly a boon to Prince Michael Romanoff who was introduced to all the royal families. He was bold as a lion, committing his heart to the part he performed every night. His claim to royalty was frequently challenged, some knew the real Romanoffs. It never lessened his zeal for the part he played. He simply found others who believed his performance.

New York went on a gambling, drinking, spending, survival binge that kept the town up and partying all night. The Europeans' obsession to celebrate every day was fueled by their grief and justified fear of annihilation. The mad, nihilistic party frenzy of World War I returned. "Live today, for tomorrow..." was a popular toast offered in saloons around town. All anyone ever talked about was the coming war.

In the kitchen corridor, Podell was starting to think he'd made a mistake. Maybe no one was coming to steal the Copa's onions after all. The little Filipino was starting to turn red. "I make piss!" he hissed at Podell. Pedro Pujal, the head chef, was coming up the hall rattling in Tagalog dialect that Podell couldn't make out. Podell whacked the stack of produce crates, "Fuck is this doing here?"

"I make piss!" the salad chef screamed at hapless Podell. Pedro heard two words in Tagalog from the Filipino and turned to Podell to explain. Podell took the top crate and flung it down the hall at the two, "Put this shit away. Put it away!" The flying crate clipped Enrique's shin and set the small man hopping and howling like a wounded dog. Pedro knew Enrique shouldn't have screamed at the man. Podell's face stiffened into a red mask. Pedro yelled back into the kitchen for the salad preps to come. He wanted them to put away the produce deliveries. The salad choppers heard the screaming and came running with their 10 inch Sabatier knives. Podell saw them with their knives out, and his snub nose .38 came out of its holster. "Come on!" He bellowed and leveled the gun. He started walking right for them. Pedro cowered and shrunk against the wall. The salad preps dropped their knives and retreated. Enrique stopped hopping and looked up into the barrel of the stubby pistol. Urine suddenly flowed down his leg onto the floor. Podell was enjoying the sudden quiet until he noticed the piss pool around his feet. "You fuckin' pig." Podell looked up and saw Monte standing squarely in the center of the corridor. Podell slowly dropped the gun to his side. Monte knew better than to speak while Podell still had the gun out. Podell pushed his chin out at Monte, "Eh." Podell holstered his gun, indicating the produce. "10 bucks a fuckin' crate." Podell walked past him.

"You okay?" Monte asked his crew. They all just looked up at Monte and said nothing. He spoke for them, "Son of a bitch."

According to LaGuardia's City Hall operating license, Jules Podell was not allowed "on the premises" of the Copa because of his long time affiliation with the underworld. The effect of the license restriction meant Podell was effectively banished to the kitchen where he could quickly exit out the service entrance when city inspectors showed up. The heat, noise and humiliation of his imprisonment ratcheted up Podell's vicious disposition. He hated the set-up. Monte got all the glory out front, Podell did all the dirty work in the back.

For Monte, as bad as the new scrutiny by the FBI and LaGuardia was, the sheer dreadfulness of cooperating day-to-day with Jules Podell was worse. As enemies, he and Podell were perfectly matched. They were the same size, build and background. Both could be pushed to physical violence, but for Podell it was a much shorter push. Like Marty Krompier but without Marty's intelligence and capacity to dream of a different life, Podell was a familiar stain that became an object of loathing in Monte's life. He was a violent sociopath who was now Monte's daily working partner.

Podell's specialty – squeezing every last nickel out of a joint and spreading the supply contracts around the right way - meant that linen, food, beverage and garbage suppliers were now directly under Podell's thumb. He was an obsessively thorough and disciplined manager. Nothing escaped his attention.

A barman was caught walking out of the Copa with a lemon in his pocket. His wife had asked him to bring it home. Podell saw him pocket it and had to be pulled off the poor man as he attempted to break the man's head open on the kitchen floor. The barman spent six weeks in the hospital recovering from Podell's attack.

Monte prepared his area of the club, the downstairs showroom and upstairs lounge entertainment. Bales of Frank's Saratoga cash bought costumes so expensive they exceeded anything seen on Broadway. Genuine mink shorts, muffs and headdresses at $4,000 a copy were purchased for each of the six anticipated showgirls and intended to be used for only one number.

This extravagance further unhinged Podell to the point where Costello got tired of hearing Podell's accusations toward Monte. He warned Podell. Monte was Frank's partner and Podell was the guy who ran the back of the house, period. Frank made it clear in the most tactful way his anger would allow, that Podell was to lay off. Monte's name was out front for a reason and Podell was to shut up about it. Podell instantly withdrew. His excess had bungled another assignment. All he could do now was watch the boss' money and hope to catch Monte stealing. That would prove he was right all along. He retreated to his lonely, tiny cocktail table in the steaming kitchen to plan his revenge.

With Podell penned-up, Monte pursued his vision for a nightclub unmolested. Money became completely unimportant. It had never been an area of great attention in his life. He had only ever had two distinctions about money - making it and spending it. He never, ever thought about money as far as investing it, leveraging it or learning even its intermediate laws. Money simply was. The more he spent, the better he felt. His habit of reckless spending was now fed from an unquenchable stream of cash. The financial reckoning he faced with Sol suddenly vanished like a bad dream. From then on, all thoughts of money settled into the twilight semi-consciousness that all gamblers maintain to shield them from the glare of hard numbers.

CHAPTER 19

OPENING NIGHT

Construction surged forward with Frank's infusion of cash. The Copa was going to open Wednesday, October 30, 1940. In the rush to hire the staff, turf battles broke out between Monte's men and Podell for control of the club. Carmine, the Maitre'd, was hired by Entratter and assigned to put together a squad of captains, who would wear blue waistcoats, a platoon of waiters who would wear red and flocks of bus boys in white. Almost every hire was matched by Podell with one of his own in a struggle for dominance. The kitchen was entirely Monte's crew, the ten Filipino cousins and brothers-in-law of Pedro Pujal, the head chef.

Podell turned to the concessions, offering people he knew to operate the lucrative businesses, people who could outbid almost anyone. Monte turned them all down. The coatroom concession, where the income was generated twenty-five cents at a time from tips, was awarded to Monte's man for $20,000 a year. The cigarette and photography concessions went to Monte's people. But the back of the house was Monte's weak spot. The linen, liquor, meat and produce vendors were all squarely in Podell's territory. They were all friends of Podell's friends, as were the truckers that delivered everything. This was a battle Monte couldn't win and didn't try. The Copa was a tribal feast on a big kill and lots of Jules Podell's friends showed up at the service entrance on 60th Street for their piece of the new partnership. The lines were drawn. Where the ovens and steam tables ended and the storage and refrigerators began, then all the way out the crooked delivery corridor to the service entrance on 60th Street, was Podell's undisputed domain. Monte held the kitchen, the showroom, the bars and the upstairs lounge. When all the pushing was over and the staff sorted out, it was clear Podell had lost. Monte's men controlled the security and main positions and for now, most of the staff. But it was only the first skirmish of what Podell knew would be a long war. Eventually everyone had to come into his storerooms. In time, he'd wear them down and fill the open positions with his people. His first objective was directly in front of him. Pedro and his staff would have to go.

Outside the club, Monte was the phenomenon of Broadway. He was hailed by every reporter he had befriended in almost 20 years of daily contact with them. Talent agents lined up to supply performers to the swankiest new place in New York, the *Copacabana*. As opening day approached, the river of publicity never let up. Every day someone was talking about it in print.

Monte had his hands full auditioning every chorus girl and singer in New York. It was pleasant duty, and it was work. The clock was ticking. The reservation book began to fill. It was clear they would have a good two weeks and the word would get out. Beyond that no one could tell. Reservations dropped off for later dates. The first two weeks would tell the story.

The plasterers and decorators moved out and the bartenders moved in. The phone rang from morning until late at night. Monte's day was devoted completely to the Copa, the *Beachcombers* were on their own until the Copa was in the clear or busted.

Monte pulled in radio personality Jack Eigen to broadcast a live radio show from the Copa's lounge every night. It was an innovation that instantly placed the Copa squarely in the spotlight. Eigen would interview a steady stream of stars coming through the club. He was a brilliant, fast talking smoothie - a man so steeped in Broadway lore and lingo that he became the voice of nightlife as-it-happened. He would be broadcasting live from the new capital of the nightclub world.

By the time Harry Gerguson got home at night, he was sick to death of talking about the Copa. Monte had Prince Mike Romanoff out and about the town having lunches, drinks and chats from noon through late at night with everybody who ever was anybody, and talking up the Copa. Harry always over-ate, over-drank and occasionally overstayed his welcome. He had been playing the part of the Prince on and off for the past year and a half, 24 hours a day. The act was becoming his real life. Harry was becoming Prince Mike. No one knew Harry anymore. No one spoke of Harry. Harry had disappeared. They all called him Prince Mike or Mike. He had changed his name legally, so his given name was now buried deep in a bureaucracy, soon to be forgotten completely. He may as well become a Prince, he wasn't going to make it as an actor.

After drumming up business in the bars and restaurants of Times Square all day, Prince Mike was due at one club or another looking rested, royal and ready for fun until the fun ended at around 3:30 in the morning. From there it was home until the next day, when it all started again at the crack of noon with a wake-up call usually from publicist Jack Diamond. Diamond had a rundown of the day's promotion assignments and was looking for ideas on more. Those morning wake up meetings were the worst part of the royal lifestyle. Prince Mike loathed them like disease. The only problem with being a Prince was the hours. He was being worked to death.

From his fifth floor penthouse on 7th Avenue, Monte looked out on the lights of Broadway and could read the familiar patterns, the incandescent landmarks of his kingdom. Near the window was an old, drink-stained Steinway piano.

He had girlfriends, a smorgasbord, from every country in the world. The finest and the plainest. He was searching and determined to do a thorough job. He was disciplined, cavalier, wary. No woman could catch him, he was a playboy. It was a development he found he could share with his father, Charles.

Charles had moved into the Taft Hotel, at Monte's insistence and expense. It was just around the corner from Monte's apartment, close to everything. Charles took to hotel life immediately. He sat on the front porch of the place and read *The Worker*, still believing in the socialist dream of economic equality. Monte joined him often. They sat on the porch, ordered meals and talked. Talk always turned to beloved Lena, mother and wife. Monte wanted to recall all the qualities that made her so dear. Charles spoke lovingly as always, gentling his voice on her name. They spoke, finally, as two men of the world. After years of battle and truce, Charles realized he could safely let the burden of leadership fall to his once wayward son. His mind was at ease, Monte would steer the family ship from now on. Charles began to stay up late, drink a bit, and visit nightclubs occasionally when Monte invited him.

Monte learned of some of his mother's qualities while they rocked and watched the street life on 50th Street. Charles always spoke of her strength and courage. Those were the qualities he admired most. From then on, Monte felt he knew what he was looking for in a woman. They spoke about youngest Leo rocketing to recognition as a writer for radio with his adaptation of the play, "Mr. Sycamore". He'd just won the equivalent of the Academy Award for dramatic writing in radio. The eldest Isabel was safely tucked away back in Baltimore as a dutiful wife to the quiet stock broker Ted Schuman. Isabel volunteered at Johns Hopkins hospital in the psychology department. Annette was Isabel's opposite. As a rabble-rousing Socialist, Annette now lived a life of outsized passion and fervor on behalf of the workers of the world. Charles enjoyed the thoughts of his children and their adult lives. Lena would have been satisfied, he thought.

The night before the Copa opened, Monte looked out his seventh story penthouse window across the constellation of lights - the Great White Way. A young lady, whose name escaped him, she might have been a dancer at the *Little Club* or the hatcheck girl, noodled away at no particular tune on the old Steinway. The diffused lights of Broadway found her milk-white breast as it hung like a half-moon the shadows of her Chinese robe. The piano was kept perfectly tuned, the action smooth but the black surface was pocked with rings of long vanished drinks.

He'd forgotten her name temporarily but wasn't concerned. Women were no longer delicate queens and he wasn't their knight in shining armor. He was a man who had lost his illusions of love. There was no perfect woman. Maybe there would only ever be his pals and Broadway. Maybe whatever wealth and fame he could manage would be enough. Maybe marriage was outmoded. All anybody really needed were a few moments of kindness and a bit of fun.

Shelves of books and untidy stacks of magazines lay around the place. There were no plants except fresh cut flowers on the dark wood dining table. The bar was fully stocked. The kitchen was full of delicatessen food and stored, prepared meals - anything a wealthy bachelor or his guests might want from Louis Sherry ice cream to covered plates of sirloin and roast potatoes from "21". The Broadway lights were the overwhelming decoration of the room.

He would be going to bed early tonight. Tomorrow the dice would finally land and foretell his future. The *Copacabana* was going to make him or break him. The chance of losing all his money didn't worry him, he'd make more. Losing all of Frank's money didn't particularly worry him either. Frank knew the score when he bought in. What worried him was his reputation. If the place bombed, they'd say he'd lost his touch, his streak was over. They'd put this together with the series of recent flops with Batch and conclude his string had finally run out. They'd say his dice were cold. It would be the beginning of the end for him as far as nightclubs. But Monte knew, as he watched the city lights and listened to his girlfriend's gentle piano playing, even if Lady Luck had abandoned him this time, she'd be back. And they'd pick up again like always, like she'd never left.

On October 30, 1940, the sun rose on a hard frost in Manhattan. The streets were silver with ice. The drone of early delivery trucks was cut first by cabs zipping to early pickups. Squealing buses and garbage trucks, then honking private cars woke up the city. Early newsboys began shouting the headlines from every street corner. Finally, police whistles and fire sirens joined in. Monte was up well before noon. He opened his bedroom window a crack to get chilled morning air. He filled his lungs slowly and completely. He did his stretching to wake up the blood and then his exercises – pressing palm against palm at full force for twenty seconds - to get the blood racing. He'd read about isometrics in a men's fitness magazine. The day had arrived. The Copa opened in about eight hours.

On the street, the war in Europe overtook all other conversations. It drove people out of their homes and into any public place where the discussion could be had and news exchanged. They read about it over morning coffee, took up the discussion at work and brought it home at dinner. America had no army to speak of, so the cost of recruiting, arming and sending one to Europe again, 20 years after the first bloody fiasco, was staggering. It was simply too much to contemplate.

As much as people were desperate to know what to do, they were equally desperate to get away from it all. Life was good and getting better. They wanted to think about that. Money flowed through America in mighty rivers and any enterprising man or woman with a little pluck could scoop up a share. They wanted to study that. Heroes with character like Franklin Roosevelt, style like Fred Astaire and Ginger Rogers, skill like Lou Gehrig, and courage like Charles Lindberg lived among the people. They wanted to live like that. But the drumbeat of the war was distracting them from their dreams. At the Copa, they could see their heroes and even sit among them. They could imagine one day they might be friends. They wanted to dream like that.

Under the navy blue awning emblazoned in white block letters *Monte Proser's Copacabana,* Nick Kelly kept an eye on the small crowd of first-nighters that had started forming before he arrived for his shift at 5 PM. When he stepped out of his cab and crossed the sidewalk to pound on the front door of the place, 30 people were stamping their feet while they milled around the front door. Entratter was inside, still in his street clothes. The door opened and Entratter let him in. Entratter shook his hand, led him down the double flight of stairs that twisted to the right and emptied into the showroom.

Toots was already down there having a cup of coffee watching Midge Fielding, the choreographer, tighten up the Copa girls' moves. Midge should've been in the line, or the star as far as Nick was concerned. She put Monte's little dancer girls in the shade. She was a real woman, a racehorse in tight pants with whom Nick had a snowball's chance in hell, like every other man in the place. The word was she didn't like men much anyhow but Nick's eyes were magnetized to her. He signed his name in an ordinary school notebook shoved under his nose by Jack Pickman's brother Milton, the back office guy.

The paint was fresh, the carpet was new and the place looked like a high class Yankee Stadium with the tiers of seats and tables piled up around the stage. He had to admit the place looked like money and the word was good on the street. It had all the earmarks of a hit. In spite of the long odds he touted after he first heard the idea, it looked like Monte's hunch was going to pay off. He was happy for the boss but happier for himself. Toots was saying they were going to be able to retire off this one.

By the time he got back outside, the crowd was spilling off the curb onto 60th Street. They were all huddled up like the awning was going to keep them warm. His first job at the new club was lining them up to the east, toward Madison. The sun was going down and a light snow dusted everything white. There were over a hundred people and more were coming in packs of three and four. Already some regulars from the *Beachcomber* and around town were angling, "Hey Nicky! How ya been, kiddo!"

"Real good, yeah. Y'gotta get in line yet. Nobody gets in." He pointed down the block. "See ya after."

"Y'gonna take care of me, right?"

"I'll take care of ya." He showed them his meaty fist, they tipped their hats. After all the clip joints and dives he'd worked on the West side, this felt like the top of the pile. He was standing across the street from a place that looked like Rockefeller's townhouse with fancy iron gates and a round driveway with a sculpture of a naked woman in the center of it. The people were coming in packs and carloads now. A mounted policeman clip-clopped up and asked if he was the man in charge.

"I guess you could say that." Nick told him.

"Keep 'em outta the street, right?"

"Do my best." Nick answered.

"Do better." The cop didn't like Nick's answer. He turned from Nick to view the swelling mob from his horseback vantage, then rode off at a fast walk down the block ordering them back into a neat line.

Podell watched the bar like a prison guard, accounting for each bottle, while having an eye to eye with the bartenders, checking to see who might be getting ready to steal. Always get to know the bartenders personally, was a lesson he learned early. How are their families? Finances? How they doing with the ponies, the broads? He had managed to get a few of his guys on the downstairs bar but Monte's people were on the main bar upstairs. They controlled the liquor closet and so they controlled the main money in and out, and set the policy. If he couldn't get Monte's people to grift a little extra from the customers in various ways, he'd be reduced to just the skim from his guys downstairs. He figured that once the boss saw the extra money coming out of the showroom, the balance of power would shift away from Monte. He was going to make sure his guys could water down a drink, inflate a check and push product better than anyone in the business. Nobody could squeeze more drinks out of a bottle of liquor than Jules Podell.

Outside, two mounted police officers tried to maintain order on 60th street. Minor scuffles broke out as people jockeyed for a place in line. The line was now a double row extending most of the way to Madison Avenue, 400 people.

Cabs and sleek, monstrously long *Packards* and *Daimlers* continued to empty people at the front door. Once Nick explained that they couldn't get in until 6 o'clock, they faced the long march down the line of other hopeful entrants. But they did it, usually without complaint. This early, before six, it wasn't a problem but after eight, people would start showing up with a load on and around midnight the nasty drunks rolled out. That's when things got dangerous. But now it was just plain confusion. No one knew the club. Everyone arrived wanting to go right in, be the first. A huge, chattering mob pooled up under the awning and had to be moved along by Nick, negotiating, then shouting orders. Some moved into line slowly, others wanted to stay and try him again, impress him with their celebrity, wit or money. Nick didn't like people who didn't step lively out of his doorway when asked. It didn't matter if you were a prince, a president, or a big boss friend of Frank's, you'd better move your ass, please. People who had greased Nick's palm over the years now expected royal treatment. It was a master class in diplomacy, Kelly the Belly style.

"Get in line, pal. I can do nothing f'you tonight. Ya see I'm working here, right?" If the guy was a real pal, he'd fall into line. If he wanted to be cute and come back again, Nicky would turn on him like a mangy dog, "Please…" the Belly would stand broad as a fence with his pointing finger like a knife in front of his face. Sane people got in line. Toots would always be there to back Nick up so it would take at least four other men to seriously challenge them. Nick carried a police department standard issue snub nose .38 on his calf, just in case.

Monte showed up at 5 PM and stared down the sidewalk at the line of people for several seconds, waving to friends. The relief was intoxicating. He was the king of Broadway for that precarious moment. He lingered, taking it in while it lasted.

"Gotta hand it to ya boss," the Belly confided, admitting his original doubt about the whole idea of an uptown club. Monte shook his hand.

"We're in clover, pal." Monte said as he walked in.

Just inside the door, Entratter was gleaming from head to toe - pomaded black hair to patent leather shoes. Ebony and gold studs bisected his chest, a perfect white shirt and vest framed in a rich black tuxedo. Everything was ready to go, more or less. The staff was there, the bars were stocked, the kitchen was hot. Now the only thing left was to turn it on and see how it worked. Monte gathered him in. They went over last minute concerns about the waiters blocking the view of the show, extra seating. Chit chat. Things looked good for the opening week, but beyond that they wouldn't discuss their chances. They both remembered a dozen other big opening weeks of places that had disappeared soon after. They were in the hands of God now.

The doors opened exactly at 6 o'clock as advertised. The flood of money rolled up to the front door and then poured in. The jinx instantly vanished from 10 East 60th Street. The first coats were checked, the first cigarettes were lit. Ice cubes clinked into a glass sounding the opening notes of a 30-year party.

Showtime. The opening night crowd settled into the showroom. Over their excited conversation and the gentle clatter of glass and silverware, the lights dimmed except for a single spotlight at center stage. The noise faded as the first bars of Joe E. Lewis' upbeat theme song "Chicago" sailed out from the bandstand. The king of nightclub comics trotted into the spot as applause overwhelmed the music. He took his moment of acknowledgement and then launched his friend's flagship nightclub on its historic voyage.

"Good evening, ladies and gentlemen and welcome to the Copacabana." He calmly surveyed the expectant crowd on three sides of him, stacked in tiers. They were silent, hanging on his next words, not wanting to miss the first gag. The exact moment he had their total concentration, when the silence became so swollen with expectation that it was about to break and not a split-second before, he jumped ahead of the crowd and broke it, "You might as well face it, *that* was my opening line." Over the relief laughter, he jumped ahead again, "For my first number... Oh yes, I want you to meet..." he glanced back to his life-long accompanist Austin Mack at the piano, "My pianist: The late George Apley." Austin rose solemnly and bowed. "Mr. Austin Mack," Joe added seriously. Austin stood for another bow.

"Austin plays a pretty good piano. I think it's a Steinway." He crossed to the piano, picked up a Scotch highball and saluted his people with it. "Post time!" he exclaimed like a racetrack announcer. His people returned his salute with drinks of their own. Joe led the way taking a long swig. His people followed and they were all off to the races together.

"Some people say I drink too much. And I resent it." He sounded genuinely annoyed. "I don't deny it. I just resent it." He took another drink to calm himself. The place was starting to percolate with laughter. He put the drink down on the piano and came back to the spotlight.

"My doctor says not to drink, it cuts down your years. Maybe... but looking around, I see more old drunks than old doctors." From the back, Austin played intro after intro nudging him toward his opening song.

"Voom! Voom!" Joe cleared his throat loudly and warmed up his wrecked vocal cords. This necessary preparation had become part of his act. "Voom! Voom!" he repeated, searching for something close to the key.

"Arrangements. Everything's arrangements." Austin continued to circle around the opening bar of the song. "The title of my first song: 'Since I Lost My Glasses, I Wonder Who's Kissing Me Now?' It's one of those songs if you want to go to the john and miss it, you won't have to shoot yourself." He stopped and listened for Austin's lead in and the dauntless pianist came around in the melody again.

"Austin is really indispensable," he said. "When I get out here with a little load, and I'm searching for a number to sing, he just gives me one cue and I'm completely lost."

Eventually he parodied Gershwin's "It Ain't Necessarily So" from Porgy and Bess. He set up the song by enacting a meeting with a young man who tells him, "Joe, You Is My Pappy Now" to which he responds, "It ain't necessarily, Joe."

My doctor says he ought to know, he told me I'm no Romeo.
He lifted my tunic and said, "Look, a eunuch,"
But it ain't necessarily so.
I'm too antiseptic, that's why I'm a skeptic.
If that kid's my moxie, I got him by proxy,
It ain't necessarily, Joe.

Joe loosened his cords with another slug of highball and returned to the mike to the opening strains of "Tea for Two".

"My next song hasn't any humorous words but the music is very funny." The first-nighters were with him no matter what and laughed along at the funny and not-so-funny just because they loved him. He sensed the door was wide open for him and poured out pure silliness.

"Everybody's breeding things. I crossed a rooster with a rooster – and got a very cross rooster."

"A friend of mine crossed a chicken with a racing form – and got a hen that lays odds." He reached into his pocket and came up with a handful of race track tickets. "I'm a great horse follower – and the horses I follow follow horses." He threw the losing stubs in the air like confetti. "A thousand bucks a day for props," he sighed. The place was rolling and he stepped it up a notch. He stepped off the stage to a ringside table and picked up a customer's highball.

"I drink to be sociable," he advised, "and I'm the biggest Socialist in town." He saluted his benefactor, raising his drink, "There is an old Norwegian saying, 'Svensky in Potorsky Grebin Novoja." He paused mid-salute and his unwitting accomplice jumped into the trap, "What's it mean?"

Joe looked at the man puzzled, "How the hell should I know? I read it on a can of sardines. I must mean something." He pulled out an empty chair at the table and sat with the dazzled couple. "Mind if I do this sitting down?" he asked, "I hate to stand up while the room is in motion." He settled in at the table, completely relaxed with only a rough idea of what he was likely to do or say next. He launched into his next musical number.

It's easy to grin when your ship comes in
And you've got the stock market beat.
But the lad worthwhile is the man who can smile
When his shorts are too tight in the seat.

Those who knew Joe's act recognized the opening stanza of his trademark ditty, "Sam, You Made the Pants Too Small."

For the next 30 minutes Joe expertly navigated the ebb and flow of the crowd's mood. The six Copa girls recently dubbed by Monte the *Samba Sirens*, were lined up on the stairs ready to make their debut to the nightclub world. Joe introduced them, "These kids kick so hard, they hit themselves in the back of the head. That's what's wrong with them." The *Sirens* came on and Joe trotted off the way he came on - to his signature song "Chicago" and well-deserved applause. The *Samba Sirens* launched into their flamboyant opening dance routine while the first night crowd caught their breath.

Monte stayed in the back nursing one scotch and soda all night, alert for any mishap. The place was soaring and he was giddy with relief. In the clanging, steaming kitchen, Podell sweated under his tuxedo, cursed his low place in life and plotted his escape.

CHAPTER 20

BROADWAY'S FAVORITE SON

A February blizzard howled down 60th Street, blowing powder snow up the skirts of several hundred ladies waiting on the sidewalk outside the Copa. The line of freezing women and their hopeful escorts, snaked halfway to Madison Avenue, then doubled back on itself. Word was out – the Copa was the hottest spot in town.

Chief of Columbia Studios, Harry Cohn, sat up front during the second show. There was a certain something about one of the Copa*'s Samba Sirens* that he thought might translate to the movies. He wanted to meet her. He called his waiter over and wanted a meeting with the Boss, now.

Upstairs in the lounge, the Boss was sitting with Abe Lastfogel, second banana under Georgie Woods at the *William Morris* talent agency.

"What am I gonna say, no?" Lastfogel leaned back into the shadows surrounding the little cocktail table. The glaring white surgical bandages over his new nose faded out like the closing credits at the end of a movie. He didn't want anyone to see him except Monte. Monte was business, maybe the most important business in New York, for his stable of singers and comedians. A shot at the Copa was almost a guaranteed screen test in

Hollywood. Abe had to come out and push for them - nose job or no nose job - or Georgie would take him apart worse than Bugsy Siegel's surgeon friend.

"Benny put up 5 g's for it, so here I am." Abe sipped his seltzer through a straw, slowly, doctor's orders. No booze and nothing strenuous. Earlier that month, at Meyer's *Clover Club* in Florida, his good friend Benny Siegel, *Bugsy* to the reporters, told Abe he was tired of looking at the curved beak attached to the front of Abe's face. He wanted it changed so that the little agent looked decent. Abe had tried every trick of negotiating he'd learned in his 20 years of agenting under the old man William Morris himself, but Benny wasn't listening. The prick. As soon as Abe heard Benny say he was going to put up the $5,000 dollars himself, he knew he was sunk. They didn't call Benny *Bugsy* for nothing. He shot people who refused to shake his hand. What would he do if Abe refused his $5,000 dollar nose job?

Benny promised it would be good for business and so far he'd been right. After the operation, Benny pulled all kinds of strings to show off the new nose he'd bought for Abe. Benny liked to joke that he'd sue Abe if he blew his own nose without Benny's permission. It was one of Benny's favorite jokes. Abe Lastfogel sipped his seltzer quietly in the shadows as the waiter from the showroom found Monte. The waiter whispered in Monte's ear and Abe knew right away he was losing his audience.

The waiter said that Cohn wanted a meeting and it couldn't wait. Monte excused himself and made his way down the stairs to the showroom. Monte didn't like Cohn, didn't like his politics or the way he did business at Columbia Studios. Cohn's business approach amounted to little more than double-dealing and blackmail in Monte's opinion. The mogul was short on taste, long on treachery, preferring to steal talent rather than try to recognize it and develop it on his own. But compared to looking at Abe, who just had his Jewish nose carved into a Gentile one at the command of a Jewish gangster, even a meeting with Cohn seemed like a good idea.

The studio chief muttered on about the great gams and also the talent of Maggie James, the most demure of all the girls and a particular favorite of Monte's. Cohn wasn't lecherous, simply crude, but this was a girl under Monte's protection he was angling towards.

Monte, in the oldest part of himself, was still a Knight of the Round Table - the image instilled by his mother. All women, especially ones under his protection, were to be treated as virtuous ladies. To hear Cohn degrading them was too much.

Cohn spoke of the girls like meat on the hoof, and worse. He was a dunce who imagined Monte was enjoying his vulgarities.

"That's the problem with people who don't drink," Monte interjected, deliberately off track.

"Wha..?" Cohn didn't waste breath on complete words.

"People who don't drink. Like you." Monte said.

"What about it?" Cohn didn't usually drink, so the champagne may have been affecting him.

"They can never tell when they've had too much." It was a stare down then, Cohn looking for the right meaning and Monte hoping to stare it into him.

"You sayin' I'm drunk?"

"That's right, pal. Sure am." This was a gentleman's insult, and one small push away from physical attack.

Cohn was shocked. No one was ever openly hostile to him. No one in Hollywood could afford it. "You're a crumb and a nobody," he answered.

The table got very quiet and it wasn't because the singer was coming on. She was a new girl, only 22, named Lena Horne. Monte was satisfied that business was settled between him and Cohn. The other studio chiefs around the table, drinking first class on the studio's tab, waited to see if the boss had had the final word.

"Pay your tab and then get the hell out," was the final word. The music swelled and Lena launched into her opening song. Monte stayed at the table and turned all his attention to Lena, enchanted like a child at Christmas. He was completely comfortable while Cohn silently fumed. When the number was over, Monte got up and left. On the way out he caught the waiter for Cohn's table and told him to give Cohn his tab for the evening. He had a hundred friends upstairs who wanted that table.

As he passed up the aisle, three hundred pairs of eyes discreetly watched him go. Monte caught the eye of a lucky dozen or so, nodding acknowledgment to them, as he moved though his club.

All thoughts of success and failure had vanished from his everyday life. The club had moved into the realm of phenomenon and Monte's place among the power brokers of show business was confirmed. He finally had the riches of America pouring into his pockets as he pictured it would as a young boy walking over the Brooklyn Bridge in his Buster Brown suit. He was now the Rockefeller, Henry Ford and Charles Lindberg of nightlife. His *Copacabana* had eclipsed every other spot in New York from its opening night and never looked back. Every seat at every table, downstairs in the showroom and upstairs in the lounge, was filled and re-filled three times a night with more waiting outside for a chance to get in. The place was the top-grossing club in New York with $14,000 coming in on an average night in tax-free 1940 dollars. His only worry was one that was familiar to his partner Frank - what to do with packing crates full of cash.

Six months after opening night even the waiters were buying expensive property around town. This was it. The top of the heap. Nothing could top it. Monte had won the biggest crap game in town, any town. He broke the house, and now he was the house.

The Copa had lost the new carpet and fresh paint smell. Now it was sharp from tobacco smoke and sour from thousands of smoking, eating, gabbing humans and their food. The smell fought with ammonia and pine oil. It was a saloon now, broken in and stained in the corners but it was also an institution. Everybody was going to the bank on this one.

It was a comforting thought while it lasted but it didn't last long. The high stakes game was over, had been for months and he had the biggest bankroll of his life in his kick. He needed a new game badly. What good was money if you didn't have a game? He sat in the manager's office pasting columns in his press book and plotting his next move as Max Siderow clicked away on the adding machine surrounded by stacks of greenbacks and bags of silver coin.

Usually, Monte showed up at the club just around noon to get to work. He always arrived with a few newspapers under his arm. Pedro, the chef, got in about the same time. Pedro went to his small office in the pantry, Monte's first stop was the manager's office just inside the front door to the left. He entered and hung his suit coat on the rack in the waiting area outside his inner office. Inside at his desk, he stacked the day's harvest of ink. He sat down to work, clipping articles while he made his phone calls to keep the talent coming and the ink flowing. An hour or two of this was as much as he could take at one sitting. He padded down the stairs, across the showroom and dropped in for a visit with Pedro. Over a glass of pineapple juice and soup bowl full of what he believed were magically health-giving lychee nuts on ice, they talked about Pedro's difficult life as Podell's constant target. The chef suffered both from the man's frustration and from his endless pursuit of corruption. Suppliers were picked by connection to the right people, not by having the best goods, so Pedro's trusted suppliers were being steadily bumped out of the competition. The pressure from Podell was constant. No dish ever went out of the kitchen that wasn't perfect by his standards. Food got flung back at the chefs with the curse, "Dat don't look fuckin' appetizin'!"

The quality of the food and the efficiency of the operation was important but money was sacred. Throughout the night, a steady stream of waiters brought him running cash totals from the bars on both floors. These happy figures he recorded in code for presentation later to boss Costello. If, at the end of the night, the figures didn't add up to the register tallies, an unlucky bartender might find a frosty ice pick laid alongside his nose, the steel point just under his eye. Money was Podell's power and he protected it with his life. Wasting Jules Podell's money was unhealthy but stealing it could be fatal.

He relentlessly devised traps and interrogated kitchen staff, looking for any hint of thievery. A pinch of salt could be worth a kitchen worker's life if Podell saw them put it in a pocket. The simple rule that Podell understood intimately was, "If you're stealing a little, you're stealing a lot." He practiced it himself. All he had to do was watch the kitchen staff and bartenders, talk to them a little and he would know for sure who was stealing and who wasn't.

More than one unlucky young Filipino was dragged through the kitchen, out the back door and onto the street by an irate Podell. Very unlucky ones made it all the way to the hospital. Pedro did not have an easy life.

Carl Erbe called up and told his old hobo pal he was now in the club business too. Carl was too sharp a businessman to just let his old protégé skim up the easy money in nightclubs all by himself. He didn't give up promoting dentists during daylight hours, he simply added a night shift, shilling for his own spot, *Club Zanzibar* on 51st street. The club took its theme from Carl's family roots in South Africa. He decorated the place in bamboo, tribal shields and zebra skins. It couldn't attract headline talent like the Copa, but the place turned a decent profit. He never once asked Monte for assistance or even guidance. Even though his protégé was now king of the nightclubs, he never paid him that deference. He simply copied the format of the Copa and dipped his cup into the river of money just downstream from his old buddy.

Months earlier, when he heard of Monte's divorce from Julie, Carl called to mend fences with his oldest friend. All the petty jealously was swept aside and soon they were back into their old, familiar orbit. They holed up in *Dave's Blue Room* again where the skewed romance had begun and where dozens of friends did their best to wipe it from Monte's mind.

It was easy living once again for the two bindlestiffs. Now they were friendly competitors, each with more than enough business of their own. The old closeness was rekindled and soon they were visiting with the old man, Monte's father, Charles, at the Taft Hotel. The three of them sat on the porch of the hotel while Carl re-told the tales of his youthful boxcar adventures with Monte. It was soon clear that Charles didn't enjoy these stories. It hurt him to know that his eldest son had squandered his youth as a vagabond rather than developing his sharp, if undisciplined mind. It was shameful. Carl soon got the stink-eye from Monte and clammed up about the old days. Charles had no use for the colorful stories of Broadway characters, even if they were about his own son. But he did appreciate some of the new found benefits of Monte's success.

The old man enjoyed seeing his son's name in the paper associated with all types of celebrated people. He mentioned reading that Robert Benchley, the noted writer, and Babe Ruth had been in the Copa on the same night recently. This was an accomplishment by his lights and a source of pride. It was also the old man's way of fishing for an invitation and introduction to Benchley since he had no interest in baseball even if it was Babe Ruth. Through Monte, Charles had been introduced to Walter Wanger, Damon Runyon, Ed Sullivan and a handful of recognizable names. He imagined Monte was a friend of everyone who came in and could arrange any introduction. He was keen to meet intellectual types like Benchley who might be roped into a discussion of his favorite topic, socialism.

During these interludes at the Taft, Monte seemed far away, fidgety. He knew his father was a bore to most people, but that wasn't what bothered him. His friends could handle themselves in any conversation. The wild success of the Copa hadn't mellowed him at all. The flood of money, the vast new power he wielded, even his father's approval that he had sought since childhood didn't finally put Monte at ease. In fact, as Carl observed, it was just the opposite.

Frank revealed the second phase of his plans for his partnership with Monte. His Saratoga casino, *Piping Rock*, could use a boost for the coming summer season from a few high-class headliners and Monte was just the guy to deliver them. The Copa show including the *Samba Sirens* and supporting acts was moved to the lobby of the *New Yorker Hotel* for the summer. The club's tables, chairs and headliner, Joe E. Lewis, were transported up to Saratoga Springs for a summer of horse racing and highballs.

The set-up couldn't have been any sweeter. Joe E. and Monte, the two Broadway bums, as they referred to themselves, took full advantage of Frank Costello's hypnotic spell over the woodland village. They amused themselves with games of croquet and cards under shady trees during the day and frolicked with the social elite of Europe and America at night. They sailed on tidy white yachts on Lake Placid, strolled the manicured gardens of bucolic country estates and enjoyed the attentions of ladies of immeasurable wealth. As sweet as the deal was, it didn't hold Monte's attention for long. He was already on to something much bigger and much bolder than even the Copa. And although the first families of Saratoga were very hospitable, it was soon clear that he and Joe were not being encouraged to spend time with the marriageable daughters of the area. Even though they were wealthy and obviously close colleagues of the powerfully fascinating Mr. Costello, they were Jews. Their summer place was the Catskills on the far side of the Hudson, certainly not the Saratoga horse country. They were entertainers and hopefully, not neighbors.

In the cities of America, jazz had broken into full swing and big bands were blasting horns and pounding tom-toms. Hepcats were jitterbugging themselves into frenzies. The dance scene had gone completely wild, almost unhinged. Girls were performing acrobatics in loose skirts that flew up revealing many of the intoxicating treasures of youth. The men encouraged and assisted these acrobatics by swinging, spinning and tossing the girls over their heads and between their legs. It was the full, primal, grunting exuberance of life and shocking sexual anarchy. War was coming. The youth of America and Europe danced against the sweeping darkness, wringing the last sweated drops of life from themselves before night closed in.

The music shouted freedom and Monte answered instantly. Here, finally, was the liberating music of his soul. It tapped his store of enthusiasm and transported him to the wild, ragtime nights of his youth. Madness was loose again in the world and he created his dream world to shut it out.

He had had a vision back then as a young boy in Brooklyn Heights, that had withered steadily under the chains of responsibility and maturity. It was a childlike vision of a place filled with music, a pure music that freed him finally from all his responsibilities. In this place he wouldn't be Jewish, or the eldest or a foreigner. He'd be exactly like everybody else. He'd be what he most wanted to be, carefree.

The new vision Monte saw was world shattering and he now had the means to make it happen. He had found his larger game to play and it would be all his, no partners need apply.

Monte's new vision was simply a nightclub for everyone. It was suddenly possible that the world might have come far enough, that this new energetic music was powerful enough and that he was now influential enough to actually create a place where everyone, for a few moments, could just have fun. It was possible that the little boy who was never allowed to just play would finally have his carefree kingdom.

The social mix of his new club would break all existing social rules, the scale of it would be magnitudes beyond anything that had ever existed. He leased Madison Square Garden from April through August for $100,000 dollars and named it *Monte Proser's Dance Carnival.* It would take another $150,000 dollars to equip and decorate the place. He was prepared to lay all the money he had - a quarter million dollars - on his new brainstorm. It was a gambler's dream, the wager of a lifetime - epic success or financial annihilation. Adrenaline flooded through him and burned a hole through any prudence he had left. It was a hole that would never heal. He was now a confirmed gambling addict and he couldn't wait to throw the dice.

The reaction from the Broadway crowd, other than the columnists who saw a madman they could exploit for catchy headlines, was stunned silence. The move cast a shadow over the entire nightclub industry. If this behemoth was half as popular as the Copa, would anyone be left for the other clubs? The rumor mill was roused from its summer slumber and thrown into high gear. Among those in the know, it was murmured that Proser had broken ranks and was bent on total domination. It was whispered that his class act was just that, an act. He had revealed his true vulgarian roots and resorted to a low-brow carnival angle. It was mass production of nightclub entertainment. It would lower standards and more importantly prices, for everyone. *Dance Carnival* - it sounded like a muddy midway where 10-cent beer was on tap.

Certain unnamed sources had it on good authority that this was a move by the mob to consolidate its hold on the business and cut out the middlemen – the club owners. The rumblings soon made their way to the ears of the Little Flower in the mayor's office. He immediately swung his tiny, wing-tipped feet off the huge mahogany mayoral desk. His nemesis, Frank Costello, was on the move again. Costello had gained a critical foothold with the Copa and now he and his front man Proser were mounting a frontal assault against the peace and prosperity of his town. A massive infection of public corruption was swelling on the West Side. If it was allowed to fester, the damage could be irreversible. New York would become another New Orleans, riddled with vice and decay.

While Frank Costello was enjoying his summer in Saratoga gratefully out of the public eye, in Manhattan, Monte was sailing affably along on a river of black ink. A torrent of giddy speculation on the nature, scope and design of Proser's extravaganza at the Garden was the topic of the moment. It was a welcome tonic for the summer news doldrums and a counter-point relief to the depressing drumbeat of war stories. In the papers, he became *Broadway's Favorite Son*, the wily *Boniface of Broadway* and the *Hobo Who Made Good*. For the first time in his career, the papers were pursuing him for material about himself. He had become his own client and his angle was spokesman and public face of New York nightlife. He was, at that moment, the authority on virtually any topic he wished to speak about. They printed it all. He had surpassed all his projects and previous clients and stepped boldly into the spotlight himself – the oracle of the Great White Way. His face, sporting owlish round black glasses, became a pen and ink caricature as distinctive and widely known as that of any Broadway star. His exploits as a boxcar bindlestiff and his rise to fame through speakeasies and later Hollywood became his legend. He was the happy-go-lucky hobo the way Jack Benny was the wealthy cheapskate or

Valentino was the sulky lover. He was the little everyman who roped the American dream through good, old-fashioned pluck and brought it down to earth for everyone to share. Winchell, Hellinger, Sullivan, all the columnists became his cheering section. He was officially welcomed into the pantheon of Broadway - a singular, unique character. From that point on, no matter what place or show or star he was promoting, he was the main attraction.

Madison Square Garden was made over into a tropical paradise, this time the scale was larger than life sized. Much larger. The focal point of the décor was a 70-foot natural rock waterfall that stood to one side of the elevated stage. At the apex of the waterfall a South Seas siren danced a striptease, a version of the *Dance of the Seven Veils*, removing layers of silk. Twenty of Monte's signature white coconut palms dotted the quarter acre dance floor. This time they were seven stories tall, like the waterfall. The largest clubs of the time accommodated a few hundred people, the *Dance Carnival* had a capacity for over 15,000 - 5,000 of whom were expected to be dancing at any one time. Three dance bands, Benny Goodman, Charlie Barnet and Larry Clinton were scheduled to play in continuous rotation while the Mutual Radio Network broadcast the music live to the nation. The only thing that wasn't large about the place was the price of admission. Tickets were 66 cents because 66 was a lucky number and mostly because it was a price anyone could afford.

Monte Proser's Dance Carnival elevated its creator to national prominence. On June 11, 1940 Monte was introduced to the nation on Fred Allen's radio show. Allen was the most popular broadcaster on the airwaves at the time. A tautly scripted "interview" was preceded by an exchange between Allen and one of the stock characters on the show, "Portland" – a naïve young woman with the voice of a wide-eyed Betty Boop. After informing his listeners that it was National Flag Week and encouraging them to display the flag at their homes and places of business, he noticed Portland who entered to audience applause.

"And now... oh hello Portland. Say, what's the big idea? What're you doing with all those traveling bags?"

The Betty Boop voice responded, "Well, I'm leaving for Hollywood."

"You're leaving for Hollywood? Don't you know that another girl in Hollywood is like one more flea on a St. Bernard dog?" The audience tittered politely. "Why go out there?"

"Well I've been on your program a long time," the starlet pouted.

"Oh, you mean you want more money?" Allen played the concerned boss.

"No, I'm getting a living wage…" the actress dropped the cutesy accent and referred to the script in front of her in her own voice, "…it says here." The audience was shocked into a genuine laugh.

"Well I'm not getting any place," she said. "Girls get ahead in Hollywood. Look at Lana Turner and Priscilla Lane?"

"Well they've got something. Those girls have glamour."

"Well how can I get glamour?"

"The quickest way to get glamour, Portland, is to hire a press agent."

"What does a press agent do?" Portland trilled, asking the question for the benefit of the audience beyond Broadway. The skit was creaking under the weight of phoniness but served its purpose of introducing what Monte did for a living.

"Well you'll find out in just a minute because our guest tonight is one of the country's leading press agents. He's a master exploiter, a café owner and only last week he turned Madison Square Garden into the biggest dance hall in the world. Ladies and Gentlemen, may I present Broadway's dynamo, Monte Proser." Brassy introduction music and applause heralded Monte's introduction to Americans at home.

"Well, good evening, Monte."

"Good evening Fred."

"Well it certainly is a pleasure to meet the man behind New York's most popular nightclubs – the Beachcomber, the Copacabana, the new Piping Rock Club at Saratoga and the new Dance Carnival at Madison Square Garden. Y'know, I don't even know what to call you Monte? Are you an entrepreneur, a restaurateur, a dance-a-teur or just what is your title?"

"I think you'd be safe in just calling me a salesman, Fred."

"Well you're rather soft spoken for a super-salesman, Monte."

"Noise doesn't get results in my business, Fred. A good salesman has to have ideas."

"Well, you say you're a salesman Monte and still you have no samples here. Now what is it that you sell?"

"Well I sort of specialize in glamour."

"Glamour. Glamour is the mystery quality suddenly acquired by a mediocre actress just before Hollywood releases her first picture. Is that right?"

"Whatever it is, I've been selling glamour for the past fifteen years."

"You mean you've been glamorizing restaurants, glorifying the Great American cover charge?"

"Not quite Fred. Until a short time ago I was a press agent out in Hollywood."

"Ahh, Hollywood. Hollywood, the home of the verbal fanfare. Where everything is glorified from a picture star to a cheese burger… which isn't such a far cry in some cases." The audience laughed at the soft joke. "For whom did you work out there in adjective-land?"

"I was with Walter Wanger at the United Artist Studios."

"And what stars did you publicize?"

"Joan Bennett, Charles Laughton, Hedy Lamarr and many others."

"Well tell me how does a publicity man go about glamorizing a person, Monte? You can't just grab a girl from behind a steam table in a cafeteria and make her a star, or can you?"

"No, if a girl wants to get any place in the theatre or Hollywood she has to have talent."

"Well all right. Well let's take a mythical case. Let's say an obscure blues singer is working in a chili bistro on 52nd Street – the El Stencho…" this struck the audience as funny too. "…and her name is Mazie Mulligan. Now you're called in as a publicity press agent to make Mazie a star. Now what happens?"

"Well in publicizing a person Fred, the first thing I look for is a gadget."

"What is a gadget?"

"Well, a gadget is sort of a thing."

"A thing? What's a thing?"

"A thing is what we call a gimmick."

"Oh now wait a minute…" The audience tittered at Fred's frustration. "…we're not getting any place. Just what is a gimmick?"

"A gimmick or a gadget is an angle, a slant."

"Oh a slant, you finally came across a word I savvy. A slant. What you mean is you have found something unique about Mazie Mulligan which you can build up?"

"Exactly. Every good press campaign is based on a gadget."

"Well Mazie has a voice range of three octaves, she's a Vassar graduate and she has red hair. Now do any of these suggest a gimmick?"

"The red hair is perfect, Fred."

"What about Mazie's three octaves and her background?"

"Well there's no glamour attached to a voice or a college education but with red hair you've got something."

"And what is the first thing you'd do with Mazie Mulligan?"

With a little laugh Monte said, "I'd get rid of that name." The audience laughed along politely.

"Get rid of the name… too long for a marquee you think? Well what would you do?"

"I'd give her a name to match her red hair."

"A name to match her red hair, for instance?"

"Well I'd call her something like uh…" Monte pretended to search for a name, "…Cherry Dare."

Fred helped Monte spell out how he would make Cherry Dare into a star, then got around to the *Dance Carnival*, "Well tell me, what about this latest venture of yours in Madison Square Garden? Isn't that supposed to be the largest nightclub in the world?"

"Yes it is, Fred. We can accommodate about fifteen thousand people. We have three name bands playing every night, five thousand jitterbuggers jitterbugging, refreshments and sandwiches. It's really quite a sight."

"It's really a Rainbow Room for John Doe."

"Yes it's the one place in New York where everybody can have a good time."

"You know if you keep doing things in a big way Monte, you'll soon be known as Billy Rose with the water drained off." This referred to the diminutive producer of the spectacular "Aquacades" at the 1939 New York World's Fair and San Francisco Expedition, an extravagant water show starring Olympic divers and swimmers like Johnny Weissmuller who had become famous as Tarzan in Hollywood.

"No, Fred, Billy's in a class all by himself."

"Yes, I hear Billy Rose is thinking about putting a floor show in the Grand Canyon with Superman as the Master of Ceremonies. Well thanks a lot for this little peak into the fabulous land of press agentry Monte."

"It's been a pleasure Fred and I might add, a gimmick."

"I get it. Thank you and goodnight, Monte Proser."

Fred Allen introduced the next act, a singer named, Wynn Murray, billed as Texaco's Girlfriend.

Monte walked out of the CBS studios on 52nd Street into the summer night and waiting gaggle of pals including Eddie Jaffe. Eddie was hot to get an item for Winchell before the great man himself corralled Monte at the club later on. Monte was officially a hot item, at least for tonight.

Eddie fell into step as his meal ticket strode out with the gang. It was the new star's victory lap around his familiar training course. It was dinner hour, Wednesday night, normally a slow night but it was the second week of June, the summer was new and still cool at night. The streets around Broadway bounced with life. Everyone seemed to be celebrating Monte's rise to fame but in fact they had more important news on their minds. Two weeks earlier, the German submarine *U-69* sank the neutral American merchant ship *Robin Moor*. President Roosevelt denounced the attack furiously. All German and Italian assets in the US were about to be frozen. Immigration quotas were cut to 25% of previous levels to stem the tide of refugees flooding into the country.

That day, June 11, the second raid on the Jews of Amsterdam had just sent hundreds more to Nazi labor camps. The only good news was that the undaunted British had swarmed with their *Swordfish* torpedo-bombers and small, V class destroyers against the German super-battleship *Bismarck*, sinking it. At least the German juggernaut was not invincible, but war was several steps closer to America's front door – injecting urgency into the celebrations of the young and able.

CHAPTER 21

JANE BALL

Jane Ball had recently left the sunlit world of high school in Kingston, New York and entered the moonlit realm of shift workers, show folk and high-class criminals at the Dorchester Hotel in London. She danced in Jack Hylton's lively musicals every night and slept in luxurious white goose down comforters until late in the morning. London was thrilling and elegant. Her mother's hand-me-down cloth coat and Jane's old dresses were soon replaced with stylish wraps trimmed in fur. She was fitted with hounds tooth Savile Row suits and gleaming calfskin ladies shoes.

She loved the Londoners who went about their business as if Hitler were just another rude braggart, someone to be ignored. She wrote to her mother that no one seemed that worried about the Germans. In the letters were always several English pound notes. To the stunning young American dancer with honey colored hair and shining green eyes, Londoners avoided speaking about the army rampaging just across the channel. They simply refused to be afraid, publicly, and Jane fell in love with them because of it. She loved their quirkiness, their plain stubborn optimism, their iron spines. She suddenly felt more at home in London than she did in Kingston. The quiet fight in the English reminded her of her beloved, tough-minded Jim Morgan who also wasn't afraid of anybody.

Months earlier, after she'd passed the audition for the Hylton show and ran into the hallway of the rehearsal hall to tell Jim Morgan, the giant Irishman stood up and hugged her for what he knew would be the last time as her mentor and protector, her adoptive father. She was part of the bigger world now and he was suddenly part of her past, her childhood. She would be traveling to Europe. She would be with new friends, starting a new life. But before Jim let her go, he took her by the hand and strode back into the dance studio to check out the head man - his final act as her protector.

Jack Hylton looked to be something of a dandy with manicured fingernails and prissiness to his greeting. He fussed like a girl but came around to business when Jim spoke directly to him.

"How much you give them to eat?" The man didn't flinch when he explained that the hotel in London provided all the meals. The girls could order anything on the menu, as long as they didn't put on weight. That was his only concern. Jim half wanted to find an excuse to queer the deal, haul his Janey out of there, back to her end stool at his *Morgan's Tavern* where she'd done her homework for years. But he knew that that time had passed. His little blond-haired, green-eyed mascot was a grown woman on her own and she was never coming back.

Jim looked the man in the eye while he held the contract in his hand. The man smiled but didn't look away. It was hopeless. He gave the document over to Jane and she signed.

He was happy for her new life and heartbroken all at once. He'd seen Jane stand up to drunks twice her size, demand and get an apology for some comment she didn't like. He saw her playing endless reading games with her younger brother Andy, doting over him, building up his confidence. He saw her dancing with her surprising fierceness, sharp and quick, so that even he could tell she was something special.

She was looking at him now and he knew she'd read his mind again or maybe his old, busted up saloonkeeper's face was giving him away again. They didn't have to say anything.

He smiled a phony smile for her that fooled no one. At least she wasn't running off with some young buck without a pot. She'd be okay, he told himself.

In London, Jane was intrigued by English men. There was none of the leering and swagger of their American counterparts. She'd seen enough of the rough-handed, braying donkeys that came around *Morgan's Tavern*, to spot a lout a mile off, so she was able to let down her guard with the English and enjoy their gentlemanly ways. Chivalry was not dead in England.

The Jack Hylton troupe took a week's engagement in Rome. It was another revelation. The Italians were shocking and completely un-English. She had never seen the fiery Italian culture up close. Social life seemed chaotic. Many Italian men were as crude about their sexuality as any New York barfly but others were deeply romantic. One in particular was quiet and Mediterranean handsome. He was like Rome – warm and completely unlike the dripping overcast of London and English propriety. It was the perfect week-long holiday from her already delightful life in London. She took the Italian as a lover. It was daring – a fling – she had never even dreamed of doing anything like it before, but the setup in Rome was a once in a lifetime chance. She had her own room in a small pensione, so gossip would be kept to a minimum.

On one of their afternoons, Jane and her Italian posed for a photograph in a café. He stared into the camera in the foreground brooding perhaps about Jane's cool, almost English reserve. He was Michaelangelo's David in flesh and black ringlet hair. Jane appeared small and delicate in the background peering over his massive shoulder. She seemed distant and resolute perhaps sanguine about her thoughts to abandon him when she returned to England, perhaps just satisfied and thoroughly relaxed with the most exotically handsome man she had ever imagined.

The week ended. Springtime was moving toward summer, generally a good season for London hotels. The Dorchester expected the return of Hylton's show. Jane and the other girls returned tanned and loaded with bags of Italian fashions. The summer production was going to be the most lavish ever. Jane tucked the tiny photo of her Italian lover away in her jewelry box intending to forget about him entirely, but even many years later, she never quite succeeded.

On May 11 word arrived. All Americans were to return to the US immediately. They were being evacuated. The day before, May 10, 1941, Rudolf Hess, the deputy Fuhrer of Nazi Germany, had flown to Scotland. He was attempting to negotiate for the safety of England, claiming that Hitler would spare the English if they would just let the Nazis have North Africa. If not, Germany would crush England by naval blockade. They would ring the British Isles in steel and let them starve through the upcoming winter. Hess was sent packing. The English resolutely refused to accept his offer. With typical English spine, they informed the representative of the vastly superior German military, that if Germany attempted to invade North Africa, they would answer to the English Army for it.

The next day the entire Jack Hylton production was put on a boat to America with a few hours' notice. By the evening of May 11th, they were sailing toward home. The magic kingdom that had opened its heart to Jane was suddenly sinking under the waves like Atlantis. It was soon a small gray dot on the horizon. And then it was gone. The perfect kingdom and just beyond it, the perfect looking man, suddenly vanished. A flame red sun set in the West splashing fire over the storm clouds. The ship teetered over the waves toward the sunset. Below it, somewhere in the black water, Nazi submarines prowled for prey.

That evening, May 11th, the Germans replied to the English rebuke of Hess. They attacked London with the full fury of the German air force. Bombs rained down on London and Portsmouth from 155 German planes. They dropped 140 tons of high explosive and over 40,000 incendiary bombs, deliberately targeting English civilian population centers. The first structure hit and set ablaze in London was the Dorchester Hotel.

The harrowing Atlantic crossing took some of the bubbles out of Jane's champagne life. The boat was jammed with refugees of all types. The high-born squeezed into the cabins above deck where they squabbled endlessly over the accommodations, while the unlucky working-class sweated together quietly down in steerage, below the waterline, where a German torpedo might strike at any moment.

    Jane had been back in New York a little over a week when she realized that the glamour of show business had faded for her. Now, dancing was simply a good paying job and the quickest way to build up cash against the coming war. Her focus was work, the more the better, and as far as sheer physical stamina, almost no one could keep up with her. She auditioned and won a job right away on the Broadway show *Panama Hattie*, directed by the highly respected George Abbott. It was the standard chorus girl schedule, two shows a day and three on Saturday and Sunday, Tuesdays off. This left most girls soaking in a hot bath all day Tuesday. Not Jane. Instead, she went looking for a second job in a nightclub after the evening show. She'd heard about a place called the Copacabana.

CHAPTER 22

THE PARLAY

The unbelievable and for some, the unspeakable, was happening. Blacks and whites were jitterbugging side by side on the dance floor of *Madison Square Garden* – thousands of them. Monte had gone over the $150,000 he had budgeted for decorations, way over, but now it all seemed worth it. Tens of thousands were marveling at the seven story indoor waterfall and its sheer rock face covered with flowers and tropical plants. High on the waterfall's cusp, a maiden performed a seductive dance of the seven veils, stripping gauzy layer after layer while the band swayed below under Monte's towering white palm trees. The action on the dance floor was spectacular, sexually charged and simmering with violence.

On opening night, Memorial Day, Friday, May 30, 1941 just over 31,500 people jammed the Garden to view the spectacle of the largest nightclub in the world. It looked like easy sailing from then on. It looked like another in the string of huge hits Monte seemed to turn out about once a year now.

Inside the Garden, the summer heat and wild swing dancing pushed up the temperature. Not long into Benny Goodman's opening number, a fight erupted. This wasn't unusual for a nightclub except that it was opening night and crowds were generally better behaved on opening nights. Kelly the Belly and his small squad of bouncers quashed the fight, but Nick reported back to Monte. He was worried. By the time he and his men had pushed through a few hundred jitterbuggers to where the trouble was, a dozen more sluggers were in the fight. Nick didn't have the odds of bouncers to bouncees that he liked - at least three to one. And there was no chance of the silent, efficient bum's rush out the door. The combatants were dragged kicking and screaming through a quarter acre of gyrating dancers. His men already had injuries. He didn't like the layout. There were no natural barriers of tables, chairs and aisles like a regular club. There were no hiding places behind a bar or serving station where weapons could be stashed for tough assignments.

Adrenaline dumped into his blood as Monte inhaled sharply. It was a bad omen. Nick was his rock. If he didn't have security he was a sitting duck. He knew how fast a nice atmosphere got queered once the wrong elements saw their advantage. Suddenly, his most fantastic success - the huge, energetic crowd of jitterbuggers - turned into a seething liability. His whole bankroll was suddenly teetering over the abyss and the band hadn't gotten through their first set.

On stage, Benny sensed the tension in the crowd and eased the pace. The music started up again on a slower, romantic theme. The jitterbuggers cooled off. They paired off, black with blacks, whites with whites. They held each other tightly and glided through slow circles. Their attention turned to the band and the beautiful jungle rock wall above the band. The lights dimmed. On cue, spotlights swung from the band to a small figure high overhead on the rocky ledge. The jungle sylph, now bathed in blue moonlight, motioned to the jungle Gods and miraculously water flowed at her feet. It cascaded down the rock face into a natural pool. The band played on and the atmosphere turned quiet. Under the music was the gentle murmur of voices and shuffling of 10,000 feet across the hardwood floor. Suddenly, the crowd backed away from the bandstand. Something was wrong. A rumble floated over to Monte who was just a few feet away. He immediately spotted the problem. The jungle pool was overflowing and spreading out over the dance floor. His gambler instinct sounded the alarm – two bad breaks in a row. There could be a jinx on the place. He headed toward the trouble.

After the pumps were turned off and the waterfall dried up, he sat down at an empty table. He grabbed a saltshaker and threw salt over his left shoulder, then his right. Salt over the right shoulder was a new twist all his own. It was his way of covering his bet, "In case of a tie." He couldn't be sure if there was a jinx on the place, best not to take chances.

At City Hall the next day, the Little Flower saw his opening. This den of corruption in the City's heart was a clear threat to the public welfare. With a little effort he could crush it. He dispatched his Westside precinct boys to find an excuse to close the place. Police precincts on the Westside had been rousting gin joints longer than Monte had been working in them. They never had a problem finding something wrong with a saloon. It was easy if you put a little effort into it.

Jane was in Ernest Carlos' tap class, a second story walk-up, above the Rialto movie theatre on Broadway by 10 AM. She and her roommate, Betsy Blair, paid a dollar for the one-hour class with 50 other professional and aspiring hoofers. They tapped and twirled until the music stopped. After class, they explored the city together. Sometimes with Betsy's boyfriend, Gene, the handsome dance director at the Billy Rose's *Diamond Horseshoe*.

As they discovered New York, Gene always picked the place for lunch, then the matinee, then the museum exhibit they just had to see and the route to walk to get to each. He couldn't stop. He inhaled New York City in great, breathless draughts, no time to waste, no time to rest. He always had the inside dope on the best new Chinese joint or cheap goulash place. He dragged Jane and Betsy along block after block, in and out of each new adventure, critiquing as he strode the world, filling almost all the available space with his opinion. He was a determined and relentless teacher. Betsy and Jane were Gene's rapt students - at least for the first few weeks. Jane gradually found herself tiring of the sound of Gene's voice before he did. She watched him sometimes with a little smile, the one she saved for the pontificating drunks who had bellied up next to her barstool at *Morgan's Tavern* spouting high and mighty ideals. Gene caught the twinge of her challenge in her half smile. He probed and caught the hard edge of her barroom manners, "Whatever you say, Gene," she said.

That was all he had to hear and his Irish was up. She responded with elevated Irish of her own and in no time the two hardheads had frayed the circle of friendship. That was the end of the long, edifying walks with Gene Kelly, the brilliant dancer and great gasbag, and Betsy. In spite of the head butting, Betsy and Jane remained close friends. Betsy even suggested they audition for a night job together uptown at the new hotspot everybody was talking about, the Copacabana. The place was due to re-open with a new season show in a few weeks.

The *Dance Carnival* steamed along through the summer heat but blew a gasket every few hours. People continued to jam the place, but Monte's dream of a dance utopia died little by little, blow by blow, each fistfight dimming its light, pushing it further toward oblivion. The Mayor had Eighth Avenue torn up in front of the place so no traffic could stop there, but still the people poured in. He ringed the place with police who scrutinized every passing man looking for mobsters, but people ignored the cops. No matter what Mayor LaGuardia did, a tide of jitterbuggers continued to pour into the Garden from every part of the city.

Finally, after the police broke up one fight too many, the Mayor claimed the place would spark a race riot and ordered it closed. That was just salt in the wound. It was already clear to Monte that the people of New York City were not ready to have a nightclub that was open to everyone. The *Dance Carnival* broke his heart and took everything he had, even his precious childhood dream that music could create a temporary utopia. The place was everything he had learned and everything he thought he knew about people. He watched it all fade, night after night, like a mirage, like fool's gold running through his clumsy fingers.

LaGuardia quickly lowered the boom, revoking his license to operate at the Garden. Publicly, the Mayor lost no time publicizing his vigilant struggle for the welfare of the people of New York City. Privately, he bragged to anyone who would listen that he had knocked Frank Costello and his front man, Monte Proser, on their keisters. The *Dance Carnival* died on June 20, 1941 after jitterbugging for just 22 days – a small death in a world on the verge of mass murder.

In France, the Vichy government under Nazi occupation banned Jews from holding positions in the government. Later that week it was reported in all the papers that Romanian troops in the town of Jassy inflicted a pogrom that killed 10,000 Jews in one day. That was the week when the world suddenly shrank to the size of Monte's penthouse and almost disappeared completely.

He had nowhere to go and no one he wanted to see. Everything was different. The world just wasn't what he thought it was. He was fundamentally wrong somehow when it came to figuring people out. His day started at a local pub with a wake-me-up, then proceeded on to one bar or another where the conversation could be found. The conversation could be found anywhere – in a taxi, from shoe shine men and shopkeepers – but Monte preferred the equalizer of a bar where liquor loosened the tongue and betrayed hidden thoughts. The conversation was the only one that mattered. It was the only conversation people were having. The conversation, at its root, was what, in the bottom of their hearts, were men? What were they capable of? How far were they willing to go with this war business in light of all that was known about war, particularly since the "War to End All Wars" was less than 20 years ago. If the answer could be found, then possibly a person might be able to guess what the future held, how bad it might get. But frustratingly, the conversation never produced a satisfactory answer. So anesthetizing liquor was ordered to help fuel the intensity of the conversation and dull the terror it produced.

Then, well into his cups, when he ran into friends on the street, he didn't know what to say to them because he wasn't sure what they wanted, not really. Men didn't constantly strive toward the light like living, growing things. That was just the carnie barker's view of things. Men's lives didn't spiral up toward the bright future of dreams, not any more. It seemed like the real direction of life was to bore into the earth like a giant iron screw, into the viciousness at the very center of men's hearts, into anti-Semitic bloodlust and madness.

Monte raged, drunk in public, looking for a fight. He found one at *Leon and Eddie's* with someone who said something about the Jews and the war. Monte went at the loudmouth at the bar, tried to drag him outside while threatening to knock the man's block off. With Monte's low center of gravity and torso built from hard labor as a young man, it took several men to pry his thick fists and forearms from the man's lapels. A lapel came off in the struggle and Monte brandished it like a scalp while he fought to get at the man.

Leon put him in a back booth instead of throwing him out as he would most fighting drunks. He spent a few hours sitting with Monte while trying to distract him from his dark thoughts. Leon was only temporarily successful.

Monte didn't stop at *Leon and Eddie's*, he was heard at *Dave's Blue Room* accusing the Mayor of sabotage, of inciting a riot so that he could take credit for stopping it, of having a personal vendetta. But no one, not even Winchell, would print the accusations. Just weeks after being the hottest name on Broadway, Monte couldn't command one column inch of news. Not only was he humiliated, libeled and about to be wiped out... worst of all, he was convicted in the court of public opinion. He was fronting for Frank Costello and the *Syndicate*. The luster suddenly faded on the *Golden Boy of Broadway*. A shadow fell across all his achievements. Overnight, he went from being a nightclub genius to a shill for the mob. It was that simple, that fast. The spotlight went out.

Monte's youngest sister Annette came when he called. He didn't call that often anymore and she knew by the softness in his voice that he was hurt deeply. He asked her to meet him for lunch at the *Beachcomber*. When she arrived, Nick Kelly wasn't at the door with his usual greeting of "How ya feelin', Sis?"

Instead Mr. Chow greeted her solemnly. His beaming smile, a trademark of the place that Monte put on the menu in a cartoon, was now barely a grin. He showed her to a back booth, dark and far from the front door. Monte got up and opened his arms for her. He kissed her on the cheek. So much had happened to him since the last time they were together.

Monte looked down at his food, picking at it as if the answer to his destruction were in it. And it was his destruction he was speaking of. He was hung-over and as low as Annette had ever seen him. He first tried to make himself feel better by talking about the people he was going to take care of, the waiters and cigarette girls who were about to be out of work. Then he talked about the musicians who were contracted through the end of the summer, they were going to be paid too. The concessionaires who provided the food and liquor, the ticket and menu printers, the decorators, electricians and Nick Kelly's security crews were all going to get paid off. His gaze was unsteady, dropping from his sister's eyes to his plate, his hands. He was beaten, like when his marriage to Julie Jenner fell apart.

"I have to take care of those people," Monte told his sister.

Then the bitter pill, the death-blow, was the remainder of the lease on Madison Square Garden. That had to be paid too. The price was all his cash and even the original source of his success, his *Beachcomber* restaurants. It all had to go. He was not only beaten, he was busted. Now he had only one source of income and that was not completely under his control.

The Copa showroom had been built out over the summer to 550 seats, air conditioning had been installed and the kitchen upgraded. It had been a good season in Saratoga. Joe E. did well with the ponies - meaning he still had some money left. Frank C. got his rest while the Mayor was busy crushing Monte's *Dance Carnival,* thinking it belonged to Frank. The Copa furniture was carted back from Saratoga and polished up for the new season.

The partners met at the club. Frank commiserated with Monte, offering to help in any way possible. All Monte had to do was ask. Frank knew LaGuardia had been aiming for him and hit Monte and he felt terrible about it. It was a point of honor now that Frank had to take care of his partner. A debt was due. All his life Frank had stood up to bullies, especially self-appointed choirboys like LaGuardia, who hid behind police badges or church robes to push around anybody in their way. But there wasn't much he could do for Monte now. The damage was done. All he could do was watch out for his partner whom he considered almost a friend.

Frank's summer vacation hadn't been over 15 minutes before he was knee-deep in problems again, including Monte's. LaGuardia's move against Monte meant the Mayor was still gunning for a gangster trophy. In a run for governor, Frank Costello behind bars would go a long way. Frank's nearly constant insomnia returned. Once again, he tried everything short of dosing himself with knock-out drops. He never liked being intoxicated in any way, it took him off his guard. Mostly he played solitaire until early morning, hoping that would tire his mind. It didn't.

Carl Erbe dragged Monte out of bed for a late afternoon breakfast and gave him a talking to like a bully older brother - telling him to snap out of it, pull himself together - he'd heard the stories of Monte's drunken rampage. Carl hadn't spoken to Monte like that since they hoboed around Yellowstone, over 20 years ago. Carl browbeat his old scuffling buddy with every insulting, degrading and humiliating criticism he could muster - in an attempt to uplift and motivate him. Monte listened while he sipped his morning tea, occasionally looking up with one eye to make sure it was Carl making the racket and not the radio. After a strenuous opening volley accusing him at long last of plain laziness, Carl took a breath and Monte asked,

"I'm that bad?"

"Worse."

"Yeah, I thought I was worse too."

That didn't please Carl who launched into another critique about what Monte should and shouldn't do. Monte forgave him because the state of the world was weighing on

Carl's mind too. Carl apparently was responding to the threat of war by cracking down on any strange behavior. It was his practical nature and Monte knew a lecture was Carl's way of showing concern.

"You're staggering around like a damn stumblebum…" Carl went on and on. Monte waved him off like a house-fly. The use of the word bum, in anger, was a stark insult between hobos, especially those of the higher bindlestiff class. Saying someone was a stumblebum, one of the lowest of all the classes of bum – a bust-out drunk - could end a friendship.

"Enough." Monte surrendered. "Carl, I'll be better. A model citizen," was Monte's answer. Carl wisely gave up and then told him to get dressed. Monte agreed, went into his bedroom and closed the door. Carl eventually knocked on the door when Monte didn't return after 10 minutes. He opened it and found Monte asleep on his bed, snoring deeply. Carl let him sleep. He would continue his lecture later. He didn't want to leave, so he lay on the couch and dozed off too. As long as he and Monte were awake by 5 in the afternoon, they could still get to work on time.

Monte surprised him. He was up and headed for a steam bath and massage before noon. The mourning period was over. The raving stumblebum and anarchist was clear-headed and unapologetic. He had blown his whole wad and then went on a bender for a few days and so what? That's the way the dice tumbled.

The steam, massage and shave revived him. He was even glad of his old, tattered friendship with Carl. In spite of their struggle for dominance, Carl had stood the test of Monte's changing fortunes. He wasn't always there to celebrate the heights but he was always at his side when the bottom fell out. It wasn't the most comfortable friendship but it was consistent. At least when Carl was around, Monte knew he was on his way up.

His old chutzpah reassembled naturally as the steam took effect. He knew how to do nightclubs. Nightclubs were the one thing he knew for sure. While the two sat sweating out last night's liquor into the steam, Monte started to roll out new ideas for the Copa. It was effortless as always, his quicksilver mind returned, one thought hitting and melding with the next, but now it was more workmanlike. It was almost routine. He saw a vision of a jewel box effect for the new show, sharp and glittering but it wasn't a new vision. It didn't break new ground. It was safe.

Once the two swells hit the street, Monte was at full power again. He had a club to re-open and a lot of money to catch up with. As visions of the *Dance Carnival* faded, Monte summed it up, "The black kids were just better dancers," he told Carl, "... and the white kids got mad." That was as deeply as he wanted to ponder the malignancy of racism. He couldn't fix it, like just about everything else, so he accepted the way things were. By calling them kids, he made them sound like they weren't responsible. It was his soft touch coming out.

"They don't fight in my place," Carl added and they both knew why. Places were either black or white. The *Zanzibar* was a place for blacks. Monte had ignored that rule. Carl had found a rich vein in catering to blacks. The *Zanzibar* was one of the few high-class places south of Harlem that welcomed all of Harlem's people. Once that was known, only whites who had business or pleasure to seek among this community showed up. Places like Carl's *Zanzibar*, that mixed a few whites into a black place avoided trouble, but places that mixed a few blacks into a white place ended up like the *Dance Carnival*.

The *Zanzibar* was black and booming. It was the hottest jitterbug joint on Broadway. Carl didn't need headliners, his place cooked six nights a week without them. This was a small worry to Monte. He worried that Carl, former publicist of the daylight world of dentists and vacuum manufacturers, might be having more fun than him.

The Copa girls were all new, with new costumes, new routines and new lighting. The whole look was glossier and brighter. The headdresses were larger, more ornate and sparkled like carnival glass. Long black and white evening gloves cuffed and ringed with jewels accented the ladies' pantomime. The dance routines were sharpened up.

Outside, it was just Nick Kelly and his boys on the door, Toots had moved on and opened his own place on 51st street. The lines formed up again on 60th snaking towards Madison. Inside, Jack Entratter greeted the folks and Joe Lopez maitre'd'd them to their tables and once again the money rained down in buckets. The audience was dotted with soldiers in sharply creased khaki and mirror shined shoes, sailors in navy blue and for the first time, WACs, the ladies of the Women's Air Corp in khaki skirts and low heels.

The guest of honor that night was Milton Blackstone. Milton had just received the Presidential Medal of Freedom from President Roosevelt for his courageous action at the Eureka shipyard a few weeks earlier. Milton was the first publicly acknowledged civilian war hero in the country and still bore the bandages on his hands that attested to his extraordinary bravery.

President Roosevelt's Lend-Lease program had been sending supplies and ships to England as fast as America could build them. Even as he was making *Grossinger's* into a small empire complete with an airstrip, man-made lake and miles of roads, Milton also began to build the desperately needed ships for England along the banks of the Hudson in Newburgh. Government contracts for his Eureka Shipyard were for tens of millions and demanded accelerated delivery dates that demanded round-the-clock production schedules. *Grossinger's* was booming and took whatever remained of his time and energy but somehow even with both these responsibilities he continued to operate his Blackstone Agency in Manhattan, exclusively to handle advertising for Jennie Grossinger and of course, Monte's Copa. The Blackstone Agency ran flawlessly even though it was now only a tiny fraction of his empire. He never disappointed either Jenny or Monte. He never missed a deadline. He always treated them like they were his only clients.

Milton quickly mastered shipbuilding as he had the hotel and advertising businesses. Once his ships were built and floated, they were loaded with cargo then sent down the Hudson and off to war. On the second ship that Milton built, things went wrong. The ship was floated and was being loaded with high explosive artillery rounds. Trucks were on the dock off-loading crates into cargo nets that were hoisted up on deck. Around noon, a fire broke out that cleared all decks. All hands ran or jumped off the ship while the flames approached and began to touch the wooden crates of the shells. Milton raced on deck. He hooked a crate with a block and tackle and began dragging it out of the flames inches at a time. Frantic calls went out to the fire department while a company bucket brigade quickly fizzled. No employee was going anywhere close to the ship. The crew began heading for the hills into the thick trees up the riverbank. Milton managed to drag the first crate of shells out of the flames and went back for another. It was clear he was not going to retreat. A few brave men rushed back in to help him. The foreman mustered a few more of the cowering crew back into a faltering bucket brigade. Some who ran to the woods found the courage to join the rescue. For nearly an hour before the fire department arrived, Milton jumped in and out of the flames, always taking the most dangerous position and burning his hands badly in the process. By late afternoon, the fire was out. England would get her ammunition and ships would continue to splash out of the Eureka shipyard into the Hudson.

Everybody from Nick at the front door, to Entratter and the staff, including Podell who made a rare appearance outside the kitchen, applauded Milton as they greeted him. The news, whispered from table to table, spread through the showroom. The nation's first bona-fide war hero was among them. Eventually Milton was forced to raise his bandaged hand in acknowledgement to the smattering of applause from his countrymen.

Joe E. and Sophie Tucker opened the second season. By now, Joe dominated all other nightclub comics. He was the sharpest professional drunk in the business, the funniest guy on two rubbery legs. Sophie was the powerhouse of the intimate stage, the grand matron of nightlife. People loved Joe and Sophie like family, like a favorite uncle and aunt, not just because they were the two top nightclub acts in the world but because Joe and Sophie loved them back. They loved the small rooms. They loved being with the night people, the familiar faces who had seen them dozens of times. They were playing to their old friends in their living room.

Of course, Joe opened the show for Sophie. As usual, he had the folks falling out of their seats laughing. "Show me a man with his two feet on the ground and I'll show you a man who can't put his pants on." People laughed at the rhythm and just because Joe was talking, the jokes didn't have to be funny. People just loved to laugh with Joe.

A half hour later, Joe introduced Miss Sophie Tucker. Sophie had toured the vaudeville circuits for 30 years. She was old and vaudeville was gone. She'd lost the only home she had known in her adult life – the dressing rooms of the old theatres. She'd lost everything, and everyone knew it.

Years before, she bought a gas station on Long Island for her husband early in their marriage. The business slowly declined over ten years while she kept pouring money in. Her handsome husband was a poor businessman and worse father. As the business failed, his drinking and abuse increased. The marriage collapsed after a dozen years.

Her only son, Bert, who had grown up with Sophie's mother while Sophie toured and his father drank, bitterly rejected her on his 21st birthday. He then disappeared and never returned. This broke Sophie's heart completely. Now old, displaced from the grand vaudeville theatres and utterly alone, she had only nightclub people to be with at night. Everyone knew what had happened to her but no one, including Sophie, ever breathed a word of it. Instead, her monstrous life story filled every beating heart in her audiences with tender love and every song with heartbreak.

She showed up every night in the most elegant gowns that money could buy and sang songs that made people blush and laugh. She belted bawdy tunes that made fun of herself because she was old and fat and had never been considered even pretty, songs like "Nobody Loves a Fat Girl but Oh, How a Fat Girl Can Love", "I Don't Want to Be Thin" and "You've Gotta See Mama Every Night (Or you Can't' See Mama at All)". After having fun and making fun of herself she drifted into the sorrowful "You've Got to Be Loved to Be Healthy" and "Aren't Women Wonderful?" When she opened up her road-weary voice, a voice that newspaper writers said could lead ships into harbor during a storm, it knocked the wind out of everyone who heard her. Tears flowed because everyone heard the voice of their own mother, or favorite spinster aunt. They heard a strong woman's heart breaking. But like a kind aunt, she dried their tears with "I'm Living Alone (And I Like It)".

Joe would come back and get them laughing again until they were exhausted. Then he'd send them home – sometimes. Sometimes not. Sometimes he'd have 3, or maybe 10 drinks first, keeping everyone, including the staff, up way too late. Joe would start having a good time and then just want the company. He'd wander among the tables telling jokes while he snatched customers' drinks. He usually proposed a toast to the room, then drank the drink himself. Bartenders poured heavily and booze flowed like a spring creek when Joe worked. He never went to bed before dawn anyway, so he'd get loaded and stay up all night croaking tunes like "Sam, You Made the Pants Too Long" and other lunacies until 5 AM, an hour and a half after the last show was supposed to end. Nobody stopped Joe and nobody walked out. People emerged from the show emotionally drained as the sky began to lighten before dawn. They were 500 people who all fell in love on the same night with Joe and Sophie. Some had been touched so deeply that they never forgot it and never stopped talking about the night they saw Sophie when Joe closed the place.

Tales of these nights flooded the channels of chatter up and down the length of Broadway. They were the foundation of the club's burgeoning legend. Joe and Sophie were simply the most staggering display of nightclub talent in the world. The evening was primal yet luxurious. The two proved that a nightclub evening could touch a human heart like nothing else and the Copa was their home.

A version of this iconic Copacabana logo created in 1940 by Wesley Morse, continues to be used by the club today, which is now located in Times Square, New York City. The Copa, after 70 years, is the only one of the great clubs of the Nightclub Era still open.

Monte and young friend in Widnes, England, circa 1912

Monte makes common train travel into a publicity event as he takes "The Most Photographed Girls in the World" to Hollywood for producer Walter Wanger in 1938. Naturally, he's in the picture as well - far right. While working as a publicist for Hollywood studios, Monte also created nightclubs. He publicized dozens of movies and created over 100 nightclubs in his career.

Jane Ball in an early publicity photo for studio 20th Century Fox. Under her contract, Jane appeared with George Sanders in "Forever Amber", Lon McAllister in "Winged Victory" and Gregory Peck in "Keys to the Kingdom".

Monte and Jane caught holding hands at the bar of El Morocco nightclub.

Monte and Jane in love at the Copa.

Jane and Monte on their wedding day - June 9, 1945 - with Jane's sister Evelyn, the Maid of Honor, in New Hope, Pennsylvania.

Movie star Gene Tierney and Prince Ali Khan make an entrance at the Copa…

…while upstairs in the lounge Joe E. Lewis and Milton Berle clown around on Jack Eigen's live nightly Copa radio show.

Eternal beauty Lena Horne breaks hearts at her Copa debut. She was the first black performer to appear in a major New York nightclub below 125th Street, Harlem.

Monte pushes the racial boundaries again by booking Nat King Cole in the Copa lounge. Cole and wife celebrate with baseball legend Roy Campanella.

Monte rescued vaudeville performers like Jimmy Durante and Sophie Tucker from obscurity. He re-introduced them at the Copa, where they were re-discovered by audiences, then television and film producers.

Jan Murray, Frank Sinatra, Jackie Gleason, Jerry Lewis and Dean Martin take over the Copa stage in an impromptu jam session

Backstage at the Copa, from a Life Magazine story, 1941

Inside the world's largest nightclub. Monte's "Dance Carnival" (1941) featured three top swing dance bands playing in rotation. He turned Madison Square Garden into a jitterbug oasis with 70 foot palm trees and a 70 foot waterfall. He invested all the money he made at the Copacabana and lost every dime of it.

Jane with her first born, Charles Morgan "Chip" Proser, 1946

The playbill for Monte's only Broadway hit, High Button Shoes, 1947, starring Phil Silvers and Nanette Fabray. This and Monte's other ventures like the "Dance Carnival" distracted him from running the Copa. Jules Podell took advantage of this and moved against Monte, seizing control of the club in 1949.

Jules Podell, the mob's enforcer and Monte's enemy at the Copa - with attorney, about to testify before the Kefauver Organized Crime Committee, 1950.

Podell's boss and Monte's involuntary partner for 35 years, Frank Costello, the architect of modern organized crime, testifying before the Kefauver Committee, 1951.

Edith Piaf, then unknown to American audiences, with fiancee Jacques Pills, on opening night at La Vie en Rose, 1950. Monte opened La Vie en Rose immediately after he was pushed out of his Copacabana by the mob. It was his only club up to that time without mob partners and his favorite.

The Farm - Monte's wedding gift to Jane and their family home near New Hope.

The Original Prosers - Isabel (left front), Monte (right front), Annette (left rear) and Leo at the Farm for 4th of July, 1951.

Jane with all 5 sons along the Delaware canal outside of New Hope in an advertisement for local merchants. From left - Timmy, Jimmy, Chip, Mike and Billy, 1956.

Postcard of Monte's "Playhouse Inn". It was supposed to be his retirement business but was taken over by local businessmen.

Monte with Johnny Rosselli, the mob's top man in Las Vegas, at Frank Costello's Tropicana Hotel, 1957. When Rosselli was asked about the budget for Monte's original show for the hotel "Tropicana Holiday" by show director Earl Barton, Rosselli said, "There ain't no budget, kid. Just make sure it's a fuckin' good show."

Publicity photo of the Broadway legend. Monte went on to bring Broadway musicals to Las Vegas for the first time starting with Cole Porter's "Anything Goes" and his own successful "High Button Shoes" playing in repertoire.

Monte's last saloon. The "Little Club" restaurant and bar in New Hope. After Frank Costello was shot in New York in 1959, detectives found a slip of paper in his coat pocket connecting him to the Tropicana Hotel casino. The Nevada gaming authorities banned Costello, a convicted felon, and everyone associated with him including Monte, from the hotel for life. Finally free of the mob, Monte retired to his beloved Bucks County and his "Little Club".

CHAPTER 23

You, I'm Gonna Marry

A few days after opening night, Carl bounded into the waiting room of the office as the club was just letting in the first people for the evening. The room was empty and the door to the inner office was closed. On the standing coat rack hung a WAC olive drab wool coat, hat and handbag. Carl was about to knock on the door to the inner office when it opened a crack. Monte peeked out. He was naked.

"Hey, pal" he said as he grabbed the WAC coat and handbag off the rack. Monte smiled, shrugged his shoulders, and closed the door. Worried about Carl's disapproval of this also, he opened the door again quickly and whispered, "You don't think I'm being unpatriotic, do you?" The old hobos smiled at each other as Monte closed the door and locked it. Carl retreated to the upstairs bar near the lounge and waited for the post-race results.

Jane auditioned the same day. She walked down the stairs and straight to Monte at his ringside table a little off to the right of center stage. He chatted with her briefly, asked where she worked, nodded, wrote down her phone number on a sheet with a dozen others. His look at Jane lingered after the conversation was over. This was nothing new for her and she stood quietly letting him get his fill. He indicated the stage and Jane joined the other auditioning girls including the twin Barnes' sisters.

Choreographer Bob Alton waited for Jane a few feet away at center stage. He asked for first position. Jane and the others assumed the ballet posture. Alton demonstrated a few steps, they all followed. He led them through a small routine, then asked each one where they had studied. He thanked them all and with a look and nod to Monte, all of them were approved.

Jane and the others waited on stage for Monte's confirmation. He saw the opening for a little personal chat, the type he had with everyone who worked for him but it started off all wrong.

"Jane Ball," he said. An awkward silence followed as butterflies rose up and fluttered inside him, closing his throat.

"Yes?" She thought he was trying to remember where they might have met but he was looking at her directly, oddly she thought.

The silence grew heavier as Monte suddenly found himself dumbstruck. They were all stuck, hanging on his next words that didn't seem in any hurry to come out. Monte was in the unfamiliar throes of infatuation. An idiot's smile came to his lips as his mind geared down to an adolescent level. He wondered with everyone else what would come next.

On stage, the clatter of the kitchen preparations swelled to fill the silence. Finally, with the innocence of a small boy or an adult fool, he pointed out each one of the girls,

"You, you and you are hired," he told them, hesitating at Jane, "And you I'm gonna marry."

The shock of it froze her to the floor. She tumbled the words over and over in her mind, trying to sense their meaning. It didn't seem to be a line, it was too plain for that. He didn't look crazy or drunk. What the hell was he saying?

Monte was as shocked as she was. The sentence had leapt out of his mouth directly from some daydream he was having. For a moment he thought he should apologize. He felt the burn of embarrassment and then felt he had to back himself up like he would back up a drunken pal who had stumbled into an insult. He held his ground. The statement stood.

Jane's smile vanished and a scowl took over. Now she was mad, just short of marching over to him and slapping him good, right across the face. It had to be some kind of line. Maybe he was just simple-minded.

The other girls warily looked at each other for a clue as to what to do next. At the bar, Jack Entratter's head came to rest in his hand. He groaned in embarrassment for his boss. The bartender froze in mid-pour as he angled a silver scoop to fill a highball glass with ice cubes. A single cube slipped from his scoop and clinked into the glass. An off-duty waiter blew out a long stream of tobacco smoke in a quietly descending whistle meant to sound like a bomb dropping – with no explosion at the end of it – a dud.

"You are not!" Jane snapped. The audition was ending badly and she hesitated, hoping for a way to save it. More awkward silence as she looked into his smiling face. Did he think it was funny?! The situation was hopeless. He just sat there, unapologetic, unmoved. With a final look of scorn she marched off, toward the stairs, not even stopping to put her coat on as she stomped up to ground level. She stopped at the landing and shot back, "And I can't work the first show. My curtain's at 8."

Jane continued her march up the stairs, out of the club. For a moment Monte was worried that she'd never come back, but he was calm, comfortable with what he'd just done. Alton moved to him, looking into his eyes,

"Are you alright?"

"Probably," he said.

"You know you hired seven girls. We only need six."

Monte nodded, "It's not fair to break up the twins," he said.

Alton mulled the logic for a moment but still didn't understand it.

"Twins are good luck," Monte offered. "In China, they're good luck."

Alton still wasn't getting it. "Seven," Monte finally said, "It's a better number." Alton gave up and turned back to the new girls.

Monte sat at his table and drew a circle around Jane Ball's name. He had just proposed marriage to a woman he didn't even know and now he decided he actually meant it. It was pure instinct and intoxicating. He decided to keep it just that way, the way it came. He was going to marry Jane Ball. It was a complete picture in a frame handed to him. All he had to do was say yes. And he did. Suddenly, there just wasn't any doubt in his mind. He would eventually be with her. If she didn't come back, he would find her. It was almost as if the decision was made for him somehow. Some mystical lever had been pulled and he was, in a moment, committed to making a life with Jane S. Ball. The whole thing made him giddy and he suddenly felt like having a drink. He was going to get married again. He had the feeling he wasn't firmly on the ground, like the song said "walking on air". He was going to marry Jane Ball, the dancer… and that stopped him cold. All the rash decisions in his life suddenly clamored for his attention. Was he really going to marry another dancer? And one he just met? He had read somewhere that normal people suddenly jumped off bridges for no apparent reason. It was an impulse, the theory went, a momentary crisis.

What was it? What had hit him so hard that he fell like two tons of bricks? He remembered she didn't wear makeup. The audition had brought the color into her cheeks. A fine mist of perspiration lined her upper lip. And then something grabbed him. Her tough rejection rang in his ears as she walked out. Slowly, the fog thinned. What she was - was unglamorous. But something else was out of place. She wasn't working an angle. Seasoned chorus girls almost always had an angle. It was either to be a star or marry well or both, and he could provide a girl with any of those. A chorine who'd been around a while would at least humor him and flirt a little, but not this one. Jane Ball didn't seem to give a good Goddamn about him or the Copa. That was obvious. She was just a hardworking, slightly sweaty girl looking for a second job. So whatever it was that sprang the lock, he decided to hell with it, he was going to marry another dancer. He felt the tickle of champagne bubbles in his blood that told him he was in another high stakes crapshoot and had come out with a tough point, a long shot. He was light headed, light hearted, like he just jumped off a bridge.

Jane waved him off like a barfly. He was just another big shot throwing his weight around, or trying to. What she really didn't like was that he was so damn cocky, like he could have whatever he asked for. And he was short, only three inches taller than her. She didn't like short men. The whole truth was that Monte's shocking proposal wasn't the only aggression launched against Jane's personal life. A famous Hollywood actress had also attacked. Obviously Monte had missed the small item in his pal Winchell's column a few months ago, "Frances Farmer's detectives are shadowing Leif Erickson of "Higher and Higher" who is going to marry Jane Ball of that show…"

Leif, who had worked with Jane the previous year in Joshua Logan's *Higher and Higher*, was warm and completely unfazed by his own extraordinary beauty. Even men were startled into admiring him. He looked straight and plainly at people with his arctic blue eyes shaded by shiny, pale hair and they instantly felt comfortable with him. He was quiet, studious, a serious actor. This was the quality that held Jane's attention. In a business filled with blowhards and poseurs, Leif quietly stood above the rest.

About Monte, Jane told her friends, "Some kinda wiseguy," and had nothing further to say on it. This was a shock for some who hadn't seen Jane's other side, the one that grew up on a barstool. To them, Jane was mature, quiet and very kind. But now they saw the sharp thorns on the delicate Irish rose. Jane knew she was going to take the Copa job anyway. She could handle herself around wiseguys.

Higher and Higher, the light-hearted romp, was grinding Jane to a nub. She barely had enough time to sleep and eat while working four shows a day on Broadway plus two a night at the Copa, six days a week. She weighed just over a hundred pounds and if she could rest would've weighed ten or twenty more. But she couldn't rest, there was a war on, and too many people in Kingston directly or indirectly shared the money she sent home every week. The three other girls sharing her apartment every night were anything but restful. Her feet and calves hurt constantly. It didn't leave much time or energy for her boyfriend Leif, but somehow they managed. They made time for each other and within a few months, she brought him home to meet the family.

In the big house on Albany Avenue he got the once-over from Nan, who had seen every sly dog and earnest suitor routinely turned away by her disinterested daughter, Jane. This one was certainly handsome as the devil, soft-spoken and obviously infatuated with her third daughter. Nan allowed her hopes to swell at the thought of a gaggle of tall, gorgeous grandchildren and Jane was as giddy as a girl around him. It certainly seemed like he could be the one.

The first afternoon with the family was planned around a ball game pitched by second daughter Shirley's new boyfriend, Bud Zoller. It was a dream afternoon in the Hudson River town. With cold beer in the hot sun, they watched young men give everything to the game of baseball. Jim Morgan, the adoptive father of all the Ball children and grim protector of Shirley's well-being, was at bat. Bud, Shirley's prospective beau, was facing Jim down and trying to strike him out. Nan, the matriarch, watched this titanic showdown with amused interest as she kept Jane and Leif in the corner of her eye. She was a bit afraid for Bud because Jim was such a fierce competitor.

Jim Morgan played ball like he ran *Morgan's Tavern*. He was known as a "scrappy" player, meaning he would slide "spikes-high" into second basemen and was as accurate as a camel with his tobacco juice. Bud got him down 3-2 and showed him some of the speed of youth. He wasn't backing off. Shirley cheered him on, "Strike the bum out!" which made the whole family laugh.

Growing up, Jane had done a lot of her homework on the last barstool in *Morgan's Tavern*, the one closest to the wall. She preferred this spot to the dining room table in the big, drafty family house on Albany Avenue where her two brothers and two sisters did their school work. She had liked the warmth and chatter of *Morgan's* and the ready help of big, Irish Jim for tough homework problems.

Jim snapped a single through the infield and showed the youngster Bud the economy of experience. Jane and Leif were relaxed and happy. They drank the local Reingold beer from paper cups and whooped like kids on a ferris wheel. Jane wiped beer foam from Leif's chin, catching his glance. A thin smile underlined his eyes that darted toward the action on the field but swung back to hers. She flicked the beer foam from her fingers into his face, laughing with him and releasing them both back to the game. They sat close and whispered inside jokes to each other, like any two young people falling in love.

On the field, Jim Morgan, checked the position of the second baseman considering a possible steal, then snapped a quick look over his shoulder into the stands, to check on his Janey and her new boyfriend. He was determined to be the only one attempting to steal anything on this ball field.

Jim knew a lot about stealing bases in baseball and a little about stealing love. In 1931, Jim Morgan and Nan had stolen their love in broad daylight right in front of the congregation of St. Joseph's parish. At the time, Nan was a married and very Catholic woman, whose husband had been committed to a sanitarium with advanced syphilis. Since Nan could not divorce, she and Jim lived their lives together with bedrooms just down the hall from each other in the house on Albany Avenue that Jim had bought for Nan and her five children. The arrangement fooled no one and caused endless public scorn from the flock but technically permitted Nan to retain her standing in the parish.

Jane saw Jim's glance from first base and knew exactly what he was thinking – and it wasn't brotherly love for Leif. She had to smile, he was so obvious. She loved the flinty, raw-boned Irish giant with a ferocity than permitted no hint of disrespect from anyone, ever. His unwavering love for her mother and generosity had saved her family from abject poverty. He stood with them in the face of public contempt for her mother, the woman with the philandering, diseased husband who barely disguised an adulterous liaison with a foul-mouthed bootlegger like Jim. Jim, of course, didn't give a goddamn what anybody thought, and Jane thought that was about the right attitude. Given the choice, she'd rather be in *Morgan's Tavern* with Jim than in the *White House* with President Roosevelt.

The plan all along had been to get Leif into *Morgan's* after the game. That way Jim could get a good look at the young man and take the measure of him. If the guy was throwing a spitball at his Janey, Jim would see it clear as day and throw the bum out.

CHAPTER 24

DECLARATION OF WAR

War split the world on December 7, 1941. Within weeks, trains filled with American men and boys poured into military training camps. Factories roared with new life. Whole mountains were torn apart, melted down and formed into piercing steel. The economy boomed and rivers of cash flowed into New York City from all over the world.

In Europe, royal families that had been quietly slipping away from the insanity in Germany for years, now ran for their lives. An avalanche of princes, dukes, barons, counts, earls, their servants, and the cousins of all these, fled to New York in great royal herds. They brought everything of value they could move. The flood of ancient wealth and power into New York tipped the world on its axis. Suddenly the 22 square miles of Manhattan Island was the new center of social gravity and the diamond necklace that wound through its heart called Broadway was the focus of all the new attention.

America's declaration of war against Japan changed the nature of human relations. Friends became precious because they would likely be gone and very soon. Idle romance lost its grip and love took hold. Life and death were the subtext of every conversation, song and picture. The sense of time vanished since each moment might be the last. The pace of life tripled overnight and crying was expected in women and excused in men. Facing the first certainty of death on a massive scale, people spoke with frank urgency. They saw who was standing and who was retreating in fear. The fearful were despised. Fear was a tool of the enemy and the fearful carried it like a plague.

Monte turned his attention to Jane, declaring his own campaign to win her. The war had turned his bold declaration of marriage into prophecy. The more he was around her the more he knew he'd made the right, and the lucky, decision. She was suddenly his salvation and his last chance for the life he had almost given up on. He had only three small problems; one, Jane had little energy left after her punishing work schedule, two, she had a boyfriend and three, she thought he was an idiot.

Monte was at the office of Dr. Rupert Hitzig being told that his flat feet, color blindness and age, at 38 years, were not things the US Army was looking for in a recruit. "To hell with it then. I'm not going where I'm not invited." Monte said. He felt as strong as he ever had in his life. He could twist an apple in half between his two thick hands and liked the idea of bringing this talent to the neck of a German soldier or one of their pogrom-inclined Russian collaborators. He was ready to do his stint. Hitzig told him to find another way to help. The Army eventually agreed with the doctor. Monte found another way to get into the war.

Ernst Hanfstaengl, known affectionately to his close friends as Putzi, an early confidant and sycophant of Adolf Hitler, was in New York. He too had fled his violent master like the other Europeans of means, but in his case an assassination attempt against him made it clear that he wasn't welcome in Hitler's inner circle anymore.

Putzi Hanfstaengl was a great, loyal friend to have. During his college days at Harvard, his American classmates, including young Franklin D. Roosevelt, loved having him around. He played the piano passionately and knew hundreds of jokes. Parties never really got going until Putzi arrived. After graduation he returned to Germany and found great success joking and performing for the power elite of German society. Before long he was entertaining a young political firebrand named Hitler. Putzi could always get a laugh out of Adolf as he had done with young FDR.

But Putzi wasn't just an entertainer. He showed his talent for mischief by brilliantly conceiving of a plot to set fire to the German parliament building, the Reichstag. Not only was it Putzi's idea, but he led the arsonists through the long tunnel from his offices late one night with the kerosene and matches. This elegantly simple ruse, gave Hitler the excuse he needed to blame the fire on Communists and declare martial law. Thanks to Putzi, Adolf and his Nazis gained a stranglehold on Germany without firing a shot.

Unfortunately, just after Putzi had helped hijack Germany for his ambitious new friend, a rival tried to detonate him into many odd pieces. He fled first to Canada, then turned to his old schoolmate, FDR, to help him. FDR had come to detest the grown-up Putzi, but guessed his value as a sycophant. Putzi would know Hitler's bent of mind and personal weaknesses intimately. Roosevelt beat back the Republicans long enough to convince key congressmen of Putzi's strategic value. Putzi was going to advise congressional and military leaders on Hitler's mindset and that of his closest advisors. FDR ignored his revulsion toward his old classmate and negotiated the type of filthy deal that the war had now made a necessity.

Putzi was back in business. He immediately set himself up in style in New York City, courtesy of the US government. The word went out that the Copa was extending a special invitation to the distinguished German fugitive. Putzi was intrigued. The *Copacabana*, owned by one of America's most prominent Jews, couldn't be ignored. It was a great opportunity to announce his availability and to show that promoting the destruction of European Jews, as he had done to win Adolf's friendship, was a thing of the past, no hard feelings. He was a new man and a loyal American. Now all he needed was someone who believed him. At the Copa, he was sure to run into someone, like FDR, who was willing to ignore his past in order to employ his special brand of dirty work. Putzi was looking forward to getting his hands dirty again for a new patron.

Monte prepared certain key members of the staff for the evening. No hint of displeasure or annoyance was to show on anyone's mug toward the German gent or the jig would be up. The staff took the assignment solemnly, even Podell signed on. For the night, he and Monte were two Jews united against a common enemy.

Putzi arrived precisely at 8 PM, the perfect civilian, attended by three grim bodyguards. They were whisked inside with the graciousness befitting a ranking statesman and seated center, three rows back from the stage, the prime vantage point to see and be seen. Monte greeted Putzi briskly and wished him a good evening. The man spoke nearly perfect British-inflected English. Putzi's unsmiling, attending muscle refused to even acknowledge Monte. The host slipped away.

The evening bobbled on with Putzi sipping champagne, while his armed escorts drank beer. The beer took its course, prompting a few of his men to excuse themselves to the men's room. This was the moment Monte had been waiting for and the trap was sprung.

Extremely attractive women were posted to intercept and delay the bodyguards once they exited the men's room. Monte watched from the shadows near the spotlights. Putzi looked like he had just stepped out of an MGM musical, every hair perfectly in place, his gaze fixed and expressionless as he watched Jimmy Durante scat-sing a little nonsense ditty that had become his theme song called *Inka Dinka Doo*. That was the signal that Jimmy was ready.

Jimmy struck up the band to a gallop, leading the charge off of Monte's cue. The spotlights both turned on Putzi, bleaching him nearly white as he shielded his eyes. The Copa girls strode into the audience and surrounded him. Open, half-empty bottles of whiskey and gin flew in on waiter's trays and plopped down on Putzi's table. Lit cigarettes appeared on his table in full ashtrays. One of the girls playfully ran her fingers through his hair and loosened his tie as other girls displayed their remarkable legs for the man. The mark went along with the big American joke. Everyone laughed. Walter Winchell's photo man snapped the picture that told a thousand words.

The next day it was revealed in Winchell's column that this reformed German refugee, in spite of his sympathetic image, was actually a drunken fool and treacherous Nazi sympathizer. Winchell pounded poor Putzi, saying that this disgusting, corrupt buffoon was indeed the perfect representative of the German government. They were both a disgrace and an affliction that the world was better off without. Putzi was quickly pulled from the limelight by FDR's staff. He went into seclusion in upstate New York. His mission was suddenly top secret. FDR's great love for Winchell was tested by this ridicule of an important intelligence asset. Winchell dropped the story and moved on. But the damage was done and Monte had gotten his licks in by guiding Winchell's poison pen. He'd done his small bit for the war effort by assassinating Putzi's character. Putzi was a pariah. He was out of action, one of the many broken hearts represented by each light on Broadway.

Dancer Harriet Wright loved her boss, Monte, "He's such a doll," she said. She went on and on as the Copa girls dressed for the second show. "Perfect gentleman, and he could throw his weight around plenty, if you know what I mean."

"Who?" Jane interrupted. She had arrived just in time from taking the curtain calls in her new show *Panama Hattie* on 46th Street.

"The Boss, honey," she said. "Don't you think so? A livin' doll."

Harriet was one of the friendlier girls. The others mostly kept their distance. The word had gotten around that the Boss had eyes only for Jane. Harriet didn't care about any of that.

"I wouldn't know." Jane peeled off her overcoat, kicking off her fine English shoes.

"Well I would. Him and Walter are thick as thieves." Jane didn't know whom she was referring to this time either. Walter Winchell had been Harriet's special friend for some time even though he was married. Harriet was introduced to him after her performance as a diver in Billy Rose's *Aquacade* at the 1939 World's Fair. Winchell brought her to Monte.

Jane wasn't interested in hearing much about the boss. She'd just read that morning in Winchell's column that she was Leif Erickson's fiancée. It was news to her. Leif called to apologize, he'd been talking to a reporter and felt he had to give the man something to write about. Jane cooled and the conversation died. Leif awkwardly said goodbye. That was at 10 AM.

Now after seven at night, Jane, faced the last two of her five shows that day, but was already exhausted. It was Wednesday, matinee day. She'd been working since 11 AM, dancing three shows. And now she dressed for the late shift at the Copa. That would take her through to 4 am – almost all of it on her toes, dancing. Both feet were covered with bandages from toe to heel. Her calves were taut as steel wire and ached from bruises and muscle knots. She'd recently started drinking coffee to keep up. Everybody was doing cups and pints of coffee especially the dancers who were moonlighting in the clubs. It made Jane jittery and cross. It had been a hellish day from the very beginning.

"Hello little people. I have arrived." June Allyson sashayed in with her usual bubbly attitude. June was one of Jane's three roommates at the *Henry Hudson*. She was in *Panama Hattie* as well so Jane couldn't avoid her almost every hour of every day. No one looked up or greeted her but that didn't faze June. She simply demanded attention whether people paid it or not.

Jane slipped on her robe and dance heels. She couldn't even go to the bathroom without her dance shoes on. She trudged past Joe E's dressing room. If she'd been even a little bit curious, she could have peeked in and seen Joe's legendary gigantic jock strap slung prominently above his mirror. The pouch had been let out by Joe's personal tailor to accommodate a tool that would have made Bigfoot proud. Some said the nasty thing was his good luck charm, some said it was just deceptive advertising. For Joe, it was simply a delight to watch the faces of well-mannered visitors as they tried not to stare at the thing.

Jane had heard the stories and was determined not to look into Joe's room. Any backstage area was treacherous for underdressed chorus girls, but she was particularly on guard at the Copa. The place was lousy with wiseguys and randy drunks. Joe was charming but not that different and she was in no mood for men.

The only good thing about the day was that the Copa was pretty much a cakewalk. The hardest thing about it was getting in and out of the costumes and walking down the stairs. They piled on headdresses and jewelry that made it impossible to do fast turns, high kicks and jumps, so the routines were gentle turns, graceful arms and, of course, Brazilian samba. Coming down the stairs from the dressing rooms took more skill than the dancing. On the fourth step the spotlights from the back of the room hit the girls straight in the face, blinding them. Normally, in a theatre, spotlights were elevated but the Copa was a cellar. The intense lights were at eye-level. Blinded, in high heels and balancing enormous headdresses, the girls navigated the last steps down to stage level by feel and faith. They were not permitted to look down. As the follow spots found them on the fourth step, a collective gasp of awe rose from the audience. They were a sparkling vision of feminine beauty and poise. On nearly the last step, a dense cloud of Chinese food and perfume enveloped the dancers. When they cleared the last steps and took center stage, they could finally see the patrons. They were only inches away.

The last show wrapped up just after 3:30 am. The girls peeled off their sequined tops, left their makeup on and dressed to go home. Jane made her way out through the show room, June followed. They were going to split a cab back to the *Henry Hudson.* At the back of the room, Monte was at the bar with Joe E. They were talking as quietly as two bankers. Monte noticed Jane immediately and watched as she crossed the room. She was too tired to do anything but keep walking and hope he didn't have any more embarrassing outbursts. It was clear she wasn't going to encourage him. She was heading for the exit.

"Thanks," he said. She looked at him.

"...For a good show," he added. She nodded an acknowledgement. She and June kept walking, up the stairs and out of the place.

Monte turned back to the bar, "She's the one, Joe," he told his old buddy morosely. Joe didn't have a snappy comeback for this one. He'd read Winchell and knew what Monte knew. Monte had no chance with her, she was engaged. Joe just took another pull on his Chesterfield, letting the smoke fill his mouth so he wouldn't have to speak. He sat with his old pal and watched him suffer, then spun his finger at the bartender for another round.

When she reached the front door Nick Kelly said, "I got a cab for ya." Jane loved Kelly the Belly, the lonely, singing Irishman, like a brother, but tonight she was too tired to do more than nod and comment, "Y'did huh?"
"Compliments of the house."
June Allyson never seemed to run out of spark, she bubbled, "Oh, goodie". She and Jane bundled into the cab. On the ride to their hotel, June let on that she knew something was up between Jane and the boss but Jane wasn't talking. She was only interested in soaking her feet and getting into bed. Tomorrow she was adding an acting class to her schedule and needed to be sharp.

In the natural progression of chorus girls, Jane began to take acting lessons in hopes of landing roles that might allow her to sit down while performing and be better paid for it. Hoping to retrieve Jane's affection, Leif recommended her to his teacher, the legendary Stella Adler. Jane passed the audition for admission to Adler's class and applied the same focus to her acting that had propelled her as a dancer. Leif encouraged and helped her with the work, slowly winning back Jane's love. He instantly saw that her Irish iron will and quiet sensitivity played well together. With a little prompting, she could bring tears or anger. She was a natural. This encouragement was the last gift he could give her.

They had been on separate schedules ever since *Higher and Higher* closed and Jane signed on with *Panama Hattie* and then the night shift at the Copa. In spite of everything they felt for each other, they rarely had a moment together anymore. But there was more to the separation, as Jane soon discovered. Leif's on and off career in the movies was on again. He had a Bob Hope picture *Nothing but the Truth* to do in California.

Ironically, this was the opportunity Leif needed to tell Jane something of the truth about their relationship.

They sat in a mid-town steakhouse, the remnants of Leif's farewell dinner in front of them. Casually, Leif confided that Frances Farmer, who had been hounding him day and night for months, was in desperate trouble. She had been taking amphetamines, a newly available drug developed to keep US bomber pilots awake on long missions. Her abrasive behavior had degenerated into violence. He had to help her if he could because she was, even after years of separation and his reported engagement to Jane, still his wife. He had been married to Farmer all along but hadn't been able to bring himself to tell Jane the truth, until now. He was not going to get a divorce.

Leif dropped this bombshell on Jane matter-of-factly, without excuse or hint of shame. Their relationship and widely publicized engagement was off. Apparently, Leif never had any real intention of marrying her or even telling her he was already married.

He was a true con artist, she decided, a professional. How else could he look at her now without a flicker of remorse? Their affair was a sham, and maybe, just a publicity gimmick and a sex holiday.

The barren truth of it snatched Jane's breath away. His betrayal was so deep, so complete, that her mind suddenly went blank and she felt like she was looking at a handsome stranger in front of her. Just as her father had betrayed and humiliated her mother, Leif had done to her. Silence descended like a curtain coming down on an extremely dull play – the type where people are too disappointed to even attempt applause. They just want to slip quietly away.

Traffic hummed along outside like always, filling in the quiet. Leif's naked ring finger lay calmly among its mates, untroubled by its part in the deception. The smoke from his cigarette was suddenly overpowering, she batted it away with her hand. Jane got up silently from this dull play, turned away from Leif and never looked back. He was instantly and forever in her past.

Leif's confession changed her personality for quite some time. Instead of her usual quiet energy and amusement with life, an impenetrable distance formed around her. She stood apart, partially paralyzed. Her roommates never heard her cry or ever mention Leif's name again. Instead, she seemed to settle into a state of waking catatonia, unable to do anything much for the next few months except work and lose herself in reading novels while lying in bed.

The delicious news of Jane's betrayal helped feed the idle Broadway gossip mill through the slow summer months of 1941. It was whispered to Monte late in the season, landing on his ear like the sound of distant rain to a man dying of thirst. Overnight, he began to prepare himself for the delicate task of winning Jane's broken heart. He limited himself to one drink a night and began retiring early, often in bed before midnight. His shocking behavior concerned running-buddy Joe E., who had been highballing with fellow drunks in Frank C's *Piping Rock* casino through the long summer nights. But Monte's sobering preparations were well-timed. Along with his quest for Jane, the war for control of the Copa was about to escalate.

That entire summer of 1941, while Monte played in the cool shade of Saratoga Springs with Joe E and Frank, and became a star with his *Dance Carnival,* Jules Podell sat in the hot, airless cellar of the *Hotel Fourteen* sucking in the dust and enduring the racket of the Copa's renovation. He knew there would be no credit for a job well done, only blame if something went wrong. His jealousy and fear of Monte festered in the heat and noise. He needed a way to set Monte up, to frame him or catch him some way that would expose him as a snake in their midst. Once that was done, Frank would give him the respect he deserved and the Copa would be his alone. He seethed under the plaster dust that whitened his skin and reddened his eyes like a Kabuki demon, searching for a strategy.

After the opening of the second season and Putzi's assassination-by-publicity, which only strengthened Monte in Frank's eyes, Podell tightened his grip on the kitchen. That much, the kitchen, was his alone and he began to run it with a tyrant's obsession. Every plate of food, every waiter and busboy that passed by his table near the swinging door, stood for inspection before they went out to the showroom. He saw everything - a pinhead-sized stain on a waiter's jacket, parsley that didn't look fresh on a plate, shoes that weren't shined enough – everything – and sometimes nothing.

It was his way of keeping up a level of anxiety among the staff and venting his frustration while he waited impatiently for a chance to prove himself to Frank. That chance seemed unlikely ever to happen.

Monte's new show was even more successful than the first year's had been. He had successfully topped himself. He found a star, Olga San Juan, a 20-year-old, big band singer and dancer in Spanish Harlem. Dressed in fashions from Rio de Janiero, the young Puerto Rican beauty became the Brazilian icon of the Copa, the spirit of the Copa in the flesh. She brought fire to the floorshow and sparked a Brazilian samba craze that spread across the country. She became a star just big enough to lift the show but not bigger than the club itself.

Theatrical agents continued to line up to present their clients at Monte's office door. The line frequently extended into the lounge where hopefuls filled all the stools at the bar, waiting for a chance to be seen and heard. It was becoming impossible to get any work done at the club. The word was out on Broadway, for a performer, the Copa was "it".

The sight of Podell continued to aggravate Monte. But Frank was not about to leave his investment unwatched. It was just a fact of life that some bloodhound from Frank's crew would be a permanent fixture in the place. All Monte could do was commiserate with his friends. In their unguarded moments while drinking in the club, Monte's closer friends referred to Podell as "Quasimodo of the kitchen" and commented on his reign of terror behind the swinging doors. Monte responded by dubbing Podell "…the Duke of Dirty Dishes" and "his lowness." The comments, although muted, found their way to Podell quickly. He was acutely aware of any slight directed toward him, since in his business, a lack of respect could get you killed. He got the gist of the attitude through his spies among the captains and busboys. The opportunity for his revenge came with the spring of 1942.

To ease his mind, Frank took up golf. He hoped the exercise and distraction might help him sleep at night. He was willing to try almost anything. The *Irish Meadows* golf course on Long Island became his temporary haven. It gave him momentary peace, a bit of fresh air. But it didn't last long. Within a few weeks of Frank's arrival, a dozen well-dressed Italian and Jewish hoods also showed up with the most expensive and often most colorful golf togs money could buy and a newly found passion for the game. There was no way and nowhere the Prime Minister of the *Syndicate* could escape his life. Once again, the competitors and sycophants of his shadow world surrounded him. Unfortunately for Frank, the men in his line of work actually enjoyed golf. They found the privacy available on the links highly useful. It was impossible for anyone to overhear conversations from 200 yards away.

Here was the opportunity Podell had waited for. He became an avid golfer. He professed his love of the game to Frank and used every chance to get them both out on the course together. There on the long walks, Jules found the hours of time with Frank that would never have been available to him any other way. He began to plant the seeds of Monte's destruction.

If Monte was going to gain any independence from Frank C and the *Syndicate*, he had to look to Broadway. Now that he was a well-publicized nightclub moneymaker, he would attract uninvited partners to any new place before the ink was dry on the liquor license. A show out of town over the summer made no money, so the fellas wouldn't catch the scent. If the show had the stuff to make it on Broadway and started making money, then they'd show up to get their hooks into him. By that time, he figured, he could be lined up with the powerful Shubert brothers. They had their own way of dealing with unwanted partners. At least the odds would be evened up slightly. Once again he called on Walter Bachelor who had recovered financially from their last attempt at mounting a production.

This time Monte put his money on a horse with a track record. Sidney Kingsley had won the Pulitzer Prize for Drama in 1934 with his play *Men in White*, directed by a youngster named Lee Strasberg. Sidney was a pal - a talented but hard luck case who had tasted early success but now suffered the bitterness of failure on Broadway. Monte looked out for Sidney who had been on the cuff for almost as long as Monte remembered knowing him. Sidney was in the club almost every night that he was physically able to keep drinking. He had been on a run of hard luck ever since winning the Pulitzer. His next two plays, the anti-war play, *Ten Million Ghosts* (1936) and the following one *The World We Make* (1939) both bombed. The third strike was his disaffection from Elia Kazan and members of the Group Theatre who had been elevated to minor stardom by his *Men in White*. They dismissed Sidney's writing and the bourgeois critics who had praised it. They felt it had been their staging and acting that had made his writing a success. They seemed vindicated as his next two efforts died very publicly. Now Sidney suffered the torments of the damned – defeat, humiliation and crushing self-doubt.

For the last two years, he had been writing only sporadically and living off the meager income of his new wife, actress Madge Evans. One night, well on his way to a full load of liquor, he mentioned he had something on his shelf he thought might work. It was a straight drama he called *The Patriots* about the struggle between Thomas Jefferson and Alexander Hamilton over the direction of the country they had just invented. The title caught Monte's attention and the play itself had something to say to wartime audiences. A straight play could get him attention, Monte decided, as a change in direction from his musical fare. The truth was also that he needed a deal. He and Batchelor didn't have the cash to finance a musical with a score, an orchestra, a chorus line and lavish costumes. This time he placed his bet on *The Patriots*. Batchelor signed on and the two were on the road again to Connecticut for a summer of hard work and small audiences.

Monte invited Jane to audition, she declined. He said the pay would be equal to both of her current paychecks, she declined. He did everything short of giving her the part without an audition, she declined. She didn't want any favors. Jane was content to keep up her punishing work schedule in the chorus of *Panama Hattie* and the Copa, rather than take a straight acting job from her boss. She just didn't trust him and acting itself was still a painful reminder of Leif's recent betrayal. She wasn't ready to be an actress.

In Connecticut, the play struggled to its feet in spite of Sidney's devotion to late nights at the Copa. Early in the production he showed up to work clear-headed and eager after the train ride from Manhattan. As time wore on, he began to come to rehearsals hungover. Monte had to arrive at Sidney's apartment hours before the long commute to Connecticut to rouse Sidney and get him sufficiently caffeinated. By night, he directed the Copa staff to water down Sidney's liquor and sat with him frequently to monitor the flow of booze. One night in early summer, after Monte was no longer amusing to, or amused by Sidney, he invited Jane to sit with them and have dinner. Surprisingly, she accepted. She respected writers.

To Sidney, she was a cool breeze that carried the scent of life. He perked up instantly when Jane approached the table and introduced herself. It was soon apparent that she was genuinely interested in his work and was an active reader. After that first meeting, Monte took the chance to ask for her help. Would she befriend Sidney and help keep him sober? It was important to a lot of people struggling in a small playhouse in Connecticut who depended on his guidance. Without much deference to Monte, Jane agreed. Helping Sidney appealed to her. She had long experience nursing heartbroken drunks into rosier frames of mind. In that moment, Monte lost any doubts he had about her.

He saw how easily this small act of kindness came to her. She had no stake in the play, no angle on a part for herself. It was pure kindness, the kind his kid sister Isabel lavished on anyone down on their luck. Over the coming weeks and their dinners together, as he saw her compassion and humor and how Sidney brightened with her conversation, he fell deeply and hopelessly in love with her. He had never felt anything close to this before. This wasn't the eccentric, dramatic rush of his marriage proposal. It was quiet, deep and overwhelming. He was forced to patiently watch her, over drinks and dinners and conversations, as she revealed herself. Suddenly, he wasn't interested in protecting or mentoring her. He didn't want to be her big brother or her manager. He was in love with her. He needed her in his life. She, on the other hand, felt nothing much for him.

"You've been very generous," Monte nearly groveled before her, his need was so great. He knew it was obvious and that made him unsure, but couldn't stop himself, "Thank you. You've helped him so much." He tried to hide his lovesickness, but everyone saw it plainly. Except, Jane. She had no interest in men in general and romance in particular.

"Thanks. Sydney's okay, a good guy." Jane said. "Goodnight," she turned, took her coat and went home. She didn't give Monte a second look.

The Patriots grew from infancy to adolescence. It was a credible piece of work but not a hit. Audiences were lukewarm. It wasn't the type of play Monte felt he could tamper with, so he and Batch had to trust that Sidney would find the missing pieces. Privately, they discussed killing the show and cutting their losses. Because the play seemed to improve a little each night, they decided to stay with it. They also decided that what the play needed more than anything else was confidence – Sidney's confidence in himself. Monte scheduled a meeting with the Shubert brothers to book a theatre and seek their investment in the show for the coming season. *The Patriots* was going to Broadway – whether anyone currently wanted it or not.

Apparently the Shuberts had a different opinion. They sensed a load of bad luck headed right for them. Monte was right that the Shubert brothers had their own effective way of dealing with unwanted partners of a certain background. They stopped them at the door. This tactic was now applied to Monte. The brothers remembered last summer's revelation from Mayor

LaGuardia that Monte was a shill for Frank Costello. The meeting to discuss possible theatres for *The Patriots* was cancelled.

Monte looked at the dead phone receiver in his hand and fell into a momentary stupor. The news shook him like the death of a close relative. Over his career, he had been hemmed in by cops, gangsters, unions, stars and movie executives but those were temporary obstacles, par for the course. This was new. The Shuberts practically owned Broadway.

Monte sensed for the first time in his life, the end of his world. A possible way out of his smoky, boozy racket was suddenly beyond his reach. In the ever-joyful heart of Broadway, his adopted home, he was suddenly unwelcome. It was the death of possibility. Lines had been drawn and he would forever be on the dark side.

He shouldered the burden of telling Batch that they were going to fail once more. It was strike three and they both knew it. It was the end of a ten-year dream they had of working together. Monte was now tainted and anyone who stood with him would be tainted as well. He had another reputation now, one that was contagious. He promised his old friend that he would make good on his half of the money. To his eternal credit in Monte's eyes, Batch didn't flinch when he heard the news and said he wouldn't accept a nickel of Monte's money. As far as Batch was concerned, personally they were closer than ever. It was conspicuous that he said nothing more about doing business together. There was nothing more to say. It was the end.

The effect was subtle at first. Monte seemed his same happy-go-lucky self, up at noon, hobnobbing and party-making until 4 in the morning. The Copa was packed to the rafters and he was praised as *"That Proser Guy; The Night Club Proprietor Broadway Can't Break"* in a four page spread in *Cue Magazine*. The article recounted his mythological beginnings as the unsinkable little hobo whose entire life was dedicated to building ephemeral empires dedicated to fun. It was the perfect antidote to the disastrous news coming back in war dispatches. America was losing the war. The *New York Times* reported via the *London Daily Telegraph* that all Jews over the age of six in occupied France were now compelled to wear a yellow Star of David and that the Nazis had already killed over 1,000,000 Jews. There was nothing in Monte's outward appearance that belied his internal upheaval. Only Walter Batchelor noticed he wanted to be at the farm in Bucks County nearly every weekend.

Once in the countryside, he didn't want to leave. Their old game of "Go west, young man." at the Main Street stop sign in New Hope began again. Monte's restless, creative spirit was being crushed inside him. He'd had his moments with movies and radio and found them cold. After nightclubs, there was only Broadway and now that was impossible. The only thing that lifted him back out of his dark thoughts was his quest for the quiet, little dancer, Jane.

CHAPTER 25

SHE LOVES ME

With little hope of escape from his partnership with the *Syndicate*, Monte retreated to the solitary endeavor of winning Jane's attention. He never mentioned another word to her about marriage but never missed a chance to compliment her and delicately press forward with his courtship. He sent all his *Samba Sirens* flowers so he could include a special note to Jane in her bouquet. The notes always invited her to have dinner or stop by for a chat with authors, playwrights, movie directors and accomplished actors who would be in the club that evening.

He was wooing her by association. After a few successful meetings, he recognized that her taste ran to serious writers like Kingsley and included newspapermen. Actors of the Hollywood variety were definitely not her cup of tea, so he loaded the appointments with his buddies including Runyon, Winchell and Mark Hellinger. One evening in the midst of a particularly high-powered group including Runyon, the socialite Brenda Frasier, actor Don Ameche and others, Monte snuck in his secret weapon. Jane arrived at the booth, all the men stood up and she took her seat next to the fragile looking and soft spoken, Isabel, Monte's sister. Sandwiched among the loud, famous and near-famous, Jane and Isabel almost immediately fell into a close confidence. For the next few hours they parried the men when addressed and held their own in the conversation but spoke most frequently to each other.

When it was over, Monte walked Isabel to the front and into a cab. She was impressed with Jane, "Oh Monte, she's lovely", she told her brother. "But does she like you?"

"We got off to a rough start, but she'll come around," he said. It didn't seem to occur to Monte that he could fail. He was possessed. Isabel saw that she could only encourage him. He wouldn't hear anything else.

Irving Lazar, the young music agent from Georgie Woods' *William Morris Agency*, was having similar discussions. Jane Ball had struck his heartstrings as she brushed by him one evening in the club and later danced seemingly just for him from her place in the Copa's chorus line. He hung around the stage door of the *46th Street Theatre*, to introduce himself to her one night after *Panama Hattie* let out. He offered her a cab ride to the Copa. She turned him down.

This only fanned the flames of his heart. He too began sending invitations backstage, specifically to Jane. Like Monte, he played his industry contacts as his opening hand. To entice Jane to his table, Irving, going then by the nickname "Swifty", procured movie producers, studio talent scouts and musicians. He didn't know she liked writers. Copa house rules forbade dancers from sitting with patrons in the audience, so Swifty's meetings with Jane were brief introductions. He was always prepared for the parlay with opening night tickets to a show or the inside scoop on a band playing at another club, but Jane never accepted his invitations. Her rejections meant nothing. Swifty, like Monte, was not deterred by failure. But unlike Monte, Swifty had a detailed plan to win Jane. Monte was an important client, so he had to work quietly. His first step was to get her away from Monte, out of New York. He was going to get her a job in Hollywood.

Monte was anything but quiet about his intentions toward Jane. His mind had always been an open book to his friends and now this romantic chapter was known to everyone who knew him, or about him. His torch for Jane was lit and he carried it like a royal scepter. It drew his mind away from the darkness of war, uninvited partners and the end of his hopes for Broadway and freedom. He turned the direction of the Copa's entertainment over to Don Loper and Maxine Barrat, two talented young Broadway dancers. They brought a fresh vision and vigor to the show, dumping Monte's glossy look for a theatrical Latin theme with wide brimmed hats, full gowns and tropical colored petticoats.

Monte moved the meetings with Jane outside the club. They met Walter Batchelor and his wife Lovee at *21*. The former speakeasy was now one of the finest restaurants in Manhattan and partners Jack and Charley had Monte on the cuff. He and whomever he came in with never received a check. The gesture of affection was not lost on Jane. And the sheer fun of having Monte around at a meal was a revelation to her.

The following week, on the two-hour break between the end of the 8 o'clock and the start of the midnight shows at the Copa, they joined Henry Nemo and friends from various bands at the *Savoy Ballroom* at Lenox and 140th Street in Harlem. The integration of blacks and whites that eluded Monte at his *Dance Carnival,* was happening every night at the *Savoy*. The jitterbugging was wilder, the music closer, the atmosphere was relaxed, fun, normal. Even with Monte's flat feet and Jane's sore ones, the music was too infectious to let them sit still. Monte invited her to dance, she did enough to learn the steps but soon thanked him and sat down. Monte was too excited and went off to dance on his own and with various girls he caught on the way. Jane was excited just to be sitting down while other people danced. Jitterbugging had reached new heights of acrobatic skill. It was wild, strenuous and fast. Girls spun like tops, got flipped into the air, slid between legs and hopped like jackhammers. It was a frenzy and Monte was totally caught up in it. Jane was amused at his lack of control. He was as wild as any of them but unpracticed. He frequently spun girls out into the crowd, many never came back.

He came and flopped at the table, slick with sweat, out of breath, his tie twisted and half-mast. Drinks came, a chatter was struck up and a friend of a friend, someone in Nemo's crowd said something about the Germans finishing the Jews off, the rest was lost in the noise. Monte motioned to the man to repeat what he just said. Monte listened for a moment, looked hard at the man, then launched himself over the table at him. He got in one solid punch and took one or two before being wrestled to the floor by the others. The music stopped and only a dozen men scuffling and swearing at each other was heard. The two were dragged up, dusted off and escorted out. Jane followed Monte.

On the trip east from Lenox and down Fifth Avenue, Monte and Jane didn't say a word. Monte stared straight ahead. He was dirty, his face was cut. He had to go to his apartment, shower and change for the midnight show. Finally as they were approaching the Copa's awning on 60th Street, he said, "I'm sorry about the trouble."

"What did he say?"

"Anti-Semite…," was all Monte would say about it. Then he added to lighten the mood, "Kind of a busman's holiday for you."

"No, I enjoyed it," Jane said. And she meant it. Monte got out of the cab and held the door for her. "Thanks," she said as she walked to Nick who opened the Copa's front door for her. Monte watched her go in, got back in the cab and went home to clean up.

The Copa made *Life Magazine,* December 1942 issue. The article was called *"Copacabana Girls".* Jane, June Allyson, Lucille Bremer, the Barnes twins, all the girls were singled out and photographed in a head and shoulders close-up that took a quarter page each. Jane's caption read, "Jane Sloane Ball, Born: October 4, 1922, Kingston, NY, Height: 5' 4", Weight: 102, Bust: 32, Hips: 34, Favorite Perfume "L'heure bleue" Ambition: to study medicine. Father: an accountant. Her "Ideal man" was a dark, tall doctor with a sense of humor.

When Monte read this he felt a momentary letdown. Seeing it in print made it impossible to ignore. He really wasn't her type, except maybe for the sense of humor. He clipped the article anyway and placed it in his files with all the others.

Jane's offer from Hollywood arrived in a telegram delivered personally by Swifty. A costume drama, *The Keys of the Kingdom* was all set to shoot but they needed a young ingénue. They had tested dozens of young women but still hadn't found someone to play opposite Gregory Peck. Jane was screen tested in New York. A week later she was summoned to 20th Century Fox in California to meet the studio people and, if all went well, sign a contract. Swifty insisted that he accompany her. He had big plans to discuss during their five-day train trip together on the *20th Century*. He'd heard many wonderful things about the rocking motion of trains and romance.

"That's wonderful news," Monte told Jane. His heart was breaking. "I can give you a few names to look up while you're there."

"Thanks," Jane said. "If something happens, I may need my old job back."

Monte waved her off, "What could happen? You'll be terrific."

Jane turned to walk out of the Copa and pack her things for Hollywood. "D'ya need a few bucks for your kick?" He immediately felt foolish, desperate. "For the tickets… the extras y'know…" He was rambling, unable to make a dignified, final goodbye.

"I'm okay," Jane said. She felt him trying to appear unemotional and failing badly. Since their first ridiculous encounter she'd come to know he wasn't the idiot he first appeared to be. She thought he was a little "cuckoo" probably because he drank too much. He had no respect for money and gambled fortunes she'd heard, but she also had to admit, finally, that he was what he appeared to be – a scrappy saloonkeeper with a soft touch for drunks and other people in trouble. He was easy to read.

"Okay then, kid. Good luck," he said. He looked calm but by then she knew he was in love with her. It was in the columns. Even though this was their goodbye, he didn't flinch, gave no hint of pain. He was staring right at her, wanting to help somehow. She hadn't seen this emotional toughness before and it rang her bell. On top of that, he was like most of the Jewish men she'd ever met, loyal as a terrier. She thought he was a Jewish Jim Morgan.

"You're okay too," she told him and walked out. It was a mistake. She thought she was saying goodbye forever by ending on a nice note. But from that tiny thread of affection, Monte began to weave a tapestry of their future. His torch for her would soon burn brighter than ever.

Jane signed with *20th Century Fox* the same day as Norma Jean Baker, the future Marilyn Monroe. To celebrate, Swifty insisted on dinner at *Mocambo* on Sunset Strip. Jane surprised herself by choking up as emotions of relief and excitement swirled through her. Swifty understood her relief and did his best to comfort her. The weeks of anticipation were over. The meat grinder of chorus work was behind her and she could hopefully provide some security to her family back in Kingston. The car ride back to her hotel with Swifty was a blur of hopeful fantasies and wonder at the sight of palm and orange trees growing in people's front yards.

When Jane walked into *Mocambo* with Swifty she thought she was back in the Copa. The owners had dropped over $100,000 on the Latin décor. Live parrots, macaws and cockatoos lined the walls. It was a swing-dance-until-dawn kind of place crowded with movie people - Myrna Loy, Louis B. Mayer, Errol Flynn and everyone else who could fit. Jane was impressed. Hollywood knew how to throw a party. Swifty worked the tables so hard, he nearly got thrown out. His overbearing New York chutzpah was annoying to a few Hollywoodites. They apparently liked promotion in small doses especially after business hours. Jane thought she'd never seen a harder working man going in the wrong direction than Swifty. But it was all for her benefit, she had to respect him. When she returned to her room at the *Chateau Marmont*, there were flowers and a telegram from New York, "Welcome to stardom, Monte."

Out front, Monte kept the drinking press informed of the Hollywood progress of his would-be, possible, unconfirmed but likely fiancée. He informed Jack Entratter and the staff that he would be taking some time to look for opportunities in Hollywood. He gave the office keys to his manager Milton

Pickman and told him whom to keep on the cuff and whom to banish.

For Jack Diamond, his press rep, he expected him to keep up the pace of lubricating columnists as needed. Diamond was not nearly the drinker or table jockey that Monte was, so the least he could do was be there to buy the drinks for the right people.

For Podell, Monte went into the kitchen, the surgically clean seat of Podell's power. He took his time inspecting every element of the stoves and set up. He looked into the walk-in freezer, the refrigerators. He walked through the snaking underground hallway, all the way to the sidewalk service entrance of the club and back. On his way back out to the show room, he stopped at Podell's table near the show room entrance, the throne of his nemesis' domain, and looked it over, as Podell stood nearby, watching. Monte wiped his index finger along Podell's chair, checked his finger for dirt.

He took a moment and then looked at Podell who was watching every movement of the performance. Monte said nothing, just stared at his enemy. Podell also didn't say a word. They were at a perfect balance of power. Both were the same size and build. Both were unable to say anything bad about the other without losing power. Both were silent toward each other because neither was interested in patching up the relationship. Both detested the other. One would go, one would stay. They stared at each other like the two bar brawlers they were, only interested in finding the other's weakness and projecting their own strength. Monte turned and walked out, offering only silence and his back to his managing partner.

In Hollywood, Monte put on a soiree every night in a different place. *Mocambo, Ciro's, The Clover Club*. He gathered the most interesting human bait he could muster to attract Jane. She showed up one night at *Ciro's* after a week of invitations. It was old home night for Monte. He was hosting all the studio publicists and crackpot screenwriters he used to run around with in the old days of promoting Harold Lloyd and then Mary Pickford.

From the first minutes, it was one wisecrack after another, directed at big shot studio heads, stars or each other. Everyone and everything was fair game. As the drinks came by the trayful, the volume of their conversation grew along with the size of their party. People gathered round them. They were the floorshow for an hour or so. It seemed like most of the room was either laughing with them or straining to hear the next crack. Jane fit in, laughing easily with everyone else.

Monte was as happy as he'd ever been. He heard her laugh and read the tone of it. He could tell where she found humor and directed his jibes toward it. She roared when stuffed shirts were deflated and the vain were tweaked. She had a love for the plainly ridiculous situations of everyday life – pants that rip at the crotch, pets with more common sense than their owners, and almost anything that happened in church. She knew people. Her eyes watered, her cheeks burned red as the tummeling continued with an occasional "zetz" skewering some movie fool.

She could see Monte was very much in the center of the circle, a ringleader but a good natured one. As much as he loved any fool for genuine entertainment, there was rarely bitterness toward them. He was an optimist.

Unfortunately, Swifty showed up halfway through the evening. It wasn't a pleasant meeting although to an outsider it might appear that the two were getting along famously. Monte and Swifty talked very fast about what great business they could do together. They were in fact dueling to show who could do the most for Jane. The tone had moved from hilarity to something a lot like work. It became quite late quite soon after Swifty arrived.

Jane drifted to thoughts of her crack of dawn appointment with the studio makeup and hair artists. *The Keys of the Kingdom* was a lush 18th century drawing room drama that needed hours for dressing. She was ready for home and bed. Monte insisted on driving her home. She accepted. They said very little on the drive home. Monte drove past the orange groves on Curson Street, through the sweet scent of orange blossoms in the night air.

CHAPTER 26

SHE LOVES ME NOT

The night at Ciro's had tired her. Jane felt it the next day. Further invitations were refused from Monte and Swifty. For the rest of the movie, she went directly home to study her scenes and rest.

Monte was adrift, but it would be too painful to return to New York to live with his heartache and idle boast of engagement to Jane Ball. He spent a few days at Santa Anita screaming at horses that ran away with some of his and his pal, Jackie Gleason's, money. Gleason was stumbling through some of Hollywood's most uninspired wartime comedies and turning in forgettable performances. The previous year he'd been fired from the movie *Navy Blues* for improvising and arguing with the director. His manager George "Bullets" Durgom, named for his pointed head, not his talent with guns, sat with them in the homestretch box seats.

He'd come to California to help keep his client as sober and cooperative as possible. Monte and Bullets had been knock-around pals for more years than they could remember, running into each other in nightclubs since the 30's. Bullets needed Monte's help. He begged Monte to help keep Gleason from exploding in frustration and destroying his career.

Day to day, Gleason simply had too much energy and wore Bullets out early. Monte was supposed to take the late shift to keep the gigantic comedian from derailing. Bullets soon realized that he could not have made a worse choice for babysitter. Generally after midnight and a quart of scotch, if Gleason wasn't shooting the next day, or sometimes even if he was, he and Monte slipped away and grabbed the train to Tijuana and the *Agua Caliente* racetrack or hopped a seaplane to the *Avalon* casino on Catalina Island. They often disappeared for days. The only one who worried about all this was poor Bullets, who suffered from constant migraine headaches and acid stomach.

The only thing that worried Monte was Podell. Copa manager Milton Pickman caught Podell's waiters padding dinner checks by adding the numbers of the year, as in $19.42, as tax. When caught by sharp-eyed patrons they easily claimed it was an innocent mix-up. This was one small victory for Milton, in a constant war that could never be won. For every scam they uncovered, there were a dozen they didn't find for months or years. One of the more bizarre grifts involved filling the bar sinks with glass ice cubes and putting a layer of real ice on top. This was intended to fool the *Coca-Cola* salesmen who checked to see that their soda was immersed in ice as specified in the distribution contract with the club. Saving a few pennies on ice by grifting the *Coca-Cola* man was a small but steady earner. It was the principle that mattered. Theft, no matter how small, was the order of the day. Every day.

Even when they caught Podell red-handed, they couldn't fire him. They couldn't call the cops or get a lawyer. The only one who might care was Frank C and he quickly got tired of hearing the complaints. After the check padding scam, Frank warned Podell and the stealing stopped for a while. But not for long.

To stay busy in Hollywood, Monte started scouting around for a site to house the *Copacabana West*. He couldn't find anything that was quite right. He met with movie people half-heartedly discussing ideas for a movie like the one his old boss Texas

Guinan made, about her life in the clubs. This would be a musical comedy not a crime thriller like Texas had tried. He lost interest in the pitch quickly. It was all a ruse to stick around, hoping for a break in Jane's schedule. The winter passed in a blur of stalled and stillborn projects. He mainly worked his connections to get on the *20th Century Fox* movie lot, so he might run into Jane at the commissary during her lunch break. It worked twice. He spent a little over an hour with Jane during his 6 months in LA.

The movie wrapped and Jane returned to Kingston for the Christmas holidays with her family. *The Keys to the Kingdom* was going to be released in the spring. She was due back in LA to start *Winged Victory* with director George Cukor right after New Year.

Homecoming for Jane was a moment of triumph that she had never felt before. When she arrived on the train platform in Poughkeepsie, Jim Morgan stood at the front of a crowd of hundreds. He grabbed her in a bear hug that knocked the wind out of her. Nan fought against tears but quickly gave up as she kissed Jane's face and pulled her toward the car. Her suitcases flew from the train platform, coddled like precious objects through the crowd of fans, family and Kingston neighbors who had come out to greet their own homegrown movie star. It was a day of laughing and crying simultaneously, the joy was so delirious. In spite of that bleak winter of 1942, the Ball home on Albany Avenue rang with the shouts of a family redeemed from shame and elevated to the status of near-royalty.

The celebration ran on for days spreading from Albany Avenue to Cornell Street where the first public party was kicked off at *Morgan's Tavern*. Surprise visits from childhood friends and anxious public officials interrupted most of Jane's conversations. It was Christmas time.

Christmas carols burst out from the most unexpected patrons and drunken jitterbugging erupted inappropriately. The wave of exuberance subsided as Christmas approached. Jane found it hard to adjust to sleeping late and being idle. She'd been working so hard for so long that physically she had to get up and move as soon as she woke up. Christmas shopping became an athletic event with her as she piled on the gifts bought with her movie money. She helped scrub, dust and sweep every corner of the rambling old Victorian house and was eager to help Jim work on his car. Relaxing was not a possibility.

Christmas Day finally came and the family other than Jane seemed content to sit and chat the day away as breakfast stretched until noon and wrapping paper was strewn from the Christmas tree across the living room and into the dining room. It was family time, private time., so it was a surprise to everyone to hear a gentle rapping on the front door. The youngest, Andy, sprang into action and opened the door to find an extremely well-dressed gentleman standing on the front porch with a small gift and friendly smile.

"Merry Christmas," the stranger said.

"Yeah, you too." Andy offered.

"Excuse me, is Jane home?" the man asked.

"Yes." Andy in his 17th year, not completely confident with social graces, stood wondering what to do next. The stranger was too polite to suggest. He simply offered up the small, wrapped gift in his hand.

Finally, "You wanna come in?" Andy asked.

"Yes, thank you." Monte stepped in from the cold porch hoping Roman Catholics didn't have some subtle Christmas tradition upon entering a house that a Jew like him might not know about. When Jane saw him, she was too stunned to speak. The powdering of snow on his overcoat melted, making him sparkle with a sheen of water. He didn't offer the gift, instead looked straight at her. Christmas lights outlined her and soft winter light flickered in her eyes. Her small, wavering smile and offer of a cup of coffee, ended his torment.

Since Monte had entertained the family all afternoon with tales of adventure as a hobo and the baseball greats who were carried drunk out of the Copa before a big game, she thought it would be interesting for him to attend High Mass with them. Out of earshot of her mother, she promised him, with a wink, it would be a barrel of laughs, better than *Ciro's*. Nan was fervent in her devotion to Catholicism. No one, not even favored daughter Jane, would dare denigrate the church in front of her.

It was an unusual Christmas all around, particularly the midnight Mass at *St. Joseph's*. The former outcast, shanty-Irish Ball family was greeted warmly. The family had produced a princess of extraordinary luminance who was fiercely championed by the wealthy rum-runner turned businessman, Jim Morgan. Now, they had money, fame, beauty, successful businesses, prominent real estate and the muscle and brains to back it all up. All eight of the clan arrived together. As they moved to a pew significantly up front near the altar, they noticed every eye was on them. It seemed that the unsettling past of syphilis, shacking up and bootlegging was bleached away by the glare of show business spotlights. Except for the dapper, Jewish-looking Monte who joined them, they might have been the perfectly redeemed Catholic family. With Monte in tow, however, it was clear the Balls were still not quite ready for an invitation to many of the church social circles and probably never would be. Jane found the social aspects of church annoying anyway. She still clung weakly to the promise of a sanctified life through prayer and ritual but it was fast losing its believability with her. She'd known too many good Catholics up to their necks in sin to have much hope for the power of the church.

In *St. Joseph's*, under the searing attention of 600 hundred parishioners, Jane regretted her invitation to Monte but was surprised by how perfectly at ease he seemed. He went through the entire interminable Latin Mass with the exception of receiving communion, like he'd been doing it all his life. Monte was surprised they didn't sing. He'd heard that Christians sang hymns.

It wasn't until the following day at the bar in *Morgan's* that they actually had the laughs Jane promised. Unfortunately some of the left over hard feelings and envy of the churchgoers followed them. Jane had joined Monte at the end of the bar where he settled. She sat on the very last stool at the end of the bar where she had done most of her homework as a girl. She felt she should keep Monte company since he didn't know anyone else.

Sometime in the late afternoon, a lone voice carried up the length of the bar over the other low conversations.

"How come all the ugly Jews get all the pretty girls?"

Jane put down her ginger ale - with just enough Scotch in it to spoil the taste - and looked at Jim. His hand wasn't going under the bar yet. He went to the patron and spoke to him quietly but directly.

"Izzat right?" the man asked and repeated, "I just wanna know why all the ugly Jews get the girls!" He could not be reasoned with. Monte stared into his drink. He stood up. Jane grabbed his arm but he was moving fast.

"Get up," he told the loudmouth. Jim's hand went under the bar for his Louisville Slugger. The man stood up and seemed to continue standing up for ten minutes. When he finally unfolded to his full height he was at least a foot over Monte's head and nearly twice as wide. He was a railroad worker who was known for shouldering a two-man load while carrying his sledge in his free hand. Monte went from fury to concern almost instantly. He started to laugh. Jim looked at the situation and scratched his chin with a little smile, "Whatta ya gonna do now?"

"I don't know," he said to Jim. "Any ideas?" A quiet laugh rumbled down the bar as Monte stood paralyzed in front of the giant. The last two in on the joke were Jane and the giant who waited for Monte to make a move. Jim came to the rescue, "Hey you!" he addressed the giant, "Sit down or get the hell out and don't ever come back here."

The man wavered. Jim tightened his grip on his bat, choking it high up on the handle, looking for a quick bunt instead of line drive. Other than the railroad yard, *Morgan's* was the only place the man had to socialize.

"And apologize to the lady," Monte demanded. In spite of the jokes to defuse the tension, Monte was still hot. He prepared mentally to kick Goliath in the nuts if he flinched. Jim didn't take his eyes off the two or his hand off the bat, "Jesus, Mary and Joseph," he mumbled.

"Screw you. The both a' yuz," the giant said. He turned back to the bar and sat down.

Monte didn't move away quickly enough so Jim shot a look at him and jerked his thumb toward the end of the bar, "You too." Laughter and a few comments like, "You sure showed him!" preceded Monte as he returned to his barstool next to Jane. He sat and looked at Jane thinking he'd made a fool of himself.

"Are you nuts?" she asked.

Monte shrugged, "Eh, whatta ya gonna do?" he said, "They're everywhere."

Jim was in a pow-wow with a few of his regulars down the bar, his baseball bat still in his hand. Jane saw Monte salute him with his drink and Jim give Monte the nod. The two saloon-keepers understood each other perfectly.

Jane was on her way back to California the next day. She allowed Monte to drive her into the city to Grand Central Station in the gleaming, cream-colored Packard he'd bought from Batch. The conversation was light between them. Monte knew a bit about train travel and advised her.

"Be sure your cabin's behind the restroom, or you'll be hearing footsteps all night."

"Yeah, thanks."

He went on with practical tips on travelling and then on to where to eat in Hollywood for a while, then they fell silent.

Jane thought a lot about her talk with Sis, the oldest sister, which had lasted most of the previous night. Sis was engaged to a young Army sergeant, Dick Rightmeyer, whom Jane disliked, so it was difficult to talk about her new feelings toward Monte without straying into dangerous territory.

"He'd be steady," Jane said without much enthusiasm.

"He's not bad looking," Sis tried to help. They sprawled across Jane's bed with the windows cracked open to let out Sis's cigarette smoke. The steam radiators clanged as incoming steam expanded inside them. The valve hissed quickly releasing pressure and musty steam into the room.

"He treats me like gold. This English manners... thing," Jane said.

"Look, if he makes good money and toes the line, what else you want? He's seems like a decent enough guy. Got a good sense of humor."

Jane thought over the last bit, the humor, and had to agree with that part.

This wasn't the kind of romantic inspiration Jane was looking for but it was on the money as far as common sense. The result was Jane got a lot of help in making a decision.

As he drove south through the frozen Hudson Valley, Monte was just a happy man in love, trying his best not to show it. As they arrived at Grand Central and a Red Cap was taking Jane's luggage, the moment of decision arrived as well. It happened instantly and silently. Monte took the lead and Jane let herself be led. He instructed the porter and gently directed Jane through the iron doors of the station. They followed the bags across the granite floor under the massive dome of Grand Central through a buzzing hive of holiday travelers. Finally on the platform, Jane was about to board. She stopped to say goodbye, turning to Monte. Somehow whatever needed to be communicated was done without speaking. A lone brass bell swung by a Salvation Army recruit cling-clanged a steady heartbeat. Boarding travelers brushed past Jane sweeping her toward the waiting train. Monte leaned in and Jane surrendered. They kissed, softly, quickly. It dissolved whatever reserve Monte had left. He started talking about calling, writing, visiting, then stopped. He was jabbering. He choked up and couldn't speak. Jane saw his embarrassment and then his half-smile acknowledging his foolishness. She saw that he was exactly what he appeared to be – an impetuous man who was completely in love with her.

New Year's Day 1943 passed quickly as Monte spent the day and a small fortune on a phone call to California. It started out nicely but soon it was clear that Jane was having a hard time reassuring him that she felt as strongly as he did. He knew the temptations of Hollywood. He knew she was getting propositioned in large and small ways several times a day. She was, after all, one of the brightest young ingénues on the scene. He hung up knowing something would have to be done. Before the call he imagined her happily making plans for their future together, like he had been doing with any friend who would listen, but he heard something very different on the phone. He was losing her.

CHAPTER 27

THE INVISIBLE WEB

On August 29th, 1943 Frank Costello's quiet and obscure reign as Prime Minister of the *Syndicate* was suddenly exposed. A banner headline shot across the front page of the New York Times, "GANGSTER BACKED AURELIO FOR BENCH, PROSECUTOR AVERS". Everyone knew of mobster Lucky Luciano through his very public trial and conviction, but up to that point not many knew of, or remembered, the former bootlegger Frank Costello. District Attorney Frank S. Hogan issued a statement in the Times that said, "Frank Costello, ex-convict and underworld leader…brought about the nomination of Magistrate Thomas A. Aurelio as candidate for Justice of the Supreme Court." Costello was now a target and a public figure. This attack by the government not only limited his ability to operate, it prompted powerful forces inside the *Syndicate* to start to move against him as well. Suddenly there were few opportunities for a leisurely game of golf or private evening on the town. Frank C was under siege.

The investigation proved that Costello had in fact financed Aurelio's bid for nomination to the bench. The Prime Minister of the *Syndicate* even held a $10,000 personal IOU from the judge. The investigation also began to uncover some of

Costello's other business arrangements. To call off the dogs, Costello agreed to withdraw from any ownership in certain businesses including several nightclubs that remained unidentified to the public. As a result, Monte's protection inside the Copa vanished.

That was all the encouragement Podell needed. With Costello out of the way, at least temporarily, he began to feel he could deal with Monte more directly. Only Joe Adonis was there to prevent him from killing the goose that laid the golden eggs… but if he roughed up the goose to get a few more eggs, Adonis didn't necessarily see the harm in that. Podell was still restricted to operating primarily from the kitchen since the club was now under closer scrutiny of the authorities, but his ambitions toward the rest of the operation now had free reign.

Soon after the headline appeared, Georgie Woods began to get calls from Podell discussing talent that might appear at the club. It was a frontal attack. Of course, Woods called Monte immediately after hanging up with Podell. He didn't want to offend either man. After Woods told him the news, Monte held back. He considered his next move carefully.

With Walter Winchell now a commissioned officer in the Navy and Joe E. having just completed an extensive tour of the Pacific entertaining Marines from the back of flatbed trucks, the war effort had finally reached into every corner of America. Victories in the Pacific and Hitler's retreat from significant public appearances signaled clearly that the tide of the war had turned. The chill terror of Nazi domination began to lift and everyone exhaled slightly. Now the war could be discussed openly, even with a bit of bravado. Heroes were emerging like General George Patton, war correspondent Ernie Pyle and everyman GI's, dogfaces, swabbies, leathernecks and flyboys from hometowns across the nation. America was on the attack. President Roosevelt spoke on the radio on the evening of September 8, to start the Third War Loan drive, with its 'Back the Attack' slogan. Its ambitious goal was to raise 15 billion dollars. By the time the drive was over in February, nearly 19 billion dollars' worth of war bonds were sold.

In the swing of the moment, the Copa presented a hopeful military theme in a few of its musical numbers. But as the first, fragile optimism about the war emerged, inside the club, the private war for dominance escalated again. Podell had waited years, silently suffering insults and humiliations, holding his ambition in check. His time had finally arrived.

Monte held the line against Podell's offensive at the *William Morris Agency* by booking and contracting the entire season through July. He filled the schedule with new performers like Jan Murray, a young comedian recruited from the Catskills, rather than leaving openings while he negotiated to fill the rest of the season. Podell was shut out, at least through the summer.

Podell launched another attack on more familiar terrain. Once the heat of the Aurelio investigation cooled, the take, the reported weekly receipts, dropped significantly on certain random nights even though the place was as packed as ever. Monte saw his 50 percent of the profits waver as Podell lowered and raised the amount of cash skimmed off the top. There seemed to be nothing he and manager Milton Pickman could do about it. Podell had too many hands working for him and too many eyes on the lookout. Without the policing effect of Frank C around the place, the Copa quickly devolved into a den of very polished and professional thieves. Monte's barely suppressed rage began exploding in pointed and public insults toward Podell, until his trusted inside security man and floor manager, Jack Entratter, had to physically pull Monte aside before someone from Adonis' crew did. Monte's low center of gravity and bull physique made it tough work for the taller Entratter to grab and hold him but he managed to hold on long enough to talk sense into him. Because of their long history around barroom scuffles, Entratter was the only one Monte would listen to when his blood was up, and the only one now standing between him and serious injury.

But the real danger to Monte wasn't from Adonis or Podell. It was from the federal government. If they could prove what Monte knew, that tens of thousands of dollars were vanishing before they hit the cash registers, it would be Monte, whose name was on the license, not Podell, who would take the fall for a tax evasion rap. He took his case to Adonis.

Adonis owed him nothing, not like Costello. Since there was no friendship to leverage against, Monte had no real strategy. All he could do was make a demand, and he did. It was a pure power play.

Monte asked Joe A. to come in early one day for a meeting. Joe was a busy and easily irritated man. He showed up in a foul mood and dispensed with the niceties that would have passed between Monte and Frank. The meeting was already going badly, as Monte expected. Monte obliged Adonis and got right to the point. He said he would close the place if the monkey-business didn't stop. He'd walk away, taking his show with him. The *Copa Revue* could play in any hotel ballroom in New York. Adonis and Podell could keep the place at 10 East 60th and "… good luck…" to them with it. Adonis sat back in his chair like he'd been slapped. He said nothing for a moment as he figured the angles. He knew of Costello's special friendship with Jews, particularly this one and the hard dollar value of the Copa partnership. The strain of holding back his natural first reaction to pistol-whip Monte into submission showed on his face. He was being threatened. It made him murderous. He leaned over the table and stuck his finger close to Monte's face. "The show stays," he said and sat back in his chair. Meeting over. Joe was ready to take a swing at the next person who spoke to him.

Monte got up and went to his office. He knew Adonis would take at least a few days to cool off, if he was going to cool off. If not, the next move was unpredictable and possibly very unhealthy for Monte. He only hoped Adonis would consult with Costello before making any rash counter-move.

Almost immediately the doctored dinner checks, watered drinks and aggressive cash skimming slowed, then stopped. Podell was being held in check. Georgie Woods reported no more phone calls. Apparently Adonis took the case to Costello because within a few days Joe A. was giving Monte grudging respect calling him "…a tough little Jew" and clapping him on the back. Costello's invisible hand still held Monte safely in its grasp. This keen awareness of his vulnerability, the fragility of life – particularly his own - propelled him for the third time toward the only thing he knew that might make it worthwhile. He was off again to Hollywood and Jane.

This time there were no publicity angles or press releases of his intentions. Jane's second picture *Winged Victory* was wrapping up and he wanted to be there when it finished. But a complication cropped up.

Jane Froman, possibly the most inspired singer of the era's musical geniuses like George and Ira Gershwin, Cole Porter and Irving Berlin, suddenly wanted to play the Copa. Froman was so singular a talent, her voice so electrifying and phrasing so dramatic, that she inspired a widely quoted comment from Billy Rose when he was asked who the top ten singers in the country were. Rose said, "Jane Froman and nine others."

Normally, Froman's request to appear at the club would have been a gratifying but fairly routine event. Schedules would be shifted, apologies made and presto – availability would appear in the club's schedule. But this request was far from routine. Six months earlier she had been paralyzed in a plane crash. It seemed then that her exceptional career was over. She had been entertaining Allied troops throughout Europe in USO shows. Flying home from her last show, her plane was shot down and crashed into the Taugus River in Portugal. 23 of the 38 performers and musicians who had lived and performed with her for months near the front lines were killed in the crash. Along with her paralysis and the tragedy of losing dozens of close friends in that gruesome nightmare, one leg was nearly severed and she suffered severe internal injuries. The fact that she was able and willing to perform again, anywhere, was simply an inspiration so powerful and an honor so humbling, that Monte could not say no. He was willing to risk his chances with his Jane over it. He had promised her he would be in California on the day she wrapped up her picture, but knew he might have to break the date if Froman needed special help, which was likely. When he told Jane the situation, she agreed immediately that he should stay if he needed to. Her agreement came a bit too fast for Monte's liking. It had taken him months to get her to agree to see him again after his last unannounced and disastrous visit. She sounded almost relieved that he might not be coming after all. Even though he felt his chances with Jane Ball slipping, he felt the need to honor Jane Froman more. He didn't tell his Jane that Froman's heroic return was going to be even more dramatic than anyone could imagine. Froman wanted the intimacy of the Copa for what she was going to attempt.

On stage at the Copa, Froman was wheeled out in a metal frame that allowed her to appear to stand by leaning back against a supporting bench and lower back brace. The audience rose to their feet to welcome her. Men and women stood up, applauding her bravery and sacrifice. The ovation went on for minutes. It had been all over the papers when her plane had been shot down. For weeks no one knew if she would live. It was assumed no one would ever see her perform again but here she was, just six months later. The broken singer stood propped up in her metal contraption with unbroken composure as the tearful applause cascaded over her.

Eventually, the wave of emotion subsided. The people sat again at their tables, staring at the stage, motionless. In dead silence, the first gentle notes of "With a Song in My Heart" rose from the piano. Froman sang from her metal cage with an intensity that caught people's breath in their throats. Among all six hundred people, not a fork was lifted or drink sipped. Attention strained to catch every inflection as if everyone was imprisoned in steel with her, and her heartache was their own. The second verse began and as it rose toward its crescendo Froman stepped unsteadily out of her cage, leaning heavily on a cane in one hand. A collective gasp leapt from the audience. Pent up emotions burst and silent tears welled up in the hundreds watching her. In the long history of emotional performances, this was possibly the most wrenching ever seen in the club. There was no containing the exuberance, the pure ecstasy that flooded the small cellar that evening. Froman performed most of her remaining songs from a comfortable armchair. It was a performance of staggering power that set the columns on fire the next day.

That night was also the debut of newcomer Jan Murray. It was the biggest break of the fledgling comedian's career. He'd been plucked from obscurity in Catskill dinner shows to perform in the hottest nightclub in the world, the Copa. Unfortunately, his big debut followed Froman that evening and was completely overshadowed by her. The next day there wasn't one word about him in any column. He was sunk. The only one who seemed to notice was Monte. He made it up to the young comic by making a few calls to friends in the press. From then on, Murray got plenty of ink. His career was launched.

When Monte finally arrived in his dusty rented sedan at the motel surrounded by high desert scrub in Taft, California, Jane was waiting for him at the office door with her bags packed. She had been living between the motel and a collection of stifling warehouses converted to movie stages for almost two months while shooting *Winged Victory*. Without ceremony she carried her own bags to the car, tossed them in the trunk and told Monte, "Get me the hell out of here." They were on their way to "any place with water and trees," which Monte determined should be separate rooms in a lakeside lodge on Lake Arrowhead. They spent the drive getting re-acquainted with each other, testing the relationship in subtle ways.

At the lake, the frantic paces of their lives vanished. The noise of human activity faded to the rustle of Ponderosa pines. Most of the first day, Jane stayed in her room. Monte checked her "do not disturb" door-hanger every few hours like a night watchman making his rounds. He took the time to find all the activities around the lake in case Jane emerged.

In her room, Jane's first full bout with severe depression stole every shred of hope and every spark of energy from her. She was pinned to her bed, staring at the ceiling and out the window, wondering why all she really wanted to do was die. On the surface, she had a beautiful life. She was a movie star, she was young, healthy and beautiful, but like Frances Farmer before her and thousands who would come later, she felt like her heart was collapsing under a weight. A black sorrow swallowed every thought. She had felt this horror nibbling at the edges of her consciousness since the second week of the movie but was able to distract herself with the focus needed for the controlled panic of moviemaking on location. Now she had no distractions. She had woken after a fitful night into a dread that sat on her heart like a block of granite, pressing her into the bed. She knew that the pills she'd taken were part of the problem.

The little white pep pills always arrived on the set with the morning coffee. The assistant directors carried white paper envelopes full of them. If the boys on the front lines could fight all night and then get up and march the next day, it was the least any patriot could do to match their energy for the war effort at home. Dexadrine, the secret weapon that kept eyes wide open at the front, were passed out at breakfast like mints at a Hollywood dinner party. Jane, who got the jitters from a cup of coffee, discovered that the pills not only gave her unlimited energy but they helped bring her emotions to the surface. She could summon tears or spitting fury on a moment's notice. Director George Cukor loved watching the hard surface of his ingénue crack and expose the sentimental Irish girl underneath. They shot scenes all night. Take after take, digging deeper into all the actors' raw emotions, then more takes, restraining the emotion until exactly the right feeling was captured on film and the actors were drained and emotionally scoured clean. In the morning, they applauded their psychic surgery that had been assisted by the little white pills. Then, on a dozen hazy, gray mornings Jane was driven from the sound stage in a fog of emotional exhaustion to her dusty motel room. She locked the door, praying for sleep to calm her nerves and hoping that some pill-addled assistant director or actor wouldn't come knocking wanting "to talk".

Now, away from her little, white morning pick-me-ups she was crying for reasons she didn't understand. Shadows of hopelessness and shame, barely remembered from years ago, pulsed through her. She was crying over nothing, and then everything. By late afternoon, she fell asleep deeply for the first time in weeks.

As the sun was setting, Monte returned from his fourth or fifth walk around the lake alone. On his door was a note from Jane, "Dinner?"

They ate early, totally off the nightlife schedule, and had no drinks, not even cocktails. The conversation was quiet, almost mundane considering they hadn't spoken, except for brief phone chats, in months. All the entertainment Monte wanted was to watch Jane eat.

She was happy to have a gentleman, one who was beyond trying to impress her, as her companion. Being cloistered with the movie company in a remote location for months, she had put up with every dim-witted, half-baked pick up line, cheap ploy for sympathy, ingratiating compliment and veiled coercion until she had finally isolated herself. She withdrew to the company of a few trusted co-workers like Lon McAllister, her young leading man who was deeply in love with his wife. She began counting the days until the job was over. Now she felt relief in being with Monte. Not complete relief, they'd been apart a long time.

There was no getting around the odd progress of their relationship and his even odder obsessions and talents. Yet, in two years of courtship that seemed as fitful and unlikely as anything she could imagine, Monte had somehow transformed from a frog into a prince. From her first impression of him as a wiseguy and masher, he had revealed himself to be a gentleman. In spite of his devotion to fun and entertainment, he had the steely grit of someone who had been given nothing, a working man. Beneath all his quirks and contradictions, he had the one quality that Jane valued above all others, he was genuine. She believed what he said. Looking back at all the men she'd known, there weren't many that she could say that about. The good ones were gone off to war, or spoken for. In her hard calculus of available men, and as she would admit many years later, "There weren't a lot of choices." Perhaps she also felt after her day of horror, that madness was in her future and she would need a strong-minded partner to survive.

Monte wasn't handsome but she'd had her share of handsome actors. His refined European manners and sense of humor made him easy enough to be around, but he was something else. He was a leader, like her beloved champion Jim Morgan. Monte, like Jim, had risen naturally by his own talents in the tough and fickle saloon business. Like Jim he was a type of king, a dispenser of favors and power. He was a king of nightclubs - self-made, self-reliant, a visionary. And somehow, in a dangerous and deceitful world, he had created his kingdom of music and celebration.

In a few days, Jane's emotional equilibrium recovered. The waking nightmare of amphetamine psychosis evaporated. Even though she now had doubts about herself, the next few days and nights at the lake allowed her to finally settle all the doubts she had about Monte. He was the man, maybe not of her dreams, but of her life.

Monte was prepared to stay at the lake forever as he saw Jane's mood improve. All the scouting he had done during the first days as Jane stayed in her room was now paying off. He outfitted them with boots and khaki and was her intrepid guide as they explored the lake. Even though Jane was the one with the dancer's athleticism, she had a hard time keeping up. In the morning, they packed a lunch and headed out on what Monte called a ramble – an English term for a stroll in the countryside. It was closer to a forced march. By evening, they returned exhausted. They leaned easily on each other. After these days together, Jane had seen and sensed everything she needed. She went to her room, packed her suitcase and carried it next door. Monte was waiting. As she entered, he closed his door behind her. Their life together began.

There has never been a happier man than Monte Proser at Lake Arrowhead. He was wildly, madly in love. He just couldn't believe his luck. The next day he proposed marriage by pushing a ring box toward her over the dinner table.

"Marry me," he asked. Fragrant pine filled the dining room, coaxed through the open windows by a passing breeze. He sat back like a poker player who was all-in and happy with his cards.

Jane pinched the small, discreet diamond ring out of the box tried it on for size. She left it on and said, "I'll think about it".

After a night thinking it over, she accepted. At the age of 39, he had been saved from a life of late nights and dissipation by the petite Irish dancer he fell for at first sight. It was too good to be true, so he moved beyond rabbit's feet and the usual good luck talismans to thanking God directly, out loud, several times. He wanted to make sure the deal stayed clinched. He was determined that everything would be first class for her, top of the line. No expense would be spared to make Jane happy.

The *Hampshire House* on Central Park's south edge was the height of elegance. It provided grand hotel services and amenities with the convenience of large, luxuriously furnished apartments. With the help of Sol Meadow, his lawyer during the set up of the Copa and resident of the *Hampshire House*, Monte took a suite of rooms on the 10th floor with a view of the park, just down the hall from Frank Sinatra. The place was decorated by Broadway show designer Miles White in dramatic art deco - white plush sofas, black enamel end tables, a black grand piano, crystal chandeliers and silver accents of candelabras and fruit bowls. It was a surprise Monte kept from Jane the entire trip back from California. When they arrived in New York, he told her they were going to visit Sol and stay at his place. Sol greeted them at the door of the new apartment. Monte suddenly swept Jane up and carried her over the threshold – they were already married in his mind – into their exquisite new home.

Until they set a date for the actual wedding, Jane would commute from California between assignments. She was booked by the studio into a series of war propaganda films in California starting in two weeks. In some she was to play an American nurse or factory worker and in some she played a German housewife. She looked forward to the unglamorous but steady work. She would also be in New York later that summer to publicize the premiere of *Winged Victory*.

His joy in winning Jane erased all his disappointments of the past. Monte was restored and reinvigorated. He returned to the Copa with a future ahead of him that was everything he ever dreamed of. Not even Jules Podell could diminish his enthusiasm.

With Frank C laying low, the summer would pass without the usual pilgrimage to Saratoga Springs and Frank's *Piping Rock* club. After Monte made sure that Podell was safely stalemated and the Copa was running normally, he and Jane joined Batch at the farm for a week of relaxation.

Jane got her first real taste of country living. Up to that time she had seen the countryside mostly from a traveling car or train window. She instantly took to the simple routines and local farm and trades people who knew nothing and cared even less about show business. She learned to shoot a .22 rifle and spent hours practicing on tin cans in the field in back of the main house. Batch remarked that she seemed to fit right in with country ways. It was obvious that she wasn't the type who needed to be amused or to stick close to the men. All she needed was a box of .22 cartridges and a few tin cans or a few dollars in a country village and Jane was completely entertained. To Monte this was the final confirmation that she was his perfect match. He had grown to depend on Bucks County to relax and restore him. Now it was clear that Jane could share his sentiment about the place.

The dream ended a dozen days later with Jane boarding the *Super Chief* at Pennsylvania Station bound for Chicago and then Los Angeles. Monte returned to the large empty rooms of the *Hampshire House*. He pined for an hour or so, looking out over Central Park, then perked up when he realized the place was the perfect set-up for a card game. With Sinatra down the hall and Gleason back on Broadway starring in the hit comedy *Follow the Girls*, the games began. But they didn't last long. Jane called a few weeks later as that particularly brilliant summer was waning. She was pregnant.

Monte and Jane stood before Don DeLacey, the town barber and only Justice of the Peace in New Hope, Pennsylvania. They had decided to get married quietly in a small civil ceremony. Jane's eldest sister, Evelyn, the one she called Sis, was the witness for Jane and Walter Batchelor stood as witness for Monte. The ceremony took about 15 minutes. Jane became Mrs. Monte Proser at 11 AM on June 4, 1944. With their small wedding party of Monte's sisters Annette and Isabel, his brother Leo, Walter Batchelor and his wife Lovee and Jane's sister, Evelyn, they walked over the canal bridge on Coryell Street toward the Delaware River and converged on the bar at the *Logan Inn*. After a light lunch and a few photos outside the place, they drove to see Jane's wedding present, the Farm. Monte had bought Batchelor's place for her.

As they drove up the long winding dirt lane between the two hayfields, the house sat off to their right, above the upper field under a 60-foot cedar. The lane turned right at the end of the fields and climbed past the renovated red barn used as guest quarters on the left and continued to the circle with a towering white pine at its center between the main house and the pool. The bride and groom with their wedding party climbed noisily out of the cars. They all settled on the front porch chatting and laughing easily as they talked about the children that would soon populate the place. Jane squatted on the stone steps in her fitted, blue serge wedding suit and white chiffon hat, chin resting in her hands, elbows on her knees. She looked out over the lower fields quietly, drifting off from the conversation. She was home.

That evening, unable to sleep with the excitement and joy he felt, Monte walked along the edge of the lawn in front of the house. His heart was as light as the fireflies rising out of the dark, fragrant fields of timothy and alfalfa that stretched out to the surrounding forest. It was an image he would never forget.

The *Roxy Theatre* on 44th and Broadway blazed with light for the premiere of *Winged Victory*. Jane and Monte strode the red carpet and chatted easily with all of his press pals lining the way. For once, Monte didn't have a ready story to sell. He let Jane do all the talking. After the opening night party at *El Morocco*, they walked the 12 blocks to the *Hampshire House*. It was the peak moment in both of their lives. Neither one could express even a fraction of their joy and gratitude, except that Monte twirled Jane briefly into a waltz on the sidewalk. As they rode the elevator to their suite on the 10th floor of the *Hampshire House*, they held hands. The ancient elevator operator watched the floor markers drift past, hypnotized into his own private thoughts. Jane laid her tired head on Monte's shoulder. Quietly, she said, "Monte."

"Hm?" He was already quietly dreaming.

"I do love you."

The elevator operator heard but stayed still as a sentry, so as not to break the spell. Monte too stayed quiet, letting the words float undisturbed like a prayer. There was just too much to be happy about. They would need years to celebrate. Life had lifted them up, wrapped them in love and now laid them gently to rest on top of the world.

CHAPTER 28

NO PEACE

Jane finished three films for the War Department in California before returning again to the *Hampshire House* to rest and await delivery of their first born, due in February. Monte was battling daily to keep control of the Copa out of Podell's hands. He campaigned with the staff for their loyalty, paying hefty bonuses out of his own pocket to entice them to treat the customers ethically and report dirty tricks to him directly. This effectively started to undermine Podell's ability to operate. The captains, waiters and busboys were his eyes and ears. Now that loyalties were fraying, he was beginning to lose confidence in the accuracy of the information he was getting. He fought back to find and punish the defectors. The stress on the staff to serve two warring masters was enormous and employee turnover began to be a problem.

Even as Podell's grip on the dining room was weakening, his pursuit of influence over talent agents was beginning to show results. He continued to cajole and subtly threaten agents with ex-communication if they didn't start to respond to his demands for information regarding the booking of talent in the club. His specific threat was that he would soon be running the place and Monte would be out. They'd better start filling him in on the details. Even if the threat had a small chance of coming true, no agent could risk the possibility that at some point his clients might be shut out of the Copa. Podell got regular calls informing him of who Monte was pursuing and who was confirmed to appear. He could then use his channels of influence to interfere with Monte's choices by making certain favorites unavailable and alternates available at bargain prices. Frank Marti, the talented bandleader from the first opening days of the club, was the first to feel the effect of Podell's assault.

The musician's union was deeply in the pocket of the *Syndicate*. No one tooted a horn or strummed a ukulele in Manhattan without the *Syndicate* getting a taste of the contract money. One by one, the members of Marti's handpicked group became unavailable and were replaced by union designees on short notice. The result was frequently chaos on the bandstand and frayed nerves among the performers and Marti. At one point late in the fourth season of the Copa, the talented young composer and arranger for Frank Sinatra and others, Skitch Henderson, described the Copa house band as "…the ten angry men." He claimed that they were trying to beat their instruments into submission. After one difficult performance, Sinatra turned to Henderson and said they should have used *The Harmonicats*, a novelty act consisting of five harmonica players, instead. By the time Monte was aware of the extent of the problem, his beautiful music machine was sounding like a rusty jalopy. He couldn't identify the source of the problem and was unsure what he could do about it. Marti managed the ongoing problem with an endless cycle of firings and hirings. It was wearing him out.

In the *Hampshire House,* Jane was unable to sleep. She was on edge and having trouble coping with even small frustrations. She had a "case of nerves", a condition attributed to people of artistic temperament, particularly actresses. Rest and quiet were the prescription most doctors offered. Some suggested she try counting sheep to hypnotize herself to sleep. None diagnosed amphetamine withdrawal or would have had anything to offer for the condition even if they had diagnosed it.

To relieve Jane of some of the household and child-care tasks that were about to become a large part of her life, Monte sought domestic help. Carrie Dawson, a tall and self-assured, mahogany-tinted daughter of the deep South, arrived from Convent Avenue in the affluent Sugar Hill section of Harlem. Carrie was recently divorced from her husband and not at all convinced that she wanted to take on caring for another woman's child. Friends of hers browbeat her into at least going to the interview. She would be living in the best possible conditions with a man known as a friend of their community, a man who still came around *Dickie Wells's Chicken Shack* late some nights and was in the clubs around Harlem looking for talent all the time. Carrie gave in, she would go for the interview. The interview in the *Hampshire House* lasted just a few minutes before Jane knew Carrie was the person she wanted to help her.

Carrie found Jane's quick decision off-putting. Jane pursued Carrie promising that she would have her own room in the suite, weekends off and could name her price. In her courtly Southern manner and soft drawl, Carrie declined to accept the generous offer until she had slept on it. She left and Jane grew anxious. She began to fret that she had pushed too hard and lost someone of great strength and stability whom she would soon need.

The following afternoon, Carrie accepted. She arrived that evening with two suitcases and her friend Mazie who conducted the final inspection of Carrie's room and gave her blessing to the arrangement. Carrie didn't sleep well that night. She awoke the next day and put on the starched blue dress and white apron of her domestic position for the first time. She made herself breakfast then sat alone in the quiet living room overlooking the park until Jane and Monte rose just before noon. Just a few hours into that first day together, Jane knew she had been right. Carrie quickly became her vital ally in managing a life that was already threatening to unravel.

Recently Milton Blackstone, who had upped his work schedule from 12 hours a day running *Grossinger's* to 16 hours in order to handle his booming ship building business and various advertising clients like the Copa, found enormous energy and stress relief from the injections of Dr. Max Jacobson. Jacobson had a small practice in Brooklyn and came to Milton's attention through long time guests of Grossinger's who swore by the "vitamin shots" the doctor administered. Milton invited the doctor to spend a weekend at the Catskills and administer his miracle shots to himself and Jennie Grossinger, who was also working herself into an early grave. The shots were indeed miracles. Milton had never felt healthier or more alert in his life. Jenny felt the initial kick that Milton had but didn't like the after-effect of irritability she felt. Jacobson patiently explained the irritability was a symptom of how exhausted she truly was. She was not convinced. Her parents, aunts and uncles all had worked the same grinding schedules for generations. She didn't believe in miracles.

But Milton did. He believed he had found something like the fountain of youth. He believed Max Jacobson was a genius. Dr. Jacobson humbly explained the key to his miracle formula was the newly available synthesized vitamin B12. Whatever it was, Milton trumpeted his restored vitality as living proof of Jacobson's wonder treatment. Jane and Monte were next in line for the injections.

Jane had immediate relief. Her withdrawal was instantly reversed into radiant good health and humor. For Monte it was an answered prayer. Jacobson became a frequent guest at the *Hampshire House* as Jane approached her delivery date for the baby. But Jane's relief was only temporary, lasting no more than 12 hours. She found herself slipping into the dark moods that had worried her so much before. This time she didn't want to tell Monte. It would worry him too much. She thought she could soldier-on and fight the creeping depression. Her iron will, the will power that had gotten her through everything so far, would get her through this too. Once the baby was born, she thought, and she was living at the farm, she would straighten out. It was the recent pressure of work and having the child that was driving her moods. In fact, what was driving her moods was the methadrine that Jacobson mixed in all his "vitamin" formulas. Jane was on amphetamines again, the liquid form of the little, white pills she had taken while working on *Winged Victory*. She just didn't know it.

With Monte spending most of his time at the club or in meetings, Jane decided to be with her mother and sisters and have the baby in Kingston. She and Carrie packed up and were on their way north to Kingston in Jim Morgan's car within a few hours of her call.

Monte reacted euphorically to the injections, as most people did. The after-effect in his case was a sort of narcolepsy. He began to fall asleep in the middle of conversations at tables full of guests in the club. It became another quirk of his rambunctious personality, part of his mythology. The new chapter in his story was that he was having so much fun that he forgot to sleep and it sometimes caught up with him. He'd sometimes awake to an empty table with three or four drinks left for him. Sometimes a friend would shake him back to consciousness and he would retire to the manager's office for a catnap. Jack Entratter was the only one who immediately recognized that something was wrong. Monte brushed off his old friend's concern attributing his behavior to the stresses of work and home life. In any case, he had a new doctor who was fixing everything. He'd be as good as new soon.

With Podell advancing at every opportunity and creating havoc in the operation, Monte moved into the manager's office to stay near the front line of the battle. He returned to the *Hampshire House* early in the morning and left before noon most days. He was determined to make a stand against Podell, to crush him or outmaneuver him somehow. The skirmishing between them was over. He wanted war.

It happened just before Christmas. As much as Monte and Podell tried to avoid actually seeing each other, they happened to be in the upstairs lounge at the same time. The lounge had always been a safe area for Monte, a Podell-free zone a few steps from his office door, unlike the main show room adjacent to Podell's kitchen downstairs. Monte was at the bar chatting easily with a few pals about plans for the upcoming holiday when he heard Podell threaten John Flaherty, the Irish bartender,

"Fuckin' mick..." the rest of the sentence was lost in the din of the bar activity.

Podell was standing next to Monte and probably didn't notice it was Monte sitting close to him. As soon as Monte heard his enemy's voice so close to him, he stopped in the middle of whatever he was saying and was still for a moment. He saw Flaherty's frightened face, and he suddenly wheeled around. He leapt off his stool and attacked Podell with a flurry of punches that knocked the man back several feet before he knew what was happening. The entire bar piled into the fight pulling the two men apart. Monte had to be pinned to the floor by five or six men before he would stop attacking. Somewhere in the event he had broken his left thumb. Podell had a dislocated jaw and multiple bruises. He only could mumble, "Dead. Dead.", as he was helped outside to cab and then to a hospital emergency room. When Jack Entratter came in for the evening and heard the story of what had happened, he turned white. He knew that attacking Podell was like attacking Frank Costello himself.

Frank Costello summoned Monte to the *Waldorf Astoria* hotel. Monte was told that the only reason he wasn't at the bottom of the East River was because Costello had put up some of his own money and lied for him, saying Monte had apologized privately for the attack and offered the money as compensation. The Prime Minister of the *Syndicate* did not say the amount he had put up. He then explained that he couldn't protect Monte if there was another attack. It also remained unsaid that in his current weakened position Costello couldn't replace Podell even if he wanted to. If he did it would look like weakness, and further weakness at that point would endanger Costello's own life. Monte couldn't quite bring himself to say he was sorry but said he appreciated what Frank had done for him.

After that meeting, in spite of Frank C's warning, Monte maintained a constant presence in the showroom, in a cast up to his elbow for his broken thumb, and ventured into the kitchen frequently. He figured Podell had gotten pretty much the same talk and was determined to gauge the man's reaction. Podell was tight as a clam whenever Monte appeared in his domain. That told Monte his theory was right. He counted his attack as a victory and was determined to provoke Podell into making a final mistake that hopefully would catapult the leg-breaker out of the club forever. All of this strategizing and probing, along with actually running the club, consumed most of Monte's waking moments. When Jane's mother called that night of February 6th from Kingston with the news that Jane had been taken to the hospital, Monte panicked, "What's wrong with her?" he asked.

"Monte," Nan explained as if to a distracted child, "She's having a baby." He had forgotten. He rushed from the club to get the next train to Kingston.

There were complications. The stresses of the past months seemed to all add up as Jane went into labor. She couldn't relax and so the pain shot through even the heavy dose of opiates she was given. The entire delivery was difficult but ultimately successful and a new baby boy let out a healthy scream on his arrival into the world. He was named Charles for Monte's father and Morgan for Jim Morgan. Almost immediately the now familiar dark mood descended on Jane as she felt herself physically torn and mentally adrift in a confusing mix of emotions. It was hard to keep up a good face even when the baby was brought to her with Monte and Carrie cooing encouragement and congratulations. She just wanted to sleep and try to lose the feeling of dread that hounded her.

"Where the hell were you?" Her eyes blazed at Monte.

Monte was taken by surprise. The sharpness of Jane's accusation stopped him cold. "I came right away, Janey. Look." He indicated the baby and then saw her look of hesitation that chilled him further. She held her arms out and was given her son. She looked at her first born as tears came into her eyes.

"You poor little boy," she said, feeling the loneliness that hounded her like a demon settle into the center of her heart. In an instant, it was communicated directly to Monte, to his deepest instinct. Something was very wrong.

Her room emptied out and she was given a sedative to help her sleep. She slept through the night, then through the early part of the morning until the day nurse noticed she was flushed and feverish. Sweat was soaking through her sheets and her breath was rapid and shallow. By the time the doctor arrived, Jane was struggling in and out of consciousness and apparently in terrible abdominal pain. She was quickly examined. She hadn't expelled the placenta and the delivering physician had neglected to remove it. She was suffering advanced sepsis and was succumbing to toxic shock. Emergency procedures in her room removed the placenta and she was infused with antibiotics as they rushed her to intensive care. There was nothing they could give her for the pain because she would need all her waking energy to fight the massive infection. She was left in intensive care to fight for her life for the next 48 hours.

After the first day of watching over Jane in intensive care, Carrie knew there was nothing she and Monte could do for her, but the baby was suffering without human connection. They took the child home to Albany Avenue. To dispel any possibility of a Jewish ceremony, Nan promptly had the boy christened Charles Morgan Proser with herself standing in for the baby's mother. But the Holy Water that ran from the boy's forehead gathered in the hollow of Carrie Dawson's palm. Carrie held the child's head for the ceremony. She carried him from the church.

Carrie fed, bathed and swaddled Charles Morgan from that moment on. The connection that was supposed to have formed between Jane and her baby snared Carrie instead. Over those next few days, in the subtle and mysterious ways of the human heart, Carrie became the child's mother in all but name.

The flow of well-wishers and gifts to the *Hampshire House* crowded even the spacious rooms. Sisters Annette and Isabel made themselves the sentries guarding the palace while Monte and the pale, subdued Jane sat next to the bassinette, receiving guests. Brother Leo poured drinks while Carrie came and went with the child as needed, eventually asserting her leadership to which Monte and Jane both instantly submitted. "This baby needs to get out in the air," she stated and fended off all objections citing the falling snow and freezing temperature. "Getting the cold on his face brings up the blood. Cold won't bother him." She proceeded to prepare the child and Monte looked to Jane for guidance.

"She knows what she's doing," Jane said, "I hope."

The new family went for a walk to the skating pond in Central Park. Jane wasn't quite strong enough yet to do more. Monte bought paper bags of hot chestnuts from a smoking cart and stuffed Jane's coat pockets with them to keep her warm. He shelled one and was about to offer a morsel to his son but cleared it with Carrie first. Carrie took the crumb, chewed it into paste and dabbed the paste on the boy's lip. They watched the baby work his lips and wonder at his first taste of roasted chestnut. Everyone had a piece of chestnut then. "Hmmm," they murmured at the boy. It was their first family meal.

Spring began to daub the treetops of Central Park pale green and Monte's attention turned with the certainty of a magnetic needle northward - to musical extravaganza. With the Copa schedule contracted out months in advance and Podell temporarily restrained, his dream world descended from the clouds again. This time he saw an outdoor public concert. This would sidestep Mayor LaGuardia's fire restrictions and occupancy rules, eliminate the rent and maintenance of a physical building. Most importantly, it might break the connection to Costello's mob and the long shadow they cast. It was one more roll of the dice to win his life-long jackpot – musical liberation. In his mind's eye he saw something like his alma mater years ago on Long Island, the Lights Club, an amphitheater. What he found was Lincoln Square, the hub of New York's Westside, directly across Central Park from the Copa. At the urging of his pal Henry Nemo, crapshooter, mixologist, hipster and music hound, he booked Dizzy Gillespie, a hot, new jazz star, to light up the event with an odd, new sound called be-bop.

Weeks earlier British troops had liberated *Bergen-Belsen* concentration camp reporting that, *"both inside and outside the huts was a carpet of dead bodies, human excreta, rags and filth."* The full extent of the Nazi genocide campaign in Europe was being revealed for the first time as the Allies converged on Germany. They liberated

Auschwitz, Dachau, Malthausen and *Therienstadt* between January and April of 1945. Early reports estimated that over 2 million people had been exterminated in the camps and 1.5 million of them had been Jews. Germany was in full retreat and Japan's bold Pacific campaign was collapsing into bloody, suicidal resistance. In New York, cautious optimism was tempered with waves of revulsion at the savagery now reported on the front pages. As with the previous war, unimaginable evil was suddenly a fact.

For Jane, a deep, emotional numbness muted her conversations as nightmare images in the newspapers and magazines overwhelmed her. It was simply too much. It was unspeakable. From an undisturbed corner of her bottom dresser drawer, she dug out the rosary beads and tiny pocket-sized Bible from her first communion, over 25 years earlier. Holding both powerless talismans between her hands, she sat motionless except for the infrequent tear sliding over her cheek, in the sunny window overlooking God's isolated rectangle of Central Park.

For Monte too, the hideous revelations ripped his emotional fabric. Too much had been lost and the fragments of horror surfacing in the news in front of his eyes confirmed it. Mankind was beyond hope. The thought drained his strength, dropping his hand like a marionette with its strings cut. His coffee cup clattered down onto its saucer like bone striking bone, cracking the stillness in the house. Jane didn't flinch, her gaze stayed fixed on the pigeons gliding above the treetops. Monte folded the morning paper, turning the photographs down, out of view. Only his family, his Janey mattered anymore. He padded across the bright carpet, kissed his suffering wife on the forehead. She turned with a smile.

"Janey," Monte prompted a response as he saw the beads draped through her fingers.

"I can't..." She may have meant, "believe it" or "talk right now" but her sentences fragmented and the cut pieces wilted into silence. He crossed to the door where Carrie held his son for him. He kissed the boy. "Thank you," he said to Carrie as he opened the front door and then stepped out into his unhappy world.

CHAPTER 29

A Changing of the Guard

Lucky Luciano shaved 12 years off his sentence at Dannemora prison by helping the US win the war. Not only had he secured the New York waterfront against German infiltration, he also provided vital intelligence and logistical help for the Allied invasion of Italy by mobilizing his Mafia connections in Sicily. This early release fulfilled a wartime deal made by New York Governor Thomas Dewey to the gangster he had prosecuted and imprisoned as State Attorney General. Governor Dewey then went one step further. He immediately deported Luciano.

This was the double-cross of all time, yet Charlie Lucky took it, uncharacteristically, without saying a word. He accepted the swindle because he had the cold comfort of knowing he had double-crossed the Governor first. The acts of German infiltration and sabotage along the New York waterfront that had brought the government to his damp prison cell to negotiate for his help were largely the work of Albert Anastasia and designed by Luciano himself. The German hoax had succeeding in suckering Governor Dewey into cutting 12 years off his sentence and that would have to be good enough. Luciano couldn't even afford the satisfaction of letting the Governor know he'd been conned, or it would be right back to the can, possibly with an additional charge of treason. In Anastasia's eagerness to execute Luciano's orders, he had gone a little too far and actually sunk the French luxury liner *S.S. Normandie* at its moorings on Manhattan's west side docks as it was being converted for use as a troop ship. As a result, Charley Lucky left the country without a peep and stayed away.

For Frank Costello, this betrayal by the Governor meant that he would have to remain the acting head of the *Syndicate*. He longed to return to his obscure supporting position as diplomat and business mastermind of the Italian/Jewish conglomerate, but for the time being, he was the top man and chief enforcer.

For Monte, this meant that the invisible hand that had always protected him would stay in place for now. But it also meant that the next generation, a Capone protégé named Johnny Rosselli, was moved into position and assets like Monte were handed over to him.

Perhaps the person most upset by this turn of events was Vito Genovese, the violently ambitious childhood colleague of Luciano. The two had grown up and made their bones together in Lower East side tenements enforcing collections for carpet joints with Bugsy Siegel and Meyer Lansky. Genovese coveted the top position and resented Costello, the uptown smoothie. The moment Luciano's decision was announced, Genovese realized that along with Costello himself, Costello's close ally Albert Anastasia would have to go too – when the time came.

The *Samba Sirens* and the Copa show remained at the club as Joe Adonis had demanded and now with the help of Johnny Rosselli, also out of Chicago, the *Sirens* themselves were much more likely to stay firmly within the sphere of the *Syndicate*. Johnny offered the ladies a ready-made path to Hollywood.

Rosselli, who had muscled in and then controlled the IATSE labor union in Hollywood for Capone in the late thirties, was now a secretive and powerful broker in the movie business. He operated officially as an "associate producer" out of the tiny

Eagle Lion Studios, with small offices and a sound stage on Santa Monica Boulevard, but held the chains of many large studio executives like Joe Schenk, head of production at 20th Century Fox. Schenk, who did 3 years in prison for tax evasion at the same time Rosselli was serving a stint for the IATSE labor racketeering bust, was forever grateful to Rosselli for his protection while he was locked up.

Monte had run across Rosselli in Hollywood years earlier as Rosselli was in the midst of consolidating the IA into his portfolio. At the Copa, Adonis made the introduction, Monte's second, to Johnny Rosselli and the new regime began. Rosselli operated from Frank C's playbook, smooth, charming, even joking at moments. He was completely comfortable in a leadership spot, unlike Frank, and so seemed like any powerful businessman. None of this did anything to relieve Monte's anxiety that the bite would soon follow their polite chat. But it never came. All Johnny wanted to do was help. He knew people, had money, and was looking for opportunities like everybody else. He was more than reasonable, he was a good businessman.

Monte understood that the introduction by Adonis announced a changing of the guard. It also became obvious that it was Frank's way of exploring a larger partnership between them. Monte politely sidestepped the implied offer, indicating his plans were all set as far as new opportunities they might work on together. Johnny steered the conversation to the West Coast, where word was that gambling might be legalized. Los Angeles Mayor Bowron had always been more than lenient with various gambling operations and Chicago's friend, Mickey Cohen, recently allied with Bugsy Siegel, was wired all the way up to the governor's office.

Johnny brought up Billy Wilkerson, the owner of the *Trocadero*, *Ciro's* and publisher of the *Hollywood Reporter*. At this point in 1947, Billy, like Monte, was a racetrack and craps addict. Whatever the two made in their businesses, they lost on slow ponies and cold dice. Monte had always liked the *Troc*. He had recently decided to make his friend Billy an offer on the club. It was unnerving that Rosselli brought it up. Exactly how much did Rosselli know about his business? Johnny tapped his cigarette leisurely on the black Copa ashtray, letting the smoke curve into question marks that hung in the air between them.

Monte's plan was to make the *Trocadero* into a showcase for Carmen Miranda. He was on his way to Hollywood in a week to sign with *Republic Pictures* for production of the movie *Copacabana* to star Groucho Marx and Miranda. She was ready to sign a long-term contract to appear at the *Trocadero* after the movie came out. The *Troc* would be a perfect spot for her. It would be the Copa *West*.

Rosselli jumped right in. He might be able to help with the negotiations since Billy owed lots of favors to his friends out there – "favors" as in thousands of dollars in gambling markers. Monte declined gracefully. Billy was his friend and he didn't want any pressure applied. Without a hint of disappointment, Johnny backed off, leaving the door open if Monte changed his mind. Meeting over, they came out of their huddle, sat back in their chairs signaling well-wishers in the club that they were free to approach. Doing business with Rosselli was a walk in the park compared to Adonis.

The new state of affairs came into focus as friends joined the table. Monte was no longer just one of Frank C's personal partners, he was now part of the *Syndicate*, one of its possessions. The Copa was no longer the personal domain of Frank C under the temporary care of Joe Adonis. It was now community property and access to Monte came with it. He was suddenly friends with all of Frank's friends, and Frank had a lot of friends.

The infiltration of gangsters into the entertainment industry and other legitimate businesses was expanding farther and faster than anyone, including Monte, could hope to outrun. Business in general was booming again with thousands of young men and women returning to the nightlife after years of scrimping and service to the nation. The ranks of the *Syndicate* swelled in every area of the country with young men trained in violence and ready for their piece of the action. The upper levels of *Syndicate* management had enjoyed ten years of uninterrupted prosperity. They used the time and money to consolidate and refine operations. The new, consolidated mob meant that the old days were gone when one gangster could be played against another and a trip out of town could avoid them. Now they were unified East to West and North to South.

Internal ethnic differences were resolved. Under the quiet leadership of Costello, the motley, diverse mob was now the smooth-running *Syndicate*. It had coalesced firmly around the Jewish/Italian axis and deliberately left the Irish out in the cold. While the Italians and Jews were integrating seamlessly, the Irish were still a mob that was split into warring factions and occasionally opposed within their own community by a large number of their own people who were employed by city police forces and political offices. The internal *Syndicate* relationship was a mirror image of Frank's long and happy marriage to his Jewish wife and, when it came to the Irish, perhaps also a reflection of the abuse he had suffered at the hands of Irish cops in his youth.

The Italians and Jews supplied the *Syndicate*'s expansion since Prohibition by bringing younger members of their own communities into the ranks and grooming them for cooperative leadership. The independents like Dutch Schultz, the hotheads like Legs Diamond and gunslingers like Mad Dog Coll were all gone, killed off. Now they were mostly like Johnny Rosselli and Joe Adonis, well-spoken, sharp-eyed businessmen and strategists, who assigned violence to specialists. They owned the best legal, financial and political talent money could buy. They diversified into entertainment, unions, trucking, construction, banking and real estate. Even without the Irish, they were now more powerful and widespread than ever. They became more like a modern corporate conglomerate every day. They planned for the future.

CHAPTER 30

HIGH BUTTON SHOES

At home, well into her second year of motherhood, Jane seemed to have recovered physically yet remained moody and quiet. She was content with her new baby who was healthy and the center of everyone's attention but she didn't spend much time actually playing with the boy. A subtle despair, that may have been part post-partum depression and part amphetamine-induced nerve damage, settled over her like a weighted net. She was still as kind and sincere as always, just quietly melancholy. Monte saw this change in her and became concerned. Younger sister Annette, who had taken up with a young, socialist firebrand and law student named Bernie Rosen, visited her brother in his dramatically un-socialist luxury apartment and saw him as nearly frantic about Jane's condition. It was the first and only time she ever saw this level of panic in him. The love of Monte's life was wilting from the inside and he was powerless to help her.

Monte became determined to bring some life, some lightheartedness into his home. He felt his father's proper name, Charles, was too ponderous for the boy. He wanted a little sidekick, someone to take his mind off of work and nicknamed the boy Chip, for chip off the old block. Jane accepted the nickname without much comment, even seeming to defer to Carrie who happily took up the new name. He saw then that something more serious than a "case of the blues" was wrong with Jane. Some part of her was always on edge, unable to enjoy life. In the last few months she had rarely ventured from the apartment and had not been keeping up even with her good friends. A psychiatrist diagnosed Jane's condition as *anhedonia* – the inability to have fun. He said it had to do with guilt about her father's adultery and shame, and would take years of therapy. Jane wasn't particularly interested in talking about her father for years to come and never went for another session.

She had extended her leave of absence from the movie studio, unsure that she would ever want to return. Hollywood had become a distant and corrupt place in her mind. Even the thought of California brought on a quiet gloom that usually ended any conversation on the subject. Monte began to spend more time with her, avoiding the late night carousing of his past, hoping he could somehow bring Jane back to herself. His personal doctor, Dr. Hitzig, advised him that she might still be recovering from the physical trauma she had suffered in giving birth. His only prescription was that she should eat highly nutritious foods and get outside for frequent walks in the park.

Monte had special meals prepared by the best chefs in New York hand delivered for Jane's dinner. He annoyed his old speakeasy buddies at "*21*" by insisting on only the freshest calves' liver, not overcooked and delivered by taxi while still hot. But nothing worked. After months of buying her everything he could think of to eat and wear and amuse herself with, and offering to take her and the boy anywhere in the world, the only remedy he knew of that could bring the life back to her eyes was the "vitamin B cocktail" in the little black bag of Dr. Max Jacobson. Jane agreed. She knew she was not herself. Once again, the good doctor was summoned to the 10th floor of the Hampshire House.

The doctor arrived, as usual, with his small, plain and silent wife, Ruth. Max Jacobson was a tall, slightly stooped, Abe Lincoln type. They strode quickly into the room with the efficiency of intent medical professionals. Ruth alighted quickly at a cocktail table closer to the picture window overlooking Central Park. Dr. Jacobson crossed to Jane and looked her squarely in the eyes, one eye at a time examining her irises and pupils. He shook hands and asked how she was feeling.

"Oh, a little tired, I think," was Jane's way of describing her condition. He agreed silently, turned to greet Monte and joined Ruth at the sunny cocktail table. Without much care, the doctor tipped his bag on the glass table and glass vials of blue, brown, clear and green liquid clattered onto the table. He separated out three or four of the three-inch vials, then reached into a pocket inside his black bag and produced a leather syringe case. He opened the case, screwed the needle onto the syringe, swabbed the needle tip with alcohol and laid it carefully on its side. He snapped the vial's glass necks with rapid-fire technique.

The syringe drew up several CC's of liquid from each vial. No one noticed at first, but once Dr. Jacobson's routine became known, it was disturbing to realize that the good doctor used little scientific process. He was experimenting without keeping records. Each injection was a brand new, fairly random combination of primarily vitamin B12 and other vitamins with different types of amphetamine. He kept no records at all of the amounts of each ingredient or how each mixture affected his patients. He relied entirely on his eye exams to assess, and then on his memory to record, what his patients' reactions were. No one cared because the shots worked miraculously.

Jane's vitality returned immediately. Monte had himself revitalized as well. He thought, "You can't get too much of a good thing." Within days, Jane relapsed into irritability and insomnia. Dr. Jacobson was called again. He was becoming very popular and hard to schedule. The doctor kept almost no written records of any kind except for his appointment book dutifully and silently inscribed by Ruth and he always preferred to be paid in cash.

High Button Shoes was the kind of solid musical comedy that struck Monte's ear and his heart simultaneously. The writers were veterans, composing songs for Frank Sinatra and others.

Monte had been bumping into both Jule Styne and Sammy Cahn at various gin mills and gatherings up and down the street for decades. Jule and Sammy acted out the story and performed the songs of *High Button Shoes* for Monte in the Copa's showroom. The book, or story, of the show would never win a Pulitzer, but the music struck Monte's ear just right. They shook hands, had a drink and a few laughs and made the deal. For the fourth time he placed his bet on Broadway. This time, to hell with the Shubert's, he'd find his own theatre. He was now a competitor.

Comedian Phil Silvers and counter-part Nanette Fabray headed the cast. It was a whimsical story about the endless search for love in a simpler time, the Gay 90's, the time of high button shoes. After three attempts and failures on Broadway with Walter Batchelor, Monte finally produced a hit. The show ran for 727 performances and won a Tony Award for the choreography of young Jerome Rabinowitz who had recently adopted the name, without Monte's help, of Jerome Robbins. Jule Styne and Sammy Cahn went on to unprecedented 30-year careers on Broadway creating classics between them like *Gentlemen Prefer Blondes, Pal Joey, Peter Pan, Gypsy, Funny Girl, Fosse* and *Thoroughly Modern Millie.*

High Button Shoes created the appearance of independence from the mob for Monte, but the opposite was true. Monte had approached fellow saloonkeeper Joe Kipness to co-produce the show with him. It was a fateful matchup. Kipness, proprietor of very successful bars and restaurants around Broadway, was from a family that controlled one of the largest trucking and cartage companies in Brooklyn. Joe was considerably lower on the food chain than Frank Costello, but was still, as they said, connected. Whether the choice was careless or calculated, it was one that silently confirmed Monte's underworld alliances.

While Monte's instinct for partners was poor, his instinct for talent continued to be infallible. He heard singer Perry Como on the radio and hired him sight unseen for the next Copa show. Como was added to the long list of performers Monte had plucked from obscurity or rescued from fading careers and placed in the Copa spotlight including Jimmy Durante, Sophie Tucker, Ethel Merman, Carmen Miranda, Danny Thomas, Jan Murray and dozens of others. He was a star-maker with a seemingly infallible touch. Confirming his taste in talent, the movies were becoming populated with Copa girls like Jane Ball, June Allyson and Lucille Bremer.

In 1947 the cameras rolled on the movie *Copacabana* while *High Button Shoes* was selling out on Broadway. This synergy helped boost the club from mere prominence to legendary status. The word Copa was entering the language as a description of a type of lively nightclub and "*copasetic*", an ancient word of unknown origin, meaning essentially "everything's going well, no problems" was becoming popular among jazz musicians. The club itself was more than ever the center of variety entertainment and prime showcase for new and rediscovered stars. If they could have expanded to 1,000 seats they could have filled them all easily, three times a night. With the expanding popularity of the nightly radio show from the Copa lounge, it seemed that Monte had conquered every medium of entertainment – Broadway, nightclub, movies and radio. He was a bigger name than many of the stars he employed. Faithless Lady Luck once again returned, and clung to his arm cooing promises of eternal love into his ear.

In spite of his standing in the entertainment business and his long history with the movies, he had virtually no power when it came to the production of *Copacabana*. Even with trusted ally Walter Batchelor signed on as associate producer, Monte's involvement in the production of Republic Picture's *Copacabana* was another lesson in humility. What had seemed like a good idea to begin with slowly devolved into a compromise of conflicting ideas that satisfied no one. Even though Batchelor had a hit two years earlier with the comedy, *It's In the Bag* starring radio star Fred Allen, based largely on Batchelor's adventures in the radio business, the same did not rub off on Republic's version of the nightclub business. Five writers came and went. The script became more implausible with each one, until the studio finally forced production to begin with the last script they had on hand. It was simply too expensive and risky to hold off production for more rewrites. Monte and Batch did their best to patch up the story line and left it to Groucho and Carmen to interject comedy where none was written. At least the filming itself was sometimes enjoyable since Monte brought in his press buddies Louis Sobel, Earl Wilson and Abel Green, the editor of Variety, to play bit parts as themselves and loaded the cast with friends and relatives including Groucho's wife, Kay, who played the cigarette girl. But it was "…God-awful" as the two Broadway buddies – Batch and Monte - watched the jokes fall flat and the musical numbers wander in and out of the story line like a drunken uncle – lurching and tuneless. It broke their hearts – not just the film – but finally facing the fact that in spite of their great love and respect for each other, nearly every project they attempted together turned to disaster. The movie *Copacabana* was no exception. Not only did he mourn the little death of his dream of working with Batch, but after more than 20 years of promising starts and disappointing outcomes, Monte believed this was his final exit from the movies. He had no hope for the film.

Shortly before filming of *Copacabana* wrapped, Jane, toddler Chip and Carrie joined Monte and Batch in Los Angeles. Jane's contract with 20th required one more picture. She was scheduled to test for an ingénue part in the upcoming *Forever Amber* starring Cornell Wilde. To surprise her, Monte bought a house on a deserted part of the beach just above Santa Monica. It was a small but comfortable two-bedroom, white, frame house with no neighbors within sight in either direction. At the time, most people felt it was impractical to live on the beach but Monte enjoyed the seclusion and thought the sound of the ocean would be soothing to Jane. Carrie came along to tend to Chip and support Jane.

Jane had begun drinking small amounts of whiskey at home "to calm her nerves". She had never before drunk hard liquor by herself and it was clear she didn't enjoy it. The recent injections by Dr. Jacobson had left her more aggravated than ever. She was often up throughout the night, going for long walks on Santa Monica beach, to tire herself. Carrie did what she could to ease Jane's tension, drawing hot baths and even calling on her friend Mazie back on Sugar Hill in Harlem to send her homemade nerve tonic made of bitter herbs. Again, nothing seemed to help for long. Jane spent much of her time reading, hoping it would tire her mind enough to let her sleep for more than a few hours a night.

She was relieved to know that her screen test and audition had won the part for her. She was anxious to fulfill her contract and put Hollywood behind her. The dozens of intense personal interactions necessary for a working movie actress were becoming overwhelming for her. She longed for the seclusion of the farm and country life. She also didn't want to be in Hollywood beyond May. She was pregnant again and due to deliver their second child in August.

In spite of his misgivings about the Copa movie, Monte decided Carmen Miranda was a big enough star to survive one bad movie and he should go ahead and buy the *Trocadero*. But instead of heading to the club to make Wilkerson the offer with a $25,000 down payment, he took the cash and went to Santa Anita racetrack. By mid-afternoon he had over $100,000. It was magic – he and Lady Luck were deeply in love. When he arrived at the *Troc* and laid the $100,000 in cash on the cocktail table in front of Billy, he said "...for the whole place and everything in it, including what's in the cash register right now." Monte was convinced his winning streak would be extended to the cash register and thousands would be there. Billy shook hands, took the 100K. There was $120 in the register. The heartless Lady Luck laughed at the fool she'd come in with. She turned seductively to Billy, took his hand with the 100k in it and whispered her undying love into his ear. Billy and the irresistible Miss Luck abruptly got up and left Monte sitting alone in the dark room.

He was right about the movie *Copacabana*. It bombed unceremoniously. It was so bad that even his sycophants weren't trying to say nice things about it. It was like it never existed and it reinforced his newly developed observation on his business, Broadway in particular, but applicable to all of show business,

"Broadway's a hard taskmaster," he said to reporters and friends, "You make good or you're forgotten." - exactly the way the movie *Copacabana* was forgotten moments after it premiered.

In spite of her new 3-year contract to perform at Monte's *Trocadero*, Carmen Miranda extended the losing streak. On top of the disaster of the Copa movie, a publicity photograph was taken while Miranda was rehearsing a dance number for the *Troc*. At the photo session, as she was being whirled around the shoulders of her dance partner, Cesar Romero, she passed the lens, feet first and a clear view up her skirt was snapped. With photographic deep focus, Miranda's reported disdain for underwear was clearly evident, particularly to those who could read lips. It somehow passed several editors unnoticed but soon came to their attention with the receipt of several irate letters and a dramatic spike in sales. The photo became an instant collector's item and was added to countless pornography collections around the world.

Miranda was so humiliated by the movie and photograph that she refused to appear in front of people on the same stage where the photo was taken. The publicity for the club turned into the story of mutual lawsuits. While the lawyers got paid, the club itself faded once it was known that Wilkerson was not there generating personal publicity in his *Hollywood Reporter* for every star that showed up. Monte closed the place two months after he bought it. The suit was settled out of court with Miranda paying to get out of her contract.

With Jane's contract to the studio fulfilled, she now wanted only to raise her sons and try to regain her emotional strength. Whatever demons had been unleashed in her from the vials of Dr. Jacobson, were temporarily in retreat. She had found her restoration in the deep, dreamless sleep of the newly popular barbiturate, Nembutal. For the first time in several years, she felt rested and normal. All she needed now was peace and quiet. The family returned to New York to await the birth of their second son.

The phone rang at 10 AM. This was shocking enough on its own, but on the other end of the line was Meyer Lansky.

Monte hadn't heard from Lansky in years and considering the hour was the middle of Monte's night, he had to ask several times before he realized who was calling. Lansky said that special guests of his had asked to see a show at the Copa and they needed very special treatment.

Meyer had moved up in the world like most of his colleagues in the *Syndicate*. He didn't just run "carpet joints" anymore. He had become an important armorer of the Jewish settlers who were struggling to establish a homeland in British controlled Palestine. Meyer had arranged for freighters full of small arms to drop anchor in the Mediterranean Sea just north of Gaza on several moonless nights. Their deadly cargoes were shuttled to shore by a small flotilla of private pleasure boats arranged by European friends of Meyer and Charlie Lucky. Meyer was now an international power broker and friendly with some of the most powerful political leaders in the world. "Not bad for a kid from Brooklyn," he liked to quip.

Jewish leaders David Ben Gurion and Golda Meir were in New York twisting arms politically at the UN for a Jewish state while raising millions of dollars to fund the proposed homeland. Their intended resurrection of the ancient Jewish nation, Israel, was becoming more likely every day. As a result, tens of thousands of Palestinian Arabs wanted them both dead. The two leaders had survived several recent assassination attempts, but they trusted Meyer enough to confide in him and allow him to arrange a night on the town for them. They wanted to go to the Copa.

Meyer confirmed security arrangements with Frank C who in turn relied on Albert Anastasia to command the operation. On the night of the Ben-Gurion/Meir visit, it was said that there were more concealed weapons in the audience of the Copa, than in the lockers of the New York City Armory a few blocks away. The two leaders arrived tired from several long days at the United Nations shuttling endlessly between world leaders and underlings. They were looking forward to a night at the famous nightclub and to meeting show business stars. A slight hitch in the plan developed on the night of the visit.

After inspecting the showroom a final time and meeting with Anastasia, the leaders' personal security team would not allow them to sit in the audience, even with Anastasia's men stationed at every vantage point. They were restricted to the kitchen of the club. The two reluctantly agreed.

In their concealed position at a private table in front of the Copa's steam table, they had to imagine most of what a night at the club was like. But even under these odd conditions, the two pioneers of Israel were thrilled to be in the legendary nightclub. They were occasionally permitted to peek at the stage between the swinging kitchen doors and could hear the show through speakers set up at Podell's table nearby.

Monte was in awe of the two leaders - in a way he hadn't felt since he was a teenager meeting his first stage performers at the Lights Club. These two were the legendary warriors who were unifying his scattered people into a mighty army – and winning for the first time in nearly two thousand years. Yet they looked like a middle-aged tourist couple from any small European village.

Meyer had given Monte a glowing recommendation and the three of them greeted each other warmly. Instantly, the awe they each felt for the other vanished in a flash of recognition and joy. They were the same people – driven nearly to extinction – now celebrating their survival and triumph together. Over plates of pineapple chicken, the first heroes of Israel avoided any discussion of politics and wanted to talk only about Monte and show business – where were his Jewish roots in Europe? How did he come to America? Did he know Charlie Chaplin?

Even Jules Podell was gentled by the visitors. He was happy to act as private headwaiter for the table and took the occasion to voice his support for the idea of Israel. He received two short, polite "thank yous" before the two politicians turned back to Monte with more questions about show business and movie stars.

One by one Monte sent for his headliners – Joe E. and Perry Como - and recruited stars from the audience to sit with the two. Suave movie comedian Dick Powell of the *The Thin Man* series was summoned for a visit and funnyman Lou Costello of the team *Abbott and Costello* was pulled in to join the party. For a few short hours, the weight of the future of their people was lifted from the shoulders of the two guerilla leaders as they joked and kibitzed with an assortment of stars from Broadway and Hollywood. The kitchen got crowded with security, busboys, waiters, an occasional cigarette and photo girl lighting up smokes for new table guests and snapping group photos while drinks and plates and more movie stars swirled around the two politicians. Everyone was a tummler that night.

By midnight, the two were laughed-out and exhausted. They had bags full of autographed Copa menus and napkins, enough pineapple chicken for two more days and were ready for bed. A phalanx of their own security and Anastasia's men trundled them down the long crooked hallway and out the back entrance onto 60th street, through a gauntlet of more security and into a waiting armored car.

The next day, a box of Havana cigars was delivered to the club addressed to Monte. A short phone message was also left with the phone operator some time that day that said, "Enjoy the cigars, Meyer."

William Sloane Proser was born on August 23, 1948 in New York City. He was a large, healthy baby topped with the reddish hair of an Irishman. In recognition of his continuance of the Irish line, he was given the family name of Sloane. And so William Sloane, second son, joined the family with great screams of outrage and shock on his arrival. The nurses predicted he would be a singer or a wrestler.

As Jane calmed herself and moved into the rhythms of motherhood, she and Monte saw less and less of each other as he returned fully to work. She was up with the children at 6 and 7, Monte was asleep until noon. In the afternoon he spent an hour or so with the children before getting ready for work. From 6 PM on, he went from meeting to meeting until the early morning. She and the children were in bed by 10 PM, the middle of Monte's workday.

It was time to retreat and build the family home in Pennsylvania. Even on the remote Jericho Mountain farm, Jane would probably see Monte as much as she did now in New

York City. At the farm, he would be all theirs, even if only a few days a month. As she was making plans for the move, Jane's friend, the vivacious, fun-loving Sharon Waye, the new fiancee' of *Hampshire House* neighbor Sol Meadow, mentioned that she was planning a cruise to Italy with her roommate Lucille Marsh. Both were dancers and friends of Jane's for some time and were going without their men. Jane suddenly asked to go with them. She would leave Chip and the new baby Billy with Carrie. The trip was for 2 months, starting with a cruise across the Atlantic. She felt it was exactly what she needed. Monte felt it was an odd decision but he agreed. A vacation, even without him, seemed like a good idea if it helped her enjoy herself. At least she was showing more interest in life. Unfortunately, she was showing less interest in her children.

Monte had no interest in seeing Europe at the moment. He was scouring the street for a musical on which to parlay the success of *High Button Shoes*. He was onto something called *Heaven on Earth*.

As a parting gift on his way out of the Mayor's office, Fiorello LaGuardia, brought an indictment against Monte for evasion of the War Tax. Accountant Israel Katz had prepared thoroughly for just this occasion and the indictment was dismissed on examination of Katz' apparently scrupulous accounting which showed Monte's wartime tax rate at 93%. The action served its purpose, not to convict, since that would take actual evidence, but to further smear Monte's reputation and clearly mark him as a target for the new regime of law and order, anti-corruption politicians gearing up in Washington for a post-war house cleaning.

The government action set Monte's nerves on edge. He'd long feared incrimination by associating with his unnamed partners. It appeared as though the government was looking for just such an angle and reliable sources had informed him that the FBI had been maintaining a file on him since the club opened. He sought relief in the same Nembutal dreams that Jane and other performer friends found so restful.

Unfortunately, the hangover of the long lasting Nembutal when combined with a drink or two often put him to sleep in mid-conversation with friends – a repeat performance of liquor induced stupors in the recent past. Ironically, this embellished his reputation even further among the jesters in his growing court of admirers.

Jack Entratter knew better. Whatever was getting to his boss, again, it was starting to affect business. Important people were unhappy with what they saw as a snub, particularly if they had greased everyone from Nick the doorman through and including Entratter himself to get an audience with Monte. They had urgent business to propose and vital favors to ask and started to request time with Podell instead. Entratter couldn't ignore the fairness of their requests. With all of Monte's other projects and interests, it might be months before they could catch him at the club, with no guarantee that he would be in a state of mind to discuss business.

Subtly and quietly at first, power began to flow away from Monte. Entratter had talked himself hoarse trying to bring his boss back to focus on the business but it was clear Monte's priorities were changing. He would only involve himself in the shows and performers. Back office and other duties were left unfinished. Wherever there was a lack of leadership, Podell stepped in and made the decisions. Once the power started shifting, Entratter had seen enough bad partnerships to know to prepare for the inevitable explosion.

Frank C's life continued to run oddly parallel with Monte's. Both had been lifted into high profile positions along with some very dangerous supporting characters, they were hounded by the authorities because of these associations and were now surrounded by their coterie of flatterers and/or assassins depending on the political climate.

Frank continued to seek his relief very secretively with Dr. Hoffer, a psychoanalyst on Park Avenue. News that he was having mental problems would have been a fatal disclosure if it got to certain people. Clearly the pressures of being *Public Enemy #1* were wearing on him. To help resolve the moral conflicts that his business forced upon him, he was advised to give back to the community, to involve himself in a civic charity. This, it was thought, would relieve the pressure in his head and allow him to finally rest and sleep through the night. He was willing to try anything, except the new sleeping pills everyone was raving about. He couldn't yet afford to be that soundly asleep. His doctor also recommended a sea cruise to give him immediate relief.

Frank had always been generous with charities, giving tens of thousands to all sorts of organizations privately. But now that he was a public figure, and under doctor's orders, he decided to make his generosity public too. He accepted an invitation to be vice-chairman of the 1949 Red Cross Fund Drive. His attorney suggested Frank host a dinner at the Waldorf for 100 people at $100 a plate. They would then give that $10,000 to the Red Cross. Drive chairman Ray Vir Den was enthusiastic about the plan and Frank dutifully compiled his list of invitations. The list included nearly every political leader in the city, a handful of judges and every top gangster in the region. After he read the list, Frank's attorney, George Wolf, pleaded with him to bar the gangsters, not to go ahead with this public relations nightmare. Frank got mad. Those "gangsters" were his close friends and he wouldn't hear another word against them. They stayed invited. And instead of Wolf's suggestion of the Waldorf, Frank said the dinner would be boring at the Waldorf. Instead, he picked the Copa.

The evening went off beautifully. Politicians and wiseguys mingled and chatted easily together. Frank made the rounds and personally put the arm on his underworld associates, like Joe Adonis, to make generous donations. Monte watched the action and ventured closer when Frank got to Joe Adonis, a notorious cheapskate.

"Joe, I want you to meet a friend of ours, Judge Hoffman. Judge, this gentleman ...

"Oh, I know Joe," the judge assured as Joe nodded from his seat.

"Stand up," Frank commanded unhappily. Adonis slowly got to his feet, extended his hand to the judge, as glum as the judge with the meeting. Joe deferred to keep up appearances, "I was just thinkin' of somethin' else, no disrespect."

"That's right," Frank said, searching for a big word to impress the judge, "And you were thinkin' about making a donation, being a benefactor like you are." Joe looked down for a long moment to hide his disgust and then pulled a big wad of bills out of his pocket. He opened the wad and started peeling off hundreds.

Frank smiled at the Judge. Joe stopped peeling, offered several hundred to Frank, Frank lost his smile. Joe kept peeling. Frank got impatient, took the whole wad out of Joe's hand.

"That's 10 G's." Joe whispered, aside to Frank. "And it ain't all mine," he pleaded.

"I completely understand," Frank nodded, patting Joe on the back, "It's discomfiting." Joe nodded, unsure of the word and sat down.

Grudgingly the money was produced in fat rolls of cash and the evening turned into a very lucrative outing for the Red Cross.

Outside the Copa, photographers were jostling to get the best position to get a shot of the famous lawmakers on the *Syndicate's* party list. There was Congressman Arthur Klein, five judges of the New York State Supreme Court, at least three other judges and a gang of Tammany Hall luminaries headed by the borough of Manhattan president, Hugo E. Rogers. As they cleared the front doors the flashes went off like the Fourth of July. The photos raced across the country, around the world and landed on the Washington D.C. desk of an up and coming congressman from Tennessee. The young lawmaker was fond of campaigning in a coonskin cap. He was a man of the people. Estes Kefauver saw his path to fame outlined in the frozen, startled expressions of the men caught exiting the Copa's front doors.

That same morning, Frank saw the papers and knew it was time for a powder. He made plans to spend some time out of town and consult with his boss Luciano – and the sooner, the better. He needed a place where no one could reach him for a while.

Later that same week, Jane kissed Monte goodbye on the pier in front of the *Queen Mary* bound from Manhattan to

Naples. Her spur-of-the-moment sea cruise, peacefully crossing the Atlantic with her girlfriends, was going to allow her to quietly sort through her thoughts. Monte still felt it was a mistake, but gave her a smiling, confident send off – no hint of concern.

He offered her a cake box tied with string. "Lindy's," he said. "Can't get it over there."

She looked at him suddenly flooded with tenderness, wanting to stay with him. "Oh Monte," her resolve to make the voyage was evaporating. She moved to him. He held her tightly, communicating with his arms, the strength his words couldn't convey.

He was such a good man, a thoughtful husband. Why was she doing this? Leaving her family, for what? "I'm not crazy," she whispered against his neck. "I'll miss you, and the boys…" The more she said, the less sure she was. Tears came to her eyes. That snapped the spell. She would not allow weakness. She straightened up, broke off from him, quickly wiping the tears away. This trip was going to make her better. "The boys won't even know I'm gone," she smiled.

Monte knew the boys would miss her and so would he, and that she had shown her poker hand. She was guilty and had damned herself for it. "Nah, they'll be fine," he agreed.

She turned, walked up the gangway to the ship's observation deck. He stayed to see her turn and wave goodbye. Sharon was waiting for her above on the deck. Sol found Monte in the crowd and the two lonely husbands stood their post, watching the gangplank hoist, the lines cast off.

On deck, Jane and Sharon waved for the last time.

"Look at these two glum chums," Sharon said, "You'd think we were going to prison."

Jane stared at Monte, she confided, "He's all I got."

On the pier, Monte and Sol watched the majestic ocean liner slip down the Hudson toward the Atlantic. "Whaddya think, pal?" Sol asked.

Monte thought to himself, "I'll never see her again" but responded quietly , "Buy you a drink."

By her second day at sea, Jane missed her husband and two boys. She telegrammed Monte an unusually upbeat note about bringing her three men presents from sunny Italy. She was coming back to herself, she thought, the trip was already working.

She and Sharon grew extremely close as Jane confided her recent battles with depression.

"It's like darkness, like cold rain. You just want to die," as she tried to describe it. To Sharon, a consistently sunny person, Jane's symptoms seemed to be some sort of blue flu going around the entertainment community. It became part of her mission on the journey to shepherd Jane through this low point and get her back on the bright side of life. Lucille was enlisted in the effort and the two protected Jane like two older sisters. Sharon would eventually trace the source of the blue flu in her show business friends back to Dr. Feelgood.

All three ladies were invited frequently to dine with a close associate of Monte's who was enjoying the crossing and seeking emotional restoration as well. Frank Costello, on his way to Naples for a conference with Luciano, recognized Jane immediately and was happy to have a familiar face on the voyage. She and her friends became his honored guests. He entertained the women with stories of his home in the old country and of his family life now in America. The only shadow on the pleasant gatherings was Frank's constant companion, a dour presence named Curly. Curly was bald and solidly built, an unsmiling and silent man who was never more than four feet away from Frank. He was always looking at the people moving toward and around his boss. Other than Curly, the women enjoyed their meals with Frank, never feeling they were in any immediate danger. They agreed that Frank was a very considerate, classy guy - a perfect gentleman who occasionally killed people, but usually only other killers. Civilians were strictly taboo. So all things considered, he was a sort of public servant, with a shadow legal system all his own.

The ladies ended up with long lists of people and places that Frank suggested they visit in Italy – from dressmakers to gelato shops. Frank seemed to know everybody.

His unerring eye for talent led Monte to try again for a management contract, this time with Mary Martin, just then starring in the smash hit *South Pacific* on Broadway. The cast was celebrating at the club with champagne on the house, when Monte fell into a rendition of the raucous drinking song, "It Was Nelly Who Kicked Kelly in the Belly in the Bar" with Martin and Jackie Gleason. The trio belted out the old barroom ditty to the surprise of the other patrons. They turned the joint into a saloon once again, with a chorus of roaring, happy drunks leading the way.

Toward the bleery end of the evening, Monte popped the question and Martin agreed to a management contract. Monte would bring her to Hollywood and the rest would be history. Within minutes he produced the document and the starlet signed on the line. It was all set then. She went home singing and Monte closed up the place that night with a crowd of friends and acquaintances, not one of whom he remembered the next day. He was put in a cab because he was too drunk to walk the four blocks to the Hampshire House.

Late the next afternoon, as his mind was clearing, he got a call, "Monte?"

"Yeah. Who's this?"

"Richard Halliday. I represent Ms. Martin as of today."

"Okay. What can I do for you Mr. Halliday?"

"I represent Miss Martin. Your napkin's no good."

That part of the previous evening suddenly became very clear. He had signed Mary Martin to a contract, but he'd handwritten it on a cocktail napkin. When Martin showed this Dewar's-stained document to her boyfriend-turned-manager, he patiently recited the reputation of Monte's unnamed partners in the club. Then he said he could make the napkin go away. And lastly, he, not someone who had made more stars than both of them had ever met, was the best person to manage her career. The young starlet leapt into his legal arms. When Monte called Mary the next day she was out. He left a message. It was 11 years before Mary called back.

Monte sat in the Copa's darkened showroom waiting for the next act to find their way through the shadows. Open auditions were a tedious necessity of the business that tested his patience. He saw a young man weave his way through the tables toward him followed by an older man carrying sheet music. They looked to be headed for a handshake and introduction, Monte cut them off, "If you're looking for the piano, it's over there." They changed direction.

17 year-old Eddie Fisher settled by the piano, introduced himself and sang six songs. Most auditioners didn't get to the second. "Sounds alright," Monte got up. "Better come upstairs let me see what you look like," he said, leading them up the stairs to the bar and lounge. In the sunlight from the open front door Monte laughed when he saw the youngster revealed, "You're just a little kid, this is a nightclub."

"I'll be eighteen in August," Eddie shot back hopefully. He was starving as a part time wedding and bar mitzvah singer. Monte looked him over and smiled a little.

"Eighteen!" Monte egged him on. Eddie stood his ground. The older man, Skipper Dawes, Eddie's mentor, saw the crack in Monte's mood and asked for a frank opinion of the young singer. Monte agreed the kid could sing. They discussed the poise, the experience Eddie would need to make it onto the Copa stage. He took another look at the awkward teenager and decided to help him. "Alright, come back in October. I'll be starting up my fall shows. I'll give you a job then." Eddie pressed on asking questions, not taking the October date as the final word. Monte laughed a little as the teenager worked him for more. The chutzpah wasn't new, there were lots of desperate singers, but something in the awkward delivery brought Monte back to his own early pitches as a young runaway and hobo. "C'mere," he walked the two to the manager's office where they sat as Monte got on the phone to Milton Blackstone at Grossinger's.

"Milt, I got a boy here I think you should meet. He's got a good voice but he's just a kid. I think he needs some on-the-job training." Monte listened to Blackstone's response, then, "Good," he said, "I'll send him up to see you. You'll know him right off. He's a skinny kid with a lot of curly hair." He hung up and became the famously "soft touch" known to Broadwayites. "Go see Milton, he'll take care of you."

With the nod from Monte, Milton went to work as the youngster's manager. Milton turned the prodigious energy and fierce loyalty that had made him a civilian war hero, shipbuilding magnate and peerless advertising executive toward managing the young singer. He proceeded to shake every tree in New York and Hollywood looking for opportunities. He managed Fisher like Bucky Harris managed the 1947 Yanks to the World Championship that year, tough and smart.

Under Milton's guidance, Fisher's popularity grew, his singing improved as he matured and transformed into a handsome, young man. His confidence and comfort level on stage soared. He even started telling jokes "tummeling" the audience a little. Suddenly, more female attention than he'd ever dreamed of came his way. And he took full advantage of it.

Milton, who was only once briefly married and an old-world conservative in his sexual behavior, was displeased with Eddie's emerging sexual gluttony. He began to impose moral instruction on his protégé, which Eddie pointedly ignored. In spite of Eddie's appetites, under Milton's direction, he became the hottest recording star in the world within 3 years.

As Eddie's star rose, Monte made good on his promise to give him a job at the Copa. Unfortunately for Eddie, another, very different Milton, was in the audience on opening night. Milton Berle started out with a little friendly heckling, then turned it into a duet. Berle zinged Eddie with one-liners and an insatiable hunger for attention. The older comedian stole the show at will and finally handed it back to the singer when he was done with it. Eddie was the straight man for Berle's punchlines, whether he liked it or not.

Berle started a trend at the club that became a tradition. Other stars began making scenes at their tables and getting into running arguments with the headliner, ad libbing in the middle of the show. Sometimes it would start with the follow spot finding a star at his table, sometimes it started with a heckle from the audience. More frequently it started with a request from the headliner for an impromptu performance in an effort to catch a star off guard at his table and embarrass him. Singers were asked to dance, dancers were asked to sing, actors were asked to tell a joke. Performers going to the club began to prepare themselves with a quip or a gag to either deflect or take advantage of the attention. MGM star Danny Kaye danced an "improvised" piece and clowned with the audience in a performance that went on for 5 minutes. With a loud sigh, Joe E., finally got a chair from the bandstand and sat down on stage waiting for Kaye to finish. It went on for 6 minutes. Joe had a cocktail table and a fresh drink delivered to the stage. Danny kept going. He couldn't stop, he was riding a tidal wave. People were laughing so hard they were wiping tears away with their dinner napkins. He passed 7 minutes. On stage, Joe was looking over the dinner menu and getting ready to order dinner. He hadn't heard this kind of sustained laughter in a while. All he could do was play the straight man perfectly by watching Kaye along with everyone else. Danny finished up at somewhere north of 8 minutes, exhausted and ready for another drink. This kind of thing was starting to happen almost every night.

The place truly went out of control when 22 year-old Jerry Lewis began attacking people's food. Lewis had his own singer and straight-man, Dean Martin and enough energy for two or three tummlers, so no one had a chance for a word edgewise as long as Martin and Lewis were on. Lewis was one of the most gifted of the Catskill comedians. He pantomimed to records so skillfully that he became an international star, particularly in France where visual humor was loved. As the straight-man, Martin was not only handsome and charming he was a great singer and to some, a comedian as good as Lewis. Martin played the sophisticated lover to Lewis' madcap loony. He provided the earthy soul and Lewis was the genius inventor, instigator and hare-brain.

No piece of silverware or food item was safe when Lewis worked. He stalked the club's aisles in search of comedic prey. He pounced on steaks, grabbed them off the plate, licked them and put them back. People roared with approval. He sat on women's laps and flirted with them. He turned the place upside down.

Sharon wrote to Sol of their shipboard dinners with Frank Costello and Curly. She wrote of the Italian spring, of the growing closeness of she and Janey, of the wealthy Count De Polignac who had invited the three adventuring American young ladies to his family villa in the south of France. Sol read this last bit with the alarming clarity gained by years of parsing legal smokescreens. He consulted Monte. This was war. The two were on the next trans-Atlantic flight.

After 24 hours of travel in various machines, the two Broadway guys arrived at the gates of the Count's rustic estate unannounced. And quite a surprise it was. The Count had supervised the creation of a magnificent outdoor feast. A table on the stone veranda overlooked the twilit vineyards that had belonged to the De Polignac's for generations. Candles glowed in the gathering darkness, lighting the ladies sun-tanned faces among the crystal and silver. Music wafted from the farmhouse, interrupted suddenly by the knock on the front gates that set the mastiffs howling.

"Surprise!" Sol offered as he cleared the gate. Monte followed, highly amused at the situation, assisted by the flask of Dewar's in his jacket pocket. Seeing the salads had just been served Monte quipped, "What timing!" To which Jane happily responded, "What the hell are you two doing here?" She'd forgotten Monte's habit of relentless pursuit and was thrilled to see it again. She was forgiven. She marched from the table to her pursuer.

"We had the day off," he said.

The Count was forcibly amused, not wanting to seem ungracious, his options reduced to one, Lucille, the unmarried guest, from three. Sharon made the introductions as Sol excused their sudden arrival mumbling about poor phone service, weather and fatigue.

"Of course, of course…" the Count accepted as he instructed places to be set at the table. Monte had new pictures of the boys out in the candlelight before he'd even sat down.

Jane wagged her head at his Storming of the Bastille, as she called it. It was, after all, Bastille Day, July 14th, Monte's birthday. They were soon lost in their own private conversation, holding hands.

The evening livened as the D'Polignac champagne racks were emptied and tales of movie stars who would love to meet the Count diverted the overwhelmed host. He was keen on an introduction to "Miss Grable" and was assured of it as Monte's guest at the Copa. Flapper dancing suddenly erupted to the *Muskrat Ramble* found in the Count's record collection. The ladies kicked the Charleston into high gear as Monte and Sol did the best they could by wobbling around them, champagne flutes firmly gripped with elegant pinky fingers extended. The seductive atmosphere the Count had so carefully prepared was completely destroyed. Towards dawn, Monte and Sol were found fully clothed and sound asleep on the Count's own bed. They were photographed by their thoroughly drunk and star-struck host and left undisturbed in their triumph.

CHAPTER 31

A Broken Heart for Every Light on Broadway

Hard on the heels of the Copacabana movie disaster, Monte's new musical *Heaven on Earth*, produced eventually with Ned Litwack instead of Joe Kipness, opened at the New Century Theatre on 58th Street on September 16, 1948. Litwack was truly a civilian, unconnected to the mob and continued the losing streak of other straight partners in Monte's career. The play closed on September 25th after 12 performances. Critic Brooks Atkinson said about *Heaven on Earth*,

"Although our stricken nation has only just recovered from "Up in Central Park," a little something has come to replace it. "Heaven on Earth," which opened at the Century last evening, sets a very high standard for mediocrity and drives all our happy dreams away."

The show was noted as a very expensive failure at its closing, pouring a total of $358,000 of Monte and Mr. Litwack's money down the drain. This followed the thankfully unnoticed disaster *Springtime in Brazil* starring Milton Berle that had closed in out of town tryouts a little over a year before. That turkey gobbled up $250,000 of Monte's cash also.

Thankfully *High Button Shoes* continued to sellout and people didn't notice his two failures in a row as much. The failures pushed him back onto the anxious path of finding a successful follow up to *High Button Shoes,* but now he had less time and much less money. The show was beginning to wobble. Ticket sales were slipping steadily.

Reinforcing Monte's superstition that bad things happen in threes, the ninth (three times three) season at the Copa brought on the crisis that Jack Entratter had been preparing for. While Monte had been busy with *Springtime in Brazil* and then *Heaven on Earth* over the summer, Podell had been busy discussing his thoughts for the new season with every talent agent in New York. When Monte finally returned to fully focus on the line-up for the year, he had a thicket of messages from agents wanting confirmation of dates he'd never agreed to for performers he'd never approved. It was the final and irrevocable straw. One way or another Podell would have to go. It was war.

Unfortunately, his greatest ally, Frank Costello, was on his relaxing cruise and was unreachable. Monte would not wait. He called Adonis and gave him an ultimatum, his second, and it had a similar reception to the first in which he threatened to take the show out of the club. This time, the deal from Monte was Podell hits the road or he would. Initially, of course, Adonis reacted badly. Podell was Frank's guy and Adonis was on dangerous ground if he got rid of him but he listened to the terms. Monte proposed a vote. He proposed that only three guys – him, Jack Entratter and Podell – knew enough about the club to make the decision on who should run the place. The three would vote and decide who stayed.

A vote? Adonis must have been half-amused at Monte's cracked logic. He knew the club was now bigger than Monte and could survive without him. He probably thought the little Jew was losing his marbles; so let him have his vote. Even if Entratter sided with Monte, the likely choice, he could always refer the matter back to Frank. Or he could get rid of Podell if he was as incompetent as Monte claimed. Either way, he'd decide later if he would honor the results of Monte's sham vote or not.

Monte told Sol Meadow what he had done and Sol was dumbfounded. It was like hearing his trusted ally calmly preparing for suicide. Sol had seen Monte negotiate with Frank and navigate successful compromises through the years, but this vote idea was madness. It betrayed a lack of power and more disturbingly, a lack of basic understanding. Monte didn't have a vote in Adonis' world and of all people, Monte knew it. But he was beyond angry. He was, in fact, irrational. He claimed Podell was everything he detested and he wouldn't live another minute with this cancer in his presence. Jane was not available to cool Monte's fever and neither was Milton Blackstone effective in convincing Monte to retract the challenge. Monte's behavior mimicked Jane's irritability and the irrational tirades of many others who would follow Dr. Jacobson's amphetamine therapy. It was all set to go down the next day as soon as Entratter showed up for work.

Monte hadn't slept well or at all. He was in the office early, attempting to get his press corps on the phone unsuccessfully. He had an earful of spiteful accusations and grand pronouncements of new management at the Copa, if anyone had been awake before noon to take his calls. As he had during the birth of the club, Sol Meadow stuck to Monte's side hoping to break through the tidal wave of emotion that drove Monte further toward disaster. He came straight from the *Hampshire House* when he realized Monte had left for the club without him. When Sol arrived the fateful play was in mid-act. All the players were on their way including Adonis, who was keen to protect his investment and tired of Monte's demands, Entratter who was unaware that he would face a life-altering decision the instant he cleared the front door and Podell who was itching for a showdown.

When Adonis arrived, the place was silent. He moved down the stairs to the showroom and saw Entratter and Monte huddled with Sol. Podell was standing at the bar. As he crossed to Monte the enclave broke up and Adonis removed his hat and coat. Without a hello, Monte launched into a summation of years of abuse and complaints about Podell with a few choice insults he'd been saving up using words like "idiot", "ape" and "leg-breaker". Sol winced as Monte dug himself in deeper with each insult. Entratter looked like he wanted to hide under his table, distancing himself in his body language from the comments. The ersatz tribunal leapt directly to its deliberation phase as Podell and Adonis calmly considered where they might dump Monte's body later if things got out of hand.

As abruptly as he had launched into his attack, Monte called for Entratter to cast the deciding vote, as the senior employee, for the future of the club. It was him or Podell but from this moment on, not both. One would go. Monte rested and sat back to collect on his years of mentorship and friendship with Entratter. Sol begged him once more to retract and reconsider his attack. Monte considered Sol's plea for a moment, nodding to his friend, meaning he understood Sol wanted to protect him. Monte turned his gaze back to Entratter, demanding a vote.

Entratter twisted in the wind for only a moment. "You're not making a lot of sense, Monte. I gotta be honest with ya."

Monte felt the world sway beneath him. The words and faces rushed together and a vortex opened up. It was all sucked away in that instant. The club, the life, the friendship he counted on.

The place was silent, even the cleaning crew wasn't in yet. Entratter looked down at his feet, unable to look Monte in the face. Adonis' stare was fixed on Monte, waiting for a move. Monte focused on the round, black Copacabana ashtray in center of the table. He reached out and tapped it gently, once, instinctively, the signal for another card in a card game. But there was no card coming. There were no drinks coming, the bar was so quiet you could hear the ice machine humming. There wasn't going to be another song. The bandstand was dark. Monte knew he'd drawn bad cards and was done, the game was over. It was all suddenly gone as Adonis closed the deal, "We're buying you out. How much?"

Monte, furious and determined to strike back, quickly miscalculated and before Sol could shut him up, threw out a number that belittled the value of the club without him, "Gimme a hundred and thirty five." It was a ridiculously small amount and Sol spoke up to stop the mistake but it was already spoken and recorded in Adonis' mental ledger. The mobster stood up without a word to anyone and walked out. It was over. Monte was out.

Monte spent a moment looking at Entratter who got up next, heading for the cover of the kitchen. Then Monte stood up with Sol, looked over the showroom one last time and walked out without acknowledging Podell who stood slack-jawed at the bar. Without publicity or even a farewell fanfare from the band, *Monte Proser's* Copacabana was over.

CHAPTER 32

SANCTUARY

Following the news of the sudden death of the Copa, a procession of Monte's closest friends came to be with him. They moped around the living room of the *Hampshire House* sitting shiva for the club. No doubt Monte would go on to other things but the loss of the iconic Copa was devastating.

"I never thought Jack would leave me," Monte told a few of the mourners, deflecting his own blame. He knew he'd overplayed his hand by relying Entratter's loyalty and by letting his hatred of Podell cloud his mind. He felt nauseous considering his own stupidity, and panic at the self-doubt now stinging him like a wasp. There was no blaming this one on bad luck. But there was something else, something deeper about his miscalculation. His agitation with Podell had gone out of control, beyond his usual flashes of anger. As the platters of cold meats and boxes of take-out Chinese food emptied, Sol was the one who made the possible connection,

"Maybe you got the Blue Flu? Seems to be going around."

It took Monte a minute to line up Sol's suggestion with other clues. His head ached from constantly replaying every comment and phone call that had created the disaster, trying piece together where he'd gone wrong. The doorbell chimed, someone let someone new into the crowded apartment. The phone rang. It had been ringing all day. Somebody picked it up for Monte.

"Johnny Rosselli," they announced. Monte waved the call off. Steamy clouds of Chinese food and the soft murmur of conversation made the place smell and sound like the Copa. Monte looked over his gaggle of pals and associates – all men, all middle-aged – his gang. Eddie Jaffe came over and reached for Monte's hand whispering soft condolences. His concern and handshake came with a hard look into Monte's eyes. Eddie, like the others, was there to support Monte but also assess the extent of his defeat. Monte was a rainmaker and they all felt a dry wind coming on. Decisions would have to be made.

Sol's puzzle piece about the Blue Flu finally fell into place. Monte turned to Sol, "Jacobson," he said. Sol turned his hands up and his lips down, "Who knows?"

Monte felt he did know at least a little more, but it barely mattered now. It was the past. What he needed help with now was the future. "What the hell am I going to tell Jane?"

Sol couldn't help him there. Another wave of nausea forced Monte to hold his forehead steady with one hand.

Batch drove Monte back to their oldest stomping grounds, Bucks County, the place where they had run wild and spent years rambling through the countryside. Monte was going home to Jane and the boys on the farm. Batch would stay in the cabana house by the pool.

That summer of 1949 passed with Monte and Jane recovering in the healing sanctuary of their farm on Jericho Mountain. Carrie gave the boys showers with the garden hose and baked apple pies and cornbread. For one week every month, Carrie went back to New York City to stay with an old friend, Momsy, and attend to her city life.

Sol came from New York and made a barbecue on the fieldstone fireplace by the pool. Monte and Jane took the boys swimming. Weeks passed unnoticed. Jane slowly came back to life. Monte recovered as well but was often deep in thought and not interested in going to the local taverns with Batch as they used to do. He was becoming a civilian, someone awake during the day. Mostly what he did was think that entire summer, often in the hammock by the pool. He had a lot of thinking to do once he realized the full enormity of his mistake. This was one blunder that he hadn't seen coming at all.

When he'd had enough of sweet corn and balmy evenings watching fireflies, when he'd forgiven himself, Monte's thinking turned naturally back to New York and the action. Toward the end of the summer they discovered Jane was pregnant again. Life just upped the ante on the next roll of the dice.

In his great spasm of frustration, Monte tore himself from the clutches of the mob. Or so it seemed. He emerged from the Copa apparently undamaged, but with barely enough cash to open a new place. Almost every dollar he'd earned in the last nine years had run off with slow racehorses and unlucky crapshoots on and off Broadway.

More losses at various racetracks and crap tables were incalculable but were at least as large as his losses on Broadway. In 1951, he estimated his total losing streak up to that time as somewhere near 6 million dollars. This seems a fairly accurate figure when considering the Copa grossed regularly $55,000 per week or nearly 3 million a year, meaning Monte's yearly take from the club was somewhere north of a million dollars.

But nine years of stratospheric success left him with little more than another chapter in his legacy. Among some, this only added to his reputation as the high-rolling, Broadway vagabond who stood up to the mob and survived. It was good publicity but like most publicity, it was the sunny side of the story.

The shadow side of the story was that Rosselli's Chicago *Outfit* and Costello's New York *Syndicate* had strengthened their mutual network to the point where almost everybody in show business, especially big earners like Monte, worked for them.

The trend was as inescapable as it was obvious to anyone who knew the players involved. It became increasingly indiscreet to ask where and how a Hollywood player or studio was bankrolled. People were simply friends of certain other people. The details were dropped in normal conversation and often replaced with a gesture – an index finger pushed the tip of the nose to one side indicating a broken nose, a tough guy, one of the boys. Business as usual, c'est la vie.

As the summer doldrums of 1950 dispersed crowds from the cities into the countryside, the post-war house cleaning of corruption in the public sector shifted into gear in Washington. Tennessee senator Estes Kefauver had seen the perfect vehicle for his presidential ambitions in the front-page *Washington Times* photograph of mobsters and lawmakers leaving the Copa after Costello's *Red Cross Fund Drive*. In May, he inaugurated his *Special Committee to Investigate Organized Crime in Interstate Commerce*. The first order of committee business was to put Frank Costello and his associates under a legal microscope while exposing them and the intrepid, crime-busting senator to ten million new TV viewers and 50 million newspaper readers. Six of those ten million TV viewers bought their first sets that year. It was estimated that a million TV sets were sold just to watch Frank Costello testify. Months of preparation and regular press releases were promising to make Costello's appearance the nation's first widely televised historical event. He was about to become the reluctant star of broadcast history – a nightmare of publicity that even his tortured imagination could never have pictured – and he was going to drag Monte along with him.

The loss of the Copa meant that now Monte had something to prove. He would show everybody that he could he take a punch and get back up stronger. Although *High Button Shoes* closed that summer also, achieving the status of second longest running show in Broadway history, he had already partnered with James Nasser of the *General Service Studio* in New York to produce a movie of the show. He acquired the movie rights to the novel *Shadow of a Hero*. He and Joe Kipness patched up their publicized differences and were developing follow up musicals *All You Need Is One Good Break* and *The Golden Hill*. He was contracted by the ABC network to produce a variety TV show to premiere in March 1950 starring Edward Everett Horton, sponsored by Packard Motor Cars.

In spite of this whirlwind of activity, he was going broke. The fees for his services as TV producer were his only income. Everything else was money going out. He was still very much in the game but this time out, with a third child on the way and his $135,000 from the Copa dwindling fast, he had to roll a seven. Naturally, he bet the entire bankroll on a long shot.

Within a few weeks of his departure from the Copa, he put money down on a large space at 49th and Broadway, the site of old pal Carl Erbe's *Club Zanzibar*. He had an idea – a way to combine the power of a Broadway production with the fun of a nightclub. The idea seized him and he was off again at a dead run, mind ablaze with this new vision, scattering money before him like seed corn, and this time with no financial partners to stem the financial bleeding.

Carl was happy to give up the *Zanzibar* lease. Characteristically, as he'd done when he and Monte were partners in their publicity business, he followed the easy money, the sure thing. He'd cautiously followed Monte into the nightlife with *Zanzibar* and was overwhelmed by the riotous profits from booze and entertainment, somewhere close to $40,000 a week, but now he was zeroing in on the big jackpot. Carl had teamed up with Ben Marden, owner and operator of gambling operations at the popular *Riviera* nightclub in Fort Lee, New Jersey and investor with Meyer and others in Generalissimo Batista's casinos in Cuba. Carl and Ben assured newly crowned Prince Rainier of Monaco that they would bring the prince's dowdy, little European kingdom into the limelight. They would inject the fast paced action of American crap tables and blackjack dealers into the Prince's staid Monte Carlo casinos that offered the traditional European games of roulette and chemin de fer. The young Prince loved all things American, particularly the Havana and Las Vegas sized gambling profits the Americans promised. Carl, the clear-sighted businessman, had recognized gambling as the one matchless business opportunity among all the industries of the night, and seized it with both hands. Monte, the visionary dreamer, saw only opportunities for entertainment.

At the new location, Monte developed his hybrid operation that would compete directly against the Copa and Broadway musicals simultaneously - in case anyone was thinking he'd been defeated. He called the place *Café Theatre*. It offered an adaptation of his "revue" concept perfected at the Copa that reduced a glamorous Ziegfeld-scale Broadway production, into the space of a 240 square foot dance floor. *Café Theatre* doubled down on this concept. The club offered an abbreviated version of the full scale Broadway musical, *Billion Dollar Baby* that would feature the original stars Jackie Gleason and Mamie Van Doren for the dinner show at 8. After that, his signature nightclub floorshow would run at 12 and 2 AM. The floorshow alone had 28 showgirls in the line. It was far and away the most outlandishly ambitious entertainment operation anyone had heard of in the nightclub field since he turned Madison Square Garden into the *Dance Carnival*. Only Lou Walter's rendition of the *Folies Bergere* at his *Latin Quarter* and Billy Rose's variety show at his *Diamond Horseshoe* came close.

In case one long shot wasn't enough, he opened a second club the following week using his reserve operating money for *Café Theatre*. He was going for broke, and nearly got there. Where *Café Theatre* overwhelmed with expensive star power and productions, and would suffer financially because of it, his second saloon reflected the quieter, forced maturity of the war generation. Instead of the sexy, fun-loving visions of tropical beaches that had made him famous at the Copa, Monte created a classy eastside supper club in the style of a Parisian bistro. Sophistication was more important than fun. Elegance overtook exuberance. Pink replaced hot, tropical reds. He opened *La Vie en Rose* at 123 East 54th street. Naturally, it took every dime that hadn't been spent on *Café Theatre* and more.

Luckily, Sol Meadow threw in as a financial partner. Ever since their storming of the D'Polignac Bastille, the two nearly-abandoned husbands had talked every day and were now joined at the heart. Their European trip had been the inspiration for *La Vie* and the source of healing for Jane and Monte's family life. Monte was more than grateful that Sol had a piece of the club. He was relieved.

Old pal Jackie Gleason put together *La Vie's* orchestra, gratis. He knew Monte was in a bind financially and jumped in to help him out. He also arranged the music and conducted the orchestra at musician's union scale. Gleason was on a roll, after repeated failures in Hollywood. The lucky streak started a few months earlier when he became the summer host of the new television show *Cavalcade of Stars* on the Dumont Network. Critic Gilbert Seldes saw in Gleason "…the traditional belief of heavy men in their own lightness and grace." After two episodes Jackie was signed as permanent host of the show. He'd hit the jackpot. The money was pouring in and he decided to share his triumph with Monte at his pal's newest joint. While *Billion Dollar Baby* was hung up on union negotiations at *Café Theatre*, it seemed the least Jackie could do for his old friend was to help get one of the places off the ground.

"Sure I'm crazy," Monte told Los Angeles Times reporter Jack Gaver, "Crazy about nightclubs. Miserable if I don't have a club to play around with."

"I was no sooner out of the place," he said, referring to the Copa, "…than I was planning a new one. One? I asked myself what would be better than one nightclub? Two, I replied. So I've got myself two clubs. If I had stopped to think about what I was getting into I probably wouldn't have done it. But that's the idea of this business – you don't think, you go ahead and do what you feel you have to do and hope for the best."

But hoping for the best was already falling short at *Café Theatre* where Actor's Equity claimed jurisdiction of his innovation – the tabloid version of Broadway shows. Because *Billion Dollar Baby* had been a successful Broadway production, the union enforced Broadway scale pay rates that were much higher than American Guild of Variety Artists rates for nightclub performers.

"I can't possibly get off the nut of each new production at the Café Theatre with its engagement there," he told Gaver. "I can only make a profit by touring the tabloid units in other nightclubs and theatres around the country after my place is through with them. I need a quiet, little place where I can go to relax," he said, "But actually this nightclub thing isn't as crazy as it sounds. I've done Broadway shows and made movies. You spend a lot of money on them and you get just one chance. In a club, all your money isn't riding on one number. You are selling food, liquor, music, a place to dance and, of course, your entertainment. Say things aren't right the night you open. The service is lousy, the show stinks. You get complaints, sure, but you've got a chance to correct the mistakes. You can even do it between shows on the same night. By the end of the week things may be looking up."

"I don't mean I'll never do another stage show or movie – I fully expect to – but give me a nightclub every time. Or two clubs."

Gleason's orchestra warmed the room up for *La Vie en Rose's* opening act, Milton Blackstone's skinny, singing waiter from Philadelphia, Eddie Fisher. Fisher had just scored rave reviews at Ben Marden's *Riviera*, the first genuine hit engagement of the young singer's life and had a hit record *"Thinking of You"*, selling out across the country. Since Milton controlled every aspect of the youngster's career and much of his private life, Monte got Fisher at the old prices - before singers with one hit record got $15,000 a week.

La Vie en Rose took off right out of the gate. Women looked beautiful and seductive in the low pink lighting. A lavish draped and raised stage took up one third of the floor including its orchestra pit down front, ala mode de Paris. The show room accommodated 450 people and was unobstructed by pillars like the Copa, where massive foundation pillars in the middle of the room were disguised as palm trees. *La Vie en Rose* was dominated by the stage. It was the ultimate cabaret showroom, overwhelming in its intimacy with the performers, and perhaps the most perfect, in his view, of all Monte's clubs. The style was romantic French, a celebration of the society that almost died in the war - the society that had created vaudeville and perfected the nightclub. The society that created romance, that smoked, drank, cursed, screwed and ate freely. A society that had survived.

As compelling as Monte's new vision was, it was small insurance against the whimsical nature of nightclub success.

The most insignificant detail could kill a club, like the smell or noise from a neighboring business, a change in a city traffic ordinance, large and small things that were unforeseeable and unimaginable that could cut the delicate thread of life on Broadway. *La Vie en Rose* had one small problem. The small, pink rosebud at the center of every pink leather seat cushion had the annoying habit of goosing guests regularly. Overcoming the rosebud, the place took off, selling out two shows, 12 and 2 AM. The 8 o'clock seating was for dinner only, another concession to rising talent costs. With a little fast thinking and help from his friends, Monte had managed to throw another seven. Once again, the river of money flowed to him. The opening weeks saw friends from every profession pay their respects by stopping in.

Frank Costello, escorting his wife Bobbie, arrived opening night to give his blessing. It was the first time they'd seen each other since the Copa blow-up. Bobbie, glamorized to the nines in diamond earrings and necklace, clutched Monte's hand to her and pulled him in for an unabashed, sisterly kiss. "Monteleh," she called him, the Yiddish endearment. Something had changed. She'd always been polite and friendly but now there was a warmth to her greeting.

Frank, almost embarrassed to ask, said, "If you need anything…", but Monte cut him off. "Nah, all set, thanks." They hadn't talked about the Copa since the split but Frank felt he owed Monte something.

"About the place and Julie, you shoulda come to me," he said.

"You weren't around," Monte replied, and another uncomfortable moment passed between them in silence. After all their summers at *Piping Rock* and seasons at the Copa, it was acknowledgement of a friendship that had been damaged as well as business partnership. Frank let Monte's shortness pass. If there was anyone in the straight world who deserved a pass it was Monte. The Prime Minister hadn't forgotten 1941 when Mayor LaGuardia privately slandered Monte, then publicly investigated and dragged him through the newspapers trying to expose Frank's connection at the Copa, or that his men,

Podell and Adonis, had mis-handled Monte at the club. But that wasn't quite all. There was more bad news coming on Frank's account. Not to ruin opening night, Frank let it wait for a day.

The following night, Johnny Rosselli arrived with his steady girlfriend. More than ever he was looking like the logical successor to Frank's throne. In the two years since his release from prison, Johnny had been a model citizen. He wouldn't drive more than 20 miles an hour to avoid any possible cross with the law and had conscientiously pursued a straight job to satisfy his parole requirements. He even humbled himself before his old co-conspirator Harry Cohn and went hat in hand to the mogul to ask for a legitimate job. To avoid the taint of association, Cohn turned him down. Johnny never forgot this betrayal and had occasion to avenge it in coming years, but in spite of Cohn's disloyalty, dozens of genuine friends like producer Bryan Foy, actress Donna Reed and screenwriter Joe Breen Jr. moved to support him, on both sides of the law. Like Frank, Johnny lived comfortably in both worlds and was respected as a man of principle – a stand-up guy. He was fiercely loyal and protective of his friends and their families, an outspoken patriot and a classy gentleman of the old school. It was easy to ignore the rumors of a vicious hidden personality and now, in humility and friendship, he spoke to Monte on Frank's behalf.

It was a pleasant exchange at first and after they'd caught up on old friends and his girlfriend left for the powder room, Johnny casually mentioned that Monte was about to be subpoenaed by the Kefauver committee. Monte sat stunned for a minute. A suicidal impulse to punch Johnny in the face forced him to keep his arms firmly planted on the table.

Johnny reassured Monte that, "Frank really feels terrible about all this but, this Kefauver, he isn't going to be a problem."

The hook was set and there was nothing Monte could do now except wait. Johnny and Frank would take care of the lawyer and anything else he needed. Monte understood, of course, that like him, Kefauver was somehow compromised, but the fiction of Monte's independence from the mob was over. Monte summoned all his power to restrain his natural reaction and excused himself.

"Enjoy the show, John," Monte told the man, then retreated to the bar for a double Dewar's before he did or said something he'd regret.

Sol, sitting at a back table with Sharon and a few friends, saw the end of the exchange. He was about to go to Monte when Rosselli came over to say hello, and maybe reassure him that his partner was in good hands. He wished Sol good luck on the club, complimented Sharon on her beauty like a diplomat visiting a foreign embassy. Smooth as silk and warmly jovial, Johnny exuded the kind of class that put everyone at ease. Except Sharon. She'd heard every Italian gigolo, French playboy and American ladies' man work flawless routines for months. She could smell a wolf. When Johnny returned to his table, she looked calmly at Sol without saying a word but the message was loud and clear. Sol joined Monte at the bar to get the real story. They stayed there, huddled together, the rest of the night.

But Johnny wasn't just blowing smoke about Kefauver. While the senator was just beginning to sharpen his meat-axe, Costello and friends had already moved to blunt it. They had known for some time that Senator Estes had two convenient problems – he couldn't keep his hands off women or dice. *New York Times* columnist Russell Baker recalled one evening as the senator's campaign bus pulled into a small town in the middle of the night. The senator told one of his aides, "I gotta fuck!" Apparently, the lawmaker had a standing order to his staff for fresh conquests in every whistle-stop on his campaign trail.

It was practically effortless to set the senator up with two dancers from the *Chez Paree* nightclub in Chicago one evening and have the encounter secretly photographed by the house dick, an off-duty cop moonlighting on the *Outfit*'s payroll. Since it happened in Chicago, it was the *Outfit*'s attorney, Sidney Korshak, who presented these photos to the senator as his committee was beginning to issue its first subpoenas against Frank Costello and other *Outfit* colleagues.

Kefauver was not the only public servant on the committee with exploitable weaknesses. Each one was visited by attorney Korshak, who held their dossiers in his hands. The committee went on to interrogate over 600 witnesses including Monte, brought no indictments and found only circumstantial evidence of organized crime operating in the United States, although it did produce several sharply worded reports. These reports would be the blueprints on which emerging, ambitious lawmakers such as Joe Kennedy's younger son, Bobby, would build their careers. The committee did generate much needed publicity for Senator Kefauver's presidential ambitions and re-ignited the public interest in gangsters that encouraged a rash of popular movies and TV series like *The Untouchables*. It also reassured gangsters everywhere that *they* were in fact, the untouchables.

In the next days, Monte booked the follow up acts to Eddie Fisher - Edith Piaf, who had made the song *La Vie en Rose* famous and then Josephine Baker, the rage of Paris and the *Stork Club* and then retreated to the country to consider his situation.

It was the melon-sweet heart of summer on the farm in Bucks County. Chip and young Billy played with the new St. Bernard puppy, *Buddha,* named for his wise, old face. Grandmother Nan, now matriarch of a growing tribe of grandchildren, moved into the cabana house by the pool to stay close to Jane, who now cradled her third son, three-month old Michael Lee Proser in her arms. They had hoped for a girl to offset their two boys and were going to call her Lena, after Monte's mother. Michael got the male version of his grandmother's name. Mike had arrived a few weeks prematurely. He contracted pneumonia in the hospital and was now recovering slowly with the help of antibiotics and round the clock care from Carrie, Nan and Jane.

Jane was on the upswing again, finding support in her friendship with Sharon and the unwavering devotion of Monte. She had returned from Europe refreshed, grateful to be home. She and Sharon had spent the last of their youth together forming a bond that was to last their entire lives, and beyond. They'd made the adjustment from young, working women to married mothers. Jane came home strong and even happy. She had even taken the burden of her third pregnancy with Michael in stride, never complaining.

To Monte, it was as if nothing had ever happened. He was too in love with his reinvigorated wife, his new son and his *La Vie en Rose*. Life was truly in the pink. After a weekend visit from Sol assured him that Kefauver was in fact a toothless lion, and that that they were going to be left alone to run the club without partners, Monte's relief was overwhelming. He felt like a man saved at the point of drowning. Every farmer, tradesman and housewife he met on his errands into the countryside was engulfed in his renewed optimism. He was his old hobo self, without a care and in love with the world and everyone in it. His ultimate relaxation was to fill the smooth riding Packard with family and go for long, slow drives down the flank of Jericho Mountain, onto the dirt and gravel Eagle Road and then over the mostly unpaved country roads where, for a few golden moments, control over his life was absolute and the world was peaceful. Cruising among the cornfields of head-high stalks with the convertible top down and seats filled with his chattering family, he had his peak moments that let him know he had finally found his reward.

For those few weeks, Jim Morgan stood watch over the whole shebang. He sat in the shade of soaring ash trees overhanging the patio next to the pool and calmly polished his rimless eyeglasses with his busted up saloonkeeper's hands. He'd brought an old ball bat and spent hours hitting small rocks out of the driveway into the mowed hayfield below the lawn of the main house. He wrestled 50-pound burlap sacks of sweet corn in and out of the trunk of his car for the family midsummer dinners of only two main courses - corn and blood red tomatoes. He was happy in the noisy main house full of small children and women. He was happier still to retire in the cool evenings to the poolside cabana house - the cabin in the woods that happened to have a full bar in the main room – a saloonkeeper's paradise. Late nights, over bottles of beer, he and Monte often talked quietly about "whatever happened to…" this bootlegger or that boss who used to run booze up and down the length of the Hudson. Now the two old scofflaws just laughed and shook their heads, remembering the mayhem of the old days, and the day the government finally wised up and took their cut of the stuff in taxes. Gambling was next. Bookies would be going the way of bootleggers as soon as the government muscled in.

The week before, Monte had done some muscling of his own. He telephoned Dr. Max Jacobson with the message that if he ever saw him again, he'd break his goddamn neck. After nearly two years of occasional treatments, the panic and distractions stopped long enough for Monte to realize the harm the doctor had done with his hare-brained potions. He knew the damage, particularly to Jane, was incalculable, and the price they had paid and would pay for trusting the doctor was high. He was deeply troubled about the future costs because he knew that his plucky, little Irish rose, Jane, as strong and valiant a fighter as she was, was not quite the same. But he also knew that he and Jane would survive. It was small comfort because so many of his closest friends were still under the doctor's spell. Unfortunately for everyone else, all he could do was warn them.

Milton Blackstone was still one of the doctor's willing victims. So was Eddie Fisher. Also Joe Kennedy's boy, young congressman Jack Kennedy, composer Alan Jay Learner, actor Dick Shawn and dozens of others in the nexus of show business and politics. Eventually Marilyn Monroe, Montgomery Clift and others felt the sting of the doctor's needle. Some, like Milton and Eddie, were invigorated, some were almost instantly raving, paranoid schizophrenics and some, like Jane, simply retreated under a black cloud with a permanent case of the blue flu. Monte couldn't convince Milton or Eddie of the danger they faced. They didn't believe him.

In years to come, at an engagement at Harrah's Lake Tahoe, Eddie Fisher stormed onto stage during Buddy Hackett's opening performance, stood just off mike and accused Buddy, in front of a full audience, of coming into his dressing room and using his hairbrush. Never at a loss for words, Hackett asked, "Eddie, can we talk about this later?" as he indicated the full house. Fisher stomped off in a fouler rage.

Milton and Eddie were on a death spiral toward madness together. Over the next years, there would be no diversion, only delay, until they both crashed at rock bottom. In the meantime, they zoomed toward their destiny at full throttle, full of amplified hope for the future as Eddie's career began to take off.

CHAPTER 33

Jules Podell's Copacabana

The old awning came down and a new one proclaiming *"Jules Podell's Copacabana"* went up at 10 East 60th Street. The change to new management was seamless. Talent and cash continued to flow through the place like Niagara Falls. The Chinese food was as good as ever and customer's wallets continued to be gutted like fresh fish. It was harvest time for the rackets and Grand Central for wiseguys from around the world.

The pressure on Podell to succeed as the sole operator of the club increased his fanatic attention to detail. Nothing missed his gaze and no one was safe from physical attack if he was angered. Waiters and busboys were routinely smacked in the face and pushed against a wall for nose-to-nose instruction about un-shined shoes and wilted parsley. The occasional explosions of violence coming from Podell's kitchen became more frequent.

Johnnie Ray, a 25 year old, white singer was suddenly the hottest act in the US. Naturally, as the latest and hottest act, he was immediately booked into the Copa. His recording of *Cry* on Columbia Records was the number one seller for 11 straight weeks. Coming from virtual obscurity singing in the *Flame Showbar*, in Detroit, Ray adopted the emotional delivery and voice quality of black performers who made up most of the *Flame's* entertainment, often falling to his knees and crying as part of his performance.

His contract, through the *William Morris Agency*, set the new benchmark for nightclub acts at $15,000 a week. The Copa was forced to collect a cover charge of $3 and enforce a minimum charge of $5 to help cover the talent expense. Making the $15,000 weekly payments "…to some little pisher." pushed Podell relentlessly toward rage. Ray's act itself pushed him the rest of the way. He just couldn't stand the sight of Ray flopping to his knees and weeping. Women wailed, soaking their handkerchiefs through with tears. Even men puddled up at Ray's show. To Podell, it was disgusting.

A week or so into the engagement, Ray walked into the kitchen before a rehearsal of some new material. Apparently, it had been a long, bad day for Jules Podell. They nearly collided in the kitchen as Podell barreled through the swinging door. Suddenly, the thought of three more weeks of Johnnie Ray and his blubbering freak show pushed the new manager over the edge.

Podell blurted, "What is it with you and the crying?" Ray, one of the gentlest and politest of men, wasn't sure how to respond. It didn't matter, Podell was so completely disgusted by him that he carried the argument all by himself.

At one point Ray made the mistake of defending himself saying, "but Mr. Podell, …It's the hottest thing." - meaning it was making him a fortune. Podell shot back, "Well maybe you need to cool off." He grabbed the singer by the throat and arm and marched him into the Copa's walk-in freezer, slamming the door closed behind him, locking it from the outside.

"Don't let him the fuck out," he warned the staff as he walked out of the kitchen to the bar. At the bar, he got his nightly highball glass of brandy a bit early that afternoon and retired to a back table to relax. No one came near him for over an hour.

Several hours passed. The banging on the freezer door had stopped long ago. Podell came back around 6 PM and let the shivering, coughing singer out without comment. Johnnie went home and immediately developed a fever with his cough, his evening appearance was cancelled. Ventriloquist Jimmy Nelson and comedy duo Betty and Jane Kean continued on without the main attraction. Soon Ray developed double pneumonia and was forced to cancel the rest of his engagement.

In spite of Podell's continued violence toward staff and performers, the Copa became *the* place for new talent and recording stars. Old timers like Durante and Joe E. appeared less frequently. The tradition of Joe E. opening each new season was over, although he and Durante continued to play the club. The Copa wasn't their home any more. Frank's friends at *William Morris* called the tune as far as who was going to appear, and it was whoever had a new record or movie to promote. Nightclub performers were now second choices unless they were making records. So they began recording albums live at the Copa. Dozens of live albums were recorded and helped to fortify the club at its position on top of the entertainment heap. The other big clubs *El Morocco*, the *Latin Quarter*, *Eden Roc* were jammed as well, but the big talent through the top agencies was locked in at the Copa.

On November 24, 1950, the new musical by Frank Loesser opened and became the runaway hit of the season. Broadway finally had its own musical, a tribute to the type of Damon Runyon characters who had made *The Main Stem* an international icon. *Guys and Dolls* parodied the horse-touting, hard-drinking, wisecracking night clubbers and gangsters of Broadway lore. The songs were funny, fresh and very singable. The street had clearly made good, and now would never be forgotten. *Guys and Dolls* was the peak expression of Broadway in its own dialect and musical art form. As Café Society celebrated itself at its apex, and the whole world applauded its quirky exuberance, it simultaneously passed into living history. *Guys and Dolls* was the newly minted archive of the images and sounds of an era about to be eclipsed.

Post war America stalled at the pinnacle of the nightclub age without the momentum to move on. People were safe and satisfied that the terrors of recent history were far behind them and for the moment, that was more than enough. Peace reigned and things, everyday things, were back to normal. Young families slept peacefully. Hospital delivery rooms and elementary schools swelled with the raucous next generation of Americans as the baby boom began booming with a new music, again coming out of the south, and a new way to hear it. Scatman Crothers cut the first record that named the new music. He recorded "I Want to Rock And Roll" with Wild Bill Moore on saxophone. It was distributed on the new 45 RPM vinyl records and the age of rock and roll began while the great nightclubs were packed to the rafters every night.

All people saw of Frank Costello on television was his hands – manicured perfectly and sporting a star sapphire pinky ring. Attorney George Wolf won the concession that his client's face wouldn't be shown. The TV audience only saw Frank's fingers rub the pinky ring as he was questioned. Late in the first long day of the hearing, after Frank's ownership in "…a certain well known nightclub" was confirmed but nothing illegal was attributed to the cordial Prime Minister, the frustrated and compromised Senator Kefauver asked, "Have you ever done one, single thing, Mr. Costello, to help your country?"

Frank thought for a second and replied, "I pay my taxes." That got a laugh from just about everyone except the chagrined Senator. As he had during Prohibition, the Prime Minister outfoxed the government. But it was a hollow victory. Although no one on TV saw Frank's face, he was on the cover of every newspaper in the country. He was now as famous and recognizable as John Wayne.

He returned to a very nervous group of colleagues. No one would meet with him in public but there was simply too much to do, too many urgent decisions that needed to be made to give the public spotlight time to cool off. Business was booming at the racetracks in Florida and the nightclubs of Hollywood. A new world was opening up in friendly Havana, and in the wild desert of Nevada, Las Vegas was blooming. Frank bore the public scrutiny that followed him with grim humor and continued to build his empire with quiet efficiency.

As the newer, less established clubs began to sputter under spiraling talent costs, Monte was forced toward the leaner, more precarious operation of *La Vie en Rose* – a trend that would become common as the economics of nightclub entertainment changed. Without the Copa's gushing cash flow, he had to cut back as well on personal expenses. He moved from the lofty *Hampshire House* to the quiet, plush comfort of the *Algonquin Hotel* on east 44th Street where Gleason stayed, now that the comedian was flush with his TV cash. Monte moved into a two-room suite down the hall from his pal on the third floor. A suite at the *Algonquin* was living well indeed, but considering the oceans of cash Monte enjoyed in the Copa years, it was relatively small potatoes. His erratic financial picture indicated not only the changing landscape of nightclub operation but his growing gambling addiction, stronger than anything Dr. Feelgood could put into a needle, which threatened to consume him.

It was sometime in November, one night toward the end of the week, that the two shared a cab to the hotel in the wee hours. They had been drinking at Toots Shor's place after closing *La Vie* for the night and Gleason was still wound up on the ride downtown. He was off for the rest of the week and the upcoming weekend and wanted to keep the party going. A fat roll of hundred dollar bills was chafing him through his hip pocket.

In the hotel, Monte retired to his room, washing his face and getting ready for bed. A knock on his door forced him to put on a bathrobe. He then found Gleason standing in the doorway, also in his bathrobe.

"Yeah, Jack?", Monte made it clear he was in for the evening and needed to rest.

The comedian as usual paid no attention "C'mon, we're going."

"What? Jackie…"

"C'mon, let's go."

"Jack, I'm in bed."

"Not yet you ain't."

Monte motioned to his bathrobe. Gleason ignored that too, "Don't worry about it." He brandished his bankroll, "You're faded," meaning his bet was covered.

"Jackie, c'mon…", Gleason roared and grabbed him by the shoulder dragging him out of the room. Monte was laughing too as they weaved down the hall toward another adventure, this time in matching snowy white bathrobes and slippers.

The cab deposited them at LaGuardia airport in the nick of time for an early morning flight. It wasn't until they were taking off that Monte bothered to ask where they were headed. He was hoping it was someplace warm enough to be comfortable in a bathrobe. They were headed to Havana, Gleason thought. At least that was what he had asked for at the ticket counter.

En route, the first class cabin attendants served them scotch and orange juice for breakfast as they cruised to a weekend on the tropical island. Gleason spent much of the flight trying to convince their stewardesses to be their guests for the weekend. It didn't work.

On the island, they checked into the presidential suite of Meyer's *Hotel Nacional* and had tailors come to the room to fit them for new clothes. Jackie paid cash, generously, for everything. Monte managed a few moments rest before he was practically carried to the jai alai courts and had a roll of cash stuffed into his pocket. Where exactly Gleason managed to pick up the four or five beautiful female escorts, Monte couldn't say. From jai alai, they went to the horse track, then on to lunch at the hotel, where they finally fell asleep by the pool. The bankroll in Monte's pocket was gone, replaced by losing ticket stubs from several gambling venues.

The cycle started again that night with Gleason leading the charge from nightclub to private party, to a moonlit cruise on the Minister of Finance's yacht. Gleason was full throttle by 2 AM, dancing the meringue in a fashion previously unknown and with complete abandon. Women were swept into his centrifugal force and the belief of heavy men in their own lightness propelled him back and forth across the beam of the ship. Monte could only hope to keep *The Great One* from seriously injuring himself but was in no real shape to prevent Jackie from doing anything. The man was a bleating, mad drunk, totally unhinged and convinced that no laws, including gravity, applied to him. They ricocheted around Havana like this for another day and a half on a bender that might have killed inexperienced men, losing somewhere around $100,000 in the process.

Finally, on Sunday afternoon, Monte found his partner unconscious, face down on the balcony of their suite, a woman's scarf shielding his head and face from the harsh sunlight. He managed to revive him and saw the full toll of the lost weekend in the greenish tint of Gleason's skin. The realization that they were both expected at work the next day - on Monday afternoon - drew the last reserves of energy from them, getting them to the airport with the assistance of several hotel employees called in especially for the task. They were both paralyzed with hangovers so fierce that it hurt to smile.

In New York, Monte took the initiative to direct the cab to Bellevue Hospital where he checked them both in and ordered a regime of oxygen therapy and blood transfusions with the help of his trusted physician, Dr. Hitzig. He'd read that it was the latest treatment for a severe hangover and was ready to try anything. They had only hours left before they were both due at work. With the help of a few stargazing nurse volunteers, Monte arranged for his barber and manicurist to tend to them in bed. Corned beef and coffees were brought in from the Stage Deli. Bullets Durgom, Jackie's long-suffering manager, delivered their clothes from the Algonquin and included with the delivery a harangue that nearly ended their relationship. As the two adventurers were barbered and buffed, while being transfused, they caught up on their business reading, peering over their oxygen masks at *Daily Variety* and the *Herald Tribune*. In the early afternoon, they slept.

By 5PM, they were rested, shaved and rejuvenated. Gleason glided into the Dumont Studios as if he'd been napping all weekend and delivered one of his funniest shows ever. He felt strong, nearly indestructible. Monte settled in at *La Vie* around 6 PM and made sure fresh flowers were in Dorothy Dandridge's dressing room. All traces of the weekend were gone from his body. He was pain-free and calm as a tropical breeze.

When Dorothy Dandridge slunk out onto *La Vie's* stage, it was like an electric current went through the heart and groin of every man in sight. Her shape, the texture and deep tint of her skin, her gracefulness, the emotions quivering in her eyes and lips, the fact that she could deliver a song from her soul, made audiences hold their breath with excitement. Starting January 21, 1952, Dorothy Dandridge electrified the club for 20 weeks straight. She was the most beautiful blend of black skin on white features that anyone had ever seen and she was the sensation of the season.

After years of watching people crowd the sidewalk to get into the club, the landlord of 123 West 54th, figured he could run a joint at the spot as well as anyone. When it came time, in 1954, to renew the lease for *La Vie en Rose*, he refused Monte and took the space for himself opening up *Gilmore's Steakhouse*. Sol Meadow was powerless to help, the snatch was perfectly legal. Monte was quietly enraged.

The last day of *La Vie en Rose* found Monte motionless in chair in the middle of the showroom as tables and pink, upholstered chairs were covered and carried out around him. The most perfect of all his clubs had been wiped out by the whim of a landlord, leaving him to sit quietly alone and wonder what all his talent, experience and fame was actually good for. He controlled nothing, he owned nothing. He lit a cigar languidly and gazed at the bare stage as if Edith Piaf were there, singing just for him. He didn't hear the moving men straining against great loads of furniture piled high on dollies all around him. The rich, sharp fragrance of his cigar kept the stink of the sweating men away while the rising rivulets of unhurried smoke were unceremoniously shredded by passing furniture.

A passing workman knocked a case of champagne glasses off the bar accidentally. The sound of muted, smashing glass didn't startle Monte from his dark musing. It seemed appropriate to his thoughts. When the men had finished and silence returned, he rose slowly and joined Sol at the barren bar at the back of the room. Without a word, he clapped his old friend on the back and then dropped the keys to the place on top of the bar. The two old pals walked out together.

Sol had found a place just down the street where the furniture was now being loaded into. It was smaller and so lacked the elegant proportions of *La Vie en Rose* but would hopefully be good enough to attract much of the old clientele. They were open the following week under the appropriately diminished name, *La Vie*.

But people who went to nightclubs were getting harder to find. They now had a choice of movies that cost only two dollars and exploded from the screen in full stereophonic sound and brilliant color, or television for free. Nightclubs, even the top ones, couldn't match the payout offered by television to headliners like Gleason, Jack Benny and Milton Berle. Along with the traditional competition of Broadway, radio and movies; television now took the largest bite out of nightlife. Married couples could be entertained by top stars at home and still get the kids to bed on time. The option to stay home made more sense, more often. Even the flow of booze, the foundation of the saloon business, was slackening as family patrons declined the second and third drink in favor of driving safely and getting kids off to school in the morning.

Pointedly, Monte's trademark of beautiful chorus girls such as the now famous Copa *Girls*, was under direct attack. Television paid chorus dancers $112.50 for a half hour show. The top clubs paid only $100 per week for eighteen shows. Monte felt the ground moving under his feet.

Only the big clubs, *Toots Shor's*, the Copa, the *Stork Club* continued to rake it in, gathering overflow crowds nightly. At the *Stork*, Billingsley began promoting heavily to colleges to entice marriageable young women into his place. He occasionally gave away a $25,000 silver and diamond bracelet as a door prize when a beautiful coed walked in his front door – and made sure it got into the columns. This strategy worked well and his place stayed packed with young ladies and their many followers.

Toots' place took the other end of the market. He ran an old-fashioned saloon, a watering hole for men - sports figures, reporters and businessmen. At Toots', the bartender's pour was generous, the food was mediocre, the meat was rare and so were women. He provided relief to the legions of men, now stripped of the noble purpose of defending the nation and reduced to petty office battles and domestic drudgery. They fled to Toots' smoky, cloistered barroom where hard liquor was still the universal social solvent, tranquilizer and truth serum.

In the middle was the Copa, the flagship of the fleet, still drawing sell-out crowds with the biggest names in recording like singers Billy Eckstine, Billy Daniels and Perry Como. Top comedians were moving to television and were priced out of the nightclub range. Soon the singers like Como, Nat King Cole and even the old timer Jimmy Durante would follow.

The first major club to fail was the venerable *Diamond Horseshoe*, Billy Rose's opulent show palace. For years, the *Horseshoe* had maintained the dazzling musical format that included elegant costumes and a large cast. Now that the economics of nightclubs included headliners pulling down tens of thousands a week, the *Horseshoe* faded in the field and was shut out of the money. Billy Rose, the impresario of Broadway since the 1920's, had his first large-scale failure. The *Diamond Horseshoe* was the dead canary in the coalmine.

La Vie en Rose had made a good showing and closed after a decent run, so Monte's reputation and ability were still intact, but the hastily put up *La Vie*, his new place down the street was struggling. There was something wrong beyond the club itself and he knew it. It was something impossible to pinpoint, like the faintest scent of a new perfume floating in a crowded showroom. No other major, new nightclub opened in New York during *La Vie's* season and a half. He had enough money in the bank to buy some time. Again, he retreated to the farm to sort out his next move.

Their first winter at the farm turned into a happy, unhurried time. Monte honed his skills as a country squire, letting New York nightlife fade to a memory. He gathered winter provisions, making sure the cellar was fully stocked with essential staples like white asparagus, lichee nuts, smoked oysters, sardines in olive oil, anchovies, capers, white cocktail onions, maraschino cocktail cherries, kosher dill pickles and pickled mushrooms. He had Benny, the handyman, busy at work on a dozen projects simultaneously, many of them having to do with preventing mice and the copperhead snakes that followed them, from moving into the cellar for the winter. The old farmhouse was in need of immediate and constant attention to contain his growing family. But Monte was busy building his nearly forgotten dream of a family life and was happy every moment of it.

Winter storms exploded in the skies over Bucks County, showering down white snow for weeks at a time. The countryside was suddenly brilliant white, soft and silent. Monte hauled the toboggan to the top of the hill by the drifted over greenhouse and the boys rode it down to the lower field. Jane even took a ride. It went on for hours, Monte happily grunting like a draft horse as he hauled the sled uphill, the boys screaming back down in seconds.

As the spring of 1953 bloomed into summer, this writer was born ten miles from the farm in a 25-bed country hospital in Doylestown, Pennsylvania. For the first time, Jane was with her husband when her child arrived. The delivery on the morning of June 15th was uncomplicated and this fourth boy arrived in good health. But the event was somewhat disappointing. After their second son Billy, they hoped for a girl. The third son, Mike, was strike one on that score. As the day approached for the fourth delivery, Jane asked every Jew and Gentile in her extended family to light candles and pray for a girl. The prayers worked slightly. James Andrew was the only son to arrive with his mother's blond hair and green eyes but once again, with his father's equipment. Strike two. Now there were Chip, Billy, Mike and new baby Jimmy, Carrie, Jane and Monte all crammed into the two bedroom farmhouse as summer went to seed and dropped into autumn. Weeks went by, the phone calls to and from New York were steady but unproductive. As the scent of another winter snow descended, *Café Theatre*, his grand experiment, closed its doors. The shows with Joe Kipness flopped or stalled in previews. His movie projects disintegrated into endless, pointless meetings and phone calls. It was the first time in 25 years that he wasn't part of some club or show on Broadway.

Milton Blackstone called with a lifeline. The fiery Italian operatic tenor and leading man, Mario Lanza, had gotten himself fired from his MGM movie contract and subsequently the bi-weekly 15 minute *Coke Time* TV program broadcasting out of New York. Coca Cola wanted Eddie Fisher, currently one of the hottest recording stars with his back to back million-sellers, *Any Time* and *Tell Me Why*. Milton got Monte on the show as Production Advisor, essentially a co-producer with Sonny Werblin, the producer assigned from the dominant agency of the new medium, Music Corporation of America, MCA. MCA was to television and movies what William Morris was to recording and nightclubs – nothing moved without them. To MCA, Monte was practically an unknown.

Coke Time zoomed to popularity along with Eddie's recording career culminating in 1954 with *Oh, My Papa* that sold 890,000 copies in the first month. Eddie signed the paper jacket on the first copy of the record to Jane, writing, "Janey, remember, he's my Papa too. Eddie." Eddie performed the song on every *Coke Time* that month – eight times. One of Monte's contributions to the show was that each number needed a set change. Since the small TV studio had no room to move backdrops in and out, he began to experiment with projecting images onto screens from behind. Other than that, it was time in purgatory, creatively. Since all of the talent came through MCA, he had little say in that. Monte also insisted that each show end with a close up of Eddie singing. The rear-projection technique and the close-up were the extent of his creative exercise.

Further dimming his creative light, the teenage girls who screamed and swooned in the audience ruined the sound quality, so the audience was eliminated. Monte soon found himself with virtually no creative outlet and little to do, locked in the daytime production routine of a lifeless sound stage – far from his friends and the intimate cabaret nightlife he loved.

CHAPTER 34

A Change of Seasons

The heavy autumn rains of 1954 washed through the gutters of Manhattan taking the era of the big nightclubs with them into oblivion. The two pioneers and leading lights of the form, Billy Rose and Monte Proser, were sidelined and would not be back. The Copa still dominated all survivors but the days of *Samba Sirens* in $4,000 costumes of mink panties and hats was over. The ebbing tide was invisible to all but a few veterans of Broadway. To night clubbers and the performers who entertained them, the Copa still delivered on the promise of spectacular entertainment and a thrilling social mix, like Sinatra said that year, "You're a show business nobody until you make the Copa and do three shows nightly under its tremendous pastel roof."

Monte watched the muddy torrent of the Delaware River rising rapidly under the gray, winter rain. He was nearly fifty. His father, Charles, had died a few months earlier, alone, in his Taft Hotel room just after he and Monte had made what seemed like a lasting peace. The Old Man had been upset, like everyone, about the loss of the Copa but had made the adjustment to *La Vie en Rose* for his nightly port and political conversation. In a way, it was a blessing the Old Man hadn't lived to see the shuttering of *La Vie en Rose*. In his eyes, Monte had truly made something of himself. He was very nearly the son he wanted, almost the lawyer he hoped for.

In his adopted village of New Hope, Monte stood on the west bank of the Delaware River in the whispering rain just south of Coryell Street, looking out over the river. 30 years of late nights, rich food and scotch whiskey bulged under his belt, weighing him down in the river mud. His fingers, still perfectly manicured, nails shining like mirrors, ached in the chill rain from the reminders of a dozen barroom scuffles etched across the knucklebones. New York City was 90 miles away, its raucous nightlife a fading echo. He watched the rushing river carry ancient trees torn out by the roots, furniture, shattered lumber. Scraps of prosperous lives and business ambitions swept past him into the growling rapids, crushing and swallowing scenery of the past. He surveyed the riverbank as the site for his new brainstorm, a first class nightspot for weekenders from New York and Philadelphia.

20 yards south of the site, the *Bucks County Playhouse* sat in a foot of water, its long-unused millwheel turning rapidly in the flow from Pidcock Creek that bisected the village of New Hope and fed into the river. Painted hatch marks on the interior walls proudly recorded the flood levels of certain exceptionally wet years when the audience seating hosted eels and large- mouth bass. As one of the great summer stock theatres in the country, the *Playhouse* had also withstood years of floods and droughts in show business.

Having *La Vie en Rose*, the favorite of all his saloons, at the height of its popularity with its own special untouchable status from Frank Costello, snatched from him by a landlord, had turned his thinking. Even the worst gangsters only took a piece of the action, not the whole place. After Sol failed to find any legal way to prevent the pinch, Monte contemplated making a phone call to Frank to fix the problem. He ranted against the landlord, "…the son of a bitch", he said, but never could pick up the phone. He put his hand on the receiver once, stared at it, but couldn't lift it and Sol did not insist. Instead, the partners quietly took the loss of hundreds of thousands or millions of future dollars.

Standing on the muddy riverbank next to the Playhouse, he envisioned his *Playhouse Inn* with a few of his trademark elements – intimate entertainment, great oriental food, a lively bar and this time the new twist - rooms by the night. Every room would have a picture window looking out over the river. He envisioned an art gallery on the premises to house the thriving school of impressionist painters who worked in the area. He saw a swimming pool and dining patio on the river's edge. The place would be a relaxing, country vacation for harried New Yorkers and an after-theatre spot for patrons of the *Playhouse*. It wouldn't break new ground, light up marquees or flood the columns with publicity ink but it might provide, finally, the steady income that Jane and their herd of 4 ravenous, energetic boys needed. And this time, he would own the real estate that housed his creation.

Jane particularly, needed some reassurance. The loss of the Copa had been greeted with quiet resolve. She knew Monte was bigger than the club and would recover. She saw how his commitment to his family had focused him, even more, on succeeding. He still had the energy of a young man but the vast experience of an older one. She believed in him, in his talent and his inner strength. Her confidence was rewarded by his quick recovery in establishing *Café Theatre* and *La Vie en Rose*. But now, with the destruction of those two places in fairly quick succession and then the slow dissipation of even the modest *La Vie*, she sensed they were entering a new era of unknown qualities. And Monte was a terrible actor when it came to appearing confident.

She had relapsed into the nervous agitation first caused by Dr. Feelgood's amphetamine injections. Over the winter, her appetite had dwindled as her weight dropped to just over 100 pounds. Outwardly she made no complaints, but the steely silence and reticence returned, shutting her off from even from the simple joys of family life. Monte returned to Bucks County after trips into New York to push *Hot Rocks*, a new musical written by his long-time pal and jazz composer Henry Nemo and to California where he was developing another show, *Good News* featuring the music of another old running buddy, Lew Brown. The telltale hesitation in Jane's voice, her slight slurring, warned him that the light of his life was dimming again and his sons were at risk.

"Hellllllooo" the word snaked slowly, softly out of the telephone receiver like a viper but rang in Monte's ears like a firehouse bell. Jane wavered on the other end of the phone half conscious, in the eighth year of a sleeping spell that came and went like the rain.

"Janey…" the rest of what he had to say suddenly dropped away. It was hopeless and he lost heart.

"Monte…" She knew she was drowning again, sinking deeper, and only he could save her.

"I'm coming in tomorrow. Can you drive?"

"Yeesss. I'm fine."

"I'll call tomorrow from New York. You can't drive if you're like this…"

"I can drive." She insisted. She just needed the strength to focus on the next 24 hours.

"The boys okay?" He couldn't disguise his concern. "They get off to school okay?"

"Everybody's fine," she shot back. She'd made soup, done the shopping, done laundry, managed somehow to keep things going. "It's no picnic up here," she let him know. "I can't do it like this… Money, no money. You're here, then you're not here." She heard how desperate and weak she sounded and regretted it.

"I know Janey," he admitted. He was neglectful, still with his head in the clouds, nearly irresponsible, and he knew it. He hadn't changed. Broadway guys like him made terrible family men.

Jane still smarted from his subtle accusation about the boys getting to school but still needed to hear strength in his voice. She needed to know he wasn't quitting on her. Sensing they were on the edge of collapse, she softened, "So, how'd it go?"

"Who knows," he stopped himself from sounding worried, it only made things worse, "It looks pretty good. Wild, you know, rock and roll." He was hoping *Hot Rocks* was his ticket to the new music taking over the scene, but didn't really have much hope for it.

She heard the doubt in his voice. "What time?" she asked.

"I'll call you from the station. Okay?"

"I'll be there."

They each clung to the phone, silently, neither one wanting to say goodbye. There was no illusion anymore of a restful, family life together in the country. At best, they were in for a long struggle against Monte's shifting tides of fortune. The only question left was could they still count on each other.

Jane cut to the heart of the matter as usual, "I love you, Monte. I do," and started to cry.

"I love you too, Janey," he said.

Jane hung up the phone and fell back onto her pillow, steeling herself against her fear and heartache and summoning all her strength. She'd be ready tomorrow.

It was late November, as Jane drove the family's massive Packard along an icy River Road, headed to the Trenton, New Jersey train station. She handled the heavy car deftly, negotiating the patchwork of ice, snow and asphalt with practiced skill. She had gotten up early that morning, cleaned the house and shopped for T-bone steaks for the special family dinner welcoming Monte home. The drug fog had mostly cleared from her mind and she outwardly seemed as normal as anyone else. Only a slight tremor in her hands was evidence of her permanently frayed nerves.

Country life had proven her to be capable and resourceful in spite of her barbiturate handicap. She could drive any truck, tractor or car in any weather, she learned how to battle the various plants and animals that routinely infested and attempted to overrun her country home and she controlled the endless line of tradesmen who restored and maintained the property like a seasoned farm wife. Even as madness shadowed her, she soldiered on, raising her 4 rambunctious sons with irregular assistance from Monte. His search for the next hit kept him on the road. Carrie was her only companion on the isolated 17 acres as the silent, gray days and long winter nights tormented her.

The Packard slid along the black ice coating the road, first the front, then the rear wheels threatening to break free of the road surface as Jane negotiated the treacherous drive south. On her left the frozen Easton-Bristol canal curved along the natural course of the Delaware River between the river and the two-lane roadway. Children skated on the canal, pulling infants behind them on sleds. The canal had been cut and dredged 12 feet deep to allow barges loaded with wood and stone to travel north from Bristol to Easton and then return south, loaded with coal. In spite of the frozen scene outside, she wore only a light sweater as she drove. The $10,000 full-length mink coat Monte had given her on the opening night of *La Vie en Rose* laid across the backseat. The coat was heavy and bulky, adding more work to clutching, gear shifting and steering. She always slipped into the spectacular coat while waiting for Monte at the train station.

As she headed into the long, half-moon turn beyond McKissick's corner, the car shot in a straight line along its path of momentum suddenly unattached to the road surface. As the car left the road, a patch of clear asphalt grabbed the left front tire, snapping the steering wheel sharply clockwise and lifting the two-ton missile into a roll toward the driver's side. Hitting the snow bank that separated the roadway from the canal, the car pitched upward, elevating and becoming completely airborne as the roll accelerated. It threaded two stout poplars and described a shallow arc as the heavy engine brought the front end of the car back to earth, or in this case, to ice. The upside down car met the ice covered canal with its headlights. It shattered the ice and dove instantly to half its length in the black water, hesitated for a moment, then quickly sank the rest of the 12 feet to the bottom.

Children scattered screaming, scrambling out of the canal to the road and houses nearby. A farmer in his pickup truck stopped to see what the problem was. The neighbors came running. No one dared step out onto the shattered ice. The farmer yelled for rope as he stared at the rim of the black hole helplessly. Another car stopped on the road as a small crowd formed around the farmer, cleaving to him as the one person who might have a plan. After a few moments, faintly, a siren came to life, miles away. It faded and surged, fading almost to silence as it wound its way toward the scene. The crowd stared at the black, oily water bubbling in the ice hole. The bubbles stopped. Then Jane shot to the surface, clearing the water with a gasp. She treaded water as she caught her breath. A rope shot out toward her but wasn't long enough to reach the hole and lay uselessly 6 feet away from the rim. Jane swam to the rim of the hole and climbed out. She laid on her stomach for a moment but the chill of the ice quickly penetrated her wet clothes. She crawled across the shifting ice to the rope and grabbed the end, winding it around her wrist and palm. They pulled her to the edge of the canal.

Blankets and coats piled in on her as her soaked sweater and wool pants were stripped away. Hands rubbed her back, arms and legs as questions poured in. A child's thermos of hot chocolate was handed to her. The siren bore down from the distance and eventually a fire truck arrived.

In the fire truck, Jane explained through chattering, blue lips that her husband was waiting for her in Trenton. The fire chief got on his radio and called the station house with the news. As the fire chief was speaking, she suddenly remembered out loud, "My coat's in the car." The fire chief and a fireman nodded sympathetically.

"My mink coat," she said, and again nodding from the firemen. It was clear they had done their duty and it did not include rescuing coats.

"T'hell with this," she told them as she unwrapped her blanket. In her damp bra and underpants, her ribs stood out under a thin layer of goose flesh.

"Where're you going?!", the firemen shouted over each other as her still powerful dancer's legs pushed her out of the truck and into 6 inches of snow. She ran across the road wearing someone's bulky wool socks, slipped down the canal bank on her butt and tip-toed gingerly across the wet, shattered and shifting ice. She stood at the edge of the hole as the fire chief yelled at her - a direct order - she had better get the hell back in the truck! After taking a few deep breaths, she dove into the black water.

Jane was always waiting for him as he came up the escalator from the passenger platform. She would be sitting behind the wheel of the huge Packard parked at the curb, the collar up on her mink coat, looking almost like a child. When Monte finally crossed the sidewalk, threw his bag in the back seat and got into the car, for those first few moments, he was free. First, they clasped hands, and then the most stunningly beautiful face of all the chorus girls he'd ever seen leaned in to kiss him. Just for those few moments, as the pressure to find success again on Broadway disappeared, he was home.

She would always do the driving back to the farm and he would relax, often saying little until they cleared Trenton's city limits. Once they crossed the bridge above the city and were on the river road, he would ask about the boys – what news, what talents did they show?

But this time, his happy daydreams thinned as he waited in the cold at the curb. Jane, in spite of her condition, was never late. He finally crossed the street to the *Trentonian Hotel* to use the pay phone and businessman's bar. An hour later, Upper Makefield township sheriff and neighbor on Jericho Mountain, Charlie Lindenmayer, arrived in his pickup truck with Jane in the front seat, hair still damp, dressed in a boy's winter coat and corduroy pants. As Monte and Jane embraced on the sidewalk, Charlie lifted the dripping mink coat from the bed of his truck.

In the city cab on the way to the farm, the excitement of Jane's adventure waned and they returned to their normal catch-up conversation. At first the conversation swayed easily, but then slowly, as they cleared Trenton, and headed into the suburbs, the conversation wilted uncomfortably. She was suffering again in the same inexpressible way. She was out of excuses for herself and embarrassed to say anything. Finally, she was silently furious and sick to death of her own frailty. She wouldn't try to fake her way through it like some phony. All she could think of was to ignore it until it passed. Her struggle was apparent.

It terrified Monte. He was so sensitive to her frequency of despair that each small silence and sigh struck Monte's ear like a stone. In the silences, she faded away before his eyes. Panic set his heart thumping.

At the house, the confirmation. Carrie pulled him aside. She'd run out of ideas, Jane was eating almost nothing. It became clear Monte would have to stay close to her again until this bout of the blue flu passed, if it did. His thoughts turned only to Jane and his home life. Opening the *Playhouse Inn* became the obvious card to play to stay close.

The *Inn* might bring Jane's friends from New York and draw her out of her retreat. She would have a place to socialize with adults away from the pressure of raising four young boys in virtual isolation. It would be a family place where the boys could come up in the trade and gain the introductions that would launch them into the world, and most importantly, it would provide for everyone if something happened to him. With a new sort of inspiration and urgency, he marshaled his energy for another roll of the dice.

Monte stood with Jane looking out at the river as 9 year-old Chip and 7 year-old Billy skimmed stones on the river, and 4 year-old Mike found the best stones for them.

"It's kinda quiet around here for a place, don't you think?" Jane asked.

"We'll make money all summer. Chinese food! Nobody's got Chinese around here."

Jane tried to see Monte's vision, "Chinese" she smiled, "Why the hell not." She gripped his hand as a tremor rumbled up her spine, letting her know her time out of the shadows was almost up.

CHAPTER 35

THE COPA ROOM

In Las Vegas, Jack Entratter finally got his reward. After his demonstration of loyalty to Podell and Adonis, against Monte, for control of the Copa, and decades of hospitality as the inside man at the club, he was given his own Copa franchise. He was made the boss of the *Copa Room* at Meyer and Frank's new *Sands Hotel*. Everything would stay the same - the food, the acts, the variety show format. It didn't even matter if the place was profitable, as long as the roulette wheels kept turning just outside the showroom. Jack was set for life.

With the *Sands*, Meyer and Frank followed Benny Siegel into the promised land of profits. After a struggling start, Benny's *Flamingo Hotel* was now turning over 4 million dollars a year, not counting the customary 20 percent tax-free skim off the top. Unfortunately, Benny was not there to participate. The founding member of the Bugs and Meyer gang had been rubbed out after costing the *Syndicate* 6 million dollars in cost overruns building the place, partially attributed to the ambitious Virginia Hill doing a bit of skimming herself. Since the vivacious Virginia hadn't been successful in winning Frank Costello after helping to drive business for him at the original

Copa, she had latched onto Siegel for her big score. The party ended badly for Virginia too, reportedly a suicide in Europe.

The beginning of the end of the nightclub era drew Monte and Frank Costello into closer parallels. The chain of events started by Senator Kefauver's hearings that damaged Monte's legitimacy also damaged Frank's control. Senator Kefauver connected Monte and Costello through the Copa and *Piping Rock*. He asked Costello if he owned any part of either club. Frank denied any connection. Whether it was true or not almost didn't matter. What had always been rumor was now part of the public record.

Once again the Shuberts publicly backed away from associating with gangster elements as they had when LaGuardia cracked down, chilling Monte's Broadway prospects. Those with something to gain, like Lou Levin, the landlord of 123 West 54th where *La Vie en Rose* was housed, were emboldened to move against Monte. Even his sanctuary in the small town of New Hope was now contaminated by the news of his mob connections.

For Frank, although the compromised Kefauver dared not indict him directly, the committee pulled a thread that began to unravel Frank's world too. Former New York Mayor Bill O'Dwyer, Costello's handpicked replacement for the nettlesome LaGuardia, was revealed clearly as Frank's man. But the real trouble started when it was also revealed that during his time as Mayor, O'Dwyer accepted a bribe from Local 94, the *Uniformed Fireman's Association*. As a result, Tammany Hall, the great nexus of New York Democratic politics, O'Dwyer's power base and Frank's prime influence brokerage, began to dissolve under continuous scrutiny. The strings that tied judges and congressmen to Frank were exposed and quickly cut.

Even as his hidden power relationships vanished, he continued to gain in public recognition – a dangerous combination. The *Greater Los Angeles Press Club* invited him to be their honored guest at their annual *Eight-Ball* dinner. Previous guests included President Harry Truman, Vice-President Alben Barkley and General Mark Clark. Frank declined the invitation, but his public exposure was nonetheless complete. His friends, business associates and even his daily habits were now common knowledge and public information.

As Frank faltered, his secret, relentless enemy, Vito Genovese, saw an opportunity. Willie Moretti, Frank's cousin, a dangerously talkative man whom Frank had protected for years and had run *Syndicate* operations in northern New Jersey, was assassinated. No one stepped up to claim the hit and directly challenge Frank but the selection of Moretti was a clear message – Frank couldn't protect anyone anymore. Weeks went by as Frank investigated and assessed his strength. Finally it was clear that if he knew the killer, he wasn't saying and further, he was not going to retaliate. This was a strategy Genovese hadn't counted on and without further provocation he was stymied. Frank had outplayed Vito again. No one would support a direct move against the leader, even in his weakened state. Strategically, Frank kept the peace and his cards close to his vest but clearly the sharks were circling.

Frank's ally, Meyer, called the first Board of Directors meeting of the *Syndicate* in eight years. Eight years before, the Board decided that Meyer's life-long friend and partner, Benny Siegel, had to die. Benny was the only one not invited to that meeting. The only one not invited to this new meeting was Frank, Meyer's other life-long friend and partner. The topic was the same.

A reduced and agitated Board met at the Waldorf Astoria. Luciano had been recently deported from Cuba back to Italy under pressure from the American government – another credit to the indirect effect of Senator Kefauver's committee. Joe Adonis, deported from the US, joined him in Italy soon after. Heat was coming from all directions as local and regional lawmen saw the possibility of landing a big Mafia fish that could get them on television. Normally these two, Luciano and Adonis, would be counted among Frank's allies. As things stood, the split for and against Costello was close to even, making Meyer's job particularly delicate.

Arguing that Costello should remain at the top and that the heat on everyone would soon pass was the instigator of the crisis, Vito Genovese. Always patient, Vito thought the Feds would do his work for him by removing Frank. By taking the initiative in appearing to support Frank, it showed him to be the clear leader and successor. Appearing to support Frank also deflected suspicion from him as the source of the Moretti hit. Of course, if asked, he stood ready to take the reins from Frank if the council decided it needed a strong leader.

With Genovese on Frank's behalf were Jerry Catena, the likely triggerman of the Moretti hit, Tony (Anthony Stollo) Bender, Longie Zwillman and naturally Albert Anastasia. Anastasia was generally opposed to anything Lansky proposed and had always resented his leadership. He resented it even more since Meyer had not invited him to wet his beak in the common well of the Havana casinos.

On the other side, arguing that Frank was a very public liability, was Vincent "Jimmy Blue Eyes" Alo, Trigger Mike Coppola of Miami Beach and his New York partners, Joey Rao of the Bronx and Fat Tony Salerno, Thomas Luchese, George Scalise, and an old enemy of Lansky's, Anthony "Little Augie" Carfano. Little Augie was known to be ambitious and was also suspected of ordering Willie Moretti's killing.

Jimmy Blue Eyes pulled Meyer aside before the meeting and warned him, "You get rid of Frank and we may have a worse problem on our hands. Little Augie hates your guts." Complicating the negotiations further, "Big Albert" Anastasia, Frank's immovable ally, made it clear he intended to get a piece of the action in Havana that had been denied to him.

As the Board heard all the arguments it became clear that Meyer Lansky, who had brought discipline and corporate structure to their criminal enterprises, was the man to take the helm from Frank as they headed into the storms of public scrutiny ahead. Despite the passionate loyalty Anastasia stated in support of Frank's leadership, the Board was not moved. Enraged, Big Albert blundered into an attempt to dissolve decades of ethnic cooperation by calling for Italian solidarity. It was a mistake. Longie Zwillman, a senior board member, former beer baron and Hollywood player, sent a note to Meyer, "The bastard don't like Jews, should I change my vote?" Lansky replied, "Stick with Costello. It looks better that way."

The vote came down. Costello was out, Lansky was in. The natural question followed – should Frank be killed or allowed to step down? Little Augie saw his opening and rose to argue for Frank's murder. Costello was drawing more heat every day and like a wounded shark, he would trigger more sharks to attack him, dividing the *Syndicate* and its loyalties. As he spoke, he looked at Anastasia, making his warning clear. Jimmy Blue Eyes, in spite of voting to retire Frank, rose in defense of Frank's life. As he saw it, the man had broken no rules. As their leader, he'd simply been the unlucky target of their enemies. He had made them all money and deserved a peaceful retirement. Let him retire in honor and Blue Eyes would personally guarantee that there would be no more trouble regarding Costello. It was clear that this was Meyer's wish as well, as the new, acting head of the *Syndicate*. A show of hands spared Frank's life. Dissenting was Little Augie and two of his lieutenants. Little Augie's vote for death was duly noted and memorized by Big Albert, who still operated *Syndicate* subsidiary, *Murder Incorporated.*

Meyer took the news to Frank in person. Not surprising to Meyer, Frank expressed his relief. He never wanted the top spot and was glad to be rid of it. Within hours of their private meeting, the uncomfortable negotiations began for the break up and distribution of Frank's operations among the other members. A dangerous stall in the process looked like it might derail Meyer's new reign as boss into a wartime administration. The Prime Minister was not going to relinquish his elegant lifestyle or shrink from the prominence in society he had achieved, and those things took money. He would step down, but he would not be dismissed with only a thank you. Frank's tone let everyone know that the old lion still had teeth if he needed them and suddenly the *Syndicate* bosses found themselves locked in negotiations with a master of the game.

Meyer broke the impasse by creating another milestone in organized crime, a retirement plan. The solution was a partnership in a new venture between Frank's longtime partner in New Orleans, "Dandy" Phil Kastel, Meyer and Frank. It would be the grandest carpet joint ever conceived. Meyer, through his Miami front man Ben Jaffe, had already bought 40 acres out on Route 91, a mile closer to Los Angeles than the rest of Las Vegas. In a sentimental gesture to their years of successful partnership in Havana, they decided to call it the *Tropicana*.

Monte's retirement plan, the *Playhouse Inn*, rose on the west bank of the Delaware River as 12 foot floodwalls of flagstone, red and gray plates of rock quarried just upriver in Lumberville. Above the floodwalls, floor to ceiling windows were framed in for the dining/showroom designed to serve 250 diners. Six-foot horizontal picture windows were framed in for each of the 12 hotel rooms. The rooms were to be named after locally prominent people instead of numbered and Monte asked readers of the local *New Hope Gazette* in its front-page story to suggest names for the rooms. "Why not?" he said light-heartedly in the story, "It's a community enterprise – let's let the community do some of the work." The article identified Monte as the president and Don Walker, the head of the *Bucks County Playhouse*, as vice president of the new corporation that would own and operate the *Playhouse Inn*. In line with Monte's commitment to give the New Hope community a stake in the place, local businessmen and community leaders Ben Snyder, Ben Bodine and Harold Getz were also included on the board.

The *Inn's* semi-circular bar faced the small dance floor at the opposite end of the long rectangle dining room. A state-of-the-art copper kitchen, replicating the *Copa's* oriental steam cooking configuration, was behind the back wall of the bar, its swinging door adjacent to the bar's service area. A triple-wide flight of stairs brought people up from the ground floor parking lot to the dining and showroom above the floodwalls. On the ground floor at the entrance, the coat checkroom shared a passageway to the cavernous storage area within the floodwalls under the dining room and kitchen.

A separate glass-fronted art gallery was built just off of Main Street at the entrance to the property. It sat on the bank of the millpond for the old mill that was now the *Bucks County Playhouse*. The riverside swimming pool and patio of the

Playhouse Inn pushed construction costs over $150,000. The cost of the average home at the time was $22,000.

Frank's retirement plan, the *Tropicana*, rose from the desert floor at a cost of $15,000,000. He spent much of that construction time fighting legal battles, including his first loss in 20 years for walking out of the Kefauver hearings. He got 18 months in jail for contempt of congress for that stunt. While inside, he learned they were also going after him for $28,000 of income he hadn't reported on his taxes. Not long after he finished his jail time for contempt, he made a pilgrimage to confer with his partner of many years and co-venturer in the *Tropicana*, "Dandy" Phil Kastel, at Kastel's plantation mansion near New Orleans. Frank was picked up at the Moissant airport and driven to Kastel's place by Chicago's golden boy and ultimate fixer Sidney Korshak. Sidney represented the five *Outfit* hotels then operating in Las Vegas. In the back seat of the car sat Meyer, completing the welcoming committee and perhaps to reassure Frank of his personal safety. There was still blood in the water from the Moretti hit and sharks like Genovese and Little Augie were never far away.

Later that day, they were joined by Johnny Rosselli and Carlos Marcello. Marcello was Kastel's direct boss, the Don of New Orleans and the newest partner in the *Tropicana*. Together Kastel and Marcello operated the most opulent carpet joint in the country, the *Beverly Club*, in Jefferson parish outside of New Orleans, where many of Costello's slot machines had been producing faithfully for years. "Dandy" Phil, with his gold tipped walking stick and silk shirts had designed the *Beverly* with Old European extravagance; dazzling, massive crystal chandeliers, marble fountains, fine china and weighty silverware in the dining rooms. He provided only top entertainers like Sophie Tucker and Tony Martin to entertain their gambling guests. He would bring the same opulence to the *Tropicana*.

Rosselli would provide the *Tropicana's* casino bosses Lou Lederer and Babe Baron to oversee the gambling operations. He would also oversee staffing the barbershop, gift shop and parking concessions. Meyer provided the front men Ben Jaffe, an Indiana insurance executive who also fronted for Meyer's *Fountainbleu* in Miami and Las Vegas resident J. Kell Houssels Sr.. That left only the entertainment to organize. Frank and Johnny Rosselli agreed there was only one producer they wanted for their showroom.

As reliable as the spring floods, the summer crowds swarmed the streets of New Hope. The *Bucks County Playhouse* boasted of a full summer season of plays including shows by George S. Kaufman and Moss Hart who both had summer homes in the area. Stars in the productions included Jerome Cowan, Basil Rathbone, Julie Harris and Moss Hart himself. Prolific Broadway producers Robert Whitehead and Alexander H. Cohen provided several of the shows that season including in August, Cohen's, *The Champagne Complex*, for which the producer arranged a first class excursion from overheated New York City to breezy New Hope. He arranged air-conditioned buses to transport theatre-goers and included a champagne dinner at the *Playhouse Inn* after the show. He sold out. Once again, the charm was working. Monte had another hit.

Treasurer of the *Playhouse Inn* Corporation, Benny Snyder, had never seen so much money come in so fast. The first summer season flew by with the *Playhouse Inn* packed solid from the first day. The place was more like a noisy, New York nightclub than a country inn. People talked over each other, smoked and drank like the world was coming to an end. Men with jeweled rings and ladies in mink stoles crowded around Monte like he was a movie star. These weren't weekenders from Camden and Philadelphia, these were a different kind of people altogether. It looked like New Hope was finally on the map.

Monte was not turning out to be like any manager Benny had ever known. For one thing, once the place was launched, he was rarely there, stopping in only for opening night galas at the *Playhouse*. Benny appointed himself assistant manager to keep tabs on the operation. He'd never managed a nightspot before but he knew business. The more difficult wrinkle was that when Monte was there, he sometimes made problems.

The root of the problems was Tuinol, the newly available barbiturate prescribed to Jane for sleeping, was now prescribed to Monte as well. The residual doping of the barbiturate when combined with a few drinks, knocked Monte into a slurring stupor. Benny noted Monte's deteriorating behavior as Monte led choruses of drunks into the kitchen to show off his pride and joy, the copper fixtures and steam plumbing that gleamed like the engine room of an ocean liner.

The absentee and drinking problems were one thing, but involvement with gangsters was quite another. Benny Snyder didn't know anything about Monte's mob connections until the rumors eventually found him. Now he felt the danger. He didn't know for sure whether he'd ever met a gangster among all the fancy characters showing up in thousand dollar suits, but he knew the chances were pretty good. Who else would leave a 100-dollar tip? And what else might they eventually want for their hundred dollars? Now that the place was raking in all this cash, how long would it be before one of Monte's big city friends moved in? Maybe one was already planning a takeover?

The two other local men on the *Inn's* board of directors heard the new plan directly from Benny. Considering the dangers the community now faced from the mob and Monte's undisciplined behavior, the fact was that Monte was a liability. A change had to be made. Benny could run the place, had been running the place. They had a decision to make. As community elders and guardians, they could continue as they were and wait for gangsters to show up, or they could nip the problem now. There was such a lot of money to consider. It was rolling in, whether Monte was there or not. Did they want to risk all that money, all that easy money, going into the wrong hands?

Coke Time started to wobble when Eddie Fisher began demanding the show be moved to California. Monte, as producer of the show, had given up trying to work with Fisher, who had fully transformed from the bashful boy singer in the Copa's sunlit doorway to a moody and unpredictable star. The program finally ended after his next five records bombed and his personal life began to teeter. His on-again, off-again engagement and marriage to Debbie Reynolds exhausted the public's patience and showed him up to be indecisive and immature. Even though Milton kept the machinery of Eddie's career in high gear, privately they both began falling apart. Even when invited to perform before the Queen of England, Eddie couldn't make the trip without Dr. Max Jacobson in his permanent 15-person entourage, all with Milton's blessing and participation.

Milton continued to work with the same extraordinary energy that had built Grossinger's from a local boarding house into an international destination and launched a half-dozen Victory ships from the little town of Newburgh. He leased an entire floor of the RCA building in Manhattan and filled it with secretaries who serviced the network of 10,000 Eddie Fisher Fan Clubs that Milton had created around the country. The secretaries personally answered 3,000 fan letters a week and sent out that many personally autographed photos of Eddie. Milton was busy doubling that effort to capture England as well. It didn't seem possible that anyone could work as hard and as long as Milton did.

Monte had to admit that at nearly 60 years old, and in spite of Dr. Feelgood, whom Milton vehemently denied played any part in his vitality, Milton was far and away the most inspiring figure Monte had ever met. One of his many genius traits besides his talent for organization and his enthusiasm, was his profound correspondence with the public through letters. The same way he had written, in many cases personally typed, letters enticing the young women of Brooklyn and the Bronx to Grossinger's to find "…young men of excellent character", he seduced young women in every state to fall in love with Eddie Fisher. And they responded with loves notes, poems with pressed flowers in them and prayers for Eddie, thousands of them every week. Failure was simply an impossibility around the man. To Monte's way of thinking, Milton was as close to a sure bet as existed in this life.

As *Coke Time* fell away and the musicals *Hot Rocks* and *Good News* sputtered and died in the planning stages, Monte felt relief at being simply a country innkeeper. His years on top as the target of praise and envy, with uncertain friends and reliable enemies, had worn his optimism to a thin, bitter humor. Like Frank, he had survived at the top much longer than anyone expected and was happy to step out of the spotlight. Monte's constant attention was now on his wife and four boys. Both he and Frank were, for the moment, content to step aside and enjoy the fruits of their many years of success.

Benny Snyder convened the *Playhouse Inn's* Board of Directors. The only one not invited was Monte. Benny knew he could count on his local friends and hoped to convince Don Walker, the other Broadway veteran like Monte, to take over the *Inn* with them. No one in the room could ignore the fact that incidents of drunk driving had increased ten times in the months they had had been operating. One local boy, a busboy at the *Inn*, had even been killed after stealing leftover drinks off the sideboard of the bar and wrapping his family's car around a tree on Windybush Road. Rumors of drunken sex parties in the *Inn's* twelve rooms had been overheard as well as tales of crap games being held in the storeroom. Benny Snyder sounded the alarm. The drinking, sex and gambling were a warning. The mafia was on their doorstep.

To Don Walker, who had knocked around Broadway almost as long as Monte, Snyder's distress was laughable. He couldn't deny Monte's history with mobsters, but instantly understood Benny's move for what it was, theft. The vote came down 3 to 2 against Monte with Benny Snyder and two other local board members voting against him. He was fired immediately as the general manager and his salary stopped. They would buy out his shares. He was out.

Monte thought he was coming to a meeting to discuss the closing date of the place for the winter and review their successful first summer. Monte climbed the stairs from the ground floor to the dining room, stopping to view the panorama of the Delaware River flowing by. Almost every day the river was a different color from muddy brown to overcast black to sunny green and gold. Monte sat facing the other board members across a dining table.

Benny and the deciding members of the Board laid out their charges of public drunkenness and foul language that poorly represented the company. Monte looked to Don Walker and saw that a snatch was about to happen. Suddenly, Monte erupted from his seat, "You're a bum and a nobody," he told Benny. Benny quickly moved to the Board's decision to fire Monte when Monte threw the table in front of him aside and moved toward Benny promising to break his neck. Benny bolted for the door as Monte screamed curses at the man in retreat. The other Board members were petrified in their seats. His frustration and hatred were inextinguishable. "You're nothing. None of you. A bunch of goddamn no-talent, nobodies. This is my place and you'll get nothing." He marched out hoping to catch Benny Snyder hiding somewhere on the ground floor. He was ready to beat the man to death and might have if he had found him.

The worst gangsters he ever knew were better partners than the pillars of the community he ended up with. For the second time in a row, first with *La Vie en Rose* and now with the *Playhouse Inn*, legitimate businessmen had taken everything he had built and there wasn't a thing he could do about it. It took the heart out of him. They took the two places he loved more than all the others. They took the security of his family, his retirement, his ace in the hole. They temporarily took his faith in people, leaving him embittered and with a burning need for men of honor.

Chapter 36

"Five boys. In China we'd be rich."

Under a regime of no alcohol, close dosage monitoring of her barbiturates and pure vitamin B injections, Jane fought her way back to a nearly normal life. Her nerves were quieted and her anxiety lifted enough to dissipate much of the depression weighing on her. This and his healthy sons were the saving graces that kept Monte afloat as he brooded over the streak of luck that seemed to have closed every door to independence and stability in his face. Monte retreated once again to the farm with no job, no prospects and no idea what the next roll of the dice might bring. He just hoped there would be another roll and soon. Jane was pregnant again.

Just after 6 PM on November 7, 1955, fifth son, Timothy Milton Proser arrived at Doylestown Hospital, weighing in at a little over 7 pounds. He was a healthy, whole and quiet baby. Since Jane had exhausted all the male names in her family, she called on her mother to find an appropriate saint. Nan suggested Saint Timothy, the son of a mixed Christian/Jewish marriage, who was a quiet and loyal friend to St. Paul. Monte added the name Milton to the boy's title in honor of Milton

Blackstone and asked his stalwart friend to be the boy's godfather. With Milton as a role model, the boy could only be successful in life. Telegrams and letters poured in from all over the world. Five boys was some kind of streak. Timmy's debut made all the columns.

Sol and Sharon called from New York with congratulations. "Five boys," Monte told Sol over the phone, "...In China we'd be rich."

It was another winter of contemplation in the old fieldstone farmhouse where every conceivable space was filled with evidence of children. Monte's family, Isabel, Annette and Leo, came out from New York City for a Christmas of turkey and gefilte fish. They had all reached middle age and successfully found their professional niche and spouses. The sisters seemed content to enjoy their five nephews rather than raise children of their own. Leo was hopeful to have a family with his young wife Connie. For Monte, it was a moment to exhale, to take stock of his family and enjoy the successes they had all achieved. Carrie had agreed to stay with the family through Christmas instead of returning to New York City as she normally did. Monte acknowledged her sacrifice with a $500 holiday bonus. Although his bank account was again dwindling and he had no immediate source to replenish it, he seemed at ease. Something would come along. It always did.

Carrie made her southern-style Christmas with sweet potato pie and collard greens, the perfect complement to gefilte fish, everyone agreed. Jane appeared briefly at Christmas dinner with baby Timmy. Isabel offered a prayer before dinner for Albert Einstein, the intellectual light of the Jewish world, who had died earlier that year. Later, Leo recalled the latest Groucho remark that he knew Monte would appreciate, "I must say that I find television very educational. The minute somebody turns it on, I go to the library and read a book."

Jane spoke quietly and kept sleeping Timmy in her arms. She wasn't going to let go of this one. She knew Tim was her last baby. He was her Christmas present to herself. She cooed to him constantly, inhaling the scent of him. Monte sent his eldest sons to kiss their mother and their new brother. This was his game for the evening. Carrie smeared a dab of sweet potato on the baby's lip and watched his reaction to it with Jane. Tim liked sweet potato. For the moment, with the pain of the *Playhouse Inn* putsch receding and an unknown future ahead of him, this was more than enough. It was Monte's private heaven on earth.

By spring he was back at work, commuting to New York, starting over. He had returned to his suite at the *Algonquin* and was making more frequent trips to Aqueduct racetrack to conduct business while he fed his adrenaline-fueled gambling addiction by risking more money than he could afford to lose. With no club or regular office to operate from, the track served as his occasional daytime base of operations. He could have rented a floor of private suites at the *Algonquin* for what it cost him in sluggish horses.

The stillborn Henry Nemo and Lew Brown musicals took $50,000 of his remaining money with them into the hole. He optioned the book for a musical comedy TAKE THIS WOMAN with a new partner, the novice producer Cork O'Keefe. In spite of the new project, prospects for having something up and running by the fall season were beginning to look grim.

The call came as summer began cooking the blacktop streets of Manhattan. Johnny Rosselli had an offer. $5,000 a week to run the entertainment at the *Tropicana* – an offer Monte wished he could refuse. He played it cute, telling Johnny he was working on something, and he'd think about, and thanks. Johnny asked about Jane and the boys. He wasn't just making polite conversation. Like Frank, Johnny was from the old school where 'la famiglia' was everything. He was especially protective of all his friends' families as well as being fiercely loyal to his friends, and Monte knew it.

Johnny attended Catholic mass regularly, gave consistently to charities and often took hard luck cases under his wing. To friends who had known him for years, Rosselli was sometimes their best and only friend, someone they regarded as a brother. Family was at the center of Rosselli's code of ethics – the bedrock of the old Italian culture. A few years earlier, when Bryan Foy's wife Vivian had been ill with cancer, he was at Vivian bedside almost around the clock. One night when Bryan was out of the house, and the kids were off somewhere, Johnny was sitting with Vivian as she died. He closed her eyes. Years later, when he learned that Bryan was fighting with one of his brothers over a business deal, Johnny confronted his old friend and told him to patch it up. When Bryan refused, Johnny became so enraged at the breach of family harmony, even though it was not his family, that he punched Foy, knocking him down.

Johnny saw himself as a gentleman soldier and man of honor. His naturally warm personality was not in conflict with the violence and law-breaking sometimes required to serve friends and family. It was natural, in Johnny's mind, that a man in his position should command both respect and fear. In fact, they were his stock and trade.

Friends speculated that his fanatic devotion to their families was because he didn't have one of his own. But in fact, unknown even to his closest friends, Johnny did have a family. One he kept hidden, along with his true identity. All his life he secretly supported his mother and sisters in Boston by sending his mother regular deliveries, packets of cash, by courier. He never saw them, never phoned, and kept them completely isolated from his criminal career even changing his name from Filippo Sacco to Johnny Rosselli.

Monte opened up to Johnny over the phone and crowed about his sons, and said all was well. Johnny made his case for the new hotel explaining the price tag of $15,000,000 was buying the classiest, most modern hotel and casino in the world, bar none. The place was on 40 acres that was going to be landscaped into a desert oasis, it would have 300 rooms, an Olympic sized pool shaped like a scallop shell. It would make Phil's own *Beverly Club* look like a horse barn. Monte got the picture, he'd let him know tomorrow. Johnny sweetened the deal, "We'll put up 250K for the show." And then the clincher, something to the effect of, "Look, Frank asked me to make the call. He says to tell you he's going to the bank on this one." Monte had to admit. Johnny was every bit as smooth as Frank.

Unless there was some magical way he could have his own place in the works by the next day, Monte would have to say yes. The way Johnny phrased it, it was more than just a sweet offer, it was a gesture of repayment from Frank. But working for Johnny, even if Frank was a partner, was jumping back into the same nasty pool he'd fought to get out of. And they might not let him out a second time.

And it was Las Vegas. The place sounded horrible. Like being on the moon, with gangsters. If he took the job, the jig was up, he was an employee. As much as he disliked the prospect of being on Johnny Rosselli's payroll, like almost everybody else he knew, the plain fact was that Johnny and his friends now owned or controlled every nightclub in the country. The offer was everything he needed, but nothing he wanted. He'd need a night to sleep on it.

Against the black desert night, a tulip shaped fountain, six stories tall, sprayed sparkling aqua and rose colored water into the air. Behind it like a giant sprawled on his back, arms flung above his head, lay the *Tropicana*. The long torso of the giant was the casino and show room. Each out-flung arm was 150 of the most lavishly furnished suites that money could buy, the arms wrapped around the huge scallop shell pool, the giant's face. The blocks of suites were terraced, three stories tall, each suite let out onto a patio overlooking the pool. They called the hotel the "Tiffany of the Strip".

In Las Vegas, the competition to provide entertainment, service and luxury was fierce. The *Trop* set new standards for all of them. The ratio of one and a half staff members to every guest insured that every detail, every whim a guest could think of was accomplished quickly and with a smile. No comfort or convenience was too large or small. The kitchen was open around the clock. A request like cherries jubilee at midnight was easily done. Two girls covered in whipped cream at 3 AM, was only slightly off the menu.

A mile down Route 91, the *Desert Inn* pool offered an underwater observation room and a deck-side bar. The *Sands* topped it with a sculpted, flowing lake of connecting pools. The *Tropicana* raised the bet with its quarter-acre scallop shell featuring underwater music and surrounded by 34 acres of tropical oasis. In the oasis it rained four times a day and once at night.

The plush carpeted casino blazed with a hundred chandeliers. It was the size of an airplane hangar. The showroom sat 450 people in the most technically advanced theatre in the world. Motorized runways could extend into the audience, catwalks materialized overhead. Even the curtain was an innovation. It was articulated by an electronic control panel and could form into almost any shape or divide into multiple curtains to create different spaces on stage. Monte had bought the rights to the curtain over the previous months. It was his little bit of independence, his private concession in the hotel. The way Johnny Rosselli got the barbershop, newsstand and parking lot for his private income, the lease on the curtain went to Monte on top of his $5000 a week paycheck. Some of the curtain was modified to carry panels for rear-projection. Monte would use curtain walls of projected images for his set walls and save the cost of construction. That left him most of the $250,000 budget to hopefully pack the show with more excitement than anyone had seen in Las Vegas before.

$250,000 was simply a figure Johnny made up to recruit Monte. When the show's director and choreographer, Earl Barton, once asked Rosselli for details of the show's budget, "What's the bottom line, John?" Rosselli looked evenly at the 26 year-old with ice blue, unmoving eyes, "There ain't no bottom line, kid. Just make sure it's a damn good show."

More than anyone else, Monte needed it to be a damn good show. There was no author, partner or star to blame if it bombed. There were no excuses. He had a blank stage and a blank check. If he bombed here, there was no place left to go. Whatever the boys didn't own outright, they controlled through legitimate companies like MCA, William Morris and City National Bank. Like Meyer said that year, "We're bigger than US Steel."

Jane and the boys were comfortably installed in the heart of Beverly Hills in a modest house on Crescent Drive. Sol and Sharon Meadows were neighbors again, in a mansion on Doheny Drive. Sol had the West Coast rights to manufacture *NO CAL*, the first sugarless soda using an artificial sweetener. He was making a fortune with it. Sharon had two children, a son Jimmy and a daughter Melissa, or Missy, who were close in age to the youngest Proser boys. It was an idyllic moment. Money was flowing steadily, not gushing as it once had, but enough to put minds at ease and Jane had been transported from the isolation of Jericho Mountain to a friendly neighborhood in the California sun. All was well.

Monte and Jane took a second honeymoon to Catalina Island. On the boat across the Pacific, the sea air brought the color up in Jane's cheeks and loosened her golden hair, still untouched by gray. She clutched Monte, her protector and savior, to her. In her eyes and smile, Monte found his sunrise.

"We're going to make it, Janey," he reassured her.

She wanted to believe him. "We got this far" she said. But deep down she knew there would be no "making it" for them. They'd been up and down so many times, been through so much money, so many "sure things" and so many grand schemes, that she couldn't really believe in anything, except Monte. She wished that she could believe in God.

All was well except for the irritating facts that Monte was now Frank's man, answering, it seemed now, directly to Johnny. He was "on the pad". He hadn't been on anyone's payroll in 25 years, since his publicity work with the studios, and it aggravated and depressed him. The $5000 a week was decent money but he had no piece of the action. He had only his reliance on Frank to assure him that he and his family would be taken care of. Everything depended on Frank. Everything relied on him being a man of honor.

Monte knew better than anyone that he'd been on a losing streak lately. All his adult life he had sensed changes in his luck like farmers sense changes of weather. Everything he'd touched in the past 4 years had turned to dust and it was time for a turn around. To test whether his luck was returning, he walked into the *Tropicana* for the first time and headed straight to the first roulette wheel he saw. A gala party of invited guests was getting the bugs worked out of the casino before the official opening. Guests were given small buckets of silver dollars to gamble with as party favors. Monte placed his entire bucket, represented by one silver dollar, on 17 black. The wheel spun, the steel ball spun in the opposite direction. It dropped on 17 black. A roar went up at the table and he knew his luck was back. The losing streak was broken. They paid him 35 to one on his bucket.

When the luck was flowing, you had to ride it. The crap tables drew him in like green islands in a shifting sea as he crossed the casino to get to the showroom. Even while ideas for the show were spinning in his head like a juggler's china plates, he walked past the crap tables reluctantly. Craps brought him vital energy and focus, and had since he was a teenager. You could feel the luck in your clenched fist and then let it fly with just the right English to set the dice spinning right into your number. In a crap game, you knew the odds, you knew the point – it was simple and fast. The world divided neatly into numbers. Everything else vanished as invisible threads of luck brushed against your hand.

Pit boss Lou Lederer spotted the fixed eyes and slack mouth of a problem in the making. He kidded Monte to play with quarters until he got the hang of the game. It was his way of warning someone he didn't want to offend, but he knew the warnings never worked. He'd known Monte since forever, since *Piping Rock*, since Havana. Monte was golden – kind of a wild guy, but fun, a guy who frequently left the price of a house or two in the stickman's crook. On those nights he'd empty his pockets, no matter how big the bankroll he came in with. And he wasn't above asking for markers, depending on how much fun he was having, which depended on how much he was drinking.

But that was Copa money back then. Monte could always go back for more. Now it was a different story, he was on the payroll with everybody else. Nobody needed a problem like the one Lou saw forming in Monte's eyes. He brought it up to his sponsor, Johnny R.

Johnny made it a point to sit in at rehearsals to catch a word with Monte when he was relaxed, in a good mood. They kibitzed. Johnny was always ordering appetizers and drinks, taking care that everyone was comfortable and had whatever they needed. The *Trop* was Johnny's place, he was the host. Monte responded and treated him like Frank's errand boy, a new guy. Johnny had to laugh, no one but Monte ever disrespected him to his face. It was hilarious. Monte was half serious like all good comedians. Frank was the man he worked for, not Johnny. So Monte barked at him, "Sit up. You slouch. It's bad for your digestion," and Johnny took it. Monte was just golden.

All money was paid out at the cage, the same cage that serviced the casino floor. Payroll for technicians and performers was given to Monte in cash in plain, brown paper lunch bags. He would take the bags across the casino to his production desk in front of the stage and divvy it up into hotel stationery envelopes. Security was never a concern. Bags of money were loaded out of the cage every few hours, wheeled through the hallways of the hotel in wheelbarrows and dumped into unlocked counting rooms heaped with piles of silver dollars, half dollars, quarters, dimes and nickels each as tall as a man.

He was perfectly safe as he crossed the casino, except from the sound of dice as they bounced across felt and clicked against a sideboard. It was the sound of luck itself, whispering to him like the Sirens once did to sailors lost at sea.

As *Tropicana Holiday* came together, Monte felt his power return. The show developed around themes – tropical romance, sex, pleasure – with no particular story beyond boy meets girl, boy likes girl, boy gets girl, or not. The songs, with words and music by Gordon Jenkins, introduced the themes, then built in intensity, from *I Feel Like a New Man*, to *Pleasure Island*, to the show-stopper *Sex*, and the denouement *In the Heat of the Day*.

But there was one tune, a sentimental ballad that Jenkins played for Monte in the composer's Malibu living room that had the most hauntingly beautiful lyrics and melody the showman had ever heard. Monte stared quietly across the Pacific through Jenkin's picture window after hearing the last fading note and knew he had a problem. It didn't fit anywhere in the show. But the song spoke to him so profoundly, it seemed to tell the story of his life.

The song began with the singer simply saying, "As I approach the prime of my life, I find I have the time of my life, learning to enjoy at my leisure, life's simple pleasures and so I happily concede – this is all I ask, this is all I need." Then, as the melody sways into time, the man sings of a few, private moments that come with maturity, "Beautiful girls, walk a little slower when you walk by me. Wandering sunsets stay a little longer by the lonely sea. Children everywhere, when you shoot at bad men, shoot at me. Take me to that strange enchanted land, that grown-ups seldom understand."

When the song was finished, Monte didn't know what to say to his friend. Jenkins knew the song didn't fit the show, since all the characters were young and in some phase of love, so he simply "let the music play" as the lyrics advised and dedicated the song to their friendship.

"It's a gift," the composer said, "You'll find a place for it someday." He handed a copy of the sheet music to Monte. At the top he'd written, "For Monte. Love, Gordon". It was one of the most astounding acts of generosity, on par with Batch's mortgaging the farm, that Monte had ever witnessed. The moment hung in the air between the two men like a thunderhead, full of rain and electricity. The hush of the Pacific washed the last notes of the melody out to sea as Monte stood still, touched with love for his friend. The emotion was more than a modest, quiet man like Monte could express.

"It's beautiful, like a dream," he said. His heart was completely full. Distant seagulls chimed in to the rhythm of the waves as salt tears came up in his eyes. The release of emotion shocked him. He turned away to hide his sudden sentimentality, crossing to an open side window to face the ocean. Salt mist blew through and across Monte's lips, bringing him back from his heart-bursting dream. He re-composed himself and turned back to Gordon at the piano. He took the musician's hand and held it, "Beautiful girls," he sang softly to his pal, "…walk a little slower when you walk by me…". Gordon enjoyed that but had liked the tears even more.

Monte drove from Malibu with the melody running through him, over and over again. The more he heard the lyrics, the more they described his inner life. He had reached that time in his life, his prime. He had everything he wanted. All that he now asked, all he needed, was for life to show itself to him in private moments of beauty.

When he arrived at the *Mocambo* for an afternoon casting session of showgirls, he gave the piano player the handwritten notations for Jenkins' *This is All I Ask*. The gentle ballad played all day so the beautiful girls would walk a little slower as they walked by Monte.

Returning to Las Vegas with the show cast and the score completed. He finalized the layout of the show. Now it was a matter of rehearsing and polishing the transitions between numbers. He was exhausted at night after a full day of making the thousands of decisions that the show needed and fell asleep without needing the pills. He awoke one morning and had the answer to a problem he'd forgotten about – what to do with the beautiful music of *This is All I Ask*. With director, Earl Barton, Monte created a showstopper, a reveal of beautiful girls, one after the other, on the catwalks around the sides of the audience. Monte auditioned hundreds of young women to find the ten most beautiful. The girls needed no previous experience or talent. They had only one job in the show and that was to strike a pose and walk a little slower while Peter Marshall sang the song. The elegant simplicity of the display highlighted the piercing beauty of the lyrics. It was a rare moment of pure poetry - the simple, everyday joy of watching beautiful girls just being beautiful.

As the story of Jenkins' gift got around and the under-stated staging of the song grew in reputation, it became the one tune associated with Monte. Like Durante's *Inka Dinka Doo,* or Jack Benny's *Love in Bloom,* it became his theme song. Monte, the lucky little hobo who charmed Broadway, didn't want money or fame. All he asked, all he needed, was for wandering rainbows to stay a little longer and for beautiful girls to walk a little slower when they walked by him.

The phone rang at the production desk.

"Monte? Sonny Werblin." Monte hadn't heard from Sonny since *Coke Time*.

"Well, Mr. Werblin. How's by you?" he said. Sonny, as an ex-newspaper man, was okay in Monte's book but as one of the top agents for MCA - the "octopus" - the most powerful and ruthless agency in the world, Sonny was more than just okay. The agent got right to the point; what did Monte think about Eddie Fisher headlining the new show? It was the first bite and was expected. Monte parried the question but already knew it was probably a lost cause.

Eddie had been signed with MCA since *Coke Time*. That put the agency in direct competition with Milton Blackstone for control of the singer's career. As Eddie said later, "MCA controlled the sponsor, the show, the guest stars and me." When the tug-of-war with Milton turned bitter and Eddie agitated to get out of his contract with *MCA*, four *MCA* agents, presumably Sonny among them, cornered the 24-year-old in his suite at the *Beverly Hills Hotel* and told him plainly, "If you leave MCA, we'll see to it that you never work again."

Monte knew if it came down to a power play no one was strong enough to tangle with *MCA*. If the *Tropicana* show was a hit, then he might have some leverage but as it was, *MCA's* power to shut off talent to all of Las Vegas meant Sonny's good idea was more than just a good idea.

What made the deal hard to swallow was that things between Monte and Eddie were not good. Eddie and Milton had been fighting ever since Eddie signed with the octopus. Monte had seen Eddie's ingratitude and disrespect toward Milton first hand. He'd heard all the stories of Eddie's sexual gluttony and weakness of character. The topper was that Eddie still brought Dr. Feelgood with him everywhere. Worse still, was that Eddie had already succumbed to the same demon that Monte was fighting for his Jane's life. The singer now sedated himself with barbiturates to salve his amphetamine-frayed nerves. It made him sometimes lethargic, sometimes exuberant and always unpredictable.

Governor of Nevada, Rex Bell, smiled for the cameras on opening day. Rex had been a reliable actor in B westerns and husband of Clara Bow, the "It Girl" of early movies. Mayor of Las Vegas, C.D. Baker, backed the Governor up and showgirls posed with the two men for the official photograph of the ribbon cutting ceremony. Meyer's man, Ben Jaffe, represented the management of the hotel in the photo and it was the only picture of the management permitted in circulation.

The ribbon fell away and a crowd of over 600 poured into the plushest European grand casino in the world. Eddie Cantor, wise elder of all stage performers, was one of the first in the crowd to stride into the deep red carpet. The cream of Hollywood and New York show business followed Cantor inside and mixed with powerful factions of California and Nevada political and business interests.

That night of April 15th, *Monte Proser's Tropicana Revue*, debuted to a packed house. It was spectacular, energetic, impressionistic. Wildly skewed and warped perspective sketches by Glen Holse, rear-projected onto curving set walls, gave the show the look of a fun-house mirror. Costumes were equally lyrical with bold circus colors and patterns. It was as light and colorful as confetti, and just as grave. This was a saloon show for patrons who wanted excitement, emotion and romance over drinks, before dinner.

Eddie Fisher, on the right mixture, was now a commanding and sure voice, completely comfortable on stage. Elaine Dunn, a powerhouse young dancer and actress, who looked like Audrey Hepburn and had the skill and legs of a prima ballerina, captured every eye in the house.

It was a smash and Monte was once again in clover. Reservations for weeks in advance started stacking up, then for months. Las Vegas columnists were reliable. Just as violent street crime would never be a problem, bad reviews didn't exist in Las Vegas.

Monte sent a ticket to Milton and reserved a suite for him, demanding that he take the next plane. Milton couldn't refuse. Monte hoped that, in the glow of success, he and Eddie would reconcile and re-unite to counter-balance MCA.

Milton arrived and was happy to see Monte but less than thrilled with the prospect of seeing Eddie. He had only come as a favor to Monte. Milton showed signs of the strain between he and Eddie, and the legacy of Dr. Feelgood. Where Milton once had total focus on their conversations, and generally a turn of good humor, he now flitted from subject to subject. Monte was familiar with the symptoms.

Monte allowed both men two days to get used to the idea that they were going to meet, with him as the referee. He made it clear to both that he expected a reconciliation. The past was to be forgotten. Period. Both agreed. Monte arranged an event that would allow both men to easily break the ice without a direct confrontation and with something to distract them if conversation became strained. He arranged for a brand new Cadillac *LaSalle*, a sky blue convertible, to be parked in front of the hotel wrapped in a red ribbon and bow. It was Eddie's gift from the hotel, a token of gratitude and success.

Milton was several minutes early for the press event as usual, impeccably dressed and groomed, smiling like a diplomat from a very wealthy and powerful country. After two days in the steam room, on the massage table and in the barber shop, Milton's skin gleamed like polished pink marble. Monte called the press conference to give Milton and Eddie their chance to let bygones be bygones, and grab a little ink in the process. Eddie arrived literally seconds before the 1:30 PM scheduled start. He was hesitant, withdrawn and Monte instantly saw trouble. Milton had relaxed, opened up and was chatting with the reporters. He caught the cue from Monte.

"Ladies and Gentlemen!" Monte interrupted, "Everyone get enough to drink?" The line always got a laugh from newspaper people who were generally proud of their industry's reputation for hard drinking and understood it was also an invitation to drinks later, on the house.

"On behalf of myself and the Tropicana, we present this little token of our appreciation to Eddie for a grand, smash success." He waited for the note taking to stop and the faces of his new friends to turn up from their notepads for more. He went on with the customary hurrah and made a slow sweeping gesture of handing the keys, wrapped in their own bow so as to be easily identified in grainy news photos, to Eddie. Photographers had plenty of time to frame and focus while the keys were swinging toward Eddie, when they finally arrived Eddie did his best "surprised" face and held it. The flashes died off. A few questions for Eddie that he shooed away like horseflies, and it was over. The press crowd dissolved and Eddie was left with the keys, the car, Monte and Milton. The silence of the deep desert returned as each man, Eddie and Milton, squirmed to find the first words, the first look at each other in months. Monte was staying out of it but began to rock on his feet like a cop waiting anxiously for the last float of a very long parade to pass.

Eddie finally said, looking at the car, "It's kind of an odd color, isn't it?"

Monte's heart sank. Milton's back stiffened. He looked straight out into the empty desert. Monte turned to Eddie, opening his arms, his face twisted into a grimace of confusion, as if to say, "That's the best you can do?" Eddie shrugged, unaware of, or unwilling to correct the ingratitude of his comment.

More moments of silence evaporated in the desert heat. Milton roasted in this new disappointment. Nothing had changed with Eddie. His anger flooded back and his face reddened. Like a kind uncle, he turned to Eddie and said, "Congratulations, Eddie." Then he turned to Monte, "I like the color, beautiful," he said. He turned and walked back into the hotel. Milton and Eddie would never speak again.

Monte turned to Eddie burdened with so much sadness that it hurt to speak, "Enjoy it, kid," he told Eddie and then followed Milton back into the hotel.

Two weeks into the bonanza in the desert, as the first blooms of May were rewarding everyone with a new year of promise and abundance, Frank Costello walked into the lobby of his home at 125 Central Park West. He'd just come from dinner with wife Bobbie and Generoso Pope, publisher of the Italian newspaper *Il Progresso*. He left Bobbie to have dessert with Generoso and took a cab home early for his routine of nightly business calls starting at 11 PM.

As Norvel, Frank's doorman, opened the lobby door for Frank, a large man rushed up from the shadows of the street, "This is for you Frank," he said. Frank turned his head and got a good look at the man who raised a .32 pistol, aimed it at his head and fired once. The impact of the bullet whipped Frank's head around and spattered blood on the wall. Frank stumbled back into the lobby, falling into a leather couch as the young man ran back to a waiting black Cadillac. The car screeched away, south on Central Park West, with its lights out. At long last, Vito Genovese had made his move.

CHAPTER 37

Broadway of the West

The bullet nicked Frank's right ear, punctured his scalp, skimmed around the back of his skull under his scalp and exited 3 inches under his left ear. It ricocheted off the stone wall and bounced to a stop on the tile floor near the center of the lobby. Frank was knocked off his feet and fell into a couch in the lobby. He was conscious and in shock, bleeding from his neck. He called out to his doorman Norvel, "Somebody tried to get me!"

Outside, Phil Kennedy, another early retiring dinner guest, had seen the whole thing from the cab he and Frank had shared from the restaurant. He rushed to his friend. When he got inside, Frank was spattered with blood and bleeding but conscious. Kennedy picked up the 66 year-old man and carried him to the cab.

In his bed in the Roosevelt Hospital emergency room, Frank sat up for NYPD Chief of Detectives, Jimmy Leggett. Jimmy pulled up a chair and stared at the white turban of bandages around Frank's head for a moment. The detective was very concerned and completely sincere when he asked, "Who could've done this, Frank?"

Frank looked back at the policeman with equal sincerity, "I don't know who could have done it. I haven't got an enemy in the world."

Jimmy knew the Prime Minister unfortunately still had all his marbles and so they were both in for a long interrogation. The detective knew that this was very likely the opening shot of a gang war, so he had no choice except to grind Frank for every scrap of information he could get. He waited patiently, asking Frank ten or fifteen times what happened at every moment of the evening. Frank's memory of the evening was perfect except for the shooting, and for the life of him, he just couldn't imagine anyone who might want to harm him. He was completely stumped. Jimmy understood, of course, then calmly started again, recounting the events of the last 24 hours, checking his notes for any changes in the story.

For evidence, Jimmy had the bullet, whatever Frank had in his pockets at the time and three eyewitnesses including Frank, but only Frank got a real good look at the assailant. After two days, the task force of 66 detectives that Jimmy assigned to the case had nothing. The case was going cold faster than a trout on ice. Among the coins and small bills in Frank's pocket was a handwritten note that read,"

Gross casino wins as of 4-27-57, $651,284.
Casino wins less markers, $434,695
Slot wins, $62,844.
Markers, $153,745.
Mike, $150 a week totaling $600
Jake, $100 a week, totaling $400
L. $30,000
H. $9,000.

Within two weeks the figures on the note were deciphered and verified. It was the tally and profit split of the *Tropicana* casino in the first 24 hours of operation. The handwriting was Lou Lederer's. Immediately, the Nevada Gaming Commission banned Frank from any connection to the hotel. The same went for "Dandy" Phil Kastel and Lou Lederer. They were all out, banned for life from participation in a casino. Only Meyer and Johnny Rosselli stayed in place of the original investor group due in part to their impenetrable front men. Those front men now included Monte.

Frank's public ban from the *Tropicana* had absolutely no effect on his participation in the profits. He'd never been to the hotel for fear of drawing attention anyway, and now was relieved of any obligation to make an appearance. His cut of the skim continued to arrive like clockwork while he battled the government over a previous charge of tax evasion stemming from the Kefauver investigation .

As always, Frank's misfortune foreshadowed Monte's. Without ever bringing formal charges, the federal government finally made their move. The Internal Revenue Service simply imposed a tax lien against the farm for $31,582. They claimed it stemmed from underpayments during the war years at the Copa. Federal prosecutors had long since learned that what couldn't be proved in court, didn't have to be with the IRS. Just give them the target and the IRS would punish without proof and often without recourse. The IRS was untouchable.

Israel Katz, through his emissary, the faithful Max Siderow, advised Monte that it was best to pay the penalty and avoid a full-blown audit of all the Copa years. The government had shackled Monte and Frank in one prosecution file under the title of Copacabana. The faster Monte disposed of the problem, the better. But the file was too rich a source for just one prosecution. It would keep government forensic accountants and prosecutors employed for years to come, shooting at Frank but hitting Monte.

Where the *Kefauver Committee* left off, a new crop of ambitious politicians began with the *Senate Labor Rackets Committee*, headed by Senator John L. McClellan, specifically investigating organized crime's infiltration of unions. Among the most active in the zealous pursuit of labor criminals were two of Joe Kennedy's boys, Jack and Bobby. Particularly Bobby had a near religious fervor in pursuing union bad guys, many of whom were former colleagues and current friends of his father. In fact, Joe still played golf with Johnny Rosselli, whom he'd known since the 1930's in Hollywood, and with Frank Costello who went all the way back to their rumrunner days together in the 20's. Joe knew very well that Rosselli, who pioneered turning unions into personal checking accounts for Al Capone, was one of the pigeons his son would be looking for, and how dangerous that was.

Bobby, as older brother Jack's campaign strategist, knew that bashing mobsters was a certain path to national public exposure that could pave the way for a possible presidential run in 1960. At the Kennedy compound in Hyannis Port, the family was shocked by an argument over the subject that spun up to a level of fury the family had never seen before. Old Joe was deeply emotional and "…a little scared." family member Jean Kennedy Smith said. A family friend who was there, Lem Billings, commented, "The old man saw this as dangerous, not the sort of thing or the sort of people to mess around with." But Bobby had already drawn first blood. He had subpoenaed teamster leader Jimmy Hoffa.

Rhonda Fleming replaced Eddie Fisher in *Tropicana Holiday* and was followed by Carol Channing. Comic actor Dick Shawn was added to the cast. The casino continued to bring in over $700,000 a week. In spite of Frank's enforced absence, everybody was happy. The show was running well, packing them in. Now all Monte had to do was replace performers as needed, the show was set.

With Frank in forced retirement, Johnny rose to overall leadership in Las Vegas as the natural liaison between the New York *Syndicate* and Chicago *Outfit*. Even independents like Moe Dalitz, of Detroit's Purple Gang, who operated the *Desert Inn*, accepted Johnny as an honest broker and reliable businessman. As Frank said later, years into his retirement, "We were always lucky to have Johnny in Las Vegas."

Since witnessing Monte's ability to create and sustain a sensation with *Monte Proser's Tropicana Holiday,* Johnny proposed a partnership to Monte that would provide entertainment to practically every casino in Las Vegas, Havana and Europe. Through Johnny's connections and Monte's reputation and talent, they could dominate the industry, the sky was the limit. The result was *Monte Proser Productions*. Within a few months, Johnny delivered a contract for the production rights to entertainment in every Hilton Hotel in the world, "the biggest deal in club entertainment history", as reported in the Hollywood Reporter.

"Janey we're in," Monte crowed over the phone to his unsteady wife. "This is the end of troubles," he said.

"That's wonderful. When are you coming home?" Jane wanted to know. Her self-imposed isolation was becoming acute. She no longer made the effort to get to know her neighbors and barely spoke even to Sharon, who was only a ten minute drive away.

"Soon. How are the boys?"

"Oh they're all fine. Driving me crazy, but they get fed. When are you coming?"

"Next week. Just got to sign the papers." Monte had given up his fight for independence from Johnny and the boys. At least he'd held out for a good price. All he cared about now was ending the boom and bust cycle of his chaotic career.

"Take it easy, honey. I'm coming home soon," he reassured her. Monte got off the phone and immediately called his friend Sy Devore, the Beverly Hills haberdasher to the stars. He ordered Jane a $10,000 diamond bracelet, figuring it was an investment, he told Sy. He told Sy to have it ready and wrapped with a bow when he came home the following week.

Hilton Hotels financier and managing partner, Arnold Kirkeby, was one of the gang, so to speak. He had been in business with Meyer since the mid-30's. They first partnered in the National Hotel of Cuba Corporation that operated the posh *Nacional* hotel and casino in Havana, Frank and Meyer's first large scale success on the island. The *Syndicate* leaders made the *Nacional* into the largest and most luxurious casino in the world, setting the standard that would play out again at the *Tropicana*. In 1946, Kirkeby merged with Conrad Hilton's holdings of 10 modest hotels located mainly in the Southwest U.S.. In the dozen years since the merger, Kirkeby had expanded the company to include 28 of the most prominent landmark hotels in the country, elite properties that were to be the homes, offices and playrooms of the mob. Hilton Hotel major investors besides Kirkeby, Meyer and Frank included New Jersey boss Longy Zwillman, Joe Adonis and Al Hart of the *Outfit's City National Bank*, of which Kirkeby was a director.

With the Hilton entertainment deal in process and *Tropicana Holiday* running smoothly, Johnny went off on an entirely new project leaving Monte on his own in the world's grandest and newest palace on the banks of the largest river of cash in the world. Las Vegas, the meadows, was flooded with money from everywhere. Young turks, who arrived with suitcases full of cash, came at Monte from every angle. Gamblers, grifters and promoters of every description arrived by the dozens from McCarran Airport and by bus, car and limousine from Los Angeles. Vegas was an open city. Everybody could come in for a taste, as long as they had good manners. And everybody came - some as armed escorts for moving vans full of swag and dirty money that needed cleaning, some as high rolling gamblers who needed a game, some as fading show business stars who needed a fresh start.

Johnny got the call for his new project from Bob Maheu, a private investigator in Washington D.C.. Maheu was on retainer from the CIA and handled difficult or unsavory tasks for the agency. As CIA security chief, Jim O'Connell phrased it before a congressional committee, he used Maheu, "...in sensitive covert operations in which I didn't want to have an agency or government person get caught." Maheu's elite clients included not only the CIA but also billionaire Howard Hughes, the Teamster's union, the Senate Banking and Currency Committee and the New York Central Railroad.

Maheu apparently had met Johnny in Las Vegas through Teamster president Jimmy Hoffa. Johnny helped Hoffa arrange investments for the Teamster's multi-million dollar pension fund. Johnny, with Sidney Korshak, helped arrange over 240 million dollars' worth of low interest loans from the retirement fund of the hard-working teamsters to friends looking to finance Las Vegas hotels. The *Stardust* and *Riviera* hotels, among others, were financed from the fund.

Maheu had known Hoffa since doing some "electronic" work for him to counter government surveillance. When

Maheu needed a favor in Las Vegas, Hoffa suggested the investigator call Johnny as the man with the keys to that town. Now the time had come to turn the tables. Maheu had something to offer his long-time friend. In spite of their friendship, Maheu took his time buttering up Johnny before presenting the job the government wanted to offer him.

Finally, over coffee at the *Brown Derby* in Los Angeles, he got to the point. The CIA wanted Johnny to kill Fidel Castro. Long moments passed as Johnny looked deeply into his companion's eyes for any flicker of fear, then discreetly inspected the patrons in the restaurant trying to spot government agents. This type of work had never been discussed with civilians, people outside the *Outfit* before. Johnny waited until the silence was painful, then waited a bit more. Maheu made it clear it was a federal request, not private. Even so, Johnny backed off. The idea was too shocking.

After some further discussion, Johnny proceeded cautiously, asking the private investigator to provide authentication. Later that month, Maheu and Johnny met with Jim O'Connor. O'Connor explained the government's offer in the scrubbed language of espionage that excluded the words "kill" and "assassinate" to achieve "plausible deniability". Nonetheless, O'Connor explained exactly what they wanted to happen to Castro, how it might be done and when they wanted it to happen, which was as soon as possible. As a patriot, Johnny felt he had to take the job. Of course, Johnny had to clear it through his new boss in Chicago, Sam Giancana.

Sam was tickled when Johnny asked permission for the hit. He had always been amused by Johnny's patriotism. He joked with his colleagues, "Give Johnny a flag and he'll follow you around the yard."

"Ladies and Gentlemen," Bobby Darin drew the audience's attention to the stage of the Copa. He cocked his head as if listening for a distant sound, then leaned on his mike stand toward the Copa's kitchen. He pulled the microphone from the stand and held it out toward the kitchen as if giving another performer a solo moment.

"You fuckin' bum!", Podell bellowed behind the kitchen doors. This was followed predictably by shattering glass and crashing silverware. Darin continued, "A word from the management." The audience and he listened for a few more action-packed moments as the violence peaked and then went silent. He turned the mike back to himself and saw immediately that his stunt of defiance, instead of winning the audience, had soured them. The illusion of the Copa was broken. People saw the dirty backstage machinery, not the beautiful illusion they paid for, and turned against Darin for it. A few jokers laughed, but overall people were uncomfortable. Bobby quickly moved into his new hit song, *Splish Splash*.

Fading columnist and icon Walter Winchell returned to his first profession, hoofer. The year he turned 61, depressed after his failure to make the transition to television with his *Walter Winchell File*, his old pal Monte threw him a lifeline. Monte created a spot for him in his spectacular new *Tropicana Holiday* and paid him $35,000 a week for his efforts. It was the highest rate of any headliner in the show. Monte knew the star salary would erase his old drinking buddy's defeat in television and hoped it might open a new door for him. Winchell ran with it and got ink from coast to coast, "They offered me $25,000 a week," he told reporters, "They said that's what Marlene gets," comparing his star salary to the one just paid to Marlene Dietrich who had just wrapped up two months in the show, "…but…" the wisecracker continued, "…I said Marlene hasn't got syndication."

Winchell gave Las Vegas everything he had. He tap-danced like a 20 year-old chorus boy and performed a dramatization of his radio program on stage for two weeks. A stentorian narrator recounted Winchell's history in quasi-Winchellese so the younger people in the audience would know who the old man was and get a flavor of his achievements.

It was awful. And it got worse. Early in the run he pulled a lower back muscle and was performing in constant pain. The newsman's stage presentation was ill-conceived and old-fashioned to begin with, and as he hobbled through to the end, pathetic. Everyone was relieved when it was over. Joe E. Lewis, locked into an exclusive contract at the Copa *Room* at the *Sands* with all the old Copa regulars, saw Winchell's performance. The dreadfulness of it lifted his spirits. Watching his old friend bomb amused him enormously. "I was a little disappointed," he said of the show," I enjoyed it."

In spite of the overwhelming power and influence of his employers, Monte didn't give up his fight for independence. He would somehow punch his way out of his velvet prison. As he'd done with Dizzy Gillespie at Lincoln Square in New York in 1945, Monte produced a summer concert that year, 1958, with Louis Armstrong at the Hollywood Bowl. Ella Fitzgerald was a guest singer. The two singers had a rivalry as to who was the best scat singer and challenged each other throughout the show. Scat history was made that night. The success of the show sparked a glimmer of hope, as though Monte had transferred his decades of success in New York clubs and music events to the West, and everything might once again be copasetic.

But at home, hope faded. The crack in his bedrock widened to a chasm and threatened to swallow them all. Jane turned for the worse, often sleeping all day, more unconscious from the barbiturates than asleep. Carrie Dawson had decided not to move west with the family, so Jane was on her own and becoming more isolated than ever. Her erratic cycle of recovery and deterioration had scared and frustrated Carrie. In spite of the love that had grown between them, Jane wasn't able to take Carrie's help, still believing that she could fix herself. Her impregnable mental toughness and independence now worked against her.

Jane called it "bucking up", fighting the growing sense of dread that dogged her. The assassination attempt on Frank, whom she considered a remote friend and family protector, shocked and sickened her. It highlighted their increasingly dangerous, unstable situation. There was no illusion about their situation, their independence, anymore. They were on the payroll. Jane had been around Broadway long enough to know that very few, especially top earners like Frank and Monte, could expect to retire peacefully - or at all.

The *Los Angeles Times* with the picture of Frank in his hospital turban stayed open on the kitchen table. Monte came down from the bedroom upstairs to find Jane making egg salad. Although frail and very thin, it had been a good week for her, one of the occasional reprieves from barbiturate prison. Margaret, the maid, stopped washing the dishes when Monte came in and left with the sink still half full.

"I'll get to these later," she told Jane on the way out.

"Good morning, Mr. Proser," she smiled as she passed Monte.

"Good morning, Margaret," he returned.

Jane turned from her salad making to face her husband.

"Good morning," Monte offered.

Jane hesitated with her reply, "Good morning," she said, fixing him for a moment with a stare and flat tone of voice that told him something was off. Turning back to the counter, she poured him a mug of perfectly brewed and properly steeped English tea from a Wedgewood teapot. She knew how to take care of him.

By the time Jane had crossed to the kitchen table, Monte was absorbed in the newspaper story of Frank's assassination attempt. She sat down and placed the mug next to the small pitcher of chilled cream and silver sugar bowl. A cloth napkin had been set for him beside a small dish with an egg cup for soft boiled eggs standing in its center. He didn't notice Jane or the special table setting. She was motionless as she watched him reading. The sound of Margaret sweeping the walkway outside filtered into the kitchen.

When he'd finished reading he sat back in his chair and took his glasses off. He massaged his eyes, maybe wanting to erase the images he'd just seen. He put his glasses back on and saw his beautiful wife smiling softly at him, being brave. He couldn't really tell her not to worry, like she was an outsider to his business. They knew that whatever was going to happen next couldn't be good for them.

Jane snatched the paper up and took it back to the counter. She piled wet egg shells on top of Frank's picture, quickly crushed the paper around the eggs and opened the cabinet door under the kitchen sink. She snatched the metal lid off the trash can, threw the bundle in and clanged the metal lid down tight. She was breathing like she'd just run a race as she rinsed her hands under the tap on the kitchen sink. She shook her hands dry and smoothed back her hair, taking the moment to restore her hair and her face to perfect poise before turning back to face Monte.

He hadn't touched his tea and was stilled leaned far back in his chair, deep in thought.

"How about some eggs?" she asked. He came back from the desperate chess game that was going on in his head.

"Yeah, let's have some eggs," he agreed.

In spite of the stigma of gangster association sticking more closely to them than ever, Jane and Monte ventured out socially in Hollywood to parties of close friends including Sharon and Sol, haberdasher Sy Devore and actress Donna Reed. At a party given by neighbor Donna Reed, they re-discovered the effect of residual barbiturate in Jane's body when combined with alcohol.

Jane was starting on her second martini when Reed relayed a story about how Johnny Rosselli, who placed family ties above all else, had involved himself in a family argument between two brothers, insisting on family unity to the point of knocking one brother down in the process.

"That's what he's good at...," Jane blasted her host for seeming to defend the mobster to her other guests.

"Jane..." Reed responded to calm her guest and rescue the conversation, "Johnny's no choir boy...."

"He's a mug. They're all a buncha mugs..." Jane slurred slightly.

"Ahhh...," Monte searched for a way out of this line of conversation.

"I'm sure you could tell her all about it, Monte," Reed teased. "I just hear these things and Johnny's, well, you know..."

Jane attacked like she was back in *Morgan's Tavern* cutting of some barroom braggart, already weaving as her balance drifted, "Then why doncha shut the hell up? You don't know what you're talkin' about."

Reed reddened and set her lips in a tight line. The conversation died and the party drifted away with Reed to other guests, leaving Monte, Sol and Sharon in a quiet circle all their own. Monte retrieved Jane's coat and purse. They made an early exit.

The next day, when Jane had recovered and Monte told her what she'd done, she was horrified. She'd always been modest, even reserved, but one drink now transformed her into a loud-mouth bully and a bore. Her embarrassment eroded her confidence and ended her social schedule. She sank further into retreat, even from Monte. Sleep seemed to be the best medicine. For a time, the clock stopped and the alarm never rang.

With the five boys ranging in age from Tim at two, up to Chip at twelve, the demands on Jane to solve every conceivable problem and issue were constant and overwhelming. She hired a maid to help with the boys and hired the woman's husband as groundskeeper and handyman. Everyone got fed, clothed, and off to school on time, but soon after the house fell quiet again, Jane took a pill. When the boys got home, the house was silent. Dinner was an irregular event. If Monte wasn't at home, the boys generally fended for themselves.

They began to suffer from her lack of attention, of seeming interest. It was slightly easier for the younger ones since they were buffered and guided by the older, but everyone missed their mother. At some point in the first months in California, all the boys realized they had been abandoned. As each one sensed the truth, their reaction, their instinct for survival, bonded them together.

Yet each one, in their turn, saw what this writer saw late one night. What I saw as a five year old boy that night cut me off from all that was safe and familiar that had gone before. Late in the evening, long after bedtime for small boys, a chill had crept through the thin walls of the house. I quietly called the names, one by one, to each of my four brothers in our communal bedroom but they were all silently wrapped in their dreams. The silence and black chill of the house moved me to leave my bed to find warmth and comfort for the fears in my active mind. I walked down the carpeted hall to the master bedroom to see if there was room in my mother's bed. In the gloom of the cavernous room, a monster was on hands and knees, crawling around my mother's bed mumbling, groaning, wild hair over her damp face and red eyes, lost and insane. For a moment she looked up at me with spittle dripping from her lips, eyes unfocused, as I stood frozen to the spot, terrified. She didn't recognize me and went back to searching the carpet for whatever monsters look for in carpets in the dead of night. I recognized her, the monster that used to be my mother. I couldn't go back to bed or anywhere else. Wandering out of her room, unable to go back to bed, I stopped at the top of the stairs that led down to the living room and sat down. Suddenly I was crying in deep sobs, trying to be quiet so my brothers wouldn't wake up and find me acting like a baby. I'd become pretty tough through the constant rough-house wrestling matches with my brothers and almost nobody could make me cry. But now I was crying desperately for my Mommy like a newborn baby and couldn't stop. I was terrified of the growling and mumbling that I heard coming from her room and then terrified the monster might come out of the room after me. Hours passed this way. Slowly I began to know, in my gut, that my mother was dead somehow. Eventually, as exhaustion ended my crying and I slumped against the stair railing, I realized that I could never again sleep in her bed. I knew for sure that our warm, safe, fragrant slumbers were gone forever.

Then the crying went on for more hours. I thought even then that this was odd and frightening in itself, I never cried this much. But the damp face of the monster continued to frighten me. It still does.

Sun lightened the windows and the terror subsided but I stayed on the steps until the others were up and coming out of the room ready for school. I passed them, looking down so they wouldn't see my crybaby eyes and went into the room, telling them I was sick and couldn't go to school that day. It was a scene that was played out dozens of times in different ways over the years for each of the boys, until the heartbreak of it no longer hurt.

Monte made the situation clear to the boys one bright Sunday morning in the walled back garden of Crescent Drive. He stormed out of the house, his robe flapping at his sides, "Hey! Get over here!" He was furious. It was 10 o'clock in the morning, a rarely seen hour of the day. The boys were deep into a terrible, violent fight. They gathered, covered in mud and blood, clothes torn, under the coconut palm in the shade. He grabbed up five slender sticks from the ground, clenched them tightly in his fist and shoved it at Chip. "Try to break them." Chip took the bundle and tried but couldn't break it. Billy tried, then Mike, Jimmy and even Timmy. He took the bundle back, selected one stick, broke it, showing it to everybody.

"One is easy to break," he said. Then, holding out the bundle, "Five is hard. Impossible." He let it sink in for a second. "You gotta stick together." He went on, speaking directly, instructing the older boys on their roles as protectors. He made sure everyone understood what he meant. It wasn't a scolding so he could get some sleep, it was a command, a direct order telling them what was needed for the family to survive. He then demanded everyone shake hands. After he retreated to the house, the boys decided they would all be firemen and the garage would be their firehouse. From then on, fighting between them was rare. They stuck together.

CHAPTER 38

CALLING IT QUITS

As he eased down in the barber chair at the St. Regis hotel barbershop in New York, Big Albert asked for a shave and a trim. His hat was taken to the rack for him, a steaming towel coiled on his face. Two men, faces covered with scarves, came in. One told the barber, "Keep your mouth shut if you don't want your head blown off." They wasted no time drawing and firing their .38's into the relaxed customer. After the first volley Albert jumped to his feet, lunged at his killers or what he thought were his killers. It was their reflection in the mirror. Several more shots finished the job. He dropped. If Frank Costello was thinking of removing the stone in his shoe that Vito Genovese had become, he would have a much harder time of it now. His Spartan guard, Albert Anastasia, was dead.

In the old days it was called going to the mattresses. Anastasia's killing brought out the dogs. The Feds were swarming and any big moves were put on hold. The combined mob was ordered to lay low. Meyer saw the move to wrap up all the entertainment at Hilton Hotels under *Monte Proser Productions* as the kind of grandstand play that would draw heat. He killed the deal outright. No discussion was ventured. Johnny couldn't help. Monte's big score became another lifeless dream. When news of Anastasia's murder reached Jane, her waking nightmare of mob cruelty came a step closer to home.

Even J. Edgar Hoover, as much as he may have wanted to stay out of it, was forced to act. He ordered increased surveillance and soon received the field report that documented Joe Kennedy visiting with friends at his Cal-Neva Lodge in Lake Tahoe. At the meeting, Old Joe cut a deal in which Frank Sinatra, Dean Martin, Peter Lawford and others got lucrative shares of the resort. One of the others in the deal with the Rat Pack was recently ascended Chicago boss Sam Giancana. Giancana, known affectionately as Momo, was an old school, pure blood Sicilian, who had always enjoyed his show business friends during the years that they made the *Outfit's Chez Paree* nightclub in Chicago such as success. Old Joe was building support for his son Jack's presidential run in 1960. He particularly hoped Momo would forgive his son Bobby's recent attacks on his business. It was nothing personal. They were going to need Mo's help with the Chicago Democratic machine.

To Jedgar, the news of Old Joe's meeting was more ammunition in his growing feud with the brash, boat-rocking Bobby Kennedy. He placed the report in his personal files. It was like money in the bank.

The young dancer, Dante D'Paulo, crossed through the *Tropicana's* casino among the blackjack tables, on his way to lunch. Monte was seated at a table, hunched over the upholstered bumper, impeccably dressed as always in the finest, almost transparent, white cotton Sulka shirt. Monte saw him.

"Hey kid, come over here and sit with me for a while," the elder producer said. Dante moved in and settled next to him. "Set'm up,' Monte instructed the dealer. The cards were laid out. As the young dancer reached into his pocket for money, Monte stopped him. "Take it easy," he said. Monte placed the bet for him. The hands of cards came and went. Monte didn't want to talk about the show or much of anything except was Dante getting enough sleep, how was the food, the human things. He was looking out for the kid, as he called him, making himself feel better by protecting the young dancer and taking a break from the hordes of needy cases and fortune-seekers that swarmed through the hotel.

Monte quietly played for both of them, paying the dealer for the losses and giving Dante the winnings. He handed over the stacks of silver dollars advising the $250-a-week contract dancer, "Put these in your kick." Dante stayed at the table filling his pockets with silver dollars as long as the invitation held, ordering lunch at Monte's invitation while he relaxed and kept his benefactor pleasant company.

Sam Melchionne, a musician who played in one of the seven house trios that provided live music throughout the hotel, became friendly with Monte and began to sit with him late at night as the dinner and show crowds dispersed and the casinos filled with action. The show had been running over a year, an album of the show had just been recorded. Monte's workload lightened and he found himself wanting company, particularly in the evenings. He established a routine of nightly, open dinner parties with normally around a dozen friends. He drew in Sam and other performers to surround him and keep his loneliness at bay. The parties rolled until late, often roaring into the small hours. As they liked to say, "Anything goes." And anything did, including the dangerous game of targeting Johnny Rosselli for sport.

"Look at you," Monte looked at Johnny's gleaming silver grey hair and dark silver, silk suit, "You're all gray," he said, "Try a little color. Something. Peach..."

"Peach?"

"Anything but gray," Monte sipped his drink, taking his time, then added to Peter Marshall at the table, "Gray... He learned that in jail." It was late enough and people were soggy enough that the jibe shot around the table in little snorts and snickers. Johnny took the tease good-naturedly, laughing along with the others.

But days later, at another dinner, after bottles of liquor had come and gone, the idea of "anything goes" went a bit too far. Tommy Noonan, the brilliant, lightning-witted ad-libbing comic, was lit like a Roman candle. That night, Tommy had people doubled-over with laughter and slapping nearby tables in an effort to control themselves. They were weeping, cheeks fully glazed, aching and hoarse from laughter. Monte had his glasses off and was attempting to clean and dry them on the tablecloth while blind with laughter. Tommy leapt onto the small lounge stage, breaking into the middle of a song being performed by Freddie Bell and the Bellboys.

"Evening, Lays and Gentlemen," he swung into an improvised routine without his usual partner, Peter Marshall, who was still at the table with Monte and pals, recovering from Tommy's humor assault for the past 20 minutes. "Y'know this place is run by gangsters, right?" Tommy announced from the stage. The laughing dwindled to almost nothing. For the first time that night, Tommy had flopped. He couldn't believe it, "No, really, you know gangsters, they're all over the place," he continued. The laughter died. Marshall heard the death rattle, and was up out of his chair. He crossed to his partner on the stage as Johnny Rosselli was crossing the casino, heading right toward Tommy.

"It's full of killers." Tommy went on blithely, unaware that Johnny was 50 feet away. "Just look around," Tommy said as Marshall made it to the stage. Peter tried to save his partner from saying something unhealthy by pulling him into a hug but Tommy thought he was still on a roll and fought his way back to the microphone. "Like him," the comedian pointed at Johnny as the mobster passed the stage and went to the newsstand. Johnny hadn't been listening to Tommy, or pretended he hadn't. He continued to the newspaper stand, paid for his paper, folded it under his arm, and then definitely heard Tommy repeat, "… he's a killer." Johnny looked up from his papers at Tommy. Peter Marshall was now fully wrestling with Tommy at the microphone but stopped as Johnny made the return trip. Johnny just looked at Tommy as he passed, gave him a little laugh, a wag of his head and continued on to bed, unfazed.

Conversation sometimes dwindled in the small hours, as diners dispersed and Monte's second and third drink was drained. His pleasant, quick observations evaporated as the liquor took hold and he sat nearly mute, thinking of someplace else, miles away. He became like a volcano erupting under the sea, only a dark cloud on the surface marking its existence, obscuring the upheaval underneath. Increasingly, as the parties broke up, Monte made his way alone to the cage for a $1,000 stake in his nightly crap game with the Sirens. They sang to him from the green felt islands, luring him into their embrace.

Without Lou Lederer watching out for him, Monte followed the sirens' song all the way into the crushing rocks. As his beautiful Janey slept her precious life away at home, leaving his boys abandoned, and the desperate loneliness of his desert exile weighed on him, his gambling increased. Within a month, he owed tens of thousands more than he had and was getting in deeper every week. Johnny finally got wind of the problem and had the talk he meant to have when Lou first mentioned it.

Naturally with Johnny, the talk started out about Jane and the boys. He knew things, more than he said, about things at home with Jane. Problems with pills and alcohol were common but very much a private matter, not something discussed openly. Johnny eventually brought out the stack of markers that had been held at the cage under Monte's name – somewhere between $50,000 and $100,000 worth.

"I'm gonna make these go away," Johnny said. "But I gotta make a deal with you." The deal was that Jane got sent $4,000 of Monte's pay every week, leaving him $1,000 to live on. Naturally, Monte took the deal. People ended up in shallow, desert graves for much less, but even so, he burned with humiliation. He couldn't even manage to thank Johnny for his protection and generosity. In his mind, he was always one new idea away from big money and only temporarily Frank's salaried employee, meaning Johnny was still an errand-boy. Monte resented the favor.

Months after their little chat, it all ended suddenly. Johnny called him from Florida and gently cut the thread. The show was too expensive, they didn't need it anymore. It had done its job, the world's most exciting carpet joint was now well established. It was time for the show and Monte to go. Meyer was cutting expenses. At least that's what Johnny said. Maybe Johnny saw a problem developing with his gambling and also maybe he was perceptive enough to recognize the signals of Monte's unhappiness in his drinking and buying dinner every night for a dozen friends.

To Monte, although he was fired, he was free. He hoped he would never see Las Vegas again. Financially, in the two years at the *Trop*, he did a little better than break even.

When the money stopped, so did Monte's regular daytime schedule. He came back to Los Angeles. He was home at night after his meetings in the afternoon. Some days he had no meetings, he was home in his robe, reading in the den, tending to Jane. She was seriously addicted and frightened by her condition. Monte couldn't console her. The boys couldn't comfort her. She'd become frightened of them, of the crushing responsibility they represented when she couldn't even help herself. Monte was reduced to nursemaid and escort to a series of doctors who examined Jane and could find nothing wrong physically.

One morning, she and Monte were having breakfast in the dining room, the kids were off to school. She asked Monte quietly, "You finding any work?" and smiled at him. She was thin but still a miracle of beauty to Monte, and most other people. She showed no ill effect of the inner damage. Staying conscious and functioning was a long, slow contest of strength between her mind and her damaged nervous system. For weeks sometimes, she seemed to be winning the match. Monte saw the smile and forgot every fear. His Jane was still there, right in front of him, she still lived. He was home.

"I'm Ziegfeld of the Desert. That can pay quite well."

"How marvelous."

"Shall we go out? A trip somewhere?" he asked. Jane considered the proposition, "We could visit Sharon and Sol?"

"Well done." Monte said and quoted his old pal Joe E's theme song, "*It's easy to grin when your ship comes in,*
And you've got the stock market beat.
But the lad worthwhile is the man who can smile,
When his shorts are too tight in the seat.

Jane laughed for the first time in months, she said, "And he sings too. Such talent."

Sol returned home from work to entertain Monte and Jane. Sol loved any excuse to be out of the office. He missed Broadway, the action, the characters. He missed Monte most of all. Predictably, Sharon captured Jane and swept her to the far side of the property for a long, heart-to-heart. Sol and Monte stayed in Sol's office, sipped scotch and swapped stories of the scuffling days, the salad days. Sol and Monte never stopped pitching ideas to each other. They started out with business but always ended up with something just fun. They re-stormed the Bastille and captured their wives for a car ride.

In separate cars, they each fetched their kids out of Hawthorne elementary school, two Meadows and five Prosers. We all drove to an enormous bicycle store in Beverly Hills where every kid got to pick whatever bike they wanted. Sharon saw the store carried biking shorts and bathing suits as well. Everyone got a suit that Sharon picked. I was humiliated by the tiger striped, skin-tight suit she picked for me. They looked like fancy underwear and when modeled for fit in the store, clearly revealed my modest pickle. Sharon loved them and I tried to act thrilled for her, I couldn't break her heart. I wore them and burned with humiliation.

The bikes we packed in a delivery truck and followed the cars back to Sol and Sharon's place on Doheny. Jane declared the day, "St. Noodnik's Day", named for the patron saint of idiots who spend money recklessly on children. Monte relished his sainthood, and blessed Jane with constant attention. The four adults sat by the pool as their seven children invented worlds and chased each other up the driveway and across the front yard. Sharon rose to chase her grey miniature poodle from the house. She'd taken to chasing the poor beast with an electric prod.

"She's gonna kill that poor dog," Jane mused. "I hope." Sol blurted a laugh and Monte followed.

"How ya feelin', kid?" Sol asked Jane.

"Pretty good, Sol. It's been one hell of a nap."

"It's a tough fight." That was about all anyone wanted to say on the subject of Jane's drug addiction, and only Sol's status as family permitted even that much. "Why don't make another picture, Jane?" Sol needled.

"Oh God," the idea was so remote to her, Jane could only add, "I don't have the talent or the temperament. I should've stayed a dancer."

"I can get you work." Monte offered.

"Stay out of it, you," she teased her husband. Their eyes met. The conversation dropped and no one re-started it. Sharon returned from poodle police duty and dropped back into her seat. Jane gently draped her hand over Monte's hand, both hands resting on the white wicker table in front of him. They both turned to Sharon.

Jane directed the name, "Sgt. Preston of the Yukon…" at her panting friend. "Can't you just tell him, "mush"?"

Sharon was still annoyed, "Oh, I don't know what to do with that stupid dog."

"She always gets her dog." Monte mimicked the announcer's voice of the popular TV series. They were teasing Sharon and she took a moment to realize it. Through the performance, as Jane and Monte grinned happily, Jane's hand gripped Monte's tightly and his hand never moved.

"You two…" Sharon chided them, then laughed at herself.

But within days, the drugs forced their way back and pinned Jane's shoulders to her bed. The fight was simply too much for her and Monte was left to sit and watch her. For hours, he laid in his bed next to her and read books while Jane slept. He roused her every few hours and asked what he could get for her. The answer was always the same, "Water. Just water."

He'd lose patience eventually, "Fight it. You've got to fight this. Jane!"

"How?"

"Get up, walk. Come on, come with me now." He grabbed her under the arm and start to lift. She pushed him off. She slurred, "No! No! Leave me alone, will ya? I just need sleep…" and then the contradiction and confusion of it would hit her like a wooden plank.

"Please," he'd beg, "Please, get up out of bed, Jane. Do it for the kids."

The words were hard to find. Her tongue was thick and slow to respond. The words slid out, off rhythm and mangled, "I'll just fall down." She'd begun having seizures when she tried to walk and bore the scars of her endless attempts. Almost every journey by foot was paid for with a bruise or cut. Her exquisitely tuned dancer's body was as slack as old guitar strings.

The boys were playing "pepper" a base running game in the backyard. Mike practiced his beautiful hook slide, perfecting his technique to nick the corner of the base with his toe. He struck an iron sprinkler head at ground level with this extended knee. The metal tore a gash just under his kneecap that exposed white tendons and gushed blood. A scream went through the air that was joined by four others as the boys picked Mike up and carried him. Monte came running from the house.

After Mike was safely in the hospital and Monte was assured that the knee would be fine except for skin scarring, he roused Jane. She had slept through the whole incident. It was late afternoon. Monte roused her from her stupor and forced her to speak, to interact. For minutes, she was disoriented. Then as the world slowly came into focus, she responded. As she spoke, her terror became clear. She was convinced she was losing her mind as her father had done. She couldn't explain her behavior otherwise. When Monte suggested it was the pills, she fought as if her life depended on them. Pills were the only thing that kept her sane. If she couldn't sleep, she couldn't survive. Monte was exasperated. He couldn't fight her for the pills, the doctors had ordered them. He flew into a rage. His world was crumbling and he was out of ideas.

Chip came into the room, upset, having overheard the discussion. He wanted to know what was going on. He wanted to know why she was like that. He was angry, he demanded to know why she slept all day. He was a brave, little boy keenly aware of what was happening. Monte focused on Jane as she approached the point of nervous collapse. She had no idea why she was the way she was. She shook with fear.

"It's because of the kids," she said.

"No!" Chip protested, "It's you! We didn't hurt you…"

The slap came fast and hard across his mouth. Monte, in his one and only act of violence toward his family, slapped Chip to shut him up as he would to a dirty-mouthed drunk. Chip had never been hit or, outside of cartoons, seen anyone hit. He was just sticking up for the boys, the way Monte had told him to. He was telling the truth and protecting the others. He was doing exactly the right thing but got attacked for it. The pain, humiliation, betrayal and confusion of the slap touched off a fury that burned white. It sent Chip off crying in a horror all his own. Monte called after him to apologize but it was too late. He felt he was losing his mind too. The slap drove another fissure through the family bedrock that would never close.

That was it. Like a show closing out of town, the family was a bomb. It was quits. Monte was powerless and in a madhouse somehow of his own creation. He called Jim Morgan. They were going to the mattresses. Jim managed the crisis, dividing up the boys among their aunts and uncles in three different houses in Kingston. Baby Timmy and eldest Chip stayed with Nan and Jim on Albany Avenue, Jimmy went to Shirley's, Mike and Billy to Uncle Bill's on Pine Street. Jane was going to a hospital for help. Monte would stay in Beverly Hills and find work. Within days the boys were at Los Angeles Airport in new clothes. They had dinner together as a family, swordfish almondine, green beans and chocolate cake for dessert. Jane, quiet and twitching nervously as the sedatives wore off, said little. The boys all had notes in their top shirt pockets. Jane kissed them one by one and said goodbye, crying but trying not to cry. Monte hugged each one and handed them over to a stewardess who escorted the boys to the plane.

Less than an hour later, Jane walked unescorted toward her own flight. Monte offered to go with her but she refused. Visibly shaking as she descended deeper into withdrawal, she fought for control of herself and snapped at Monte that she was "not helpless" and could "face the music" on her own. Shouldering her shame, her devastation at the separation from her children and her terror of the madness now clattering through her bones, she asked her husband only once, looking down, quietly,

"Forgive me?"

He didn't hesitate. "Of course." He reached and pulled her into his arms. He did forgive her, "Always, Janey," he said, "… Always."

They kissed urgently, then broke off. She turned and walked toward her two-month sentence at Philadelphia General Hospital with a Catholic's lonely penitence knowing that she was a danger to her family and a failure as a mother and wife. As she walked from the terminal and crossed the runway toward the plane, a seizure convulsed her muscles and threw her hard onto the cement. An open gash that would need seven stitches poured blood over her twitching face under the morning sun. She was taken away by ambulance and a new diagnosis was added to her medical history, epilepsy. With her continuing luck of the Irish, a new drug had recently come on the market that appeared to be effective against seizures. It was called Tuinal, a combination of amobarbital and secobarbital, two barbiturates of the previous generation of drugs.

CHAPTER 39

THE NEW BREED

Jack Kennedy squeaked into office with Mo Giancana's help stuffing ballot boxes in Chicago and after Skinny D'Amato from Atlantic City drove down South with a few friends and a truckload of Old Joe's imported *Cutty Sark*. Skinny and friends greased the voters of West Virginia with bribes of either $20 cash and a quart of whiskey or straight cash of $40. The senior Kennedy bought these thousands of West Virginia primary votes right out from under Hubert Humphrey and set his son Jack up as the Democratic candidate. Mo then delivered the crucial Chicago districts, as promised in the Cal-Neva deal, which made candidate Kennedy into President Kennedy. It was a feat of ruthless political gamesmanship that stunned nearly everyone. Particularly the defeated Richard Nixon who felt he was simply out-robbed by people who were willing to use professional gangsters.

The young, handsome, fearless war hero strode into the oval office and the hearts of almost every American. He brought hope, eloquence and glamour to the Presidency. He brought the era they called Camelot. The achievement of the highest office in the world sent ripples of congratulations to Chicago from mobsters around the world. Everybody finally had a friend in the White House. And with their friend Old Joe behind the White House, they had a pipeline directly to the top man - a man who partied in Las Vegas and Hollywood as only the sex-addicted can. The only one not fully in the parade was hard-headed Bobby Kennedy – a stone in everyone's shoe.

To Jane in her hospital room in Philadelphia, Jack Kennedy was hope. He showed everybody that Irish Catholics were as good as anybody else. Unfortunately, she knew that he was every bit his father's son. Joe had been a wolf who devoured tender young actresses in Hollywood for years while playing power politics with the boys in backrooms, and Jack showed all the same traits. But as often happened in large Irish Catholic clans, one brother would carry a bag for the boys and another carried a gun for the cops. Perhaps the new Attorney General Bobby Kennedy would keep a lid on things. At any rate, Sinatra, one of the old Copa gang, was now a guest in the White House. How bad could things be? The news tickled both Jane and Monte who enjoyed watching the anti-Semitic and anti-Catholic Mayflower Republican bluebloods take a beating.

Jane made steady progress as she was gradually transferred to Tuinal. Epilepsy after the age of 30 was extremely rare, the cause and cure were unknown, but the new combination barbiturate seemed to be working at controlling her seizures. It wouldn't be known for years that withdrawal from barbiturates was the cause of first-time epileptic seizures in many adults. The cause of Jane's seizures was now being prescribed as the cure for her non-existent epilepsy, locking her forever into a twilight world of sedation enforced by her doctors.

Jane was one of about 5 million Americans, mostly women, who were now barbiturate addicts. Following Tuinal, a new compound, brand named Nembutal, was targeted toward women with a wide variety of indications including - *"...anxiety, restlessness, irritability, and adjunctive use in dermatosis, allergies, hyperthyroidism, psychoneuroses, cardiovascular disorders, toxemia of pregnancy, menopausal syndrome, pre-menstrual tension, nausea and vomiting, motion sickness, gastro-intestinal disturbances."* 852,000 pounds of barbiturates were manufactured that year of 1961, enough raw material for 6 billion one-grain barbiturate pills, or about 33 for every man, woman and child in the United States. For Jane, and coincidentally, the starlet who had signed on at Fox Studios on the same day, Marilyn Monroe, the comforting medication was now a necessity.

The good news was that, once again, Jane's short-circuited nerves were quieted. She was determined to fight her way back to her family and took strength from the news of the triumph of her once-shunned and despised people. An Irish Catholic Kennedy was in the White House.

Monte started over in the new Kennedy era. He went all the way back to the model of his first joint, *Monte's Clam House*. *Lucey's New Orleans* had a sparkling white and cobalt blue mosaic tile clam bar among 40 tables with a back corner of the dining area left open for musicians. It was a New Orleans clam house with walls of lush hanging plants copied from the *Mocambo*. The back tables were in the cool shade of stylish banana fronds, away from the sunlight dazzled bar. Ceiling fans turned slow circles.

The place was relatively cheap to put together and hopefully the cash mill that Monte needed quickly to keep up with the mortgage on Crescent Drive, hospital bills in Philadelphia and five boys at large. Located across the street from Paramount Studios, the place was a lunchtime destination for above-the-line artists and executives from the studio. Jimmy Cantillon, Johnny Rosselli's attorney, helped Monte set it up and Marshall Edson, the last owner of Billy Reed's *Little Club* in New York, was a partner.

The problem was almost everybody in Los Angeles went home at night. Especially actors, writers and directors who had early calls at the studio the next morning. Melrose Avenue was a ghost town after 6 PM. On top of that, a writer's strike that was supposed to last a week or two at the most, continued for five months, effectively shuttering the studio. Monte sat at the clam bar night after night and bought drinks for newspaper pals who would have no story to write about except what Monte could spin out of thin air. Failure hung over the place. Within a few months of its opening night, *Lucey's* was gone.

This time the call came from Frank himself. The two men hadn't spoken since the opening night of *La Vie en Rose*. Monte had written his old partner off after being passed on to his waterboy, Johnny, but was still relieved to hear from Frank and know that he wasn't badly damaged from the shooting. Frank was as polite as ever but distant. A lot had happened to both of them and neither wanted to talk about any of it. Monte was sorry he'd ever met Frank and Frank knew it. Government tax persecution on top of everything else was something Monte lived with like a disease, caught from Frank.

The call was Frank's way of continuing to pay his debt. He offered Monte the job of Entertainment Director at his and Meyer's first investment in Las Vegas, the *Thunderbird Hotel*. The job came with same pay, $5000 a week. Monte thought for only few seconds before signing on. He didn't have the energy or interest to play it cute with Frank, he knew him too well. Monte thanked his old partner. They quickly moved on to news of each other, then family news. Monte's news wasn't good and he didn't try to hide it. Dr. Feelgood had destroyed his Janey and there wasn't much anyone could do for her. Frank already knew most of it. Drugs were ruining friends of his and his business in general. He'd always been against them. They talked for a few minutes, all about family.

The black stillness of Beverly Hills at night was like the desert silence of Las Vegas. The wide, immaculate streets were empty and silent as Monte walked them before going to bed for the night. He slept alone in the Beverly Hills house that Saturday night. The house groaned when the temperature dropped and the sea air from the Pacific settled on the thin, shingle roof. Where had everybody gone? In Manhattan, he could wander into any bar and knock into a dozen drinking buddies on a Saturday. Where do you get a nightcap in Beverly Hills?

Have Gun Will Travel on CBS was over at 10:30. All three black and white channels went to static or a test pattern with an Indian chief's head at the center like a target. He switched the set off. In his separate double bed, he looked over at Jane's empty bed and thought he heard the sound of his five little monkeys clambering into their beds down the hall. But it was just the big house, emptied of life, contracting in the cold. What the boys loved the most was putting on shows for him in the living room. They threw themselves into a series of skits they made up on the spot. The singing was nonsense, the dancing was insane. It was the best show in town. The best he'd ever seen.

Monte brought Broadway musicals to Las Vegas and provided the moniker *"Broadway of the West"* for his newspaper pals to identify the Thunderbird's new attraction. *Flower Drum Song*, the Tony Award winning musical of 1959, opened Monte's run at the hotel. The orchestra was conducted by Richard Rodgers, the surviving member of *Flower Drum's* legendary creative duo, Rodgers and Hammerstein. *Flower Drum* was followed by *High Button Shoes* and *Anything Goes* playing alternately for the 8 and 11 PM shows. Monte brought Broadway to Las Vegas with one slight modification. Each show was cut down to 90 minutes. He knew his drinking, dining and gambling audience. They'd filled his saloons for years.

Chapter 40

Rain in the Desert

When Rosemary Clooney sang, it was like rain falling in the desert. Monte soaked in her voice and was moved beyond his usual enthusiasm for emotional melody. It was the singer that moved him now, sweeping over him suddenly like a cloudburst. He was shocked by the heartache as his impossible love sang only to him. He felt like he was a young man again, seeing his future wife for the first time, and then just as suddenly a married fool in love with someone else's wife. It didn't help that she was blond and Irish, like Jane, and had the same plain-spoken, good nature that grounded conversations in the immediate and familiar. She sparkled. She was a mirage, an oasis to his dying eyes, a salve for his breaking heart.

Neither one would share the unhappiness they knew at home, she with an abusive, jealous husband and he with a disintegrating wife. A shadow romance welled up between them. Flowers arrived at her room with no note attached. A jeweled bracelet, a "gift of the hotel", Monte presented to her over dinner. He could never, personally, give her such a gift. Yet as he made the romantic presentation, he read her face like a love sonnet, memorizing each expression of delight for his dark nights alone. It was a mute and stoic love, unsubstantial as mist, an unlit candle. Late one night, after dinner with a table full of noisy friends, Rosemary gave Monte the only love she could. Without accompaniment, she sang the song that told the story of Monte's life, the one his pal Gordon Jenkins gave to him, the one that became Gordon's own favorite and a classic for a few of the singers Monte had helped through the years like Sinatra and Nat King Cole. "As I approach the prime of my life," she sang, "I find I have the time of my life." It was her parting gift. She sang the whole song, all the verses, to him. Then kissed him goodnight, and goodbye.

Rosemary's engagement at the hotel ended the next day with a taxi disappearing into the heat waves radiating off of Route 91. Monte watched her taxi evaporate and then returned to his silent, dark hotel room. Rain never lasted long in Las Vegas.

The eccentric multi-millionaire caught up with Monte in rehearsals. He came into the showroom, looking slightly agitated, his wet shirt wet rumpled and askew. Howard Hughes took a seat next to Monte and re-introduced himself. They'd met before in several places around Hollywood but Howard was bad at recalling social details, so he made sure whomever he was talking to knew who he was. Monte asked what the story was with the wet shirt. Hughes looked at his shirt as if he'd just noticed it himself but didn't respond to the question.

Howard had moved into the *Thunderbird* several months earlier on the recommendation of his private investigator on retainer, Bob Maheu, but had only recently developed the habit of washing his shirt several times a day in the sink of the men's room just off the casino floor. It was one of the several odd habits the man was now exhibiting. Hughes didn't seem to think Monte was at all busy as he launched into his idea for picking up the pieces of the dashed Hilton Hotels contract. Monte explained patiently that it was over, ancient history. Hughes heard him but kept offering ways to make the deal work including his idea for a movie featuring a Hilton hotel as the setting for a Broadway musical. If Hilton didn't want it, someone else would. Monte listened and kept one ear on the rehearsal of

Anything Goes because you could never tell when Howard was in his right mind with a million dollar idea.

A few months earlier Howard had beaten Sidney Korshak and a few Chicago friends out of a cool million dollars. Howard had bought RKO Studios from Joe Kennedy two years earlier but didn't seem to be able to make it work. Where Joe had made steady money with modest thrillers and mysteries, Howard seemed to go off the deep end with one flop after another attributed to his incessant meddling in the productions. On one movie, he held up production for weeks while he designed the perfect brassiere to highlight Jane Russell's breasts. He brought in his best airplane engineers to design the garment with aerospace precision and materials. Oddly, that film also flopped. Howard put the studio up for sale and welcomed the offer from Korshak and friends - who had always been lucky in Hollywood. After Howard took the Chicago deposit of $1,000,000 dollars against a $3,500,000 dollar purchase price, he slyly let slip the provenance of the new owners to Billy Wilkerson of the *Hollywood Reporter*. The leak was not immediately traced back to Hughes and the public outcry over a major studio being covertly owned by shady out-of-town characters was predictably a deal-killer for the publicity-averse Chicagoans. Billy kept the secret of his source and Howard kept the million. But the Windy City boys were not fooled for long. In earlier times, Howard might have gotten a visit from Mickey Cohen offering a .45 caliber lozenge to help him cough up the deposit, but now Sidney Korshak advised his clients patience. A whale the size of Howard Hughes, who swam in the same waters as the *Outfit*, would eventually make a mistake and Sidney would be waiting. Howard's first punishment was that he was not welcome at any of the Chicago controlled hotels in Vegas, thus forcing the millionaire to Frank and Meyer's *Thunderbird*. His second punishment took longer but validated Korshak's strategy.

Revenge for RKO came in the form of fleecing Hughes out of over $5,000,000 by inflating the price of the *Desert Inn* when the millionaire was in the process of buying that hotel. Within three years, Sidney Korshak had not only recouped his clients'

$1,000,000 loss, he added a dividend of $4,000,000 more. This revenge robbery further boosted Sidney's position from wise counsel to rainmaker. His coronation also accelerated the *Outfit's* transition into legitimacy, as Meyer had done for the *Syndicate*. It was increasingly clear to the two organizations, that like many other large conglomerates, more money could be made with lawyers than with leg-breakers. Violence was to be used only when all legal means were exhausted and blackmail, intimidation and corruption had failed.

For the time being, as persona non-grata throughout most of Las Vegas, Howard kept Monte company at the *Thunderbird* while he bounced from one increasingly bizarre idea to the next. Monte's soft spot for misfits pushed him to protect Howard while the man continued to show up at rehearsals to ply Monte with ideas. Now that he had RKO back, he was anxious to find something that would make a good movie and also full of ideas to improve Monte's stage shows. Monte continued to assure Howard that his ideas were "really something" while making sure the man had a dry shirt from the show's wardrobe so he wouldn't develop pneumonia in the hotel's air conditioning. The casts of the shows began referring to Howard as Monte's pet millionaire and offered to help feed him while Monte got some work done.

In New York City, Toots Shor took a $7,000,000 loan from Hoffa's Teamster's Fund to open his new joint next to "21" at 33 East 52nd Street. Within weeks he was wondering where his staple of nightcrawling sports writers and their subjects had gone and how he was going to cover the nut of the place. Nearly alone at the bar that he had recreated exactly from his old saloon, he lamented, *"On fight nights you couldn't get close to the bar. Now all those sportswriters live in New Jersey or someplace like New Rochelle. Now these young crums cover something at the Garden or a ball park and rush home for their malted milk and go to sleep, I guess. Show me ten of these new crums and I don't recognize but five or six. What's happening to the world?"*

Lew Walter's had closed his *Latin Quarter* the year before and followed Monte to Las Vegas where his *Folies Bergere* had taken the place of Monte's *Tropicana Holiday* at the *Tropicana*. *El Morocco*, the only true competitor to the Copa of the first class nightclubs, was uprooted and moved two blocks west to a new, dowdier home at 307 East 54th. The younger people who once would have filled the *Latin Quarter* and *El Morocco* were now flocking to see Elvis Presley's new movie *Blue Hawaii*. The soundtrack to the film reached #1 on the album charts, where it stayed for 20 weeks. It sold an unprecedented 2,000,000 copies and was Presley's best-selling album to date.

The very heartbeat of night time entertainment quickened and moved from Broadway to Las Vegas – for young and old. Elvis had taken to hard, late-night partying while shooting his new movie *Viva Las Vegas* with the help of energy and mood enhancing injections. Nearby at the *Sands*, the Rat Pack with Peter Lawford, recently President Kennedy's brother-in-law, wrote a new chapter in nightlife. Lawford secretly ushered the new commander-in-chief into and out of non-stop Vegas parties, setting him up with starlets including Marilyn Monroe and Judith Exner, Mo Giancana's sometime girlfriend. The Prez was also helped along by "vitamin shots" that made him forget about his bad back.

In New York, prospects for the Copa under the reign of Little Augie continued to dim along with the other nightclubs. Augie had thrown his allegiance to Frank Costello, deserting Vito Genovese's crew, after Frank's botched assassination. He calculated that Genovese would be on the run, desperate and with a short expiration date. He was enjoying the Copa one spring evening in spite of the dark skin of the newest Columbia Records artist Johnny Mathis, a younger, velvet-voiced Nat King Cole, crooning on stage. Mathis carefully recreated the silky sound of his new hit record in the club by bringing his own orchestra with him. The Copa, alone among the top clubs, could still afford this extravagance. Little Augie and Jules Podell reluctantly tolerated Mathis under the mob's newly evolved policy of racial tolerance for moneymakers. Augie did his best to ignore the handsome, dark-skinned Mathis, while his escort, the beautiful Janice Drake, enjoyed the music. Augie's purgatory of racial integration was interrupted by a call, an invitation to a restaurant in Queens with news about his push to get a piece of Meyer's Havana gambling operations. He and Drake left Mathis in mid-song. They climbed into Augie's black Cadillac that was always illegally parked in front of the Copa. Little Augie never made it to the meeting. He and Drake were found later near LaGuardia airport with several bullet holes in their heads. He had miscalculated Vito's desperation and Frank's waning power. With Little Augie gone and Frank pushed further into retirement, the Copa became essentially unaligned. Even as it continued to enjoy sell-out weeks with the hottest new singers and comedians, it couldn't match the profit margins of even the smallest casino and so declined in importance along with Frank's position in the *Syndicate*.

Jules Podell finally held all the cards but in a losing hand. His strategy was to just hold on, keep the quality of the food up and hope that someday, somehow, things would turn around. He clung to the familiar, to people who knew entertainment, booking anybody *William Morris* sent him without comment - even Johnny Mathis - the melancholy crooner and black fairy he detested almost as much as weepy Johnny Ray.

Downtown from the Copa, in the venerable *Stork Club*, Don Bader, bandleader at the club for years, held up an ad he saw in the *New York Times* offering hamburgers and French fries for $1.95. It was an ad Billingsley had placed to boost the once-exclusive *Stork's* lunch traffic.

Bader held up the ad for his musicians to see and said sadly, "Guys, look at this. It's all over."

CHAPTER 41

LIGHTS OUT

Jane arrived at the great, white, wedding cake house at 346 Albany Avenue in the pouring rain. The budded lilac bushes nodding under the spring downpour partially concealed Nan waiting on the side porch, anxious to see her gentle daughter again. She needed to see for herself, to look deeply into the green eyes the color of sunlight on the Irish Sea and make sure the strong, confident fighter she had raised and surrendered to the tentacled world of glamour was fully restored.

Jane crossed the lawn, shrouded against the rain, steady and sure. She glided up the porch steps and suddenly stood like a waking dream before her mother. The effect was electric. Jane looked like a movie star. She looked like the girl of 21 who was off to Hollywood for the first time, but there she stood, defying the lost years, the mother of five, 42 years old, without a line on her face or a gray hair. Fat tears of relief and joy spilled down Nan's cheeks as she hugged her Janey to her. Everything was going to be alright. The years of darkness were gone now and Jane's sons were waiting in the house to see her.

Quietly as always, from the first bedroom on the right at the top of the curved stairs, where she and five-year-old Timmy now slept, Jane once again included herself into the housework of the rambling mansion. There was always plenty of housework with four adults including a single gentleman boarder and various bands of children marauding through the grand house – one of the procession of impressive, hotel-sized homes surrounded by vast lawns that presided like well-fed bankers over the traffic on Albany Avenue.

On Sundays the population in the house swelled to ten children, half of them named Proser, and eight adults, all of them loading up plates for their biggest meal of the week from a lace covered dining table the size of a small truck – pancakes, scrambled eggs, bacon, sausage, biscuits, oatmeal, cornmeal, milk and coffee – all you could eat, sit anywhere. For the Ball women, half of Sunday morning was devoted to church and cooking, the late morning went to cleaning up the morning meal. This was their day of rest. Even so, the sisters jockeyed for position to take on the grittiest job of scrubbing the pots and pans, showing the readiness for mean work learned at their mother's side.

Jane was nearly silent, speaking only a little to her sisters and usually only when encouraged by them. She ate almost nothing, often only bread and retired to her room soon after the cleaning chores were done. She was a ghost of herself, a penitent who blamed herself for sins only she knew of. Late at night she wandered the big house, sometimes reading alone in the kitchen.

The Proser boys finished their school year in Kingston, while Jane came around again to the heavy harness of day-to-day management of her five energetic boys. As summer rolled in, Jane's eldest sister, Sis, and her family of four boys and one girl, who had been caretaking at the farm, moved into a 3 story frame house in Lumberville, 2 miles north of New Hope on the Delaware. The Proser family packed once again for the car trip from Kingston, down the Hudson, past New York City and through the farmlands of central New Jersey. Jane saw the trip clearly in her mind and was anxious to start, afraid her nerves would falter and scuttle her return to normalcy forever. She saw them drive cross the Delaware on the narrow iron bridge from New Jersey into Pennsylvania and turn down the river road through New Hope. The final leg was the steep dirt road to the top of Jericho Mountain, to home.

Monte had come the day before to double-check on Jane's readiness and pilot the car that would carry everything he loved in the world. No one, not even Jane herself, could know whether she was truly ready but no one doubted her determination.

In their bedroom the night before, even Monte seemed to finally lose his confidence in her. He'd let himself hope too many times.

"How can this work, Janey, leaving you alone again," he meant during the long intervals between his returns from Nevada and New York.

"It just has to, that's all." She had nothing but her stubbornness to rely on.

Monte circled around again cautiously. He'd glimpsed another life, even though it was sheer fantasy, with Rosemary Clooney. They didn't have to torture Jane with a responsibility she couldn't meet. He tested her to see if the woman he loved still existed. "The boys can stay in school here. You don't have to take all this on…"

But she was having none of it, "Why don't I just die? And you can just go if you want to. You're sick of this." That was all the confirmation he needed. She was still fighting, even against him, if necessary. "I'm going to be fine," she stated flatly.

Monte was relieved, "Okay," he said, "Okay, Janey."

The farm welcomed them again into its quiet, fragrant and lonely embrace. The swarms of children and cars of Kingston were replaced by the endless, rasping monotony of crickets broadcasting their coded messages all day and into the night. Summer smells of the city, of tar and grease, were now pine and hay and well-water on hot fieldstone as the swimming pool took endless days to fill from a garden hose, lilac near the house and skunk cabbage in the tiny marsh at the bottom of the lower field. Sidewalks and fire hydrants faded from memory before open fields and spring-fed ponds sprouted with watercress and golden-eyed frogs.

Monte's weeks in Nevada always ended with a plane trip to New York, then a one-hour train ride to Trenton. The exhausting trip was aided by a prescription of the latest sleeping pill, Nembutal. On the first drive back from Trenton to Jericho Mountain and his reunited family, he teased his wife, "Once more, with feeling," he said as she once-again drove toward home.

Carrie Dawson sat in the back seat, her black felt traveling hat shading her mahogany face, her eyes drawn to the passing bright, green corn fields. Monte had assured her that all was well again, that Jane's illness had been diagnosed and cured, that the boys were all asking for her. He knew that this was her weak spot and almost nothing else he said mattered. The boys, Carrie's boys, needed her. She had seen them growing in her dreams and in the letters that had kept arriving from them to 400 Convent Avenue. She remembered them as she watched her Harlem neighborhood of Sugar Hill turn ugly and fierce from the plague of heroin. Her own future retreated to long nights alone and a lonely pew seat in the Abyssinian Baptist Church. All the good men seemed to have left Harlem. Only the innocent love of her boys and the eternal love of Jesus Christ gave her a reason to hope for better days. And now the bright faces and unstained hearts of her boys were coming back to her.

The farm rang again with new life. Monte drank in the spring air swirling down through the giant cypress by his bedroom window. Resting late into the morning, he awoke into a state of grace, a feeling of hope. Jane was returned to them. She would hold together this time, he thought. The doctors had finally found the problem and had the medication to help her. He allowed himself the thought, rolled it over in his mind like a soothing balm, a delicious dream. It was possible. They'd somehow found their way back together. They'd pulled the family back from the brink of disintegration.

The vision persisted as Jane took charge of getting the house re-stocked and sorted out and Carrie re-established discipline in the boys. Carrie attempted a similar enforcement with Jane, who yielded to Carrie's rules in the kitchen, but never fully capitulated. Outside the kitchen, Jane still commanded. Fields needed mowing, handymen were called. Jane bought the boys clothes and as the summer lengthened, registered them all for school, getting everyone their immunization shots, lunch bags and the thousand other items of a student – times five.

Monte put his mind to the buildings on the property, first insisting that the boys help paint the barn that was long ago renovated by Walter Bachelor into guest quarters. The boys were apprenticed to a professional painter and somehow the project got done in spite of them. Every two hours or so, they ran off to take a swimming break. They were an incorrigible and undisciplined rabble when out of Carrie's direct supervision, a ravenous, roaming horde of mischief-makers over whom Monte ruled with benign neglect and little discipline.

Horace Greeley McNab, a bantam-sized Boston Irishman of inestimable blarney, an advance publicity agent for touring Broadway productions, had moved into the little stone farmhouse next door, down the mountain overlooking Eagle Road. He and his performer wife, Hilda, visited often for afternoon tea and brought news of show business and the wider world. They looked out for the boys and helped Jane with everything. McNab was loud, brash and most completely entertained when confounding children. He claimed to have the most beautiful feet in the world and was eager to display them on a special red velvet pillow to the boys' classmates at school, if he was invited to. The boys always declined. He gave his Bassett Hound, Saucy, frequent rides in the front seat of his Jaguar XK 150, claiming it cheered her up. Mary Margaret McNab, a gray poodle, sat in his lap at home, reportedly consulting with him on the great questions of the day by telepathy. Horace and Hilda, and Monte's friend Harry Rubin, the sculptor who lived nearby, just beyond the covered bridge, were the neighborhood. Harry's Covered Bridge Road ran for a half mile up and down the hilly cornfields then over a woodland creek and into the shadow of the sacred covered bridge where all wishes, if wished hard, silently and secretly, came true. The road dropped off steeply after the bridge, then curved into the woods up to where Harry and his exquisite Japanese wife and baby daughter lived. Just up the hill from Harry's house, George Nakashima, also a well-known artist, fashioned the local black oak into museum-collectible furniture. Writer Pearl Buck, Oscar Hammerstein, Richard Rogers and Moss Hart all lived nearby.

Life couldn't be more pleasant, Monte observed. Even with his 2000 mile bi-weekly commute, it was a life of infinite pleasure. It colored every day. Even the ones in Las Vegas.

"Every day is Christmas," Bill Collins said, greeting Monte in the lobby of the *Thunderbird*. Bill directed shows around town, usually musical revues using large girls in very small costumes. The two fast friends were off to breakfast at the new *Thunderbird Downs*, a quarterhorse racetrack newly built sparing no expense. The quarter-mile oval was a small-scale thoroughbred track where the cheetah of horses raced in blistering sprints that were over in about 30 seconds. In the afternoon, Bill and Monte would return from the track, get some steam and a massage at the hotel and then have lunch. A very agreeable schedule.

Lunches, like dinners, were generally large social and business events. Lunch was where the business of running two Broadway shows simultaneously was reviewed and analyzed. Orders were issued and proposals were heard. Preparations were made for the arrival of *South Pacific* to replace *Anything Goes* in the rotation of shows as Monte's *"Broadway of the West"* continued to populate the *Thunderbird's* showroom. Through it all, Bill marveled at the energetic joy, the elemental delight Monte had in being alive and among friends. The Broadway veteran was precise and thorough in his stagecraft and sure of himself when it came to the art of musicals. He knew what he wanted and how to ignore outbursts from temperamental artists. He was an old pro, grateful when he succeeded and philosophical when he failed and scrupulously honest with himself about both. Bill Collins watched and learned simple happiness from his mentor – a man comfortably at the controls of his life and cheerful in his journey. Every day was Christmas and every night was New Year's Eve.

But a racetrack, even a small one, was a racetrack, and to Monte it qualified as an investment. He never invested money in the back of the house for ownership, only into the front cashier's window for luck. That was his very unprofitable line in the sand. He wanted no part of the gambling business. His likely partners in any gambling venture soured him immediately to the idea of ownership. He would never invest with his employers or invite them into true partnership, even though the return was plentiful and assured. They could only buy his services, never his allegiance.

So gambling remained an open drain that sucked away whatever money he had in his pocket, and being on a salary, what he had to play with was small change - a constant aggravation. Throwing money at horses or dice scratched that growing itch for as long as the winning lasted, then predictably, plunged him into the hangover of losing. Like his pals Billy Wilkerson, Joe E. Lewis and dozens of others, gambling had become an adrenalin addiction that was steadily eroding his future. Billy was eventually able to kick the obsession, Monte and Joe E. never could. It nearly cost Joe E. his life.

The comedian was playing the Beverly Hills Country Club in Cheviot, Ohio for his customary $15,000 a week. Practically all of it was going to the local racetrack operators or blackjack tables at the club. He commented on his luck in his act, "I've been on such a losing streak that if I had been around I would have taken General Custer and given points."

The fever of losing was on him so badly one evening, that he insulted his blackjack dealer for dealing too slowly. He had to quickly catch up to the money that he'd lost, knowing his luck had to turn soon. "Faster, goddammit!" he yelled. He lost. He doubled his bet into the next slow-arriving hand and lost again. He exploded at the cards, the dealer and his foolish self. The dealer talked back and Joe went around the bend, creating such a public scene that the dealer, John Augustine, was fired on the spot. That night Augustine bought himself a seat in the front row for Joe's act. He started in on Joe as soon as the comedian walked on stage. The heckler was loud and hateful. Joe was used to tipping over happy drunks, not stalkers, and was caught off-guard. The bouncers got to Augustine and had him half way out the door when he shook them off and pulled a .45. Joe hit the deck and crawled offstage before Augustine got off a shot.

"You only live once," Joe E. later said, "but if you do it right, once is enough." Long after the gunplay was forgotten, his money troubles got even worse. He added to his act, "I don't like money, but it quiets the nerves." and "It doesn't matter if you're rich or poor, as long as you've got money." Monte and Joe had both been at the gambling tables far too long and now were on the wrong side of the house odds.

CHAPTER 42

THE CONCERTINA CLOSES

In his early retirement, Frank Costello could still afford the luxury of playing the horses, but with so much time on his hands, even days at the track couldn't absorb it all. Golf took up much of the rest. What had once been a tactic to avoid surveillance became his devotion. Occasionally he would still take Jules Podell along to keep tabs on the Copa for old time's sake, but mostly he played slow rounds with his uncle, also named Frank, childhood friends from the old neighborhood in Manhattan, representatives from Meyer and neighbors from Sands Point, Long Island. Like Monte, he now had a very agreeable schedule. At least it had been since he and Meyer had outfoxed Vito Genovese for the final time.

They maneuvered the ambitious Vito into the middle of a heroin bust they had organized with the Feds. With Vito now enduring his retirement in a federal penitentiary, Frank enjoyed his own retirement on the links while Meyer feigned retirement in his modest tract home in Florida. That lasted until Bobby Kennedy turned Joe Valachi, a low-level button man and new prison colleague of Vito's, into a state's witness. Now Frank's phone was ringing again.

Things were getting out of hand as Valachi sang like Caruso and Bobby pounced on every scrap of information Valachi offered, hoping to rouse Congress to action. It worked. Valachi's last words to Congress before he stepped down from his testimony made headlines. The gangster looked slowly across the faces of the senators and said, "Gentlemen, I'll say this. Someday the mob is going to put a man in the White House, and he's not going to know it until they present him with the bill." That day had already arrived, as Bobby knew very well. He was frantic to destroy the men who held the bill before they presented it to his brother.

With Congress' backing, Kennedy launched a full frontal attack. Six new federal investigative bureaus were opened in major cities and seven new anti-crime laws were passed that resulted in, among other things, the dismantling of the nationwide telegraphic betting system, the wire services - an important income to many of Frank's friends. Even so, at 6 billion in yearly income, the *Commission* – the union of Frank and Meyer's New York *Syndicate* with Giancana's Chicago *Outfit* - was now not only larger than U.S. Steel, it was larger than the U.S. Department of Defense – a $4.5 billion budget for Defense versus the $6 billion in *Commission* income.

The loss of the race wire was small potatoes. The real threat was that Bobby Kennedy wasn't going to stop. He had declared his intentions in his first press conference, but everyone thought it was for show, like attorney general Tom Clarke before him. Bobby said, "If we do not on a national scale attack organized criminals with weapons and techniques as effective as their own, they will destroy us."

The weapon he chose had been expertly sharpened by Kefauver, McLellan and Hoover. He chose the IRS and plunged it straight at the heart of the *Commission*. IRS man-hours in organized crime cases went from under 9,000 to over 96,000 in two years, resulting in 288 tax cases in 1963 against the nearly 5,000 members and associates of the *Commission*.

The phone callers were getting desperate. They wanted Frank to work his magic, to somehow get to Bobby, through Old Joe Kennedy. Frank was dragged back in to do these favors and mend the bridges that had been burned with the Genovese unpleasantness. But no sooner had Frank gotten Joe Kennedy on the golf course for a good talking-to, than both Kennedy boys committed a much bigger and completely unforgivable sin. They had double-crossed everyone - Meyer, Sam Giancana, Carlos Marcello, Santos Trafficante and Johnny Rosselli - by not backing them up at the Bay of Pigs.

Because Jack and Bobby Kennedy went weak when the time came for action, Havana was lost forever. Adding injury to the insult of disloyalty, Johnny was nearly killed during the pre-invasion phase. The Cuban Navy sank his speedboat carrying him and his handpicked sniper team. The team had been tasked with the "executive action" of the invasion, which was to assassinate Castro in a triangulated cross-fire, decapitating the Cuban government. This was a standard operating procedure perfected in Central America to secure compliant governments and cheap fruit for *Commission* affiliate, United Fruit.

Johnny was fished out of the Caribbean with two of his surviving snipers, narrowly avoiding capture by the Cubans. Meyer, Sam, Carlos and Santos lost millions on the small army of Cuban fighters recruited from Miami that lay scattered across the Cuban beaches.

Jack and Bobby Kennedy had betrayed everyone, and now not even Frank could help them. The news of all this was so devastating to Old Joe that soon after he heard it, after two weeks of frantic phone calls and screaming arguments with Bobby, he had a stroke that paralyzed his right side and robbed him of speech. Unfortunately for him, it didn't affect his comprehension. He knew something had to happen to settle this score, but he was powerless to negotiate or even beg for forgiveness. The merciless stroke left him with just enough power to watch and suffer.

Carlos Marcello had a nightclub in Dallas managed by Jack Ruby, a local operator in gambling and protection – a hot-tempered but reliable man originally from Chicago. It would happen there.

From Las Vegas, Monte ran his family as well as he could over the phone. Jane was often lucid when he called, but sporadically too groggy to speak for more than a few minutes. When he heard her slurring, it put him in such a flat panic that he snapped orders at anyone who then spoke to him. She was slipping away again and he could only blame himself for believing yet again, that she'd finally put her demons behind her. The pressure set him to pacing in his room, smoothing his hair compulsively, as if putting every hair on his head in order also might help put his world in order. Eventually he paced directly to the nearest crap table where he could scream at his filthy luck.

His growing agitation was not overlooked. Bill Collins bought him a polished, alabaster disk called a Worry Stone. The egg shaped disk was flat on one side, indented on the other for a thumb. The device was reputed to be a medically effective stress-reliever. Monte held it in his pocket as he'd once done with a rabbit's foot for luck, rubbing it constantly. The rabbit's foot worked better, his dice stayed ice cold.

Eddie Fisher hadn't sold many records since Milton left him standing in front of the Tropicana years ago. Since then, Milton had also begun to disintegrate. He accused Eddie of sabotaging him and cutting him out of deals. Monte's rock in stormy seas, Milton Blackstone, was crumbling into the same dark ocean of madness that was consuming Jane. There were no deals to steal. Eddie's records sat on store shelves until RCA eventually came around and took them back.

But the years of failure and humiliation had a wonderful effect on Eddie. He finally grew up. He recorded an album As Long As There's Music with recent hits from Broadway including Maria and Tonight from West Side Story, a cover of Darin's hit Mack the Knife and even the Catskill perennial Hava Nagila. He'd dropped his boyish over-emoting and sang in deeper, more comfortable ranges, delivering insightful interpretations of the lyrics. But no one bought the new album. At 29, Eddie was a confirmed has-been, except for his one, original, true believer. Milton heard the maturity that had developed in his protégé and ignored the years of failure. He wanted Eddie working for their company again but was temporarily stymied. He would not speak to Eddie directly. Instead, he asked Monte to speak for him, to be the go-between. Together they would come up with something for Eddie, a comeback.

To Monte, this sounded like the kind of long shot that was a loser, even if you won. Milton spoke at Monte without breathing, words clattering out of him like a machine. Monte's level-headed, unassuming friend stated his intentions as if they were commands, almost like a different person without the charm and generosity Milton had practiced for so many years. Monte had no choice. He had to help. He couldn't afford to lose Milton too. He told him to send Eddie's record before he'd agree to anything.

Eddie's next record, Eddie Fisher; Live at the Winter Garden is by most accounts, the best album the singer ever made. The young veteran of countless nightclub and theatre performances sang with confidence and ease, achieving a bell-like tone that rang clearly. He had finally become a man and a very good singer. But that didn't help sales. The album came out on a warm day in May, 1963 and laid on store shelves like unrefrigerated lox. There would be no comeback for Eddie.

Monte's string had also run out. Jane was in an unstoppable downward spiral again, medicating herself at will and overdosing. The money was gone and only a tenuous salary from Las Vegas supported them. The world had changed so much that even Toots, with his brand new multi-million dollar joint couldn't make a go of it, and everybody in the world loved Toots Shor.

But still, in spite of everything, it was early spring and the earth bounded into life with his five boys commanding all they surveyed at the tops of their voices. His oldest, Chip, was bright and ambitious like his father, and would be going on to Boston University the following year, something that grandfather Charles would finally have acknowledged as success. As grim as his marriage and his prospects outside of Las Vegas were, Monte rested like a hobo in a hayfield, seemingly undisturbed by his ragged life. When he was home, Jane forced herself back to life. In spite of quaking hands and a haunted mind, she rehearsed the part of housewife hoping to become authentic one day.

Monte had enough for now. He stood by his tottering wife and waited. The great concertina would open again someday and breathe music and possibilities back into the world. Until then, he read books by the armload while sitting on his front porch, trolling for his next project. Tiring of that, he directed whichever son was closest to make him tea or, if he already had tea, to do 20 push-ups. Eventually the regular commutes to Las Vegas drove him from his daydreams and his hobo's itinerary. Whatever was next would come, somehow, it always did.

The days of summer shortened and lost their color. The boys were all in school and the house on the hill, Jericho Mountain, fell silent again. Even the crickets left, leaving only the lonely crows in barren trees. Monte was in Vegas, sending money sporadically - Johnny was no longer his chaperone, sending his salary home while putting him on an allowance.

As the nights of late November stretched out, the isolation crept in under the front door of the old farmhouse with the winter chill. Stealthily, the trembling fear came for her again and alone, without Monte by her side, Jane was powerless against it. Something was turning over inside her, spilling thoughts that had been so calmly arranged back into chaos. It now took two capsules to get to sleep instead of the single capsule she'd been prescribed.

The news arrived from the principal of Woodhill Elementary School. The phone rang and Jane listened while the principal told her that classes were being suspended for the rest of the day. She should come and pick up her two youngest boys, President Kennedy had been shot and killed.

She turned on the television to Walter Cronkite, listening to the narration of the end of hope. Horror was loose again in the world, shattering skulls with high-powered bullets and spraying gore over any daydreams of happiness. The brutality of the attack was overwhelming. It stopped her breath. She wept for the man and for herself, for the world that would never find peace and for the hope that could never return. The hardhearted world was a useless place, too evil to bother with, too painful and frightening to endure any longer than necessary.

Bobby Kennedy got the news in Washington. "I always thought it would be me," he said. "I didn't think they'd go after Jack." He didn't elaborate on who "they" were.

Jane drove up to the front of Woodhill Elementary in the Ford station wagon, silk scarf over her hair, tied under her chin, in mourning. Her eyes were stung red with salt, like everyone else in America. The ride home was silent. November had the final word that day – barely a whisper through the dry grass. It was lockdown and lights out, winter.

No sound came from her bedroom for two days. If she was up at all, it was late at night after everyone else had been asleep for hours. When Monte called from the *Trentonian Hotel,* Jane was too far gone to pick him up. He hired a cab to get home.

He found Jane sprawled as she usually was in a chaos of bed sheets, kicked and tossed off in her restless sleep. He revived her, first picking her up out of bed and cradling her in his arms like a newborn baby, pacing the bedroom while he gently shook her awake. He cooed to her, dissolving the sticking tar of anesthesia. He sat her up on the edge of her bed and ordered soup from Chip, who made a beeline for the kitchen. The house went on alert, no fighting, no yelling.

When she had eaten a few spoonfuls of soup and had a drink of water, she asked, "How did it happen?" as if Monte could tell her everything she needed to know. He had no idea how the president had been assassinated. A nut, a Communist, he'd heard. But by the end of the week, when Jack Ruby silenced Lee Harvey Oswald, the angles pointed to the *Commission.* How or why, he didn't want to know, but Jane did. She had to know. "How did it happen?" she asked a dozen different ways. Eventually, she figured out what Monte was then hiding. Somehow, his employers had a hand in what happened. The realization dried the words in her mouth and exhausted her. It laid her out like a lead vest. She now had no interest to do anything, even when awake.

Monte was reduced to begging, "Please Jane, you can't stay like this. Please. Janey. Please." Like the times before, Jane was beyond words. Monte forced her through the motions of life, refusing her all but one pill a day and hectoring her with food that she refused. He was losing the same battle that he and each of his sons had fought and lost a thousand times before, but he would not admit defeat.

In spite of his efforts to clean out the pills and face her screaming wrath in withdrawal, Jane had pills hidden everywhere. When briefly awake, her heart felt only grief at her hero's assassination while her mind sensed only fear, and she was soon gone again. She simply left, abandoning all but the most essential duties of her life to sleep in her own, shadowed world. Her sons and her husband waited without hope. Every few hours Jane would try to make it to the bathroom, but would only make it a few steps before collapsing and injuring herself. If Monte was out of the house, it was up to whichever son or sons heard the collision to go upstairs and face the scene of blood and sometimes broken bones.

Monte'd been home for a week and was exhausted from tending to Jane. It seemed that no matter what he did, Jane soon slipped back into an emotional catatonia, joyless and silent. He got her functioning again, but without enthusiasm. She was bruised and broken but speaking finally. As he did on alternate weeks, he turned his life over to Carrie for safekeeping and got in the car to begin the 9-hour commute to Las Vegas. He drove himself to the parking lot across from the Trenton station, an unlit, cement rectangle next to a low-rent residence hotel.

He stepped from the car and before he could lock the door with his key, the first blow from an iron pipe glanced off his head, nearly breaking his wrist and knocking him backwards. Two slender young men rushed at him from the shadows, one came up from behind but hesitated. As the first attacker reached him, Monte saw the second swing coming at his head and dodged just enough so the pipe missed his head and shoulder and landed on his side, breaking two ribs. Monte swung his leg up into the crotch of the pipe-swinger, lifting the boy off the ground and collapsing him like a broken balloon, sending the pipe flying against the car. The second attacker was on Monte, landing his full body weight and momentum into Monte's cheek with his fist. Two lower teeth flew into the air. Monte wrapped the arm that hit him into a bear hug and broke it at the elbow. The third jumped him from behind and wrestled him off balance, head first into the concrete. Monte found this man's groin with his elbow, several times, then turned over and went to work on the man's ribs with his left hook. Powered by shoulders and a forearm as thick as a blacksmith's, his pile-driver fist stove-in the man's right side, breaking almost every rib.

When the police arrived, Monte was sitting up against the back wheel of the Ford. Two slender, young men lay in the clutches of agony ten feet away. The second attacker had hobbled away before they arrived, cradling his broken arm.

At the hospital, they cleaned and stitched Monte's scalp, wrapped his ribs and wrist and gave him a cane. They told him to see his dentist about the missing teeth. They gave him painkillers and Tuinal and told him to get some sleep. On the ride back to the train station in the cops' cruiser, he narrated his victory for the officers like it was a prizefight. The painkillers numbed him and loosened his tongue as he proudly waved the fat fold of 800 dollars in cash he had successfully defended from the muggers. The two cops laughed with him as they carried his bags to the train platform while he finished the story for their report, adding color where he thought it needed it. He was on a roll and felt 20 years younger. He invited the two officers to look him up at the *Thunderbird* whenever they came to Vegas. The ecstasy of surviving mortal combat lifted him up. He'd just beaten the living shit out of three much younger men and wasn't feeling much pain. All in all, it was a pretty good night.

After the train ride, he missed his flight and stayed up most of the night at LaGuardia airport. Thirteen unlucky hours later, he limped out of the desert sun into the cool, hushed *Thunderbird* casino. He'd left his luggage at the baggage claim of McCarren airport and gotten straight into a cab, arriving at the hotel at 10 AM, that filthy hour when sensible people are fast asleep. The painkillers, a few shots of Dewar's on the plane and a Tuinal or two made walking nearly impossible. He got as far as the first crap table. He steadied himself for a moment while pulling the $800 in cash out of his pocket. He threw it to the stickman and said, "Put it all on 17 black," then collapsed into unconsciousness.

In Sunrise Hospital, they were able to fix everything except the sciatic nerve damage to his legs. His doctors informed him he had also recently developed diabetes. Since bad things always came in threes, he expected another surprise soon. Four weeks after checking in, Monte walked with a cane back into the Nevada sunshine and directly into a cab back to the airport. The jig was up at the hotel. A new show had been put up and they didn't need him anymore. He flew home. Jane was waiting for him, just like the old days, except that the sight of her tired eyes, on top of getting mugged and getting fired, landed the third and knockout punch.

Then they hit him when he was down. Bobby Kennedy finally reached the front door of the farm. On a quiet, mid-summer day, two IRS agents cruised up the long lane to the circular drive around the pine tree, parking close to the front door. They knocked at the screen door while Monte was reading the *New York Times* at the kitchen table. He probably thought they were Horace and Hilda coming up for their regular afternoon tea and chat, until they said, "Hello, Mr. Monte Proser?" When he answered yes, they asked to be let in. Monte looked over at his two sons who had come in to greet the visitors, but who looked back at him for an explanation. "Stick around," he commanded. Billy, 16, and Mike, 14, stood-to like the good soldiers they were. They had fought countless Nazis in the lower field for years and were ready for any trouble.

The agents came in dressed like William Morris agents, dark suits and ties, except cheap and worn. The first one introduced them both, showed his identification. He asked if they could sit, Monte didn't answer. They sat.

Apparently Monte had been severely under-taxed all during the four years of World War II. New figures they had on the estimated income of the Copa during the war were several times greater than the $32,000 that had been assessed years before and paid off. With 18 years of accruing interest and penalties, he now owed just over $850,000. Monte's head dipped toward his tea mug for a moment like he was hit with an invisible stick, then came back up. He turned to his two sons and told them to go upstairs. He warned them not to disturb their mother. Billy and Mike swaggered off with their toughest "fuck you" expressions toward the G-men, then scrambled up the stairs.

The boys slipped into Carrie's bedroom directly over the kitchen and listened at the open window. The men below explained they had the power to take the farm unless Monte paid his taxes immediately. They were sure Monte had stashed away millions and was holding out. He had it somewhere. They asked him over and over again, where it was, what had he done with all that nightclub money.

"Look around 48th and Broadway," he finally said. "I left quite a bit around there."

No laugh. The second agent quoted numbers and dates to jog Monte's memory, while the first one threatened then cajoled, repeating himself, expanding the threats and sweetening his cajoling, probing for a path to the money he knew was hidden.

"Come on, Monte, you have to have some of this money stashed. What happened to it?" the man pleaded.

This first interrogation lasted just over two hours. At the end of it, Monte sat at the table silent and motionless. He took off his glasses and rubbed his eyes. The boys came down to check on him. He told them, "It's gonna be okay," as he made his way upstairs. In his bedroom, he made a few calls and then slept.

When Tom Jones sang at the Copa, women's panties sailed across the audience and hit him in the face. Some lay strewn about the stage with hotel room keys tied in them like bouquets. A new standard of social behavior suddenly descended in front of Jules Podell's astonished eyes and something other than Chanel No. 5 was in the air.

The first shock wave of the sexual revolution had just hit the Copa. Jones had encouraged the ladies' attention with his thin, black satin, skin-tight pants and athletic pelvic thrusts while Podell just stared at the phenomenon, unsure what to do. He thought he'd left that sort of show behind forever at the *Kit Kat Club*, but now every kid in the country seemed to have lost all decency. He decided to make a stand for the old ways.

He pulled the singer aside after his show and ordered him to lose the tight pants. Jones, a practiced Welsh bar-brawler and 25 years younger than Podell, told the icon of nightlife, flatly, to go fuck himself. Jones had 5 gold records for his last five albums and hadn't heard a lot about the Copa before he got there, other than the received wisdom that if you played the club, you'd "made it". But Jones had "made it" long before he ever saw Podell's red face staring at him. He brushed past the hapless man and walked toward his dressing room, taking the last, lingering perfume of the club's greatness with him. By the end of the week, his manager gave Podell notice. They weren't going to accept an extended engagement at the club. They could make a lot more money playing amphitheaters and stadiums. The economics of the place just didn't work anymore.

Downtown, in the Bowery Mission Shelter, Milton Blackstone found his bed for the night, a piss-stained cot among 250 others like it. The cots were so close together they seemed to float over the floor like a formation of flimsy life-rafts. Seven nights a week, the rafts mercifully floated the remnants of once proud and loved men like Milton away from the shipwrecks of their daily lives.

Milton clutched the tattered corpse of a contract against his chest, he knew this one, shredded bit of evidence was all that kept him from total ruin. He knew there was still farther he could fall. He could be in the street, and that would be his death. Somehow the contract proved that he was once a taxpayer and successful business man and was owed, at least, a bed for the night.

His days were filled with impromptu business meetings, often trying to convince the doormen of the fine hotels and apartment buildings he once patronized to help him in his legal battle to recover his fortune. The doormen didn't have the heart to give him the bum's rush. Instead, they watched out for him with a few kind words and often a few bucks of *walkin'-around* money so he could get a cab to his next important meeting.

Friends and acquaintances he met on the street were always too busy to talk. His rivals openly despised him when they caught sight of each other. Even Monte, the closest of his powerful friends, couldn't help him anymore. He had been cheated and robbed, and no one could do a thing about it. At least Eddie was off the hook on that charge. In Milton's ravaged mind, it was now his secretary who had been cheating him all along.

In the men's shelter, the lights shut off and a thousand human holes exhaled. Milton prayed to the god that had forsaken him. All that he once was had vanished, like a dream of youth. He dared not sleep right away, until he made sure all the dangerous characters had fallen asleep first. Only when the floor was completely, safely silent, could he risk sleep. A few cots away a man stealthily unfastened his belt and slipped out of his pants. Milton recognized the sounds and the direction. Moments later a whisper passed between two men next to him. A different belt and pants were shed and dropped on the floor. One man turned face down in his cot and the second mounted him quietly. Milton knew that when the two finished, if nothing had happened to them, it would finally be safe to fall asleep.

Monte and Jane, wounded and exhausted, slept as if under an evil spell. Days passed in soft focus, unformed and listless. Months rolled under their beds leaving balls of hair and dust. Seasons faded, marked by little more than the windows of their bedroom opening and closing.

The boys were now old enough so that the older ones could take care of the younger. Carrie had held on for almost a year without pay, but eventually had to give up when Monte asked her to go. The shame of owing her money was too much for him to live with. He told her they might be moving back to California, and if so, he'd call for her to join them again.

The day came and she stood in the kitchen holding Jane's hand for several minutes as they said a long goodbye. She kissed her remaining boys, Mike, Jimmy and the youngest, ten-year old Timmy, goodbye. Chip was in college and Billy had joined the Army at Fort Dix, New Jersey. Fixing her black traveling hat with a long pin, she walked out of the kitchen with the boys carrying her suitcases. Outside, she stepped into the front seat of her old friend, Charlie Lindenmayer's pickup truck.

She and Sheriff Charlie had become close friends in all the years on the mountain as neighbors. He took her bags from the boys, and swung them into the bed of his truck, then climbed behind the wheel where his *Colt Peacemaker* and bullet-studded gun belt hung on the steering column. The truck rumbled to life and rolled away, down the curve of driveway to the left and then crossed the lower field. The boys waved from the lawn as the truck cleared the field and passed around the bend in the driveway, disappearing into the shady woods, taking the last warmth of sunlight with it.

The period of family life that followed made it impossible for any of the Proser boys to ever watch Eugene O'Neill's *Long Day's Journey into Night*. Independently, years later, in different cities at different times in their lives, when they encountered the work, they all recoiled and put down the book or walked out of the theatre. The images of addiction and hopelessness shot them dead-center through the heart.

At the farm, they grew wild and undisciplined, finding comfort in the normal behavior witnessed in their friends' homes or in television families. The house degenerated into squalor with only grim humor to deflect their abandonment. Among their school friends the watchword while in the Proser house was, "Never eat in the dark" because anything could be living on or in the food. It became known as the house where you had to wipe your feet before you went outside.

Monte had one job during that dark time. He accepted the position of greeter at Meyer and Frank's *Fountainebleu* in Miami Beach. It paid $500 a week on the books, so the IRS would have an income to record.

What the IRS missed were the envelopes that had started arriving every few months, delivered by Larry, an impeccably groomed man with the face of a well-fed cherub and snow-white, oiled hair. Larry arrived in a Cadillac limousine from New York, always sporting a box of Cuban cigars and an onyx in gold pinky ring. The boys always got exotic candies and Jane usually got a piece of jewelry. He smelled beautifully, incense and flowers wafted from his soft pink hands. He stayed and chatted with Monte for a few moments, presenting the cigars but always refusing to stay and smoke one. Frank Costello never forgot his debt to Monte. He always paid in cash and in style.

A day or so after Larry left, a new car often appeared in the driveway. The new cars were needed to replace the cars that the IRS frequently towed away. IRS agents in a government Chevy had begun arriving unannounced, leading a tow-truck to the most valuable car on the property. They would check with Monte to make sure it was his car and if so, give the signal to hook it up. Monte got a receipt for the vehicle and usually another notice to appear at the IRS offices, an hour away in Bristol, to answer for the money he found to buy a car. They always left the old Jeep.

The visits to Bristol required Jane's attendance since she was an accomplice to the presumed theft of government tax revenue. At the IRS offices, Monte and Jane could be glimpsed from the parking lot, through the exterior window of their case agent's small office that looked like a school principal's office.

The appointments were never less than an hour long. By the end of some of them, Monte could be seen laying his face in his hands that rested on the agent's desk while Jane was folded over in the metal chair next to him. The ordeal always left Jane completely drained of life. The walk from the office back to the Jeep was sometimes a wobbly one for her. Monte steadied her as he burned in humiliation and fury – particularly once he realized that the assigned parking spaces for agents were filled with cars he once owned. Apparently at government auction, the cars went for 10 to 20 cents on the dollar, affordable even for civil servants.

Over the next year, there were dozens of appointments in Bristol, visits at the farm and car-nappings but nothing equaled the height of peevishness of the newest tactic. A *Notice of Intent to Levy*, a lurid legal document the size of a tabloid newspaper, was tacked to the kitchen door. The small type in red at the bottom warned of a $25,000 fine and 3-year imprisonment for removing or destroying the document. The banner headline was in bold, scarlet letters.

Something about the document stirred the Christmas spirit in Monte. He called it "the spirit of giving" that made him commission a thick Christmas wreath from the local florist, in mid-September, and hang it on the front door. He seemed happy that the wreath was protecting the government's notice from being removed or destroyed, and even more so when the agents could not order him to take it down. It was his wife's religious expression. A pal from the Copa, famed trial lawyer and author of the new bestseller *My Life in Court*, Louis Nizer, explained to the agents that they'd need to talk to the Supreme Court about taking down the wreath. The wreath aged to a summery brown and became a conversation piece for new visitors to the house. To the inevitable questions, my family adopted the standard reply, "Every day is Christmas."

When Monte walked into the place his new partner had leased, he felt like he once did at the mean, dirty little roadhouses that survived toward the end of Prohibition. Places where you risked your life to drink whatever the house had just brewed in the back. The only difference was the size of the place, with 15-foot ceilings it felt as impersonal and lifeless as the warehouse it had been just a few weeks earlier. Dark, empty nightclubs never scared him before but this one told him he'd hit absolute rock bottom. The one, truly hideous attempt at decoration was a series of drab, flat, cutout figures fixed to the walls. They were cowboys - Western figures in chaps, ten-gallon hats and six-shooters – and badly drawn. In mid-December, in Hightstown, New Jersey, in a chilly industrial building, the ten foot swaggering cowboys were not only incongruous, they were ridiculous bordering on hideous. Monte's newest partner and the designer of the place, Johnny Francis, a local restaurateur in New Hope, made a few lighthearted attempts to assure Monte that the drawings could be changed. Monte looked at the paper napkins on the tables.

"Paper napkins?" he asked, secretly horrified.

Francis nodded innocently. About the decorations, he could change them. He'd do whatever Monte wanted, up to a certain budget, of course. Monte couldn't convincingly muster even his standard dodge, "That's really something," to avoid hurt feelings. He was done-for, this time for sure. He fell silent, turning his paper napkin over and over in his hands. He didn't even want a drink. He wanted to get away from the place as fast and as far as possible.

An early blizzard coated the roads with ice as Monte made his way back toward the farm from the meeting. He drove through the blowing snow in a small, white Pontiac station-wagon that he'd bought used for $500 cash. There was no sense spending money on a car that an IRS agent would be driving in three months anyway, so Monte bought disposable cars for cash.

I sat in the front passenger seat peering through the blizzard trying to see the side of the road. The Pontiac's heater blew only cold air but the radio was in perfect shape. With the battered car's almost treadless tires and Tony Bennett swinging hard through the radio, the ride back to New Hope, and then up the sledding side of Jericho Mountain in a blizzard, had many elements of ballet to it.

After a year or so of living at the pleasure of the IRS, with no real prospects for work in sight, Monte called another time-out. He couldn't properly care for Jane and run the house alone. He called Kingston again for help.

Nan agreed with Monte's plan. She was anxious to get her daughter under her own roof again. She knew she could help her. So the deal was made and Jane was told of the plan. Mike had just been accepted at Temple University in Philadephia, he would go to an apartment near school. Jane would take Timmy with her to Kingston, I would live with my father in a hotel in New Hope.

Sheriff Charlie let the plumber out and turned off the lights in the kitchen. The plumber had just drained the water pipes for the winter. Charlie locked the kitchen door with the tattered gray wreath still hiding the yellowed document underneath it. He had promised Monte to keep an eye on the place while he and Jane sorted out their lives. The farm went dark and was surrendered to the field mice.

The Logan Inn, site of the Monte and Jane's wedding reception 25 years earlier, rented rooms by the week. Monte and

I stayed there while I attended New Hope High School as a junior. My second responsibility, after my schoolwork, was to massage my father's feet and calves to relieve the sciatic nerve pain he still suffered from his beating in Trenton.

I had brought from the farm, a length of ash sapling just over an inch in diameter and about 14 inches in length. It was knotted into a wooden ball on one end by the work of a strangling vine on the young tree. I had stripped the bark on the thin end making a comfortable handgrip, transforming it into a practical weapon, something my hero, James Bond, might have done in my circumstances. Monte confiscated it immediately and hefted it with great satisfaction, flicking it at the shadows of his attackers. He called it his shillelagh and kept it close at hand on his night table.

Over that winter and spring, I massaged my father's feet while he read from an endless pile of paperback novels. Occasionally, after he checked in on my progress as a new student at New Hope High School, we talked about the future. "When your mother is better," began every discussion. If there was going to be a future at all, that was clearly his first condition.

He called Kingston frequently and spoke with my mother, gaining hope, as she seemed to regain her strength. He lay with his head propped on a pillow resting against the majestic, dark wood headboard of his antique bed. Everything in the Logan was dark wood and two hundred years old. His bed lay directly above the bar where they had celebrated their wedding 25 years ago. Most nights, before bed, he was at that same bar, nursing a scotch if he felt good, or a seltzer if not. His seat was on the leading corner, first seat as you came through the front door, the spot that was once dead center in the gaggle of friends and family who had leaned over both lengths of the bar all those years ago.

"Hi ya, Janey," he greeted her calmly, "How you doing today?", always making his question current so she could find something easy and recent to point toward. He listened to her then, just letting her talk, seeming to drift off at the sound of her voice, maybe remembering the gorgeous, intensely vital woman he'd married just up the street at DeLacey's barbershop. I massaged his feet while they talked, trying to detect any change in the situation. I wanted my mother to be with us. I wanted her to help, to give my father a reason to get up out of bed. "I'm coming back, I am," she reassured him. "How's Jimmy doing?"

He'd look down at me, nod his head and smile, "He's doing okay." Then he lied, "We're doing fine, Janey, you just take care of yourself."

We weren't doing fine. He was drinking paregoric, a drugstore opiate, straight from the bottle as a general anesthetic on some days when the pain in his legs was too much. Money for everything we needed came from a shoe box full of fifty dollar bills that he kept under the bed. The box never seemed to empty. The beautiful smelling man from New York must have arrived in his limousine at the hotel during the day while I was at school.

It was late February. Killing storms had been dropping ice over all of Bucks County for weeks. I was walking close to an hour every night, crossing the river, to *Phil and Dan's*, an Italian restaurant in the living room of a small row house in Lambertville. We ate from *Phil and Dan's* five nights a week. I'd sit and warm myself near the kitchen as they made our dinners. The cook was one of the many kind strangers who recognized me as some kind of orphan. She gave us extra portions, small tastes of her other dishes. Then it was back to the Logan with the food, through the winds over the Delaware. The food was barely warm by the time I got back to the hotel. I realized my father didn't enjoy Italian food that much, he just wanted me to get the exercise. It was the same as his constant suggestions for me to run laps in the lower field at home. He was making me strong and putting up with cold pasta to do it.

A little surprise crossed my father's face as he listened to the phone perched on his pillow. My mother had told him, "Thank you for forgiving me, darling. Thank you." He took that in and savored it, then he said, "I will always love you, Jane. Always." I hadn't heard that before. He always called her Janey, not Jane. It was the clue I was listening for. Mom was coming back. We were headed back to the farm.

CHAPTER 43

THE CONCERTINA OPENS AGAIN

In the spring of 1969, Texas real estate developer Jerry Finn broke ground on top of the highest hill in New Hope. His planned community, named *Village 2*, was going to be constructed there, on the site of the old Hahn farm, keeping only the pre-Revolutionary War fieldstone farmhouse intact. Finn's vision was a modern planned community of town homes around a recreation center of large pools and tennis courts. He christened the main road into the development *Oscar Hammerstein Way*, honoring the artistic tradition of the area. At the center of the recreation area, the farmhouse would be transformed into a world-class bar and restaurant. No expense would be spared. The great concertina of fortune opened again at the touch of the Texan Irishman, Jerry Finn, bringing the music of possibilities back into Monte's world.

In the midst of a muddy construction site with heavy equipment roaring around the old farmhouse, Monte and I sat with Finn in a rented limousine and looked out at the farmhouse. Monte was seeing an intimate country inn, the kind of place he and Batch had rolled into for years to avoid going back to work in New York.

"The Little Club," Monte said, naming it after his friend, the stylish British dancer and club operator, Billy Reed's place in New York City.

"It's gonna be great," Monte sold the Texan, "I got the guy for the food."

"What about makin' it sorta like the Copa? We can tear the thing down, start from scratch."

"Nah, it's perfect, just like that. Put a patio on the side for the summer. It'll work great."

"Monte, you're the boss. You got the touch."

My father turned to me and smiled, nodding his slowly in agreement with the Texan, letting me know that things were going to be better now.

On prom nights, the Copa showroom looked like a sampler box of pastel candies as Bobby Vinton, Dionne Warwick, Petula Clark, Paul Anka and Jerry Vale thrilled prom night audiences of high school seniors in chiffon and organza silk. Even the boys were in pastel tuxedos. They also wore long hair and peace signs. They noisily munched hamburgers and French fries. Wealthy ones ordered steaks. Jules Podell hated prom nights and was in the showroom only as long as it took to walk through into the kitchen. He then disappeared upstairs to the lounge for the rest of the evening. Proms kept the seats full, food expenses low and booze flowing but he just couldn't bear to watch jerky kids getting drunk for the first time.

On an April night in 1972, as Tony Orlando and Dawn belted out an encore of *Tie a Yellow Ribbon* downstairs, Podell broke out the champagne for the 43rd birthday party of Joey Gallo upstairs in the lounge. Joey had been bucking for top man in New York since Vito Genovese went away, but Crazy Joe, one of the trigger-men on the Anastasia hit, had made too many corpses and not enough friends on his way up. Just after 2 AM, Joey thanked his host and moved his party, including his wife and several friends, from the Copa to *Umberto's Clam House* in Little Italy.

Inside *Umberto's*, three gunmen interrupted the party. Joey ran for it, drawing fire away from his wife and friends, but only made it as far as the street in front of the restaurant where he was finished off with a final, close-range volley from all three men. The Copa was getting to be unlucky for people like Little Augie and Joey. Even for Frank C, the tables had turned. The place lost money for the first time in the 32 years since it opened.

In July, as opening day approached for *The Little Club*, the news reached Monte. Joe E., who had been the guest of honor or main attraction at every joint he had opened in over 30 years, had died in New York after a short illness. The Clown Prince of nightclubs was gone, and the big, belly laughs-until-you-cried went with him.

Monte attended Joe E's final appearance at the Riverside Chapel at 76th and Amsterdam Avenue, and as always Joe E. had them lined up to get in. 300 were in the chapel, another 400 waited out on the street for a last glimpse of the guy who had knocked them silly with laughter for all those years. Georgie Jessel delivered the eulogy to Joe's friends including Monte, Alan King, Jack Dempsey, George Burns, Phil Silvers, Ed Sullivan, Connie Francis, Myron Cohen and Henny Youngman. After saying a prayer for his great friend and the heart and soul of the nightclub business, Monte turned away and was about to leave when he saw for the last time, his greatest enemy. Jules Podell passed within inches as he approached Joe's casket. Monte saw how the years had softened the bulldog jowls and settled into the dark bags under the man's eyes. His hair was steel grey, not black, but slicked to his head as always. Their eyes met. Podell straightened up defensively as they passed, keeping Monte in sight. As always, Monte gave away nothing, staring at the man like he would at a filthy drunk staggering toward him, making sure there was distance between them, listening to the man's footsteps for clues of aggression or hesitation. Other eyes followed Podell out of old habits of self-protection but only a few bothered to greet the man. Podell broke the stare down with Monte and continued on, his footfalls becoming lost in the shuffle of mourners. Monte watched the man's back until Joe Russell, tapped Monte's elbow.

"Hey, Monte," Joe said. "How ya been?"

Monte turned away from Podell finally and took Joe's hand in his. "How you doin' Joe?" he asked his old, bird-dogging friend, who had uncovered more gossip for Walter Winchell than any other three people combined.

"Eh, gettin' by," Joe said, which meant he had nothing at all going on.

The farm was sold for $1 to a corporation that Israel Katz invented, giving the IRS an entirely new target to focus on. The scarlet letters came off the kitchen door and were carried up to the dump with the dust and mouse shit accumulated from a year of abandonment.

In the heat of late summer, Jane went at the cleaning of the place with a singular intention – things would be put right. The home she had left to the mice would be reclaimed. From late morning until the fields faded to black and fireflies rose on the exhaled breath of the sun-warmed earth, she worked with the quiet determination of a recently paroled convict. The terror that haunted her, that she was following her father into madness, had been quelled by time and the steady devotion of her three immovable lighthouses - Monte, Nan and Jim Morgan. In her luggage from Kingston, she brought a stack of pale blue booklets on nursing, her long-ago intended profession once dancing had played itself out. With this one delicate thread of connection to the world outside herself, she began again to feel her way back toward the bruised hearts of her family.

Mike returned from Philadelphia and took charge of cleaning, re-painting and filling the pool although it was already late in the summer. Billy was on leave from the Army. He split his time between his girlfriend Dee's house and a room he had commandeered in the cabana house by the pool. Chip was on a similar circuit to Bill's, staying most nights with friends in the area but stopping in for afternoons and meals. Timmy and I chased Becky and Robin Riss, our neighbors, back and forth across their gigantic hayloft until we were bright red, sweaty and itching like outside dogs.

The farm suddenly roared to life again. Friends of the boys slept off various parties in different buildings on the property and attacked the refrigerator without mercy. The phone rang through the day. Cars came and went in groups. Life was noisy but sweet and full again. Monte could sense his luck returning like a sailor feels the pull of the moon on the tides. But the flood tide of activity made communication difficult. Things needed to get done around the place and the boys were running off in all directions without discussion.

Dave Brady, my best friend, stayed frequently at the farm. Dave made tea as well as any true son and learned the precise formula of a special mixture of milk and seltzer that settled Monte's stomach. He ran errands and could fix cars, all in all quite a handy chap to have around. He became Monte's accepted major domo and occasional manservant.

When the phone rang one afternoon, Dave picked it up and said hello.

"Hello. Is Monte there?"

"He's sleeping," Dave told the caller.

"Oh. Well, could you wake him up? Tell him Howard Hughes is calling."

"No, I don't think so."

"You can wake him. I think he'll want to take the call."

"Nah, better not. What's your name?"

"Howard Hughes."

"Call back later, okay?"

"No. Wake Monte up now. It's okay."

"No, you call back. He'll be up later."

"Don't you hang up…," Howard ordered.

Dave hesitated, "I should go, mister. Sorry." and hung up.

Several days later, Monte came down from his room for his afternoon tea. Dave was around and made the tea for him.

"Dave," Monte asked, "did you take a call from a guy named Howard Hughes?"

"Yeah. You were sleeping."

Monte started to smile and laughed as he stirred his tea. "Did you know, he's the richest man in the world?"

Dave shook his head, "No."

"He said you hung up on him."

"I told him to call back." Dave defended himself.

"You may be only one in the world who ever said that to him." Monte continued to laugh to himself as he stirred his tea.

On June 4, 1969, crickets serenaded Jane and Monte on the front porch of their farm. 25 years ago they had sealed their marriage here with friends and family, laughter and teasing about the children who would soon inhabit the place. Now those children ran amok over at the pool by the cabana house with half a dozen cousins from Kingston. Adults drifted in and out of the kitchen passing close to the pair but saying nothing to them. The united families had made them a steak dinner with cake and ice cream for dessert and left them alone on the porch to enjoy the rising fireflies for their anniversary celebration.

"Whaddya think?" Monte finally asked.

"About what?" Jane looked straight ahead. She knew she would have to answer eventually but first took the time to see herself in her blue serge wedding outfit, young and healthy, all those years ago looking out over the same scene. "25 years," she said. "Had enough?"

Monte smiled. She would never forgive herself, but he did, and knew that he always would forgive her. "Almost," he said. "Almost enough."

Young men, reporters from the *Philadelphia Inquirer*, sat with Monte in the *Little Club's* dining room interviewing him for a feature story. I was working as a busboy and general help in the new place. I'd begun to think that I'd like to be a newspaper reporter one day, so I stood by as my father struggled to find a story angle the reporters could use.

All the headlines and stories he'd created over 40 years seemed to him to be just that, old stories, with no more significance than a child's fairy tale. He had stories about how a friend once showed him a picture of a Brazilian beach called Copacabana, about love in the time when people wore high button shoes but that wouldn't mean much to these young men from Philadelphia. They'd had never been in the Copa, the real Copa, or seen a show on Broadway before 1965. They knew discos, they'd seen *Hair*. They'd never heard of *Leon and Eddie's*, never seen Joe E. perform, barely recognized the name of Sophie Tucker. It was hard to come up with something for them.

"I should do a book," he told them, "Wanna know the title?"

"Sure," one of the reporters said.

"*Whatever Happened to Me?*" Monte heard his idea land with a soft thud behind their eyes.

A black man in gray driver's livery came into the room, cap in hand.

"Mr. Proser?" he asked.

"Yeah," Monte answered. He saw the driver and looked out the window of the dining room. A black Cadillac limousine with New York plates sat at the top of the walkway to the front door.

"Excuse me, do you have a moment?" the driver asked.

Monte turned to the reporters, "Have a drink," he told them and got up, following the driver outside. The reporters ordered Cokes as they went over their notes together. I went to the kitchen for the drinks.

Outside, the back window rolled down as Monte approached the car. Frank Costello, in a dark suit and tie, looked out from the back seat. He nodded welcome and smiled as Monte climbed into the back of the limousine with him. The window rolled back up.

Frank just wanted to say hello, check in on his old partner and wish him luck. Small talk. Was Monte happy with the new place, how was Jane?

"She's good," Monte said. "Thanks." He meant for everything.

Frank nodded, said nothing. He paid his debts, there was no need to thank him. Monte returned the courtesy, asking about Bobbie and what the hell Frank did all day.

"Nothin'," Frank answered glumly. "Nothin' fun."

"I'd invite you in but I got reporters inside."

Frank shrugged it off, "Yeah, that's all you need, me showing up."

Monte let the conversation fall off.

Frank said, "If I was starting again, today, I'd get a degree. I'd go to school and get a certificate, makes it all legal. They give you a license to rob. Like the OTB."

The first two *Off Track Betting* offices had opened two weeks earlier in Manhattan, wiping out the last of the bookies and racetrack touts that were hanging on from the old days. Like booze, the government finally wised up, legalized the vice and took over another one of Frank's businesses. The first day take for both OTB offices was $66,091.

"OTB," Monte shook his head, "They watch it on TV."

Both men snorted in disgust. Frank looked out the window, "On TV…," he said, shaking his head. "So anyway, fortuna buona, you alright?"

"Yeah, I'm okay." Monte offered his hand, Frank took it. "Thanks for making the drive."

"Forget it." Frank held Monte's hand, looked him in the eye and gave the handshake a few more bounces, lingering for a few extra seconds. Monte understood the Prime Minister was saying goodbye. His lips were pressed hard against each other for support against the emotions or maybe the confessions that threatened to split them apart. Frank's face was paler and had lost the healthy sheen he used to get from his regimen of steamed barber's towels and astringent cologne.

"See ya, Frank," Monte said. Frank nodded and finally let go of Monte's hand. It was over. Thirty years of off and on partnership was finished. Frank sat back in his seat, lit up a cigarette. Monte opened the door and climbed out. He walked down the flagstone walkway toward the front door as the limousine rolled slowly away.

Monte came in and walked past the kitchen on his way back to the interviewers. In an hour or so, people with reservations would start arriving for cocktails and dinner. The piano player was due in a few minutes. From the kitchen, Rudy, an extremely high-strung chorus boy-turned-chef, screamed "Fuck!" and could be heard throwing a stack of metal serving dishes. Then, "Oh, no!" Monte walked by the calamity, whatever it was, unconcerned. He inhaled the nutmeg from Rudy's creamed radishes cooking as he passed, making him thankful he was back on properly chef-prepared meals. He was looking forward to hearing the piano player and having dinner with Batch and a few of the other old bums he knew from around Broadway. He returned to the table and settled in.

"Yeah, what was I saying?" he asked the young men.

"*What Ever Happened to Me?*" one of them said.

"Right. Or, "*This is All I Ask*", like the song." He looked at them for a response. They were blank, never heard of it. "Anyway…" he trailed off. He looked out the window again to where the limousine had been and quietly sang the first few bars of the melody for them, "Beautiful girls, walk a little slower when you walk by me…"

~ The End ~

EPILOGUE

On February 18, 1973, Frank Costello died peacefully in his bed, the ultimate sign of respect for the gangster who had advocated nonviolence all his life. Dutifully following his boss' example, in September, Jules Podell also died at his home near Frank's place on Long Island. That same year, the Copacabana finally went dark and stayed vacant for three years until 1976 when it opened again as a disco, keeping the name of the vanished nightclub.

After nearly 2 years on the streets of Manhattan, Milton Blackstone was taken in by the Catholic sisters of the Mary Manning Walsh Home on East 76th Street. He lived out the last 12 years of his life there under the sisters' devoted and attentive care. He carried the tattered contract with him until the last day of his life, never doubting its power to one day restore him to his former influence. He called Monte the day he read in the newspaper that Podell had died. It was the last time they spoke.

In 1976, Johnny Rosselli was murdered on the orders of his close friend and long-time mentor, Santo Trafficante just weeks before he was to testify before the United States Senate Select Committee to Study Governmental Operations with Respect to Intelligence Activities, the Church Committee. His body was dismembered and sealed in a steel drum that was supposed to disappear under the waves of the Gulf of Mexico. Instead, the drum floated to the surface and was retrieved by Dade County Police.

Eddie Fisher continued to deteriorate under the influence of drugs, ending up singing in second-tier tourist bars in Europe for just enough money to get a nightly fix. His story is told in his autobiography, "*Been There, Done That*".

On October 6, 1973, having outlived both his mob protector, Frank Costello, and sworn enemy, Jules Podell, while enjoying his new song playing on the concertina of life, Monte died peacefully in his sleep at the Farm with Jane and Timmy nearby in the house and the other boys successfully off to college and careers. By his bed was a new rabbit's foot.

Jane went on to graduate first in her class and received certification as a licensed practical nurse. She practiced nursing for the next 15 years, retiring in 1988. She never remarried. She died in October, 2005 and is buried with Monte in the cemetery of St. Martin's Catholic Church in New Hope. On their headstone is inscribed, *"La Vie en Rose."*

Made in the USA
Charleston, SC
07 January 2016